RHS
PLANTS
— FOR EVERY —
SEASON

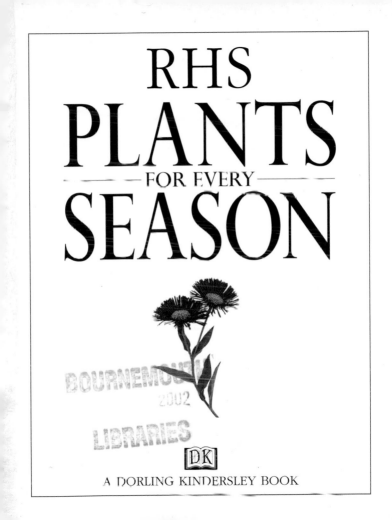

DK

A DORLING KINDERSLEY BOOK

Dorling **DK** Kindersley

LONDON, NEW YORK, MUNICH, MELBOURNE, DELHI

WRITERS **Martin Page, Andrea Loom**
PROJECT EDITOR **Helen Fewster**
ART EDITOR **Ann Thompson**
PROJECT ART EDITOR **Alison Lotinga**
MANAGING EDITOR **Anna Kruger**
MANAGING ART EDITOR **Lee Griffiths**
DTP DESIGN **Louise Waller**
PRODUCTION **Mandy Inness**

First edition published in Great Britain in 2002 by
Dorling Kindersley Limited
80 Strand
London WC2R 0RL

2 4 6 8 10 9 7 5 3 1

A CIP catalogue record for this book is available from
the British Library.

ISBN 0-7513-4644-6

Colour reproduction by Colourscan.
Printed and bound in Italy by Graphicom.

see our complete catalogue at
www.dk.com

CONTENTS

INTRODUCTION *6-11*

USING THE GUIDE

The AIM OF THIS BOOK is to help you to select plants for your garden that will provide colour and interest throughout the year. There are seven chapters, based on the six seasons of the gardening year, plus a final section suggesting plants that offer year round interest. This 'All Seasons' chapter will help you to choose some plants that give shape and structure to the garden, or that have evergreen foliage. They may be used to create a permanent framework, into which other flowering plants can be introduced.

It will come as no surprise to learn that the largest chapters relate to late spring, and to early and late summer, but you may be interested to discover how many plants are in flower at other times of year. Use this book to plan ahead so your garden has autumn interest as well as colour in winter and early spring.

In each chapter, the plants have been divided into colour categories – white, pink, red, purple, blue, green, yellow and orange – and then presented in alphabetical order. Some may flower over a long period or have several seasons of interest, but here they are placed in the season in which they make the

most significant impact. Thus a flowering cherry may have found its way into 'Autumn' due to its attractive foliage, while pyracanthas may be grown for their early summer flowers as well as their bright clusters of winter berries.

SYMBOLS USED

♀ The RHS Award of Garden Merit

SOIL MOISTURE PREFERENCES/TOLERANCES
◊ Well-drained soil
◐ Moist soil
● Wet soil

SUN/SHADE PREFERENCE/TOLERANCES
☀ Full sun
◑ Partial shade; either dappled shade or shade for part of the day
● Full shade
NB *Where two symbols appear from the same category, the plant is suitable for a range of conditions.*

HARDINESS RATINGS
❋ Plants requiring the protection of a heated glasshouse over winter but may be placed outdoors in sheltered sites in summer.
❋❋ Plants that survive outside in mild regions or in favoured sites, or those that, in temperate countries, are usually grown outside in summer but need frost-protection over winter.
❋❋❋ Fully hardy plants.

PLANNING YOUR GARDEN

IT IS A GOOD IDEA to plan before you plant by making a rough drawing of your existing garden and plotting in various permanent plants and features like paths, patio or shed. Computer programs are available to help you visualise how your garden will look, but a sheet of squared paper and a pencil can perform the same task, at a much lower cost. Hard landscaping in the form of paths and patios, should be done before the garden is planted. It is also important to take into account your garden's use: whether you need space for entertaining, or areas for pets and children to play. Once your priorities are established, you can turn to the plants.

SELECT IN ORDER

Start by choosing trees and shrubs. These provide the permanent backbone of the garden. Boundary hedges or mixed shrub screens give shelter from wind, privacy and buffer noise. Specimen shrubs and especially trees need enough room to develop unhindered. They can grow to a considerable size, so it is usually better to plant one or two modest specimens and allow them to grow naturally rather than spoil

their appearance by heavy pruning, or removing them after a few years.

Once these long-term plants are in place you can turn your attention to the small shrubs and herbaceous perennials. Often simplicity is the key to achieving a harmonious garden. Rather than using lots of different plants it is better to plant groups of three or five of the same variety, which will merge together and create more impact. The final elements are the bulbs and annuals, all of which give instant colour in their first year, and are invaluable for filling gaps. Hardy annuals can be sown *in situ* and bulbs can be naturalized under trees and in grass.

YEAR-ROUND INTEREST

There are no set times when the seasons begin and end. It depends on the climate where you live, your garden situation and the weather. In mild years, flowers start to open between one and two weeks earlier than in others; summers can be brought to an abrupt halt by severe drought or an unseasonable frost.

To achieve year-round interest in the garden, start by choosing a few plants for winter, when the choice is most limited: perhaps a tree with

DUAL PURPOSE
Bergenias are easy-going good ground cover plants for sun or light shade. This one has bright pink spring flowers and the foliage colours in winter.

interesting bark, or a cluster of winter-flowering shrubs and some early bulbs. Then select for early spring and autumn; some plants will double up with spring flowers and bright autumn tints. Move on to make your selection for late spring, before looking through the summer sections. Consider planting up a few containers for each season; again there is a huge choice for summer, but different varieties of plants like pansies go throughout the year.

COLOUR

Many people enjoy lots of colour, but some of the most appealing borders, containers or garden areas have a colour theme. You might choose shades of one colour, but this can be dull, or use a limited palette. White and pastel colours are cool and show up well at dusk – good near a patio or path. Blues and mauves are hazy and give a sense of distance, whereas hot reds, oranges and yellows appear closer.

ASSESSING YOUR SITE

P LANTING A NEW GARDEN can be an exciting prospect, but before you rush to the garden centre it is wise to assess your site by testing the soil and identifying areas of sun and shade. If your site is bare, one way of finding out what grows well in your locality is to look at what succeeds in neighbouring gardens, or ask at the garden centre. Try to select plants that suit the conditions rather than fighting against nature;

this helps to prevent expensive disappointments, and the plants will be healthier and need less attention.

If you have acquired a garden that is well established, try to stem your enthusiasm and observe it for

FOCAL POINTS
The variegated Yucca gloriosa *is a superb architectural plant, and provides a strong focus in a border in well-drained sunny gardens. It may also be grown in containers.*

a year. In doing so, you discover its hidden delights, such as bulbs, and see how plants perform through the seasons. Only then should you consider changes. If possible, keep established trees for the maturity they give, but smaller plants can be moved, ideally in early spring.

TESTING THE SOIL

The soil is critical in determining which plants will grow well in your garden and you need to establish its characteristics. Sandy soil is free draining, low in nutrients and feels gritty as you rub it between your fingers. At the other extreme is clay soil, which is smooth and malleable when handled. It is nutrient rich, but sticky when wet, becomes rock hard when dry and often has poor drainage. The ideal soil is moist and well drained, retaining water, but without becoming waterlogged. Much can be done to ameliorate soil conditions. Sandy soils can be improved by adding plenty of well-rotted manure or garden compost on a regular basis. Clay soil may be lightened by deep digging, adding grit and organic matter such as garden compost or leafmould.

To test whether your soil has poor drainage dig a hole about 1m (3ft) square and fill it with water. If the water has not drained away within a few hours the site is badly drained. You then have the option of growing moisture-loving plants and perhaps creating a bog garden or installing sub-surface drainage.

You should also test the pH of your soil to find out whether it is acid or alkaline. Soil-testing kits are available from most garden centres and this simple test can save you money in the long term, as some plants, like rhododendrons and many heathers, will thrive on acid or neutral soil.

ASPECT

The orientation of your house and garden is another important factor that determines which plants grow best. In a north-facing garden the area close to the house will always be in shadow, and it is likely to be cold and windy in winter. This limits the choice of plants to those that are hardy and tolerate shade. South-facing gardens are more sheltered but can be hot in summer, so unless you plant shading trees, confine your choice to sun-lovers. South-west-facing gardens are ideal because they offer full sun and some shade throughout the year. In windy situations it advisable to plant a sheltering hedge or screen.

CARING FOR PLANTS

ALL PERENNIALS, especially trees and shrubs, need well-prepared sites. Dig over the ground, remove all traces of perennial weeds and incorporate plenty of well-rotted organic matter. Although most plants are sold in containers throughout the year, deciduous trees and shrubs, including roses, are best planted in the dormant season between late autumn and early spring, when the soil is neither frozen or sodden. Conifers and evergreens are best left until spring. Plant herbaceous perennials in autumn, while the soil is still warm, or (better for plants of borderline hardiness) in spring.

PLANTING

Water plants in containers an hour or two before transplanting them; after planting, water again. Then cover the root area, particularly around shrubs and trees, with a thick mulch of organic matter or composted bark to conserve soil moisture and suppress weeds. Make sure they never go short of water in dry periods during the first year, or two or three years for shrubs and trees. Bulbs are normally planted in autumn, but some are planted in spring. They need a well-drained site and, as a rule of thumb, plant them at twice their depth.

AFTERCARE

In spring remove winter debris, clearing away the dead growth of perennials and cutting back ornamental grasses as new shoots begin to show. Weed and prick over the bare soil of beds and borders with a fork to aerate it, taking care not to pierce emerging bulbs. Rake in balanced fertilizer and then, when the soil is moist and temperatures rising, mulch with organic matter. Insert stakes and supports so they will be covered by the new foliage of perennials.

Once frosts are over, bedding and tender plants, such as dahlias, gladiolus, begonias and cannas can be put out, but be prepared to drape them with fleece in case temperatures fall at night.

Deadheading is the main job for summer: it keeps plants tidy and stimulates the development of new buds and more flowers. Containers and hanging baskets will need daily watering and feeding every 10-14 days unless a slow-release fertilizer was mixed in at the time of planting. Water plants in borders, particularly those recently planted. Irrigate thoroughly to encourage deep roots; watering little and often results in surface roots, and exposes plants to drought and damage.

In autumn the remains of annuals can be cleared away and perennials tidied for the winter. Perennials with hollow stems like delphiniums and lupins should be cut down to the ground but others including grasses and those not entirely hardy, like kniphofias, are better left intact for

protection. These and shrubs of borderline hardiness benefit from a protective mulch of straw or bracken in all but mild areas; keep it in position throughout winter. Move tender plants under glass for winter and lift dahlias, begonias, cannas, gladiolus to store in a cool frost-free place over winter.

REPEAT PERFORMANCE
Large herbaceous borders are glorious during the summer. Deadhead plants regularly to extend the display.

EARLY SPRING

WINTER'S COLD GRIP seems to loosen as the bulbs begin to flower. Their growth initially can be quite slow, but the first warm day stirs them from their slumber. It is often very cold at night and some early flowers, like magnolias and camellias, may be damaged in exposed areas. Keep newspaper and fleece at hand to protect plants from overnight frost.

The flowers opening beneath deciduous trees and shrubs are a feature of early spring. Bulbs, hellebores, primroses and starry blue hepaticas in mixed and woodland borders take advantage of the light before the leaves on overhanging branches unfurl. In more open sites and lawns, naturalized crocuses and daffodils make drifts of mauve, white or sunny yellow. Allow the foliage of bulbs to die down naturally wherever they grow to ensure they flower well in future.

Magnolias are the monarchs of the spring garden, but not all are large or slow to flower; 'Star Wars' will bloom from a very young age, and the smaller *M. stellata*, is ideal in an urban garden. Other trees and shrubs in blossom at this time are fragrant coryopsis and daphnes, early-flowering apricots and cherries (*Prunus*), and the tangled shoots of Japanese quince (*Chaenomeles*).

FOLIAGE FOUNDATIONS
Dramatic foliage is always an asset. The bright purple-red leaves of *Photinia* x *fraseri* 'Red Robin' stand out like beacons in spring sunshine, and it makes an unusual hedge. Many pieris, such as 'Wakehurst', also boast brilliant red leaves but they turn shades of pink and cream before maturing to green.

Hellebores have flowers in a wide range of subtle colours, but *Helleborus foetidus* and *H* x *sternii* also make valuable foliage plants, adding height and structure to the garden at the start of the year.

ANEMONE BLANDA
'White Splendour' ♀

Perennial

A spreading plant, with knobbly tubers and irregularly lobed leaves, the petals of the flowers are white, with a pink tint underneath. It enjoys a sunny site and well-drained soil, and will quickly spread to form a large clump. Plant the tubers in autumn, at a depth of about 8cm (3in), and then leave undisturbed to naturalize.

◊ ☼ ❀ ❀ ❀
‡ to 10cm (4in) ↔ to 15cm (6in)

ERICA ARBOREA *VAR.*
ALPINA ♀

Evergreen shrub

This attractive tree heather bears masses of fragrant flowers from the end of the winter to mid-spring. Perfect for adding height to a rock or heather garden, this variety prefers to be grown in full sun in well-drained, slightly acid (lime-free) soil, but will tolerate mildly alkaline conditions. The first year after planting, prune back by about two thirds after flowering to form a bushy plant. After that, further pruning is not necessary.

◊ ☼ ❀ ❀ ❀
‡ to 2m (6ft) ↔ to 85cm (34in)

ERICA X DARLEYENSIS
'White Glow'

Evergreen shrub

The Darley Dale heath is compact and
bushy with fine, lance-shaped leaves.
Masses of white flowers with reddish-
brown tips appear in late winter and
early spring. It benefits from a sunny
position and well-drained, preferably
acid (lime-free) soil, although slightly
alkaline soils are acceptable. Trim off
the previous season's growth after it
has flowered to keep the plant neat.

◊ ☼ ❈ ❈ ❈
‡ to 25cm (10in) ↔ to 50cm (20in)

HELLEBORUS X HYBRIDUS

Perennial

These hybrid hellebores have leathery,
green leaves. The nodding flowers are
white, pink, green or purple and are
often covered with small red spots.
Vigorous, variable plants, they prefer
heavy, moist, neutral or alkaline soil
that is rich in organic matter. They will
tolerate full sun, but are best planted
in the dappled shade of a woodland
border, or beneath the branches of
deciduous trees or shrubs. Although
they regularly self seed, the best plants
are purchased from specialist nurseries.

◊ ☼ ☼ ❈ ❈ ❈
‡ ↔ to 45cm (18in)

HYACINTHUS ORIENTALIS *'White Pearl'*

Perennial bulb

The large pure white, rather waxy, bell-shaped flowers of this bulbous plant are intensely fragrant, and emerge in early spring on stiff stems among bright green leaves. Plant the bulbs at a depth of 10cm (4in), about 8cm (3in) apart, in sun or partial shade in deep, well-drained fertile soil, and group them in clumps or use in a bedding scheme. Bulbs planted in pots of bulb fibre can be forced into flower early to create an indoor show for the winter months.

⚪ ☼ ☀ ✿ ✿ ✿

↕ to 30cm (12in) ↔ to 8cm (3in)

LEUCOJUM VERNUM ♀

Perennial bulb

The spring snowflake is one of the earliest bulbs to bloom. Leafless stalks produce one or two green-tipped white flowers amid clumps of strap-shaped glossy green leaves. For the greatest impact, plant groups of bulbs in moist soil, rich in organic matter, in the partial shade below deciduous trees or shrubs. Propagate by division in the spring, or sow seed in the autumn.

⚪ ☀ ✿ ✿ ✿

↕ to 15cm (6in) ↔ to 10cm (4in)

LYSICHITON CAMTSCHATCENSIS ♀

Perennial

The white skunk cabbage bears large white, hooded flowerheads in the early spring. Large, dark green leaves follow shortly after, which eventually grow taller than the flowers. The thick roots require deep, permanently moist, fertile soil, so it is not suitable for growing in containers, but it can be used beside a pond as a marginal plant, or planted in a bog garden. Allow space for clumps to develop and the leaves to expand.

◊ ◐ ☼ ☀ ❀ ❀ ❀
‡ to 75cm (30in) ↔ to 60cm (24in)

MAGNOLIA STELLATA ♀

Deciduous shrub

The star magnolia is a vigorous and free-flowering shrub or tree, suitable for even the smallest of gardens. Left to its own devices it forms a broad-spreading shrub, covered in winter with fat, silky-haired flower buds. The star shaped spring flowers open on bare branches and are composed of numerous narrow white petals. Plant this magnolia in a sheltered position in sun or light shade, and moist, well-drained, fertile soil. It requires no pruning.

◊ ◐ ☼ ☀ ❀ ❀ ❀
‡ to 3m (10ft) ↔ to 4m (12ft)

NARCISSUS
'Cheerfulness' ♀

Perennial bulb

An attractive, early-flowering daffodil
with white outer petals that surround
clusters of smaller petals in the centre.
The long-lasting blooms have a strong
fragrance and are good for cutting. For
maximum visual impact, plant the bulbs
in bold groups in late summer to early
autumn in well-drained, fertile soil. The
bulbs should be planted at one and a
half times their depth below the soil.

◊ ☼ ❀ ❀ ❀
‡ to 40cm (16in) ↔ to 15cm (6in)

NARCISSUS
'Merlin' ♀

Perennial bulb

The blooms of this dainty daffodil are
good for cutting and have pure white,
rounded petals and a flat cup-shaped,
yellow trumpet with a reddish-orange
rim. It prefers a sunny site and well-
drained soil, and flowers in the middle
of spring. The bulbs should be planted
as for 'Cheerfulness' (see above) in a
herbaceous border, or it can be grown
in grass and left to naturalize.

◊ ☼ ❀ ❀ ❀
‡ to 45cm (18in) ↔ to 15cm (6in)

NARCISSUS
'Thalia'

Perennial bulb

This vigorous daffodil will form large
clumps, and is suitable for naturalizing
in the border or rock garden. Deep,
long-lasting, funnel-shaped flowers with
milky-white petals, often with three or
more blooms per stem, are produced
in early to mid-spring. They also make
excellent cut flowers. Plant the bulbs as
for 'Cheerfulness' (see left) in a sunny
position, and well-drained, fertile soil.

○ ☼ ❀ ❀ ❀
‡ to 35cm (14in) ↔ to 15cm (6in)

NARCISSUS TRIANDRUS ♀

Perennial bulb

Angel's tears is a dwarf narcissus that
bears nodding, pale cream flowers with
reflexed petals and rounded cups. The
leaves are green and strap-shaped. A
small-growing plant, it performs well
in containers, and will naturalize, if the
conditions are right, in a sunny rock
garden or raised bed in well-drained
soil. There is also a white-flowered
variety, *albus* Plant the bulbs as for
'Cheerfulness' (see above left).

○ ☼ ❀ ❀
‡ to 25cm (10in) ↔ to 8cm (3in)

ORNITHOGALUM OLIGOPHYLLUM

Perennial bulb

In early spring, this slender perennial produces up to five, star-shaped, white flowers with a yellowish-green stripe down the outside of each petal. It also bears a pair of leaves that are placed close to the ground. Plant the bulbs in groups in the autumn in a sunny site and well-drained soil.

◊ ☼ ❋ ❋ ❋
‡ to 8cm (3in) ↔ to 10cm (4in)

OSMANTHUS X BURKWOODII ♀

Evergreen shrub

This slow-growing shrub has oval, dark green, slightly glossy, leathery leaves. In mid-spring it produces small clusters of fragrant white flowers which, on a still sunny day, will fill the garden with a sweet scent. Plant this shrub in full sun or partial shade in fertile, well-drained soil. It can be used as a hedging plant, which will need clipping once a year in the summer.

◊ ☼ ◑ ❋ ❋ ❋
‡ ↔ to 3m (10ft)

PRUNUS SPINOSA

Deciduous tree

Blackthorn is nature's answer to the
barbed wire fence. A vigorous shrub or
small tree, it bears star-shaped, white
flowers that open on bare branches in
early and mid-spring. The branches are
armed with sharp thorns, and it makes
a superb impenetrable hedge. It bears
purple fruits, or sloes, in autumn, which
can be used to make a comforting
liquor. It grows happily in full sun on
moist, well-drained soils, and can be
cut back hard in early spring. Hedges
can be pruned at anytime.

◊ ◊ ☼ ❋ ❋ ❋
‡ to 5m (15ft) ↔ to 4m (12ft)

PULMONARIA
'Sissinghurst White' ♥

Perennial

The leaves of this lungwort are elliptic
and covered with small white spots.
The flowers are pale pink when in bud
and open in spring to form pure white
funnel-shaped blooms. It makes good
ground cover and is ideal for planting
beneath deciduous trees in humus-rich,
moist, but well drained soil. Clip over
after it has flowered to encourage fresh
foliage. To keep the plant vigorous it is
a good idea to divide and replant it
every few years.

◊ ◊ ◐ ◑ ❋ ❋ ❋
‡ to 30cm (12in) ↔ to 45cm (18in)

SANGUINARIA CANADENSIS 'Plena' ♀

Perennial

Bloodroot is aptly named, as its fleshy roots exude a red sap when cut. The white spring flowers, often tinted pink on the reverse, are succeeded by waxy, heart- or kidney-shaped, greyish-green leaves that provide excellent ground cover in damp, shaded sites. Divide large clumps after flowering.

◊ ☼ ◐ ✿ ✿ ✿
‡ to 15cm (6in) ↔ to 30cm (12in)

TULIPA BIFLORA

Perennial bulb

Well suited to a sunny site in a rock garden, the fragrant, star-shaped flowers of this dwarf tulip are creamy-white, or ivory, with bright yellow centres. The blooms are produced from late winter and persist through early spring. Plant the bulbs in groups in late autumn in a light, fertile, well-drained soil, and leave undisturbed so clumps can develop. The bulbs like to be dry in the summer, so do not plant where neighbours may need watering.

◊ ☼ ✿ ✿ ✿
‡ to 10cm (4in) ↔ to13cm (5in)

TULIPA
'Schoonoord'
Perennial bulb

This is a relatively small tulip, ideal for
an urban garden where space is at a
premium. The wide-spreading, double,
pure white flowers open in the middle
of spring. The bulbs need a sunny site,
and should be planted in late autumn
in a well-drained, fertile soil. *Tulipa*
'Peach Blossom', which grows to the
same height, has double deep rose-pink
flowers and makes a complementary
planting companion for displays in tubs
and bedding schemes.

○ ☼ ❀ ❀ ❀
‡ to 30cm (12in)

TULIPA TURKESTANICA ♀
Perennial bulb

A tulip with star-shaped white flowers
and a yellow or occasionally orange
centre. The flowers have an unpleasant
aroma, and are produced in early or
mid-spring. Choose a sunny site that is
dry in summer, such as a hot border or
by a sunny wall, and plant the bulbs in
autumn in groups in well-drained, light,
reasonably fertile soil.

○ ☼ ❀ ❀ ❀
‡ to 30cm (12in)

ANEMONE BLANDA
'Radar' ♀

Perennial

The leaves of this spreading perennial are deeply divided, and in early spring it produces star-shaped, deep magenta flowers with white centres. It grows best on very well-drained sandy soil, in full sunshine. Plant the small, knobbly tubers in autumn in groups and leave undisturbed to naturalize.

◊ ☼ ❀ ❀ ❀
‡ to 10cm (4in) ↔ to 15cm (6in)

BELLIS PERENNIS
'Pomponette'

Perennial

A selected form of the common daisy, this perennial is frequently grown as a biennial for spring bedding. The double pink, white or red flowers have quill-like petals, and measure up to 4cm (1½in) across. Grow in a sunny position, in a well drained, fertile soil, in spring bedding schemes, as edging, or in pots or window boxes. Deadhead regularly to extend the flowering period.

◊ ☼ ◑ ❀ ❀ ❀
‡ ↔ to 20cm (8in)

BERGENIA
'Sunningdale'

Evergreen perennial

An early flowering plant, the deep pink
spring blooms of which are borne on
stiff red stems. The rounded, leathery
leaves become bronze-coloured in the
autumn. It should be grown in full sun
or partial shade, and is suitable for
planting beneath shrubs and deciduous
trees. Propagate it by division in the
spring after the flowers have finished,
and remove tatty leaves at this time too.

⋀ ⋀ ☼ ☀ ❄ ❄ ❄
‡ to 45cm (18in) ↔ to 60cm (24in)

CAMELLIA × WILLIAMSII
'Donation' ♀

Evergreen shrub

This camellia is valued for its deep
pink, double flowers which appear in
late winter and persist through spring.
A vigorous, tree-flowering shrub, it also
boasts glossy, dark green foliage. Plant
it in partial shade, away from the early
morning sun, in moist, but well-drained
neutral or acid (lime-free) soil, mixed
with plenty of organic matter, or grow
it in containers of ericaceous compost.
For perfect blooms, stand pots in an
unheated greenhouse or conservatory.

⋀ ⋀ ☀ ❄ ❄ ❄
‡ to 5m (15ft) ↔ to 2.5m (8ft)

CHAENOMELES SPECIOSA
'Moerloosei' ♀

Deciduous shrub

This flowering quince can be used as
a free-standing shrub or trained along
a wall. It produces a tangle of spiny
stems, covered with glossy, dark green
leaves, while clusters of saucer-shaped,
white and pink flowers appear in early
spring. The blooms are followed in the
autumn by edible greenish-yellow fruits
that can be made into jelly. Cut back
after flowering if grown against a wall.

◊ ☼ ☀ ✽ ✽ ✽
‡ to 2.5m (8ft) ↔ to 5m (15ft)

CHIONODOXA
'Pink Giant'

Perennial bulb

This medium-sized bulbous perennial
produces soft pink, star-shaped flowers
with white centres in early spring. It is
ideal for a rock garden or for planting
beneath shrubs where the bulbs can be
left to naturalize. It prefers a sunny site
and well-drained soil. Plant bulbs in the
autumn in groups, and propagate by
dividing established clumps or by seed.

◊ ☼ ✽ ✽ ✽
‡ to 25cm (10in) ↔ to 5cm (2in)

CLEMATIS ARMANDII
'Apple Blossom' ♀

Climber

The glossy dark evergreen leaves of this vigorous climber are accompanied in spring by large clusters of pink-tinged, scented white flowers with deeper pink undersides that pale to pinkish-white. It is fairly hardy but should be planted in a sunny position against a south- or west-facing wall in a well-drained soil. Purchase plants from a reputable source as there are a lot of inferior seedlings available. It can be pruned back after flowering, but not into old dark wood.

◊ ☼ ✿ ✿
‡ to 5m (15ft)

DAPHNE CNEORUM
'Eximia' ♀

Evergreen shrub

A prostrate shrub with small oval, dark green leaves. The rose pink flowers are highly fragrant and borne in clusters at the end of the branches. To grow well it needs a rich soil, which should be mixed with well-rotted garden compost or leafmould when planting. All parts of the plant are harmful if ingested, and the sap can irritate the skin on contact.

◊ ☼ ✿ ✿ ✿
‡ to 10cm (4in) ↔ to 50cm (20in)

ERICA × DARLEYENSIS
'Kramer's Rote' ♀

Evergreen shrub

Bronze-tinted green foliage and bright magenta spring flowers are features of this bushy heather. It should be grown in moist, but well-drained, humus-rich or peaty soil. It prefers acid (lime-free) conditions but tolerates slightly alkaline soil, and is a useful ground-cover plant. Trim off the previous season's growth after flowering to keep the plant neat. 'Archie Graham' is similar heather, but with mauve-pink flowers.

� ◐ ☼ ❋ ❋ ❋
‡ to 30cm (12in) ↔ to 60cm (24in)

HYACINTHUS ORIENTALIS
'Queen of the Pinks'

Perennial bulb

This is one of the best pink hyacinths, with bright green leaves and highly fragrant flowers borne on robust stems in spring. Plant the bulbs outside in the autumn where they should flower the following year, in fertile, well-drained soil at a depth of 10cm (4in), and about 8cm (3in) apart. They can be grown in informal clumps, used in a bedding scheme, or grown in pots. Feed after flowering to help the bulbs build up their strength.

◐ ☼ ◑ ❋ ❋ ❋
‡ to 30cm (12in) ↔ to 8cm (3in)

MAGNOLIA × LOEBNERI
'Leonard Messel' ♀

Deciduous shrub

A substantial shrub or small tree with
large, rounded leaves, in spring it bears
fragrant flowers, which boast a dozen
lilac-pink, strap-shaped petals, the
colour of which is most intense during
warm springs. It grows happily on most
soils and tolerates alkaline conditions.
Plant where it has adequate space to
spread, as magnolias resent disturbance.
It need no pruning.

◊ ◊ ☼ ☀ ❄ ❄ ❄
‡ to 8m (25ft) ↔ to 6m (20ft)

MAGNOLIA
'Star Wars' ♀

Deciduous tree

This recently introduced magnolia bears
massive deep pink blooms at a very
early age. It was named after the shape
of the flowers, which can measure up
to 30cm (12in) across, and have petals
pointing in many different directions.
'Star Wars' suits most soils and, in time,
this vigorous plant may grow to form a
medium-sized, pyramid-shaped tree.
Plant where it has plenty of space to
develop unhindered.

◊ ◊ ☼ ☀ ❄ ❄ ❄
‡ to 10m (30ft) ↔ to 8m (25ft)

NARCISSUS
'Passionale' ♀

Perennial bulb

This vigorous spring-flowering daffodil
has milky-white petals and a large pink
cup, and makes a superb cut flower. In
late summer or early autumn, plant the
bulbs in well-drained, fertile soil at one
and a half times their depth. They will
perform well in a sunny situation, and
can be used in a border planting, or a
formal bedding scheme. Deadhead the
plants after flowering, and divide large
clumps after 3-5 years.

◊ ☼ ❁ ❁ ❁
‡ to 40cm (16in) ↔ to 15cm (6in)

PAEONIA CAMBESSEDESII ♀

Perennial

The Majorcan peony is one of the first
to bloom in early spring. It has greyish-
green leaves, with deep red undersides
and wavy margins, while the flowers
have five pale magenta-pink petals and
deeper pink veins. Plant it in full sun in
a well-drained soil. It needs protection
from late frosts, and is best grown in
the shelter of a south-facing wall, or
under a cloche in winter.

◊ ☼ ❁ ❁
‡ ↔ to 55cm (22in)

PRUNUS
'Accolade' ♀

Deciduous tree

A beautiful flowering cherry, 'Accolade' has mid-green leaves that turn orange-red in autumn before they fall. Its wide-spreading branches produce clusters of three semi-double, pale pink flowers in early spring, which emerge from deep pink buds. It needs a sunny situation and should be planted in deep, well-drained, fertile soil. This tree does not require pruning.

◊ ☼ ❋ ❋ ❋
↕↔ to 8m (25ft)

PRUNUS MUME
'Beni-chidori'

Deciduous tree

Japanese apricots are spreading trees, suitable for small gardens. The almond-scented, double, deep pink flowers of 'Beni-chidori' appear in late winter or early spring and become paler as they age. The tree may also later produce small orange fruit, which look a little like apricots, but are very bitter. Plant it in a sunny, sheltered position, where frost is unlikely to damage the blooms, in deep, well-drained, fertile soil. No pruning is required.

◊ ☼ ❋ ❋ ❋
↕↔ to 9m (20ft)

PRUNUS
'Okame' ♀

Deciduous tree

The toothed, oval, dark green leaves
of this flowering cherry in autumn turn
brilliant shades of orange and red. The
cup-shaped, single, deep pink flowers
are produced in early spring. It is best
planted in a sunny position, in a deep,
moist, well-drained, fertile soil, and will
not need to be pruned.

◊ ◊ ☼ ❋ ❋ ❋
‡ to 10m (30ft) ↔ to 8m (25ft)

PRUNUS × YEDOENSIS ♀

Deciduous tree

The beautiful Yoshino cherry grows to
form a medium-sized, round-headed
tree with gently arching branches. In
early spring it bears clusters of five or
six single, pale pink flowers, which
gradually fade to white in the sun. It
should be planted in deep, fertile, well-
drained soil. No pruning is required.

◊ ☼ ❋ ❋ ❋
‡ to 15m (50ft) ↔ to 10m (30ft)

TULIPA
'Pink Beauty'

Perennial bulb

Tulips are an invaluable addition to the spring border, and are used to create a spectrum of colour relatively early in the year. There is plenty of choice, with different varieties bursting into flower throughout spring and early summer, providing a range of sizes, colours and flower shapes. The deep pink petals, with a brush stroke of white, and cup-shaped flowers of 'Pink Beauty' appear early, and it makes a particularly eye-catching bedding plant.

◊ ☼ ✿ ✿ ✿
‡ to 60cm (24in) ↔ to 13cm (5in)

VIOLA × WITTROCKIANA
Ultima Series

Perennial

These violets, more commonly known as pansies, have been widely hybridised to produce a range of long-flowering plants. The Ultima Series start to flower in winter and continue through spring. They are available in a range of bright colours, including pink, and make a superb choice for brightening up the garden during early spring. Use them as bedding, and in tubs and window boxes, and grow them in a sunny site in fertile, well-drained soil.

◊ ☼ ✿ ✿ ✿
‡ to 23cm (9in) ↔ to 30cm (12in)

CAMELLIA JAPONICA
'Coquettii' ♛

Evergreen shrub

In early to mid-spring the arching stems of this slow-growing shrub are covered with deep red, semi-double or double flowers. It makes an elegant addition to a border and will complement plantings in a woodland garden, but it can also be grown as a specimen in containers or in open ground. Choose a partially shaded site, out of the early morning sun, in moist, but well-drained, humus-rich acid soil. Use an ericaceous (lime-free) compost in containers.

○ ◐ ☀ ❋ ❋ ❋
‡ to 9m (28ft) ↔ to 8m (25ft)

CHAENOMELES × SUPERBA
'Crimson and Gold' ♛

Deciduous shrub

The deep crimson flowers with golden yellow anthers are produced by this Japanese quince from spring to early summer, and are often followed in the autumn by yellow-green fruit. Its wide, spreading habit makes it a useful shrub for ground cover, planting against walls or in a border, or it can be grown as an informal, low flowering hedge. Quinces trained against walls or used as hedges should be cut back after flowering.

○ ☀ ❋ ❋ ❋
‡ to 1m (3ft) ↔ to 2m (6ft)

CORYDALIS SOLIDA
'George Baker' ♀

Perennial

This attractive tuberous perennial has deeply dissected greyish-green leaves. In spring, it produces bright red, with a hint of orange, tubular flowers. Plant it in a rock or gravel garden in full sun or partial shade, in well-drained fertile soil. 'George Baker' can be divided in the autumn if clumps become too large.

◊ ☼ ☀ ❊ ❊ ❊
‡ to 25cm (10in) ↔ to 20cm (8in)

ERYSIMUM
'Blood Red'

Perennial

Although perennial, wallflowers are often grown as biennial bedding plants, and planted in combination with tall-stemmed tulips. Left alone, they will live for several years, but can become woody and leggy with age. This variety has vivid, deep red flowers in spring, and is ideal for growing against a dry wall, or to brighten up the front of a sunny border or raised bed. Plant it in autumn in very well-drained, neutral to alkaline soil.

◊ ☼ ❊ ❊ ❊
‡ ↔ to 30cm (12in)

PAEONIA TENUIFOLIA

Evergreen shrub

Fern-leaf peonies are among the earliest species to flower, producing beautiful deep red, single flowers in spring, amid dark green ferny leaves. There are also other forms with double white, red and pink flowers. Plant it in a sunny site, in well-drained, sandy soil. This delicate-looking plant may be grown in rock or gravel gardens or a herbaceous border.

◊ ☼ ❋ ❋ ❋

↕↔ to 70cm (28in)

PHOTINIA X FRASERI
'Red Robin' ♀

Evergreen shrub

The glossy young leaves of this shrub are bright purplish-red, and turn dark bronze-green as the season progresses. From mid-spring it produces clusters of small white flowers. It prefers fertile, well-drained soil; the foliage is easily damaged by cold winds, so plant it in a sunny, sheltered position. It can be used as a hedging plant or free-standing shrub. Trim hedges two to three times a year to keep up the show of bright young foliage.

◊ ◊ ☼ ☼ ❋ ❋ ❋

↕↔ to 5m (15ft)

PIERIS FORMOSA
'Wakehurst' ♀

Evergreen shrub

The brilliant red young foliage of this
beautiful shrub gradually turns various
shades of pink and creamy-white, and
then finally goes dark green. Small, urn-
shaped, white flowers are borne in mid-
spring and hang in pendent clusters.
'Wakehurst' does best in semi-shade,
and needs protection from cold winds
and frost. Plant it in moist, slightly acid
(lime-free), humus-rich soil in a shrub
or woodland border. Prune lightly after
it has flowered to maintain its shape.

◊ ◊ ☼ ☀ ❀ ❀ ❀
‡ to 5m (15ft) ↔ to 4m (12ft)

PRIMULA JAPONICA

Perennial

The Japanese primrose is a robust
perennial with a rosette of spoon-
shaped, pale green leaves. In spring it
produces a stout stem with up to six
tiers of as many as 25 white, pink, red
or purplish red flowers. It needs
humus-rich, damp soil and is ideally
suited to the bog garden and areas of
damp woodland or waterside plantings.

◊ ◊ ☼ ☀ ❀ ❀ ❀
‡ ↔ to 45cm (18in)

PRIMULA
'Crescendo Bright Red' ♥

Evergreen perennial

Polyanthus are vigorous primulas which should be planted in the autumn for a spring bedding display. They produce rosettes of evergreen leaves and often start flowering at the end of winter. The Crescendo Series is available in a range of bright colours, including vivid red. Polyanthus prefer a sunny position, but will tolerate some shade, and should be planted in reasonably fertile, moist, but well-drained, soil.

◊ ◊ ☼ ☀ ✿ ✿ ✿
‡ to 15cm (6in) ↔ to 30cm (12in)

PULMONARIA RUBRA
'Redstart'

Perennial

This attractive herbaceous perennial has bright green, hairy leaves and funnel-shaped, coral-red flowers. It begins to flower early in the year, with blooms often appearing in the middle of winter and continuing into spring. It forms a loose clump, and provides excellent ground cover for damp shady positions. Young plants are vigorous, and should be divided after four or five years. Clip over after flowering to encourage a flush of bright new foliage.

◊ ☼ ☀ ✿ ✿ ✿
‡ to 40cm (16in) ↔ to 90cm (36in)

TULIPA
'Red Riding Hood' ♀

Perennial bulb

The bright red flowers of this striking
tulip have black marks at the base of
the petals, and its lance-shaped leaves
are strongly marked with purple stripes.
Plant bulbs in late autumn in a sunny
situation in well-drained, fertile soil, in
a border, or rock garden, where they
can be left for years. Alternatively, plant
them in containers and move the bulbs
out into the garden after flowering. For
a bold bedding display, plant with a
deep-yellow tulip, such as 'Yokahama'.

◊ ☼ ❋ ❋ ❋
‡ to 20cm (8in) ↔ to 15cm (6in)

TULIPA
'Apeldoorn'

Perennial bulb

Darwin tulips, such as 'Apeldoorn', are
easy to grow and their rounded flowers
look equally at home in spring bedding
displays as they do when used as cut
flowers. 'Apeldoorn' has scarlet-red
flowers with black centres, surrounded
by yellow. Plant bulbs in late autumn,
in a sunny site in well-drained, fertile
soil. It looks superb when partnered
with a yellow tulip, such as 'Daydream'.

◊ ☼ ❋ ❋ ❋
‡ to 60cm (24in) ↔ to 13cm (5in)

CROCUS
TOMMASINIANUS ♀

Perennial corm

This crocus gives the impression of being rather delicate, but its slender appearance is deceptive. It produces purple, violet or lilac flowers from late winter to early spring, and grows easily from seed. Choose a sunny site with well-drained soil, and in autumn plant the corms in groups to create drifts of colour at the front of a border, or to naturalize in short grass.

◊ ☼ ❋ ❋ ❋
‡ to 10cm (4in) ↔ to 2.5cm (1in)

HARDENBERGIA
COMPTONIANA ♀

Climber

Clusters of small, mauve or purplish-blue flowers appear on this vigorous climber with woody stems from early spring. It prefers a sunny position, in moist, well-drained, neutral or acid soil, but it is not hardy and may have to be kept in a greenhouse or conservatory over winter. In mild areas, it can be used to complement exisiting plantings by growing it through larger shrubs and up small trees, or train it on a wall.

◊ ◗ ☼ ❋
‡ to 2.5m (8ft)

HELLEBORUS ORIENTALIS
Early Purple Group

Perennial

Often sold under its former name of
H. atrorubens, this variable hellebore
flowers very early in the year. It has
deep purple, saucer-shaped, pendent
flowers that emerge from late winter
to early spring. The deciduous, palm-
shaped leaves are mid-green, flushed
with purple. It thrives on rich, moist,
well-drained soil, and its preference for
partial shade makes it a good choice for
a shrub border or a woodland garden.

◊ ◊ ☼ ❄ ❄ ❄
‡ to 30cm (12in) ↔ to 45cm (18in)

PRIMULA AURICULA
'Adrian'

Evergreen perennial

A rosette forming perennial, this alpine
auricula has fleshy pale green leaves,
and in spring bears beautiful flowers
with purple-blue petals, slightly paler
edges and a white eye. Alpine auriculas
are extremely hardy plants, but will do
best in a sunny or partially shaded site
in moist, well drained soil. Grow them
in a rock or gravel garden, raised beds,
an unheated greenhouse, or in pots of
gritty, loam-based compost.

◊ ◊ ☼ ☼ ❄ ❄ ❄
‡↔ to 10cm (4in)

RHODODENDRON DAURICUM

Evergreen shrub

The leaves of this semi-evergreen shrub are green with a dark brown underside. It starts flowering in late winter when the funnel-shaped, bright pinkish-purple blooms bring a dramatic burst of colour to an otherwise gloomy garden. Plant it in a sunny site, in well-drained, humus-rich, acid (lime-free) soil, and mulch it annually with leafmould or chipped bark. This very hardy rhododendron is suitable for exposed sites, and may be used to create an informal screen.

◊ ◊ ☼ ☼ ✳ ✳ ✳
‡ ↔ to 1.5m (5ft)

RHODODENDRON 'Praecox' ♀

Evergreen shrub

This is among the first rhododendrons to bloom, flowering from late winter and continuing into early spring. It is normally evergreen, but sheds some of its leaves during winter. The flowers are pinkish-purple, and appear in clusters of two or three. Although generally hardy, the flowers may be damaged by severe frost. It makes a spectacular flowering hedge, but is equally at home in the border. Plant in full sun or partial shade, in moist, well-drained, acid soil.

◊ ◊ ☼ ☼ ✳ ✳ ✳
‡ ↔ to 1.3m (4½ft)

TULIPA HUMILIS
Violacea Group

Perennial bulb

This early, spring-flowering tulip has
large purple star-shaped flowers with a
bright yellow blotch at the base of the
petals, and narrow greyish-green leaves.
Plant bulbs in late autumn, in a sunny
position in light, well-drained soil. It is
ideal for the rock garden, or makes a
colourful display in raised beds. Leave
undisturbed so clumps can build up *in
situ*; they like to be dry during summer.

◊ ☼ ❀ ❀ ❀
‡↔ to 25cm (10in) ↔ to 13cm (5in)

VIOLA ODORATA

Perennial

Sweet violets may be small, but their
very aromatic bluey-purple or white
flowers will perfume the garden from
late winter and throughout early spring.
They self-seed, and will quickly become
established, particularly when allowed
to naturalize in a woodland setting
or by deciduous shrubs. Plant in a sunny
position or in dappled shade, in well-
drained, humus-rich soil. They can also
be divided and replanted in spring.

◊ ☼ ☼ ❀ ❀ ❀
↑ to 20cm (8in) ↔ to 30cm (12in)

ANEMONE BLANDA
'Atrocaerulea'

Perennial

The deep-blue, daisy-like flowers of this anemone are striking when naturalized in grass or beneath the bare branches of deciduous trees. It has a low, clump-forming habit which also makes it a suitable plant for the front of a border. Plant the knobbly tubers in autumn, in full sun or partial shade and humus-rich, well-drained soil.

◊ ☼ ☀ ✿ ✿ ✿
‡ to 10cm (4in) ↔ to 15cm (6in)

ANEMONE NEMOROSA
'Robinsoniana' ♀

Perennial

This wood anemone bears numerous pale lavender-blue flowers with a light grey reverse to the petals. The mid-green leaves die back after flowering. It is a low, creeping plant, useful for underplanting or naturalizing. A native of European woods, it does best in a woodland situation, but it will grow in most positions, given dappled or partial shade and a moist, but well-drained, humus-rich soil.

◊ ◊ ☼ ✿ ✿ ✿
‡ to 15cm (6in) ↔ to 30cm (12in)

AUBRIETA
'Cobalt Violet'

Perennial

A mat-forming perennial with masses of
small hairy leaves. In spring it produces
profuse quantities of small, violet-blue
flowers, and is ideal for trailing over the
edge of a raised bed or stone wall, or
for growing in a rock garden. Plant it in
fertile, well-drained, neutral or alkaline
soil, and trim it over with secateurs
after flowering to keep it neat and tidy.

○ ☼ ❁ ❁ ❁
‡ to 10cm (4in) ↔ to 20cm (8in)

BRUNNERA MACROPHYLLA ♀

Perennial

This spreading perennial has coarse,
long-stalked, heart-shaped leaves and
bright blue flowers in spring. It will
eventually form a large clump and is
good for providing ground cover in
semi-shaded situations. It needs moist,
well-drained, humus-rich soil. 'Hadspen
Cream' has partially variegated leaves
with creamy-white margins, which will
brighten a dull corner. Propagate it by
seed in autumn, or division in spring.

○ ◑ ☼ ❄ ❄ ❄
‡ to 45cm (18in) ↔ to 60cm (24in)

CHIONODOXA LUCILIAE ♀

Perennial bulb

In spring, glory-of-the-snow bears up
to three violet-blue, star-shaped flowers,
each with a small white eye. It comes
from the stony slopes of Turkey, and is
most at home in a rock garden, raised
bed, or naturalized under deciduous
trees or at the front of a border. Plant
the bulbs in autumn, in a sunny site in
well-drained soil. Established clumps
benefit from a mulch with well-rotted
compost in autumn.

⚪ ☼ ✽ ✽ ✽
‡ to 15cm (6in) ↔ to 3cm (1¼in)

CLEMATIS ALPINA
'Frances Rivis' ♀

Climber

A deciduous, early flowering climber
with mid-blue, bell-shaped flowers in
spring to early summer, and feathery
seed heads in autumn. It is very hardy
and tolerates fairly exposed situations.
Prune it back after flowering. Provide
support in the form of wires or trellis
attached to a wall or fence, or train it
over an arch or tripod. Grow it in well-
drained, fertile, preferably alkaline soil,
with the roots in shade and its head in
the sun.

⚪ ☼ ☀ ✽ ✽ ✽
‡ to 3m (10ft) ↔ to 1.5m (5ft)

HEPATICA NOBILIS *VAR.* JAPONICA

Perennial

This is a slow-growing perennial which retains it leathery leaves during most winters. The star-shaped flowers, with blue-purple, pink or white petals that open in spring, sit above three small dark green leaves. It requires partial shade and moist, humus-rich soil, and is well suited to a woodland setting or a shady border.

◊ ☼ ❋ ❋ ❋
‡ to 8cm (3in) ↔ to 12cm (5in)

HYACINTHUS ORIENTALIS *'Blue Jacket'* ♀

Perennial bulb

This is one of the best blue flowered hyacinths, with wonderfully fragrant, navy-blue blooms The petals have a waxy texture and purple veins. Plant it in autumn, in deep, well-drained, fertile soil in sun or partial shade. Hyacinths are perfect for creating colourful spring bedding displays, and are also useful container or window box plants. Grow them either outside, or forced in bowls of bulb fibre for display in the home.

◊ ☼ ☼ ❋ ❋ ❋
‡ to 30cm (12in) ↔ to 8cm (3in)

IRIS HISTRIOIDES
'Major'

Perennial bulb

The vivid blue flowers of this vigorous dwarf iris open in early spring. Its lower petals are marked with a bright yellow ridge, which is surrounded by dark blue lines, and the square leaves are very short at the beginning of the year, but extend to 30cm (12in) after flowering. Plant it in a sunny location, in well-drained, fertile soil. Dwarf irises are an excellent choice for the rock garden, raised beds or containers.

◊ ☼ ✿✿✿

↕ to 15cm (6in) ↔ to 7cm (3in)

IRIS
'Joyce'

Perennial bulb

A superb plant for a rock garden, this is a reticulata iris which flowers very early in the spring. It bears sky blue flowers with a bold yellow flare down the centre of the petals. Plant bulbs in autumn, in a sunny situation and well-drained, neutral or alkaline soil. 'Joyce' will also grow happily in containers or troughs of gritty, loam-based compost. Keep the bulbs on the dry side during the summer.

◊ ☼ ✿✿✿

↕ to 12cm (5in) ↔ to 7cm (3in)

IRIS
'Katharine Hodgkin' ♀

Perennial bulb

This vigorous dwarf iris flowers from
late winter. Its upper petals are covered
with fine, deep blue veins, while the
broad lower petals have a yellow centre
and are heavily marked with blue lines
and speckles. Plant the bulbs in autumn
and grow this iris on a sunny bank or
in other well-drained situations, making
sure the bulbs are kept on the dry side
during the summer. It enjoys neutral or
slightly alkaline soil.

○ ☼ ❀ ❀ ❀
‡ to 12cm (5in) ↔ to 7cm (3in)

IRIS
'Cantab'

Perennial bulb

Another reticulata iris (see 'Joyce'), this
one has pale blue flowers with slightly
darker lower petals, marked by a deep
yellow crest. The blooms start to appear
in late winter. These iris are vigorous
but the bulbs often divide after it has
flowered and then take a couple of
years to grow large enough to bloom
again. Plant the bulbs in autumn in a
sunny situation and fertile, well-drained
soil, such as in a rock garden or trough
filled with gritty loam-based compost.

○ ☼ ❀ ❀ ❀
‡ to 12cm (5in) ↔ to 7cm (3in)

MUSCARI ARMENIACUM ♀

Perennial bulb

The grape hyacinth is one of the most widely grown spring-flowering bulbs, used to create spectacular bedding displays and in the border. Each stem carries a dense spike of small, deep blue flowers above narrow, bright green leaves. In the right conditions, it spreads quickly and may occasionally be invasive. The bulbs can become overcrowded and will benefit from division in summer every few years. Plant bulbs in autumn, in full sun, in fertile, moist but well-drained soil.

◊ ◊ ☼ ❋ ❋ ❋
‡ to 20cm (8in) ↔ to 10cm (4in)

OMPHALODES CAPPADOCICA ♀

Evergreen perennial

The forget-me-not-like flowers of this evergreen are azure blue with white eyes, and borne on slender stems from early spring. It has creeping roots and forms clumps of heart-shaped, slightly hairy leaves, and makes ideal ground cover for shady places. Grow it in full or partial shade and slightly moist, well-drained, humus-rich fertile soil.

◊ ◊ ☼ ☀ ❋ ❋ ❋
‡ to 25cm (10in) ↔ to 40cm (16in)

PULMONARIA
'Lewis Palmer' ♀

Perennial

This deciduous ground-cover plant has slightly hairy, lance-shaped leaves with greenish-white spots and small funnel-shaped flowers that are pink when they open in spring and then turn a vibrant blue. Lungwort should be grown in humus-rich, moist soil in partial or full shade. It attracts bees, and makes an excellent choice for a wildlife garden, or use it to enhance a shady woodland or shrub border. Clip it over after it has flowered to refresh the foliage.

◑ ☼ ☀ ❉ ❉ ❉
‡ to 35cm (14in) ↔ to 45cm (18in)

PUSCHKINIA SCILLOIDES

Perennial bulb

The pale blue, bell-like flowers of this bulbous perennial are set off by a fine blue line down the centre of each petal. Its compact spikes make an attractive addition to the rock garden or a shrub border. Plant it in a sunny or partially shaded site, in well-drained, fertile soil.

◐ ☼ ☀ ❉ ❉ ❉
‡ to 15cm (6in) ↔ to 5cm (2in)

RHODODENDRON
Blue Tit Group

Evergreen shrub

A remarkably compact rhododendron, which in early spring bears abundant small, funnel-shaped greyish-blue flowers. Its leaves are initially yellow-green but darken to a mid-green colour as the plant matures. Like many dwarf rhododendrons, 'Blue Tit' will bloom happily in a container or in a rock or gravel garden, given full sunshine and moist, well-drained, acid soil or ericaceous (lime-free) compost.

◊ ◊ ☼ ☼ ❄ ❄ ❄
↕ ↔ to 1m (3ft)

SCILLA BIFOLIA ♛

Perennial bulb

This is a distinctive early spring flowering bulb that looks wonderful naturalized in grass or under deciduous shrubs and trees. It has narrow strap-shaped, bright green leaves and star-shaped flowers, borne on one side of the stem. This species has blue or violet-blue flowers, but there are also varieties with white ('Alba') and pink ('Rosea') blooms. Plant it in fertile, humus rich, well-drained soil, in full sunshine or partial shade.

◊ ☼ ❄ ❄ ❄
↕ ↔ to 15cm (6in)

Scilla mischtschenkoana

Perennial bulb

The pale blue, bell-shaped flowers of
this bulbous perennial have a dark blue
stripe down the centre of each petal.
They are carried above broad, strap-
shaped arching leaves on rather short
stems, which grow longer as the
flowers open in early spring. Naturalize
it in grass or plant in a rock or gravel
garden or raised bed in a sunny
position with well-drained soil. Plant
bulbs in autumn.

◊ ☼ ❀ ❀ ❀
‡ to 15cm (6in) ↔ to 5cm (2in)

Scilla siberica
'Spring Beauty'

Perennial bulb

This bulbous perennial has small spikes
of bell-shaped, violet-tinted, deep blue
flowers arranged on one side of the
stem. Ideal for a rock garden or a
mixed herbaceous border beneath
deciduous shrubs or trees, it prefers
sandy, well-drained, fertile soil in slight
shade or full sun. Divide large clumps
after flowering during the summer.
Plant bulbs in autumn.

◊ ☼ ☼ ❀ ❀ ❀
‡ to 20cm (8in) ↔ to 5cm (2in)

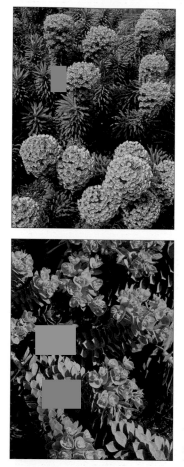

EUPHORBIA CHARACIAS
SUBSP. WULFENII ♀

Evergreen shrub

A large rounded bush with greyish-green leaves. The huge, globe-shaped heads pocked with small yellow-green flowers appear from early spring. It is ideal for the back of a border, gravel garden, or gaps in paving, but needs a sunny site and well-drained soil. Buy young plants from a reliable source to avoid inferior, less brightly coloured seedlings. Cut out the old flowerheads in autumn, and wear gloves as the sap may cause an allergic skin reaction.

◊ ☼ ✤ ✤ ✤
↕↔ to 1.2m (4ft)

EUPHORBIA MYRSINITES ♀

Evergreen perennial

This is a sprawling evergreen perennial, suitable for planting in a rock or gravel garden, gaps in paving, or at the edge of a raised bed or on a stone wall. The fleshy, blue-green leaves are arranged in a spiral around the stems. In spring, the stems are topped with clusters of yellowish-green flowers, which turn a greyish-pink as they fade. Plant it full sun, in well-drained soil. It may self-seed if the dead heads are not removed after flowering.

◊ ☼ ✤ ✤ ✤
↕ to 10cm (4in) ↔ to 30cm (12in)

HELLEBORUS ARGUTIFOLIUS ♀

Evergreen perennial

The Corsican hellebore bears bright green, slightly nodding, cup-shaped flowers from late winter to early spring. Its evergreen leaves are divided into three toothed, greyish-green leaflets. One of the largest hellebores, it grows best on moist, well-drained, alkaline or neutral soil, in full sun or partial shade. Choose it for a mixed border or allow to naturalize in a woodland setting as it self-seeds freely.

○ ☼ ☀ ❋ ❋ ❋
‡ to 1.2m (4ft) ↔ to 90cm (36in)

HELLEBORUS FOETIDUS ♀

Evergreen perennial

The stinking hellebore is a vigorous, clump-forming perennial with dark evergreen, deeply divided, somewhat leathery leaves; it is named for the unpleasant smell that emanates from them when they are crushed. The bell-shaped, slightly fragrant, green flowers are produced in clusters on tall, erect stems from late winter to early spring. Equally at home in full sunshine or partial shade, it can be planted in a variety of situations in the garden and is happy on moist, alkaline soils.

○ ☼ ☀ ❋ ❋ ❋
‡ to 80cm (32in) ↔ to 45cm (18in)

ADONIS VERNALIS

Perennial

This hardy clump-forming perennial originates from Europe, where it is often found in rocky, exposed sites. In spring it produces golden yellow flowers above deeply dissected bright green leaves. Grow it in a raised bed, rock or gravel garden in full sun and well-drained, preferably alkaline soil.

○ ☼ ❀ ❀ ❀
‡↔ to 30cm (12in)

ANEMONE × LIPSIENSIS

Perennial

The pale, sulphur-yellow flowers of this carpet-forming wood anemone appear in spring. Its dark green leaves are deeply toothed and lie close to the soil surface. Best grown in partially shaded situations beneath deciduous trees or shrubs, this natural hybrid prefers a humus-rich, well-drained soil, and will tolerate chalky conditions.

○ ◐ ☼ ❀ ❀ ❀
‡ to 15cm (6in) ↔ to 45cm (18in)

ANEMONE RANUNCULOIDES ♛

Perennial

This spreading perennial received its
name because of its similarity to the
buttercup. It has deeply divided mid-
green leaves and bright yellow flowers
with five or six petals. It enjoys a site
in partial shade and is ideal for a mixed
border or naturalizing in a woodland or
wild garden. Plant it in moist, but well-
drained, humus-rich soil.

◊ ◐ ☼ ❋ ❋ ❋
‡ to 10cm (4in) ↔ to 45cm (18in)

CALTHA PALUSTRIS ♛

Perennial

The kingcup, or marsh marigold, is a
vigorous clump-forming perennial with
serrated glossy green leaves. It is one of
the earliest aquatic plants to come into
bloom, and has large bright golden
yellow flowers. Thriving in full sun in
wet soil, it makes an excellent choice
for a bog garden, but may also be
grown in a permanently moist border,
or shallow water at the edge of a pond,
contained in a perforated basket. 'Flore
Pleno' is slightly less vigorous, and has
double yellow flowers.

◐ ◐ ☼ ❋ ❋ ❋
‡ to 40cm (16in) ↔ to 45cm (18in)

CORYLOPSIS PAUCIFLORA ♀

Deciduous shrub

This bushy, deciduous plant produces small, very fragrant, pale yellow, bell-shaped flowers in spring. The young leaves appear after the flowers, and are pink when they open, but turn green as they age. Although other corylopsis species tolerate alkaline conditions, *C. pauciflora* requires acid soil. Given plenty of room, it will grow into a pleasing, spreading shape, and enhance a woodland garden or a shrub border in dappled shade. The flowers can be damaged by hard frosts.

⚫💧☼ ✳✳✳
‡ to 1.5m (5ft) ↔ to 2.5m (8ft)

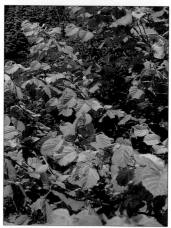

CORYLUS AVELLANA
'Aurea'

Deciduous shrub

In late winter and early spring this decorative hazel bears dangling yellow catkins. It forms a broad, spreading shrub or small tree, with bright yellow-green, sharply toothed leaves, and in late summer the rounded hazelnuts are favoured by squirrels. A relatively small variety, it is suitable for a shrub border, and contrasts well with the purple-leaved hazel, *C. avellana* 'Purpurea'.

💧 ☼ ☼ ✳✳✳
‡↔ to 5m (15ft)

CROCUS CHRYSANTHUS
'E.A. Bowles' ♀

Perennial corm

This dainty crocus has deep lemon-
yellow, goblet-shaped flowers, with
purple feathering on the outer petals.
The leaves are dark green with a white
stripe. Plant the corms in groups in the
autumn in well-drained soil at the front
of a sunny border for an early splash
of spring colour, or grow in raised beds
and containers.

◊ ☼ ✿ ✿ ✿
↕ to 7cm (3in) ↔ to 5cm (2in)

CROCUS CHRYSANTIIUS
'Cream Beauty'

Perennial corm

A compact, spring-flowering crocus
with rich cream-coloured flowers that
darken at the base to a greenish-gold,
and have a golden throat. Plant the
bulbs as for 'E.A Bowles' (above) in a
sunny position in well drained, gritty
soil. It suits a rock garden, and may
also be naturalized in grass.

◊ ☼ ✿ ✿ ✿
↕ to 7cm (3in) ↔ to 5cm (2in)

ERANTHIS HYEMALIS ♀

Perennial

The winter aconite begins flowering
in late winter and continues into early
spring. Its bright yellow blooms perch
on a ruff of deeply divided, leaf-like
bracts. Ideal for naturalizing in grass
and woodland borders, it will create
a colourful carpet beneath deciduous
trees and shrubs. Plant the tubers in
autumn in fertile, moist, well-drained
soil that does not dry out in summer.
Large clumps can be divided after it
has flowered.

○ ◐ ☀ ❄ ❄ ❄
‡ to 8cm (3in) ↔ to 5cm (2in)

ERYSIMUM
'Moonlight'

Evergreen perennial

A mat-forming perennial wallflower
with evergreen, greyish-green, lance-
shaped leaves. Throughout spring and
early summer it produces clusters of
slightly fragrant, pale sulphur-yellow
flowers. It is rather short-lived, but it
makes an excellent subject for a dry
wall, gravel or raised bed, or a rock
garden. Plant it in full sunshine, in
poor, gritty, very well-drained soil.

○ ☀ ❄ ❄ ❄
‡ to 30cm (12in) ↔ to 45cm (18in)

ERYTHRONIUM
'Pagoda' ♀

Perennial bulb

This dog's-tooth violet bears drooping clusters of up to five sulphur-yellow flowers in spring. A vigorous plant with mottled, glossy green leaves, it is suitable for planting beneath shrubs or in the dappled shade of a woodland garden in moist, humus-rich, well-drained soil. Plant the bulbs in autumn. Large clumps can be divided after the leaves have died; replant immediately to prevent the bulbs from drying out.

◊ ◊ ☼ ❋ ❋ ❋

‡ to 35cm (14in) ↔ to 20cm (8in)

FORSYTHIA × INTERMEDIA
'Lynwood' ♀

Deciduous shrub

Forsythias are free flowering, medium-sized shrubs, the upright branches of which are covered with large bright yellow flowers during spring before the leaves unfurl. Plant them in a row to create a spectacular hedge, or grow one as a freestanding shrub in a border. Cut hedges and prune back the shoots of shrubs after flowering to promote new growth and flowers the following year. Choose a site in full sun or light shade in fertile, well-drained soil.

◊ ☼ ☀ ❋ ❋ ❋

‡ ↔ to 3m (10ft)

HYACINTHUS ORIENTALIS
'City of Haarlem' ♥

Perennial bulb

With spikes of primrose-yellow, waxy, bell-shaped flowers, this is one of only a few yellow hyacinths. Its intense scent makes it an appealing houseplant when forced into bloom early in the winter months. Outdoors, it looks wonderful in spring bedding displays, and needs full sun and free-draining soil. Forced bulbs grown for indoor display should be fed regularly after flowering, and then planted outside. The flowers will be smaller in subsequent years.

◊ ☼ ❁ ❁ ❁
‡ to 30cm (12in) ↔ to 8cm (3in)

IRIS DANFORDIAE

Perennial bulb

This is an extremely attractive dwarf iris with bright yellow spring flowers. It is best considered as a disposable plant, because although it flowers well in the first season, the bulb then splits into tiny bulblets which rarely bloom again. Ideal for containers, troughs or raised beds, the bulbs should be planted in late summer or early autumn in a sunny position and well-drained soil.

◊ ☼ ❁ ❁ ❁
‡ to 10cm (4in) ↔ to 5cm (2in)

IRIS WINOGRADOWII ♥

Perennial bulb

The pale yellow flowers of this dwarf
iris emerge in early spring. Its leaves
are very short at flowering time, but
lengthen afterwards. Suitable for a rock
or gravel garden or a raised bed, grow
it in full sunshine, in well-drained,
moisture-retentive soil. Do not allow
the bulbs to dry out during summer.

△ ◊ ☼ ✿ ✿ ✿
‡ to 10cm (4in) ↔ to 7cm (3in)

MAHONIA AQUIFOLIUM
'Apollo' ♥

Evergreen shrub

This suckering shrub has large leaves,
divided into spiny leaflets, with red
stalks. Its bright yellow flowers are
carried in compact clusters, which are
succeeded by bluish-black berries. The
Oregon grape will thrive in the dry soil
beneath trees; grown in sun or shade,
it provides superb ground cover and
should be clipped to the ground after
flowering every other year. The leaves
take on coppery tones in autumn.

△ ◊ ☼ ☀ ✿ ✿ ✿
‡ to 60cm (24in) ↔ to 1.2m (4ft)

NARCISSUS
'Ambergate'

Perennial bulb

This striking daffodil bears flowers with a large, deep orange cup, surrounded by warm yellow petals from mid-spring. The flowers can measure as much as 10cm (4in) across, making it a dramatic choice for a display of cut flowers. It may also be planted in groups in a mixed border or naturalized in grass. Plant bulbs in late summer to one and a half times their depth in a sunny site in well-drained, reasonably fertile soil.

◊ ☼ ❀ ❀ ❀
‡ to 40cm (16in) ↔ to 15cm (6in)

NARCISSUS BULBOCODIUM ♀
Perennial bulb

The diminutive hoop-petticoat daffodil produces dark green, almost cylindrical leaves, and yellow, funnel-shaped early spring flowers. Tiny, pointed petals appear half way down the flower funnel, so that it looks rather like a lady wearing a long yellow ball gown. It grows best in a sunny position, and can be planted among fine-leaved grasses or in a raised bed. The variety *conspicuus* bears deep golden-yellow flowers. Plant bulbs as for 'Ambergate' (see above).

◊ ☼ ❀ ❀ ❀
‡ to 15cm (6in) ↔ to 5cm (2in)

NARCISSUS CYCLAMINEUS ♀
Perennial bulb

This early-flowering daffodil produces deep yellow, vase-shaped flowers, with strongly swept-back petals, and bright green leaves. Grow in a sunny position, in well-drained neutral to acid (lime-free) soil. It makes an excellent choice for containers, a woodland border, or for naturalizing in grass. Plant bulbs as for 'Ambergate' (see left).

○ ☼ ❋ ❋ ❋
↕ to 20cm (8in) ↔ to 8cm (3in)

NARCISSUS 'February Gold' ♀
Perennial bulb

A widely grown daffodil, 'February Gold' is extremely vigorous and in the early spring produces nodding, large golden-yellow flowers with slightly swept-back petals. The flowers are set off by mid-green, strap-shaped leaves. It is suitable for planting in borders or for naturalizing in grass. Plant bulbs as for 'Ambergate' (see above left)

○ ☼ ❋ ❋ ❋
↕ to 30cm (12in) ↔ to 8cm (3in)

PRIMULA PALINURI

Evergreen perennial

This is an attractive rosette-forming primula with rather fleshy, spoon-shaped leaves. In early spring it bears often large, cowslip-like clusters of slightly fragrant yellow flowers. Grow it in a sunny site in reasonably fertile, moist, well-drained, preferably alkaline soil, and mulch with grit. It suffers in cold, wet winters, so it is best to grow it in pots of gritty loam-based compost.

⚪💧☼ ✤ ✤ ✤
‡↔ to 30cm (12in)

PRIMULA VULGARIS ♀

Evergreen perennial

The primrose is often regarded as the true harbinger of spring. Each stem of this rosette-forming perennial carries up to 25 single, pale yellow flowers with an orange spot at the base of each petal. It prefers a position in partial shade and moist, well-drained, humus-rich soil. An excellent plant for growing in containers, it will also be happy in woodland and shrub borders, and rock gardens. Propagate it from seed, or divide during early spring or autumn; never collect bulbs from the wild.

⚪💧☼ ✤ ✤ ✤
‡ to 20cm (8in) ↔ to 35cm (14in)

RANUNCULUS FICARIA 'Brazen Hussy'

Perennial

This celandine boasts glossy, bronze-coloured, heart-shaped leaves that lie close to the ground, and bright yellow flowers which emerge in spring. Given wet soil in winter it can be invasive, but it is easy to remove unwanted portions, and it dies back completely during the summer. It will thrive in partial shade and moist soil in a shrub border, at the base of a hedge, or in a woodland setting. The variety *aurantiacus* bears single orange flowers.

◊ ☼ ❋ ❋ ❋
‡ to 5cm (2in) ↔ to 20cm (8in)

RHODODENDRON LUTESCENS

Evergreen shrub

An attractive medium to-large evergreen shrub, with bronzy-green leaves, its clusters of primrose-yellow flowers start to open in late winter and continue into early spring. Ideal for brightening up a shady woodland situation, it should be protected from cold winds and planted in moist, well-drained, humus-rich, acid (lime-free) soil. Mulch it annually with leaf mould or chipped bark.

◊ ◊ ☼ ☼ ❋ ❋ ❋
‡ ↔ to 5m (15ft)

SALIX CAPREA 'Kilmarnock'

Deciduous tree

Salix caprea is usually a tall, vigorous tree, but the Kilmarnock willow rarely exceeds a height of 2m (6ft), making it ideal for planting in small gardens or large containers. It has a weeping habit and bears numerous rounded yellow catkins in late winter and early spring. Plant it in deep, moist, well-drained soil in a sunny site. The branches can become congested; in late winter prune out surplus ones, and removing shoots that appear on the trunk.

◊ ◊ ☼ ❋ ❋ ❋
↕↔ to 2m (6ft)

TULIPA KAUFMANNIANA

Perennial bulb

The flowers of the water-lily tulip have narrow, pointed, yellow or cream petals, that are tinted orange or pink on the outside. Its tall stems bear up to five blooms, carried above lance-shaped greyish-green leaves. A long-lived bulb, it is best grown in a rock garden. Plant the bulbs in late autumn in full sun, in fertile, well-drained soil at a depth of at least 10cm (4in).

◊ ☼ ❋ ❋ ❋
↕ to 25cm (10in) ↔ to 15cm (6in)

TULIPA URUMIENSIS ♛

Perennial bulb

The cheerful golden yellow star-shaped
flowers of this low-growing tulip appear
in early spring above a rosette of waxy
green leaves; much of its stem remains
below ground. Its petals are flushed
with green and red on the outside.
Grow it in a raised bed or rock garden
where clumps can develop undisturbed
and the soil is well drained and fairly
dry in summer. Plant the bulbs in late
autumn at a depth of about 10cm (4in).

◊ ☼ ❁ ❁ ❁
↕ to 15cm (6in) ↔ to 13cm (5in)

VALERIANA PHU
'Aurea'
Perennial

The main feature of valerian is its bright
butter-yellow foliage, which appears in
early spring. The leaves turn lime-green
after a few weeks and then mature to
mid-green. After these exciting foliage
effects, its small white summer flowers
are rather unimpressive. It provides the
perfect foil for blue spring flowers in
the herbaceous border. Plant it in full
sun in any reasonably fertile, well-
drained soil, and divide it in autumn.

◊ ☼ ❁ ❁ ❁
↕ ↔ to 38cm (15in)

LATE SPRING

As TEMPERATURES RISE and light levels increase, the garden seems to burst into life. Blossom buds open, and spring-flowering shrubs with bright new foliage add colour and scent to borders and beds. As the bulbs continue their seasonal show, leaves of perennials pushing through the soil hint at the drama to come.

However, new growth can be damaged by late frosts, so keep fleece handy to protect young plants, and do not be tempted to put out tender bedding or summer displays in containers too early. Slugs and snails are about in the damp conditions and the succulent shoots of many perennials are vulnerable to their attentions. Entice birds, toads and hedgehogs to help control the pests by providing a pond; with candelabra primulas and other moisture loving plants in bloom there is plenty for the gardener to enjoy too.

Easy-growing, blossoming ornamental cherries (*Prunus*) and crab apples (*Malus*) are great value; many will reward you with autumn interest. The massive blooms of tree peonies make real impact, but the rhododendrons, with hundreds to choose from, and flowers in almost every shade provide the most excitement. If you lack the acid conditions they enjoy, try early-flowering clematis and fragrant lilacs (*Syringa*).

ALPINES AND BULBS

The rock garden is at its best as the season begins, studded with jewel-like flowers of arabis, gold dust (*Aurinia*), spring gentians and small species tulips. Tulips also dominate late spring bulb displays with larger-flowered varieties creating bold swathes of colour in beds, borders and containers. Clumps of quamash (*Camassia*), and tall, stately crown imperials (*Fritillaria imperialis*) make imposing centrepieces in the border, while the delicate snake's head fritillary (*Fritillaria meleagris*) is superb naturalized in grass.

ARABIS ALPINA *SUBSP.* CAUCASICA *'Variegata'*

Evergreen perennial

This mat-forming plant has rosettes of greyish-green, spoon-shaped leaves. The white fragrant flowers are produced in loose clusters over a long period from late spring to early autumn. It is very hardy and will flower well when grown in poor, well-drained soil in full sun, making it ideal for a rock or scree garden. 'Variegata' has the added bonus of green leaves with pale yellow margins.

○ ☼ ❀ ❀ ❀
‡ ↔ to 15cm (6in)

CAMASSIA LEICHTLINII ♥

Perennial bulb

The white form of quamash flowers from late spring to early summer. The tall flowering stems make a striking addition to the herbaceous border. The bulbs should be planted at a depth of 10cm (4in) in autumn. Plant quamash in groups in deep, moist but well-drained soil in a sunny or slightly shaded position. In areas prone to long periods of frost, place a thick mulch over the area where the bulbs have been planted.

○ ◑ ☼ ◐ ❀ ❀ ❀
‡ to 1.3m (4.5ft) ↔ to 30cm (12in)

CASSIOPE
'Edinburgh' ♀

Evergreen shrub

This compact plant has small, slightly
hairy, dark green leaves, and in late
spring produces nodding white bell
shaped flowers with swept-back tips,
similar to those of lily-of-the-valley. It
is closely related to heathers and needs
a moist, fertile, acid soil in a sunny or
partially shaded spot. Cassiopes are
fairly demanding plants, requiring the
right growing conditions to flourish;
'Edinburgh' is the least fussiest.

◐ ☼ ☀ ❀ ❀ ❀
↕ ↔ to 20cm (8in)

CHOISYA TERNATA ♀

Evergreen shrub

The Mexican orange blossom is a fast-
growing shrub with dark green, glossy
foliage. The leaves are aromatic when
crushed. It produces a profusion of
fragrant, star-shaped, white flowers in
late spring — a light pruning after these
have faded can often stimulate a second
flush of blooms in autumn. Grow in
fertile, well drained soil in full sun.
'Sundance' has bright yellow-green leaves.

◐ ☼ ❀ ❀ ❀
↕ ↔ to 2.5m (8ft)

CONVALLARIA MAJALIS ♀

Perennial bulb

Lily-of-the-valley is a delightful spring-
flowering plant with arching stems of
white, sweetly scented, bell-shaped
flowers that appear between the dark
green leaves. It makes an ideal ground-
cover plant for shady, damp situations
and spreads very quickly by means of
creeping roots. 'Albostriata' has gold-
striped leaves, and 'Fortin's Giant' is
slightly taller, growing to a height of
30cm (12in).

◊ ☼ ☼ ✿ ✿ ✿

‡ to 23cm (9in) ↔ to 30cm (12in)

CORNUS FLORIDA
'White Cloud'

Deciduous tree

The flowering dogwood forms an
attractive spreading tree that looks as
if it is adorned with large white flowers
in late spring. In fact, these "blooms"
comprise four creamy-white, petal-like
bracts surrounding a cluster of tiny
green flowers. An additional feature of
this beautiful plant is the slightly
twisted green leaves which, in autumn,
turn bright orange and red.

◊ ☼ ✿ ✿ ✿

‡ to 6m (20ft) ↔ to 8m (25ft)

DAVIDIA INVOLUCRATA ♥

Deciduous tree

In late spring, the branches of the pocket
handkerchief tree are hung with what
look like hundreds of crisp, white linen
squares. These are, in fact, showy bracts
that surround the tiny flowerheads.
Although fully hardy, it needs shelter
from strong winds. It will grow in most
situations but prefers moist but well-
drained, fertile soil and a sunny position.
When mature it can become quite large,
making it less suitable for small gardens.

◊ ◊ ☼ ❄ ❄ ❄
‡ to 15m (50ft) ↔ to 10m (30ft)

ERYTHRONIUM OREGONUM

Perennial bulb

This dog's-tooth violet forms a clump of
unusual dark green leaves with paler
mottling. In spring, it produces stems
bearing two or three pendent flowers
with creamy-white reflexed petals and
yellow anthers. Suitable for a woodland
garden or beneath deciduous shrubs,
grow it in fertile, moist but well-drained
soil. Divide clumps in summer after the
flowers have faded.

◊ ◊ ☼ ❄ ❄ ❄
‡ to 35cm (14in) ↔ to 12cm (5in)

HALESIA MONTICOLA

Deciduous tree

The fast-growing snowdrop tree forms an attractive cone shape. In late spring, often before the leaves emerge, white, bell-shaped blooms appear in clusters along the branches. These are followed in summer by green, winged fruit, measuring up to 5cm (2in) long. In autumn the leaves take on a strong yellow colour before falling. Plant in moist but well-drained, neutral or slightly acid (lime-free) soil, in a sunny or partially shaded, sheltered position.

○ ○ ○ ☼ ☼ ✽ ✽ ✽

‡ to 12m (40ft) ↔ to 8m (25ft)

IRIS CONFUSA ♥

Perennial

This is one of the crested irises with flattened flowers. The leaves, which are green and sword-shaped, are held in fans on bamboo-like stems. In late spring and early summer, it bears abundant small white flowers, measuring just 5cm (2in) across. *Iris confusa* is not entirely hardy and should be grown in a sunny or slightly shaded, sheltered position. Soil should be moist and fertile. Every year mulch after flowering.

○ ☼ ☼ ✽ ✽

‡ to 1m (3ft) ↔ to indefinite

MAGNOLIA STELLATA
'Waterlily' ♀

Deciduous tree

The star magnolia is a fairly compact
tree that is suitable for smaller gardens.
Just ensure it has sufficient space to
spread its branches. 'Waterlily' bears
an abundance of pure white, slightly
fragrant flowers in late spring. These
are made up of numerous strap-like
petals. This magnolia needs a sunny or
partially shaded spot, and moist, well-
drained soil.

◊◊ ☼ ☼ ❋ ❋ ❋
‡ to 3m (10ft) ↔ to 4m (12ft)

MAGNOLIA WILSONII ♀

Deciduous tree

This elegant magnolia forms a large
shrub or small tree, and in late spring
and early summer produces fragrant,
white flowers with a ring of crimson-
red in the centre. It can be damaged
by frost and needs a sheltered spot in
full sun or light shade. It also requires
a moist, well drained soil. As with all
magnolias, give it plenty of space to
develop unhindered.

◊◊ ☼ ☼ ❋ ❋ ❋
‡ ↔ to 6m (20ft)

MALUS TORINGO *SUBSP.* SARGENTII

Deciduous tree

This crab apple produces a profusion of white flowers in spring, giving rise in the autumn to bright red fruit. It has dark green, three-lobed leaves. Give it a spot in full sun or light shade and, although tolerant of a wide range of soil types, it prefers moderately fertile, moist, well-drained soil.

○ ◐ ☼ ☀ ✽ ✽ ✽
‡ to 4m (12ft) ↔ to 5m (15ft)

NARCISSUS POETICUS *VAR.* RECURVUS ♀

Perennial bulb

The old pheasant's eye narcissus obtained its common name from the short, red-rimmed, yellow cup in the centre of the flower. This particular variety has fragrant, long-lasting flowers with swept-back, pure white petals, and greenish-yellow throats. It flowers slightly later in spring than many other daffodils, and can be grown in borders, large containers, or naturalized in grass. Plant it in well-drained soil in full sun or dappled shade.

○ ☼ ☀ ✽ ✽ ✽
‡ to 35cm (14in) ↔ to 10cm (4in)

OSMANTHUS DELAVAYI ♛

Evergreen shrub

A large, rounded, evergreen, this plant
has arching stems from which hang
clusters of tubular flowers in mid- to
late spring. The highly, fragrant white
blooms are set off by dark green,
glossy, toothed foliage. Later in the
year, small blue-black berries appear.
Grow this bush in well-drained soil in
full sun or partial shade, and protect it
from drying winds. Prune it after the
flowers have faded.

◊ ☼ ☀ ✿ ✿ ✿
‡ to 6m (20ft) ↔ to 4m (12ft)

PAEONIA SUFFRUTICOSA
'Godaishu'

Perennial

This decorative white tree peony is well
worth searching for. It has dark green,
slightly waxy leaves, and large semi-
double flowers with pure white soft
petals that surround yellow stamens.
For the best results, plant it in well-
drained soil in full sun or partial shade.

◊ ☼ ☀ ✿ ✿ ✿
‡ ↔ to 2m (6ft)

POLYGONATUM × HYBRIDUM ♀

Perennial

Solomon's seal is an elegant plant, with small tubular white flowers that hang gracefully from arching green stems. It adds a touch of class to late spring herbaceous borders and woodland gardens, and needs a cool, shaded position, and fertile, well-drained soil. Solomon's seal may be attacked by sawfly caterpillars, which can quickly reduce the leaves to a skeleton. 'Striatum' has variegated leaves. Divide clumps in spring.

◊ ☼ ✽ ✽ ✽
‡ to 1.2m (4ft) ↔ to 1m (3ft)

PRIMULA DENTICULATA
VAR. ALBA

Perennial

Drumstick primulas have neat, globe-shaped flowerheads composed of many small blooms. This variety has white flowers, each with a bright yellow eye, although drumstick primulas also come in shades of pale lilac, pink and deep purple. All thrive in moist, well-drained, neutral to slightly acid soil, and fare best if the soil dries out a little in the summer months. They are ideal for use in a herbaceous border or among shrubs, and are easy to raise from seed.

◊ ◊ ☼ ☼ ✽ ✽ ✽
‡ ↔ to 45cm (18in)

PRUNUS LUSITANICA
SUBSP. AZORICA

Evergreen tree

This vigorous Portugal laurel forms an evergreen shrub or small tree, and bears large glossy leaves. It produces free-flowering spikes of small, white, scented blooms in late spring and early summer. In autumn, it bears red cherry-like fruits that turn black when ripe. This plant grows well even on shallow chalky soil, and will flourish when planted in a sheltered position in full sun. It makes a good specimen plant, but it is often trimmed as a hedge.

△ ◑ ☼ ❈ ❈
‡ ↔ to 20m (70ft)

PRUNUS PADUS
'Watereri' ♀

Deciduous tree

The bird cherry has a decorative habit, with spreading branches that carry pendent stems of cup-shaped, almond-scented, white flowers in late spring. These are then followed by small black fruits, which are loved by birds. This vigorous tree should be grown in full sun or light shade, in a well-drained, moist soil. The bird cherry makes an excellent specimen for the middle of a lawn or in a mixed border.

△ ◑ ☼ ♀ ❈ ❈ ❈
‡ to 15m (50ft) ↔ to 10m (30ft)

PYRUS SALICIFOLIA
'Pendula' ♀

Deciduous tree

An ornamental pear, 'Pendula' has attractive weeping branches covered with oval, silvery leaves. These are accompanied in mid- to late spring by clusters of creamy-white flowers. Small, green, inedible fruit may also appear in late summer. It needs full sun and well-drained soil and makes a decorative specimen for a lawn or a mixed border.

◊ ☼ ❀ ❀ ❀
‡ to 8m (25ft) ↔ to 6m (20ft)

RHODODENDRON
'Fragrantissimum' ♀

Evergreen shrub

This rhododendron has highly fragrant, white, funnel-shaped spring flowers that contrast beautifully with the slightly hairy evergreen foliage. It is suitable for mild gardens and warm sheltered sites; where frost is likely it is better grown in a container and taken under cover for winter. Grow it in sun or partial shade in a well-drained, acid (lime-free) to neutral soil, or ericaceous compost. Outdoors, mulch generously with bark or leafmould.

◊◊ ☼ ◐ ❀ ❀
‡ ↔ to 2m (6ft)

RHODODENDRON
'Loderi King George' ♀

Evergreen shrub

One of the best white rhododendrons,
this slow-growing plant can grow to 4m
(12ft) in height. The pale pink flower
buds open in late spring to form large
trusses of white, fragrant flowers with
green markings. It is best planted in
a woodland garden, and, like most
rhododendrons, needs a moist, well
drained acid (lime-free) soil. Mulch
it every year with bark or leafmould,
especially when young.

○◔☼✸✳✳✳
‡ ↔ to 4m (12ft)

SAXIFRAGA
'Southside Seedling' ♀

Perennial

This saxifrage bears densely packed
rosettes of pale green, spoon-shaped
leaves. It flowers freely, and in late
spring produces branched stems of red
centred white blooms. The leaf rosettes
die after flowering. 'Southside Seedling'
requires a very well-drained, slightly
alkaline soil, preferably with grit added
to it, and prefers a sunny position.

○☼✳✳✳
‡ to 30cm (12in) ↔ to 20cm (8in)

SMILACINA RACEMOSA ♀

Perennial

The false spikenard is a slow-spreading plant with tall stems topped in late spring with conical clusters of small, slightly scented white flowers. The large leaves are also an attractive feature. To grow well, false spikenard requires a shady site, and suits a woodland garden setting or a moist shady border. It will perform well in a moist, slightly acid (lime-free) soil. Divide large clumps in the spring.

💧 ☼ ☀ ✳ ✳ ✳
‡ to 90cm (36in) ↔ to 60cm (24in)

SPIRAEA
'Arguta' ♀

Deciduous shrub

Known as bridal wreath because of its arching stems that are covered in late spring with small, white flowers that create a light, delicate effect. The blooms are borne among lance-shaped, bright green leaves. Bridal wreath is perfect for a low hedge or in a mixed shrub border, and needs a moist, well-drained soil in full sun. The flowers are produced on the previous year's wood, and the stems should be pruned back in early summer after flowering.

◊ 💧 ☼ ✳ ✳ ✳
‡ to 2m (6ft) ↔ to 1.5m (5ft)

SYRINGA VULGARIS
'Madame Lemoine' ♀

Deciduous shrub

Lilacs are large shrubs with branched,
upright stems, covered with dark green,
heart-shaped leaves. 'Madame Lemoine'
has large, cone-shaped clusters of pure
white, highly scented flowers, which
are produced in abundance during the
spring. Tolerant of pollution and most
soils, except very acid soil, it is ideal for
growing in an urban garden. If lilacs
become leggy, cut them back hard to
1m (3ft) above the ground after they
have flowered

◊◊�●☼ ✿✿✿
‡ ↔ to 7m (22ft)

TRILLIUM GRANDIFLORUM ♀
Perennial

Wake-robin produces large flowers with
three distinctive clear white petals and
bright yellow stamens, which turn pale
pink as they age. The blooms contrast
beautifully with the deep green leaves
that will eventually form a large clump.
Trilliums need moist, well-drained soil
and a slightly shaded position. They are
best suited to deciduous woodland, but
can also be used in a rock garden.

◊ ◊ ☼ ✿✿✿
‡ to 40cm (16in) ↔ to 30cm (12in)

TROLLIUS X CULTORUM
'Alabaster'

Perennial

Most globeflowers have bright yellow or orange flowers, but those of 'Alabaster' are much paler. It has bowl-shaped, deep cream-coloured flowers, held on slim, upright stems. It will grow happily in wet soil, as long as it dries out slightly in summer, and is suitable for waterside plantings or bog gardens. Large clumps can be divided in early summer, immediately after flowering.

◐ ◐ ☼ ☼ ✿ ✿ ✿
‡ to 60cm (24in) ↔ to 40cm (16in)

TULIPA
'White Triumphator' ♀

Perennial bulb

This elegant lily-flowered tulip blooms in the late spring and has pure white flowers. Plant *en masse* in a mixed herbaceous border, or use in bedding schemes. Alternatively, plant a few in a large containers for a sophisticated patio display. The bulbs should be planted in late autumn in full sun and fertile, well-drained soil. In bedding displays it is often easier to lift bulbs and discard them after flowering rather than letting the foliage die naturally.

◐ ☼ ✿ ✿ ✿
‡ to 70cm (28in)

VIBURNUM PLICATUM
'Mariesii' ♀

Deciduous shrub

The broad-spreading branches of this
viburnum are held in several layers,
one above the other. In late spring it
bears clusters of small, fertile flowers
surrounded by sterile, saucer-shaped
flowers with large white petals. The
flowers are followed by small red fruits,
which turn black in the autumn. Plant it
in a shrub border or woodland garden,
in full sun or partial shade, and moist,
well-drained soil.

◊◊ ☼ ☼ ❄ ❄ ❄
‡ to 3m (10ft) ↔ to 4m (12ft)

WISTERIA SINENSIS
'Alba' ♀

Climber

The Chinese wisteria – one of the most
beautiful of the hardy, spring-flowering
climbers – can be grown against a wall,
on a large sturdy trellis or pergola, or
through a tree. Twisted stems produce
large leaves with up to 13 leaflets, and
the white, scented, pea-like blooms are
borne on long, pendent flower stems.
Plant it in a fertile, well-drained, moist
soil in sun or partial shade, and prune
back new shoots in summer after it has
flowered to restrict their growth.

◊◊ ☼ ☼ ❄ ❄ ❄
‡ to 9m (28ft)

AESCULUS × NEGLECTA
'Erythroblastos' ♀

Deciduous tree

The emerging spring foliage of the aptly named sunrise horse chestnut is bright pink, and later turns pale green. Just after the leaves have unfurled in late spring, 'Erythroblastos' produces cones of pink or peach flowers. This slow-growing tree also puts on an impressive autumn display with bright yellow and orange leaves. Grow it in deep, moist, well-drained soil in full sun or partial shade.

○ ◐ ☼ ◑ ❋ ❋ ❋
‡ to 10m (30ft) ↔ to 8m (25ft)

ANAGALLIS TENELLA
'Studland'

Perennial

This bog pimpernel forms a low mat of bright green leaves, and in late spring is covered with small, lightly scented, deep pink flowers. It requires a moist, free-draining soil to survive and will die if it is allowed to dry out in summer. Suitable for a rock garden where the soil is moist, this dainty plant can also be used as ground cover. A short-lived plant, it can be propagated by taking cuttings in late summer.

◐ ☼ ❋ ❋ ❋
‡ to 1cm (½in) ↔ to 15cm (6in)

AQUILEGIA VULGARIS
'Nora Barlow' ♀

Perennial

This unusual aquilegia has double pink
and white flowers, with pale green-
tipped petals, which are slightly swept
back when the flower is fully open. It
needs a well-drained, moist soil in full
sun, and makes a stunning addition to
a spring herbaceous border. Plant it in
bold groups of at least 3-5 plants for
the best effect.

○ ◑ ☼ ❊ ❊ ❊
‡ to 75cm (30in) ↔ to 50cm (20in)

ARMERIA MARITIMA
'Vindictive' ♀

Evergreen perennial

Thrift is a seaside plant, and will grow
happily in a rock garden. It forms a
rounded cushion of deep green, grass-
like leaves, and bears large numbers of
bright pink flowers in the spring. Its
deep taproot allows it to survive the
driest of summers, and care should be
taken when weeding to avoid damage
to this root, which may kill the plant.
Thrift is suitable for either coastal or
inland gardens, as long as it is given
a sunny site and well-drained soil.

○ ☼ ❊ ❊ ❊
‡ to 10cm (4in) ↔ to 15cm (6in)

CERCIS SILIQUASTRUM ♀

Deciduous tree

The Judas tree opens its flowers in the
late spring before the heart-shaped
leaves emerge. The pea-like blooms are
magenta in bud, turning pink as they
open, and are followed by purple seed
pods during the summer. The leaves
turn yellow in autumn. The Judas tree
comes from the Mediterranean, and
flowers best after a long hot summer.
Give it a sheltered site as late frosts
may damage the young leaves and
buds. Plant it in moist, free-draining
soil in sun or partial shade.

◊ ◑ ☼ ❀ ❀ ❀
‡↔ to 10m (30ft)

CLEMATIS MACROPETALA
'Markham's Pink' ♀

Climber

Deep pink, semi-double flowers adorn
this beautiful plant in late spring and
early summer. Not as vigorous as many
early-flowering clematis, it is ideal for
a small urban garden. It blooms on the
previous year's wood, and if necessary
should be pruned after flowering to
remove any dead wood and to keep
it within bounds. This clematis is very
hardy and will tolerate an exposed site
in sun or partial shade. It prefers well-
drained soil.

◊ ☼ ◑ ❀ ❀ ❀
‡ to 3m (10ft)

CLEMATIS MONTANA
'Elizabeth' ♀

Climber

Like all *Clematis montana*, this vigorous plant is perfect for growing up a large, sturdy trellis, a large, mature tree, or up wires fixed to a house or boundary wall. In late spring, just as the lobed leaves unfurl, it produces masses of fragrant pink blooms along its climbing stems. It needs a sheltered situation in full sun, and a well drained soil. It may need pruning after it has flowered to keep it under control.

◊ ☼ ◑ ❄ ❄ ❄
‡ to 7m (22ft)

CLEMATIS MONTANA VAR. RUBENS

Climber

This vigorous plant will soon cover an ugly wall or scramble up a large mature tree. In late spring, it produces a huge number of single, pale pink flowers with creamy-yellow anthers. Grow it in free draining soil in a sunny or partially shaded site, and prune it after flowering to keep it in check.

◊ ☼ ◑ ❄ ❄ ❄
‡ to 10m (30ft)

DARMERA PELTATA ♀

Perennial

The umbrella plant is a waterside plant that flowers before the large umbrella-shaped leaves emerge. Clusters of tiny, pale pink blooms, held on stout stems, are produced in late spring. Grow it in permanently wet soil, beside a pool or in a bog garden, in a sunny or partially shaded position. In time, it will spread to cover a large area.

◊ ◗ ☼ ◑ ❈ ❈ ❈
‡ to 2m (6ft) ↔ to 1m (3ft)

DICENTRA SPECTABILIS ♀

Perennial

This elegant plant has many common names, including bleeding heart, lady's locket and lady-in-the-bath. The leaves are pale green and deeply-lobed, and delicate pink and white heart-shaped flowers hang from long arching stems. For the best results plant it in a partially shaded position, in moist, well-drained, fertile soil. In hot, dry summers it may die down early.

◊ ◗ ◑ ❈ ❈ ❈
‡ to 1.2m (4ft) ↔ to 45cm (18in)

EPIMEDIUM X RUBRUM ♟

Perennial

This carpet-forming plant has attractive, heart-shaped leaves tinted reddish brown in spring as they unfurl, which then colour yellow in the autumn. In late spring it bears small crimson-pink, star-shaped flowers with long yellow spurs. Epimediums need a partially shaded position, and moist, but well-drained, fertile soil. Propagate clumps by division in early spring or autumn.

◊ ◊ ☼ ❄ ❄ ❄
↕ ↔ to 30cm (12in)

ERICA AUSTRALIS ♟

Evergreen shrub

The Spanish heath produces small, bell-shaped, purple-pink flowers from mid-spring to the beginning of summer, and has dark green, needle-like foliage. It is not completely hardy so plant it in a sheltered position. Young plants benefit from some winter protection until they are established. Although tolerant of alkaline conditions, it prefers slightly moist acid or neutral soil, and full sun.

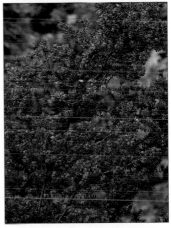

◊ ☼ ❄ ❄
↕ to 2m (6ft) ↔ to 1m (3ft)

ERYTHRONIUM DENS-CANIS ♀

Perennial bulb

The dog's-tooth violet has distinctive purple, pink or white pendent flowers, with reflexed petals. The decorative oval-shaped, green leaves have pinkish-brown mottling on the upper surface. Dog's-tooth violets can be planted in woodland or grass, and grow best in well-drained, fertile soil in partial shade. To propagate, lift and divide the clumps of bulbs after flowering and replant them immediately in fertile soil.

◊ ☼ ✿ ✿ ✿
‡ to 15cm (6in) ↔ to 10cm (4in)

GERANIUM CINEREUM 'Ballerina' ♀

Perennial

This semi-evergreen, mound-forming hardy geranium, or cranesbill, has deeply divided grey-green leaves. One of the first cranesbills to bloom in late spring, it bears many cup-shaped, pinkish-purple flowers, with distinctive purple veins and dark eyes. It makes a good rock- or gravel-garden plant, and flowers over a long period. Plant it in full sun in well-drained soil, and divide plants in the spring.

◊ ☼ ✿ ✿ ✿
‡ to 10cm (4in) ↔ to 30cm (12in)

KOLKWITZIA AMABILIS
'Pink Cloud' ♀
Deciduous shrub

One of the prettiest of the spring
flowering shrubs, *Kolkwitzia* deserves
its common name – the beauty bush.
It has arching branches, clothed with
tapering, dark green leaves. In late
spring, it bears clusters of bell-shaped
deep pink flowers with yellow-tinted
throats. Plant it in a sunny site in fertile,
well-drained soil. Although hardy, the
new leaves may be damaged by late
frosts, so it is best to choose a sheltered
site in cold or exposed gardens.

◊ ☼ ❈ ❈ ❈
‡ to 3m (10ft) ↔ to 4m (12ft)

LAMIUM ORVALA
Perennial

This pretty variety of dead nettle forms
clumps of triangular, mid-green leaves.
The hooded flowers are bronzy-pink,
and borne in tiers around the stem. It
needs shade and a moist, well-drained
soil to do well, and is never invasive,
unlike other dead nettles. There is
also an attractive white-flowered form
called 'Album'.

◊ ◊ ☼ ❈ ❈ ❈
‡ to 60cm (24in) ↔ to 30cm (12in)

LEWISIA COTYLEDON ♟

Evergreen perennial

Lewisias are rosette-forming alpines from the mountains of North America. The funnel-shaped flowers of this species are produced in vivid pink, white, red, apricot or yellow, and are borne from late spring to early summer. Unlike many lewisias, which need to be grown under glass, *L. cotyledon* can be planted outside in crevices, a dry-stone wall, or a rock garden. Plant it in full sun and a very well-drained, fertile soil.

◊ ☼ ✿ ✿ ✿
‡ to 30cm (12in) ↔ to 15cm (6in)

MAGNOLIA X SOULANGEANA

Deciduous tree

This is probably the most widely grown of all magnolias. Fast growing, it will quickly form a small tree with wide spreading branches. The goblet-shaped flowers are pink to pinkish-purple, but there are also forms with white and reddish-purple blooms. The flowers appear in the spring, before the leaves. Select a planting position in full sun or partial shade, where the tree has plenty of space to develop its spreading shape. It also needs a moist, well-drained soil.

◊ ◊ ☼ ☼ ✿ ✿ ✿
‡ ↔ to 6m (20ft)

MALUS FLORIBUNDA ♀

Deciduous tree

The Japanese crab apple grows to form a large shrub or small, spreading tree with graceful, pendent branches. The flower buds are red, opening in mid- to late spring to a very pale pink, with small fruits ripening yellow in autumn. It is not fussy about the soil conditions, as long as the site is not waterlogged. Grow this crab apple in sun or partial shade, and use it as a specimen tree in a lawn or in a mixed border.

○ ☼ ☀ ❉ ❉ ❉
↕ ↔ to 10m (30ft)

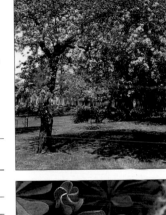

OXALIS ADENOPHYLLA ♀

Perennial

This mat-forming, tuberous perennial has greyish-green leaves, divided into heart-shaped leaflets. In late spring it produces purplish-pink flowers with conspicuous purple veins. Plant the tubers in a rock or gravel garden, or in troughs, in well-drained, gritty soil, in full sun. It is easily propagated by division in the autumn or early spring.

○ ☼ ❉ ❉ ❉
↕ to 5cm (2in) ↔ to 10cm (4in)

PAULOWNIA TOMENTOSA ♀

Deciduous tree

The foxglove tree has extremely large, rounded leaves. In late spring, the lilac, foxglove-like, scented flowers appear. The tree is not entirely hardy, and the flowers may be damaged by frost. In cold areas, it can be treated as a foliage plant by cutting it down to ground level in late winter or early spring, which stimulates growth of even larger leaves the following spring. If this is done annually, apply a balanced fertilizer and mulch after pruning. Plant it in well-drained soil in a sunny, sheltered site.

◊ ☼ ❀ ❀
‡ to 12m (40ft) ↔ to 10m (30ft)

PHLOX SUBULATA
'Marjorie'

Perennial

A pretty cushion-forming plant with narrow green leaves, the rose-pink flowers of this moss phlox have five notched petals and a dark eye. It is ideal for a spring display in a rock or gravel garden or raised bed, and will perform well when planted in well-drained, fertile soil, in a sunny position.

◊ ☼ ❀ ❀ ❀
‡ to 10cm (4in) ↔ to 20cm (8in)

PRIMULA ROSEA ♀

Perennial

This primula forms a rosette of toothed, bronze-green leaves, and produces clusters of beautiful clear pink flowers in late spring. It needs moist, neutral to acid, fertile soil, and will suit a bog garden or the damp soil beside a pond. It can be grown in full sun, as long as the soil is permanently wet.

♦ ◊ ☼ ☀ ❄ ❄ ❄
‡ ↔ to 20cm (8in)

PRIMULA SIEBOLDII ♀

Perennial

This primula has long been cultivated in Japan, and there are many different forms from which to choose. The wild plant has pinkish-purple flowers with white eyes, but there are also cultivars with pink or white flowers. The blooms are held above a rosette of bright green leaves. Plant it in a moist, fertile soil, preferably in partial shade, or full sun if the soil remains moist all summer.

◊ ☼ ☀ ❄ ❄ ❄
‡ to 30cm (12in) ↔ to 45cm (18in)

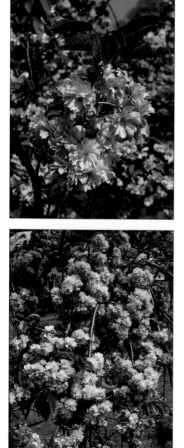

PRUNUS
'Kanzan' ♀

Deciduous tree

This pretty flowering cherry has upright
branches when young, which spread
more widely as the tree matures, and
this habit must be considered before
planting. Double, deep pink flowers are
produced just before the reddish-brown
leaves appear in mid- to late spring.
Grow it in moist, fertile, well-drained
soil in full sun.

◊ ◊ ☼ ❈ ❈ ❈
‡ ↔ to 10m (30ft)

PRUNUS
'Kiku-shidare-zakura' ♀

Deciduous tree

Often sold as 'Cheal's Weeping', the
graceful, weeping branches of this
flowering cherry are covered in spring
with clusters of double, bright pink
flowers. It is quite tolerant of pollution,
and is often planted in avenues along
urban roads. Pruning should be avoided
to prevent peach leaf curl disease from
entering through the wounds. Where
pruning has to be carried out, it should
be performed in the summer when the
sap is rising.

◊ ◊ ☼ ❈ ❈ ❈
‡ ↔ to 3m (12ft)

RHODODENDRON
'Pink Pearl'

Evergreen shrub

This is a very popular rhododendron, grown for its large trusses of pale pink spring flowers. While the plant is generally very vigorous, the branches are rather weak and have a tendency to droop. Plant it among other shrubs or in a woodland garden. It should be grown in a sunny or partially shaded position in deep, moist, well-drained, acid soil. Mulch annually with chipped bark or leafmould.

○ ◐ ☼ ☀ ❋ ❋ ❋
‡ ↔ to 4m (12ft)

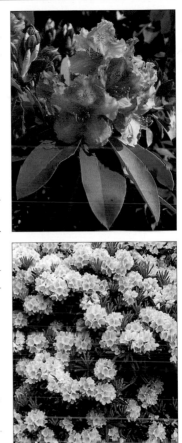

RHODODENDRON
YAKUSHIMANUM

Evergreen shrub

A compact, hardy rhododendron, this variety forms a domed bush of dark green, glossy leaves. In late spring, it is covered with funnel-shaped, rose pink flowers, which fade to pale pink and then white. Plant it in full sun or partial shade, in moist, well-drained, fertile, acid soil, and mulch annually with chipped bark or leafmould. This shrub is suitable for containers if grown in ericaceous compost.

○ ◐ ☼ ☀ ❋ ❋ ❋
‡ ↔ to 2m (6ft)

SYMPHYTUM × UPLANDICUM
'Variegatum' ♀

Perennial

Russian comfrey is a vigorous, clump-forming perennial, ideal for ground cover in wild gardens. 'Variegatum' has rather coarse, hairy green leaves, with a broad cream margin. The small, pink, tubular flowers are borne on tall stems and eventually turn blue. 'Variegatum' is far less vigorous than the normal green form, and will flourish in moist soil in sun or partial shade. It can be divided in the early spring.

◐ ☼ ☼ ❉ ❉ ❉
‡ to 1m (3ft) ↔ to 60cm (2ft)

SYRINGA MEYERI
'Palibin' ♀

Deciduous shrub

This slow-growing lilac is the perfect choice for a small garden, where the common form (*Syringa vulgaris*) may grow too large. It forms a compact bush, which is covered from late spring to early summer with clusters of very fragrant, pale lavender-pink flowers. Plant it in full sun in well-drained soil, or in a large container of loam-based potting compost.

◐☼ ❉ ❉ ❉
‡↔ to 1.5m (5ft)

TULIPA
'Don Quichotte' ♀

Perennial bulb

This bright cherry-pink tulip makes a
dramatic statement when planted in
large groups and used as a bedding
plant. Its vivid colour combines well
with cream or white tulips, such as
'White Triumphator' (see page 86), or
forget-me-nots. Plant the bulbs in late
autumn in well-drained soil in full sun.

◊ ☼ ✿ ✿ ✿
‡ to 40cm (16in)

TULIPA
'Groenland'

Perennial bulb

The viridiflora tulips are named for
the bright green stripe in the middle
of the outer petals. 'Groenland' has soft
pink petals marked with a triangular
green brush stroke. It can be used in
groups in a herbaceous border, or as a
bedding plant. Like all tulips, the bulbs
need to be planted in late autumn in a
sunny position, in well-drained soil.

◊ ☼ ✿ ✿ ✿
‡ to 45cm (18in)

ACER PALMATUM 'Corallinum'

Deciduous tree

A compact form of *Acer palmatum* that grows slowly to form a bushy shrub or small tree. It is particularly dramatic in spring when young bright red shoots appear, together with vivid shrimp-pink leaves, which gradually turn pale green. In autumn the leaves turn orange, red and yellow. It is best planted in sun or partial shade in moist, well-drained acid (lime-free) soil.

◊ ◑ ☼ ❋ ❋ ❋
‡ to 1.2m (4ft) ↔ to 1m (3ft)

ANEMONE × FULGENS

Perennial

This striking tuberous plant bears vivid scarlet flowers with black centres that resemble poppies. The late spring flowers are held on stout stems above deeply-lobed leaves. For the best effect, plant it in groups in sandy, well-drained soil and a sunny position, as it can be damaged while dormant in summer by persistent rain and wet soil conditions.

◊ ☼ ❋ ❋ ❋
‡ to 30cm (12in) ↔ to 10cm (4in)

CAMELLIA JAPONICA
'Rubescens Major' ♀

Evergreen shrub

This is a very old form of the Japanese
camellia, and produces double crimson-
red flowers with darker veins. It forms
a compact bush, with glossy, rounded
dark green leaves. There are several
other good camellias with red flowers,
such as the semi-double 'Paul's Apollo'
and 'R. L. Wheeler'. Plant 'Rubescens
Major' in a slightly shaded site, away
from early morning sun, in deep, moist,
well-drained, acid (lime-free) soil.

◊ ◊ ☼ ❉ ❉ ❉
‡↔ to 10m (30ft)

CRATAEGUS LAEVIGATA
'Paul's Scarlet' ♀

Deciduous tree

Similar in shape to the common native
hawthorn, this small tree is covered
in late spring with double, deep pink
flowers. These are sometimes followed
in the late summer by small red fruits.
The leaves are shiny and deeply lobed.
It will grow well in most soils, as long
as they are not waterlogged, in a sunny
or lightly shaded location. Mature trees
are particularly attractive.

◊ ◊ ☼ ❉ ❉ ❉
‡↔ to 8m (25ft)

DICENTRA
'Bacchanal' ♀

Perennial

Bleeding hearts are perennial herbs with finely divided leaves. 'Bacchanal' bears its dangling, deep crimson-red flowers on arching stems in late spring. Plant it in fertile soil in partial shade below shrubs or in a mixed border. Try to combine it with plants that will hide its dying foliage in the summer.

◊ ◊ ☼ ❋ ❋ ❋
‡ to 35cm (14in) ↔ to 45cm (18in)

GEUM RIVALE

Perennial

Water avens grows naturally beside rivers and streams, making them ideal for bog gardens and pool-sides. This species produces clumps of hairy, dark green divided leaves and, in late spring, it bears single, nodding, bell-shaped flowers on arching stems. Plant it in damp soil in full sunshine, and divide clumps in autumn.

◊ ◊ ☼ ❋ ❋ ❋
‡ ↔ to 60cm (24in)

LEPTOSPERMUM SCOPARIUM
'Red Damask' ♀

Evergreen shrub

The New Zealand tea tree has arching branches covered with aromatic, lance-shaped leaves. From late spring to early summer it produces masses of beautiful red, double, saucer-shaped flowers. It is not completely hardy, and should be planted with the protection of a south- or west-facing wall. In cold areas, grow it in a container of soil based potting compost and move it under cover for the winter. This shrub also needs a free-draining soil.

○ ☼ ✿ ❀
‡ ↔ to 3m (10ft)

PAEONIA
'Buckeye Belle'

Perennial

'Buckeye Belle' is a spring-flowering peony with semi-double, deep red flowers. It is a vigorous plant, and will eventually form a large clump. Peonies need to be grown in well-drained, fertile soil, but require relatively little aftercare. They are generally pest free, but may be attacked by the fungal disease, peony blight. *Paeonia* 'Belle Center' is very similar to 'Buckeye Belle', but flowers two weeks later, making them good companions.

○ ◐ ☼ ☀ ❀ ❀ ❀
‡ ↔ to 85cm (34in)

PRIMULA JAPONICA
'Miller's Crimson' ♀

Perennial

Candelabra primulas are ideal for a bog garden or planting by a pool, and are grown for their colourful flowers which are arranged in tiers up the stem. The leaves of *Primula japonica* are rounded with finely serrated edges, and in late spring 'Miller's Crimson' bears striking crimson-red flowers. It prefers a shaded spot in moist soil, and looks best when planted in a group. Divide candelabra primulas in early spring.

◊ ● ☼ ❉ ❉ ❉
‡ ↔ to 45cm (18in)

RHODODENDRON
'Elizabeth'

Evergreen shrub

'Elizabeth' is a dwarf rhododendron, making it an excellent choice for small gardens. In late spring, it bears trumpet-shaped, bright red flowers that measure up to 7.5cm (3in) across. These large blooms are borne in clusters of five or six, and create an eye-catching display. Grow this shrub in sun or partial shade in moist, well-drained, acid (lime-free) soil, and mulch annually with leafmould or chipped bark.

◊ ◊ ☼ ☼ ❉ ❉ ❉
‡ ↔ to 1.5m (5ft)

RHODODENDRON
'Hotspur'

Deciduous shrub

Deciduous azaleas are unsurpassed for vivid spring colour, and 'Hotspur' is no exception, with its clusters of flame-red flowers. The brightly coloured autumn foliage adds to this plant's decorative qualities. Plant it in full sun or partial shade, in moist, fertile, acid (lime-free) soil and mulch annually with leafmould or chipped bark. 'Silver Slipper' is a similar azalea, but bears white flowers.

◐ ☼ ☀ ❀ ❀ ❀
‡ ↔ to 2m (6ft)

RHODOHYPOXIS
'Douglas'

Perennial

This is a clump forming plant with narrow, lance-shaped, greyish-green leaves. In late spring and early summer it produces masses of deep red flowers on short stems. It should be grown in a sunny situation, in slightly fertile, well-drained soil. It is suitable for a rock or gravel garden, or a screebed, where its roots will be protected from excessive rainfall in winter.

◐ ☼ ❀ ❀ ❀
‡ ↔ to 10cm (4in)

RIBES SANGUINEUM
'Pulborough Scarlet' ♀

Deciduous shrub

The flowering currants create a dazzling display in late spring when their stems are clothed in masses of tiny flowers, arranged in clusters. This variety has an upright habit, dark green, aromatic leaves, and dark red pendent flowers with white centres. It is suitable for an informal hedge that needs only a light trim after flowering. Flowering currants will grow almost anywhere, but prefer a sunny site and moderately fertile soil.

◊ ◊ ☼ ☀ ✽ ✽ ✽
‡ to 2m (6ft) ↔ to 2.5m (8ft)

SCHISANDRA RUBRIFLORA

Climber

This climber has red shoots and lance-shaped or oval dark green leaves. In late spring, it produces striking deep red flowers, measuring up to 2.5cm (1in) across, followed on female plants by red fleshy fruits. Contrary to appearances, it is also fully hardy, and grows well in moist, well-drained soil, in sun or partial shade.

◊ ◊ ☀ ✽ ✽ ✽
‡ to 6m (20ft)

TRILLIUM SESSILE

Perennial

Wake robin is a clump-forming plant,
with three large, irregularly marked
leaves. The flowers are borne in late
spring and consist of three upright,
narrow, maroon-red petals, surrounded
by three smaller spreading sepals. It
will do well when grown in dappled
shade or woodland, in moist, fertile,
well-drained soil. It benefits from an
annual mulch of leaf mould or well-
rotted compost. Divide it after the
leaves have died.

◊ ◊ ☼ ✻ ✻ ✻
‡ to 38cm (15in) ↔ to 45cm (18in)

TULIPA SPRENGERI ♀

Perennial bulb

The species tulips are very underrated,
with a simplicity and elegance that is
hard to beat. This species is one of the
latest to flower in spring and has single,
bright red flowers with sharply pointed
petals. It self seeds and will naturalize
if planted in deciduous woodland, and
prefers a sunny or lightly shaded site
and well-drained, acid (lime-free) soil.

◊ ☼ ◊ ✻ ✻ ✻
‡ to 50cm (20in)

ALLIUM HOLLANDICUM *'Purple Sensation'* ♀

Perennial bulb

This is a superb, ornamental flowering onion, with long strap-shaped greyish-green leaves. In late spring and early summer it produces large flowerheads that are good for cutting, comprised of 50 or more tiny, star-shaped, deep violet florets. The decorative seedheads last well into late summer, although any self-sown plants that result may be inferior to the original. Plant the bulbs in autumn in a sunny position in fertile, well-drained soil.

◊ ☼ ❀ ❀ ❀
‡ to 75cm (30in) ↔ to 20cm (8in)

ALLIUM UNIFOLIUM ♀

Perennial bulb

This is a decorative ornamental onion from Oregon, in the USA. Each small bulb produces a single greyish-green leaf, which dies before bright pinkish-purple, six-petalled flowers appear in late spring. Plant the bulbs in autumn in a sheltered, sunny position, in well-drained, fertile soil. It suits a rock or gravel garden, and should be grown in bold groups for the best effect.

◊ ☼ ❀ ❀
‡ to 30cm (12in) ↔ to 10cm (4in)

FRITILLARIA MELEAGRIS
Perennial bulb

In late spring, the snake's head fritillary produces pendent, bell-shaped, purple or white flowers, with a distinctive checkerboard pattern on the petals. It grows well when naturalized in grass, and will often self seed. Take care when mowing, as the young seedlings look very much like grasses. It should be planted in a moist, well-drained soil, and prefers slightly alkaline conditions. If the bulbs become congested, mark the position and they can be lifted in the autumn and replanted elsewhere.

◊ ◊ ☼ ✤ ❄ ❄ ❄
‡ to 30cm (12in) ↔ to 8cm (3in)

FRITILLARIA GRAECA
Perennial bulb

This unusual fritillary is a native of Southern Greece. It has a delicate habit, bearing slim flower stems from which hang pendent, brownish-purple, bell-shaped flowers with a bold green stripe down the centre of the petals. Despite its place of origin, it is very hardy, but needs to be planted in a sunny site and in soil with very good drainage. It will add interest to a rock garden or raised bed, and the bulbs should be planted in groups in the autumn.

◊ ☼ ❄ ❄ ❄
‡ to 20cm (8in) ↔ to 5cm (2in)

IPHEION UNIFLORUM

Perennial bulb

In the late spring, this vigorous clump-forming plant produces violet, blue or white star-shaped flowers. The narrow, leaves smell of onions when bruised. Plant bulbs in autumn in a sheltered spot where they can naturalize. They prefer a fertile, moist, well-drained soil, in a sunny situation. In cold gardens, mulch in winter, as plants may be killed by hard frost.

◊ ◊ ☼ ❋ ❋
‡ to 20cm (8in) ↔ to 2cm (8in)

LUNARIA ANNUA

Biennial

Honesty is a fast-growing biennial that will often flower in its first year. It has tall stems, and toothed, heart-shaped, dark green leaves. Small spring flowers with four petals are borne in late spring and come in shades of either purple or white. It often self seeds and will thrive in a woodland garden or at the bottom of a hedge, preferring a site in partial shade or sun, and moist, well-drained soil. Honesty is frequently grown for its round, silvery seed pods, used in dried flower arrangements.

◊ ◊ ☼ ☼ ❋ ❋ ❋
‡ to 75cm (30in) ↔ to 30cm (12in)

PHLOX DOUGLASII 'Crackerjack' ♀

Perennial

A reliable plant, this dwarf phlox forms a mound of narrow dark green leaves, and in spring is covered with small, bright purplish-magenta flowers. Grow this variety in full sun, in well-drained, fertile soil. It is ideally suited to a rock garden, the cracks of a dry stone wall or between the slabs of a stone path.

◊ ☼ ❄ ❄ ❄
‡ to 8cm (3in) ↔ to 20cm (8in)

PRIMULA PULVERULENTA ♀

Perennial

This species is one of the most striking of the candelabra primulas. In late spring it bears tiers of deep reddish-purple flowers with a bright red or purple eye. The plants form rosettes of toothed, mid-green leaves, and their stems are covered with a greyish-green downy material called 'farina'. Plant it in partial shade, in fertile, moist soil. It will tolerate full sun, as long as the soil remains damp throughout the summer. Candelabra primulas look best when they are planted in a group near water.

◊ ☼ ☼ ❄ ❄ ❄
‡ to 1m (3ft) ↔ to 60cm (24in)

PULSATILLA VULGARIS ♛

Perennial

This is an extremely beautiful clump-forming pasque flower, with attractive divided, feathery foliage. The pendent, bell-shaped flowers have bright purple petals and golden yellow stamens. Ideal for a rock garden, it needs gritty, very well-drained soil and a sunny position, and grows best on alkaline soil. Pasque flowers do not like to have their roots disturbed and are best left undisturbed after planting. Propagate by seed.

◊ ☼ ❄ ❄ ❄
‡↔ to 20cm (8in)

RHODODENDRON *'Hatsugiri'*

Evergreen shrub

This small, compact evergreen azalea in late spring produces a profusion of bright reddish-purple flowers, borne in clusters of three blooms. It is suitable for a container on a patio, or the front of a border, and will tolerate full sun, unlike many of its cousins. Plant it in a free-draining, humus rich, acid (lime-free) soil or ericaceous compost. In the open garden mulch it generously with leafmould or bark.

◊ ☼ ☼ ❄ ❄ ❄
‡↔ to 60cm (24in)

TULIPA
'Blue Parrot'

Perennial bulb

This robust tulip is not truly blue but more violet. It has single flowers with slightly twisted petals, and blooms in late spring. Use it in borders and as a cut flower. *Tulipa* 'Greuze' also has violet-purple flowers, but they are more uniform in shape. The bulbs of both should be planted in late autumn in free draining soil in full sun.

◊ ☼ ❋ ❋ ❋
↑ to 60cm (24in)

TULIPA
'Queen of Night'

Perennial bulb

'Queen of Night' is an elegant hybrid tulip with large, dark maroon-purple flowers. The single cup-shaped blooms are borne on elegant long green stems above lance-shaped, greyish green leaves. It looks particularly effective when planted with an ivory-coloured variety, such as 'Maureen'. Plant bulbs of this reliably perennial tulip in late autumn in a sunny position and free-draining soil.

◊ ☼ ❋ ❋ ❋
↑ to 60cm (24in)

ANEMONE CORONARIA
'Lord Lieutenant'

Perennial

This striking plant originates from the Mediterranean region. The cultivar 'Lord Lieutenant' bears superb, velvety semi-double, deep blue flowers with black eyes, which open in mid- to late spring and are good for cutting. The divided foliage adds to this plant's charms. Plant the small tubers in autumn, preferably in light, sandy soil in full sun.

◊ ☼ ✽✽✽
‡ to 45cm (18in) ↔ to 15cm (6in)

AQUILEGIA ALPINA

Perennial

The alpine columbine has an upright habit, and is suitable for planting in a herbaceous border, rock garden or raised bed. It blooms in late spring and produces long stems that bear slightly nodding, deep blue flowers. The stems thrust up above finely-divided, bluish-green, ferny foliage. Grow it in a sunny or partially shaded position, in fertile, moist, well-drained, gritty soil.

◊ ◐ ☼ ◑ ✽✽✽
‡ to 45cm (18in) ↔ to 30cm (12in)

CEANOTHUS ARBOREUS
'Trewithen Blue' ♀

Evergreen shrub

There are very few blue-flowered large
shrubs or small trees that will grow well
in a temperate climate. The Californian
lilacs are among the best of these, and
are suitable for a wide range of soils,
including chalk. 'Trewithen Blue' is one
of the most vigorous, and soon forms
a small tree. It produces large heads of
mid-blue flowers from late spring to
early summer, and while it is generally
hardy, in cold areas, it is best to grow
it against a warm wall.

◊ ◑ ☼ ☀ ❄ ❄ ❄
‡ to 6m (20ft) ↔ to 8m (25ft)

CORYDALIS FLEXUOSA ♀
Perennial

This plant has waxy, light green, ferny
leaves, and produces clusters of long,
tubular, bright blue flowers in late
spring. The growing position should be
marked to avoid damaging the delicate
rootstock during cultivations in autumn
and winter. It needs partial shade and
should be grown in fertile, moist, well-
drained soil.

◊ ◑ ☀ ❄ ❄ ❄
‡ to 30cm (12in) ↔ to 20cm (8in)

GENTIANA ACAULIS ♀

Evergreen perennial

The trumpet gentian is a beautiful rock plant that bears vivid, trumpet-shaped, deep blue flowers with green spotted throats. The late spring blooms appear above rosettes of evergreen, glossy leaves that form a slightly raised mound. 'Coelestina' has Cambridge-blue blooms. The trumpet gentian needs to be planted in moist, very well-drained, acid soil in a partly shaded situation.

○ ◐ ☼ ❋ ❋ ❋
‡ to 8cm (3in) ↔ to 30cm (12in)

HYACINTHOIDES NON-SCRIPTA

Perennial bulb

In late spring, few sights compare with the beauty of a deciduous woodland carpeted with the fragrant flowers of English bluebells. Replicate these shady conditions, and bluebells will self seed and spread throughout the garden. For the best results, plant the bulbs in the autumn in moist, acid (lime-free), fertile soil, although they will tolerate slightly alkaline conditions. Cultivars with white and mauve flowers are also available.

◐ ☼ ❋ ❋ ❋
‡ to 40cm (16in) ↔ to 8cm (3in)

MUSCARI LATIFOLIUM

Perennial bulb

This is an unusual grape hyacinth, with
a spike of tiny, bicoloured, urn-shaped
flowers. The lower flowers are purplish-
black, while the upper, smaller, infertile
flowers are pale blue. The lance-shaped
leaves are broader than those of most
other muscaris. Plant the small bulbs in
a sunny, sheltered site in a well-drained
soil, and use at the front of a border or
in a rock garden. Established clumps
can be divided, or sow seed in summer.
This variety is not fully hardy and may
be killed by prolonged, hard frosts.

○ ☼ ❈ ❈
‡ to 20cm (8in) ↔ to 5cm (2in)

ROSMARINUS OFFICINALIS
'Sissinghurst Blue' ♛

Evergreen shrub

Widely grown as a culinary herb and
for its aromatic foliage, rosemary makes
a decorative shrub, and can be grown
as a low hedge. 'Sissinghurst Blue' is a
dwarf variety that bears small, pale blue
flowers in late spring. It suits a sunny,
sheltered location and well-drained soil.
Rosemary will respond well to pruning,
and old straggly plants can be cut back
hard in the spring. Propagate by semi-
ripe cuttings in the summer.

○ ☼ ❈ ❈
‡ ↔ to 50cm (20in)

SYRINGA VULGARIS
'Katherine Havemeyer' ♀

Deciduous shrub

A double-flowered form of the common lilac that produces clusters of pink buds that develop into lavender-blue, sweetly perfumed flowers. It grows quickly to form a spreading shrub or small tree, and will perform well when planted in a moist, well-drained fertile soil in full sun or partial shade. Young plants do not need pruning, but rejuvenate old lilac bushes by cutting them back hard after they have flowered. Lilacs are also tolerant of pollution.

○ ◐ ☼ ◑ ❄ ❄ ❄
‡ ↔ to 7m (22ft)

TECOPHILAEA
CYANOCROCUS ♀

Perennial corm

This low-growing plant has slightly erect, lance-shaped leaves, and in the spring produces one or two brilliant gentian-blue flowers with white throats. Grow it in a sunny site, in very well-drained, sandy soil in a rock garden or raised bed. This perennial is on the border of hardiness, and young foliage may be damaged by frost. In colder areas, it is better grown in a cold frame.

○ ☼ ❄ ❄
‡ to 10cm (4in) ↔ to 8cm (3in)

VERONICA PEDUNCULARIS

Perennial

Masses of small, saucer-shaped, deep
blue flowers open over a long period
from spring to early summer on this
mat-forming, low-growing veronica.
The glossy, purple-tinted green leaves
are also an attractive feature. Grow it in
a well-drained soil in a sunny location,
such as a rock garden or raised bed.
Stocks can be increased by dividing it
in the autumn.

◊ ☼ ❀ ❀ ❀
‡ to 10cm (4in) ↔ to 60cm (24in)

WISTERIA SINENSIS ♀

Climber

Chinese wisteria is a stunning climber,
suitable for growing against a wall, up
a large, mature tree or over a pergola.
The brilliant lilac blue, fragrant, pea-like
flowers are produced in long pendent
clusters during the late spring and early
summer. It is a vigorous plant, but can
be restricted by careful pruning in the
summer after flowering and in winter.
Plant it in full sun or partial shade in
fertile, moist, well-drained soil.

◊◊ ☼ ◐ ❀ ❀ ❀
‡ to 30m (100ft)

ARUM CRETICUM
Perennial

This spring-flowering arum is a native
of Crete. It has a large yellow or white
bract, or spathe, from which protrudes
a deep yellow spike, composed of a
mass of tiny, slightly fragrant flowers.
The large, arrow-shaped, glossy leaves
contrast well with the spring blooms.
Plant tubers in full sun in well-drained,
fertile soil. Large clumps can be divided
or plants raised from seed sown in the
early autumn.

◊ ☼ ✳ ✳
‡ to 50cm (20in) ↔ to 30cm (12in)

AURINIA SAXATILIS ♀
Evergreen perennial

Gold dust, formerly known as *Alyssum
saxatile*, is an evergreen with greyish-
green leaves. In early spring it produces
masses of small, bright yellow flowers.
Other gold dusts include 'Citrina', which
bears bright lemon-yellow flowers, and
'Compacta', a small variety with golden-
yellow blooms. It needs a sunny, well-
drained situation, and can be grown on
a wall, to spill over the front of a raised
bed, or in a rock garden.

◊ ☼ ✳ ✳ ✳
‡ to 23cm (9in) ↔ to 30cm (12in)

BERBERIS × STENOPHYLLA ♥

Evergreen shrub

This vigorous, spiny plant forms an elegant, spreading bush with arching branches covered with clusters of deep yellow flowers. The blooms appear in late spring, and are followed in summer by waxy black fruit. Plant it in full sun in a well-drained, fertile soil. It is most useful when grown as a dense intruder-proof hedge, which should be clipped after flowering has finished.

○ ☼ ❀ ❀ ❀
‡ to 3m (10ft) ↔ to 5m (15ft)

BERBERIS THUNBERGII
'Aurea'

Deciduous shrub

A beautiful barberry with bright golden-yellow leaves, it is much shorter than other varieties, and is suitable for small gardens. In late spring it bears clusters of pink-tinged, pale yellow flowers, which are followed in autumn by bright red berries. While it needs good light, bright sun can scorch the yellow leaves, but in dense shade the foliage will turn green. It grows happily in most soils.

○ ◐ ☼ ☼ ❀ ❀ ❀
‡ to 1.5m (5ft) ↔ to 2m (6ft)

COLCHICUM LUTEUM

Perennial corm

Colchicums are best known for their bright pink flowers, produced in the autumn, but this species is different. It has golden-yellow, goblet-shaped flowers that appear in late spring. It needs very good drainage and should be planted in gritty, fertile soil in full sun. It can be quite difficult to grow outdoors because the corms need to be kept completely dry when they are dormant. In wet climes, grow it in pots in a cold frame and take it outside in the spring.

◊ ☼ ❀ ❀ ❀

‡ to 10cm (4in) ↔ to 8cm (3in)

CYTISUS × PRAECOX
'Allgold' ♀

Evergreen shrub

This small, free-flowering broom bears a profusion of dark yellow blooms from mid- to late spring. Ideal for growing in a sunny mixed border, it needs a deep, slightly fertile, well-drained soil. After flowering, it can be trimmed back to keep it in shape, although pruning is not essential. 'Warminster' has a similar habit to 'Allgold', but produces creamy-yellow flowers.

◊ ☼ ❀ ❀ ❀

‡ to 1.2m (4ft) ↔ to 1.5m (5ft)

DIONYSIA TAPETODES

Evergreen perennial

This alpine plant forms a tight cushion of small, greyish-green leaves, and in the late spring and early summer bright yellow, upward facing flowers appear above the foliage. It is hardy, but needs dry, very well-drained soil and full sun to succeed. In its natural environment, it grows in the crevices of rocks, and is best suited to growing in pots of alpine compost under glass to protect it from a damp environment and winter rains.

○ ☼ ❀ ❀ ❀
‡ to 5cm (2in) ↔ to 20cm (8in)

DORONICUM X EXCELSUM
'Harpur Crewe'

Perennial

Bright, golden-yellow, daisy-like flowers adorn this leopard's bane in late spring. The blooms are held on tall erect stems above decorative, heart-shaped, basal leaves. Plant it in a moist, fertile soil in partial shade, and grow it in groups to enliven an early herbaceous border or woodland garden with dazzling colour. Leopard's bane can be propagated by division in autumn.

◐ ☼ ❀ ❀ ❀
‡ ↔ to 80cm (24in)

ENKIANTHUS
CAMPANULATUS ♀

Deciduous shrub

A member of the heather family, this
shrub can grow to form a small tree.
In late spring, the stems are covered
with dense clusters of pale creamy-
yellow, bell-shaped flowers with pink
tips and pink veins. The toothed foliage
turns wonderful shades of red, yellow
and orange in the autumn. It will grow
well in a sunny or partially shaded site
in a fertile, acid (lime-free), moist, but
well-drained soil.

○ ◐ ☼ ☀ ✿ ✿ ✿
‡↔ to 5m (15ft)

EPIMEDIUM PINNATUM
SUBSP. COLCHICUM ♀

Evergreen perennial

An attractive clump-former, this plant
produces rounded leaves divided into
five leaflets, and golden-yellow single
flowers, which are relatively large for
an epimedium, measuring up to 18mm
(¾in) across. It prefers a semi-shaded
situation and heavy, moisture-retentive,
fertile soil. Although slower to spread
than the species, the leaves still make
excellent ground cover. The appearance
of the plant will be improved if the old
foliage is clipped over in late winter.

◐ ☀ ✿ ✿ ✿
‡↔ to 30cm (12in)

ERIGERON AUREUS
'Canary Bird' ♀

Perennial

A slow-growing fleabane, this form has
rounded greyish green leaves, and in
late spring and early summer it bears
daisy-like, canary-yellow flowers. Grow
it in a sunny site, where there is some
protection from the full strength of the
summer sun, and plant it in moist, well-
drained soil, which does not dry out.
When plants begin to lose their vigour,
divide them in spring.

◊ ◊ ☼ ❊ ❊ ❊
‡ to 10cm (4in) ↔ to 15cm (6in)

EUPHORBIA POLYCHROMA ♀

Perennial

This plant is guaranteed to brighten up
a dull spring morning. The stems are
clothed in bright green leaves, which
form a rounded clump, and from late
spring and well into summer it bears
acid yellow flowers, surrounded by a
collar of striking greenish-yellow bracts.
A tolerant plant, it will grow on most
well-drained soils, and can be used at
the front of a border or in a woodland
garden. Care should be taken when
pruning the stems, because the latex
they exude can irritate the skin.

◊ ☼ ❊ ❊ ❊ ❊
‡ ↔ to 50cm (20in)

FREMONTODENDRON
'California Glory' ♀

Evergreen shrub

While not completely hardy, this shrub
will survive most winters if it is trained
against a sheltered, south-facing wall.
The large golden-yellow flowers bloom
from late spring to mid-autumn, and are
set off by dark green, five-lobed foliage,
making this plant a valuable addition to
any garden. It grows happily on chalky,
free-draining soil, and can be pruned
lightly in early spring. Contact with the
foliage may cause an allergic reaction.

◊ ☼ ❀ ❀
‡ to 6m (20ft) ↔ to 4m (12ft)

FRITILLARIA IMPERIALIS
'Maxima Lutea' ♀

Perennial bulb

The value of crown imperials in the late
spring garden is beyond question. The
tall stems carry a tuft of shiny, green
leafy bracts at the top, beneath which
hang a number of bright yellow, bell-
shaped flowers. The bulbs should be
planted in late summer in full sun and
a deep, well-drained soil, where they
will not be disturbed. 'Rubra' is more
robust, with orange-red flowers and
purple stems.

◊ ☼ ❀ ❀ ❀
‡ to 1.5m (5ft) ↔ to 30cm (12in)

GENISTA HISPANICA

Deciduous shrub

A mound-forming shrub, Spanish gorse
produces a profusion of golden-yellow,
pea-like, small flowers on green prickly
stems in late spring and early summer.
Plant it in a well-drained soil and sunny
position, such as the front of a raised
bed. Spanish gorse is not totally hardy
and may be killed by severe frosts, so
in colder gardens, plant it in a sheltered
position by a warm wall to prevent it
from being damaged.

○ ☼ ❄ ❄
‡ to 75cm (30in) ↔ to 1.5m (5ft)

IRIS
'Golden Harvest'

Perennial bulb

This iris produces pure golden-yellow
flowers, that are good for cutting from
the middle of spring to early summer.
It requires a very well-drained neutral
or slightly alkaline soil and a sunny site,
as bulbs may not survive wet conditions
while they are dormant. Large clumps
should be divided as soon as possible
after flowering.

○ ☼ ❄ ❄ ❄
‡ to 80cm (32in) ↔ to 15cm (6in)

KERRIA JAPONICA
'Golden Guinea' ♀

Deciduous shrub

Kerria is an easy-to-grow and vigorous shrub, with graceful, arching green stems. One of the most popular forms is 'Pleniflora', which has double, deep yellow flowers. 'Golden Guinea' is less vigorous, with single yellow blooms. It grows best in free-draining soil and full sun, but can tolerate light shade. Kerria spreads by suckers, which can be dug up in the autumn to propagate it. Cut back the stems after flowering to keep it within bounds.

○ ☼ ◑ ✻ ✻ ✻
‡ to 2m (6ft) ↔ to 2.5m (8ft)

LABURNUM ANAGYROIDES

Deciduous tree

The laburnum is a widely-grown garden plant and in late spring produces long, pendent clusters of pea-like, bright yellow flowers. Laburnums will grow in almost any soil, as long as it is not waterlogged, but they need full sun to flourish. They are easily propagated from seed sown in the autumn – but remember that laburnum seeds are very poisonous. *L.* x *watereri* 'Vossii' has larger blooms held in longer clusters.

○ ◐ ☼ ✻ ✻ ✻
‡ ↔ to 8m (25ft)

MECONOPSIS CAMBRICA

Perennial

The Welsh poppy has single lemon-yellow or orange flowers, and blooms from late spring to the autumn. The flowers are borne on long stems above fern-like, greyish-green foliage. 'Floro Pleno' has double yellow flowers, and comes true from seed. Welsh poppies are happiest in partial shade and moist, acid (lime-free) soil, although they will tolerate alkaline conditions. They have a tendency to self seed and will spread quickly, unless the seedheads are cut off before they ripen.

◊ ☼ ✿ ✿ ✿
‡ to 45cm (18in) ↔ to 30cm (12in)

NARCISSUS JONQUILLA ♀

Perennial bulb

Wild jonquils are valued for their sweet fragrance and small yellow blooms that appear in spring. Each stem produces five or six bright yellow, single flowers above linear, almost cylindrical leaves. These narcissi look lovely naturalized in grass or beneath deciduous trees, and also make wonderful container plants for a patio, where their fragrance can be enjoyed at close range. Plant the bulbs in free-draining soil in sun for the best results.

◊ ☼ ✿ ✿ ✿
‡ to 30cm (12in) ↔ to 8cm (3in)

PAEONIA DELAVAYI
VAR. LUDLOWII ♧

Deciduous shrub

When given the correct conditions, the Tibetan tree peony will eventually form a broad, spreading bush. In late spring, it bears bright yellow flowers, and has decorative, lobed, deeply-cut foliage, borne on graceful arching stems. Grow this tree peony in a full sun or light shade on moist, well-drained soil. It is easily propagated from seed. Cut out one or two of the older stems in late winter to rejuvenate established plants.

◊ ◊ ☼ ☀ ❊ ❊ ❊
‡ to 2m (6ft) ↔ to 3m (9ft)

PAEONIA
MLOKOSEWITSCHII ♧

Perennial

There are few more desirable plants than 'Molly-the-Witch', with its large primrose-yellow flowers and glaucous green divided foliage. The stems are tinted pink or red. Slow-growing at first, it can eventually form a wide-spreading clump. It grows happily in full sun or dappled shade, although a well-drained soil is essential. Propagate it from seed. Although peonies tend to resent being disturbed, large clumps can be divided in the autumn.

◊ ☼ ☀ ❊ ❊ ❊
‡ ↔ to 75cm (30in)

PRIMULA PROLIFERA ♥

Evergreen perennial

This candelabra primula forms rosettes of pale evergreen leaves with serrated edges. The fragrant, golden-yellow flowers appear in late spring. Like all candelabra primulas, it requires deep, fertile, neutral or slightly acid (lime-free) soil, which does not dry out in summer. It looks particularly striking when planted in a large group near water. Divide congested clumps in the early spring, or grow plants from seed

◊ ☼ ❋ ❋ ❋
‡ ↔ to 60cm (24in)

PRIMULA VERIS ♥

Evergreen perennial

The cowslip is one of the best loved spring flowers, and produces clusters of pale yellow, fragrant blooms throughout the season. The erect flower stems are surrounded by a rosette of evergreen, deeply-veined leaves. Cowslips should be planted in a partly shaded site, in well-drained, moist soil. They can be grown in full sun, as long as the soil remains permanently moist. Grow it from seed in spring, or divide large clumps in the autumn or early spring.

△◊ ☼ ☼ ❋ ❋ ❋
‡ ↔ to 25cm (10in)

RHODODENDRON LUTEUM ♀

Deciduous shrub

This widely-grown deciduous azalea in spring bears large numbers of strongly fragrant, funnel-shaped, bright yellow flowers. The lance-shaped leaves turn shades of purple, red and orange in the autumn. This azalea prefers full sun, but will tolerate a little shade. Plant it with the root ball just proud of the surface in moist, well-drained acid (lime-free) soil, and mulch annually with leafmould or chipped bark.

⚬💧☼ ☀ ❄ ❄ ❄
↕ ↔ to 4m (12ft)

RHODODENDRON MACABEANUM ♀

Evergreen tree

Many people consider this to be the best of all the yellow rhododendrons. In mid- to late spring it produces large trusses of deep yellow flowers with purple spots on the inside. Very hardy, it eventually grows into a substantial tree, making it only really suitable for large gardens, where it is best planted in dappled shade beneath deciduous trees. It enjoys moist, well-drained acid (lime-free) soil. Mulch annually with leafmould or chipped bark.

⚬💧 ☀ ❄ ❄ ❄
↕ to 13.5m (45ft) ↔ to 13.5m (45ft)

RIBES ODORATUM

Deciduous shrub

The buffalo currant is an upright shrub with attractive three-lobed, bright green leaves. From mid- to late spring clusters of small fragrant, tubular, golden-yellow flowers with bright red anthers appear, followed in summer by black berries. In autumn its foliage turns various shades of red and purple. Plant it in full sun or light shade in well-drained soil. It is easy to propagate by taking hardwood cuttings during the winter.

◊ ☼ ☀ ❋ ❋ ❋
↕ ↔ to 2m (6ft)

SAXIFRAGA × ELIZABETHAE

Perennial

A free-flowering, cushion-forming plant, in late spring this saxifrage is covered in bright yellow flowers, borne on very short stems which rarely exceed 2.5cm (1in) in height. Plant it in a semi-shaded situation in well-drained soil. It makes a superb rock garden plant, and thrives in the gaps between the boulders

◊ ☼ ❋ ❋ ❋
↕ to 2.5cm (1in) ↔ to 15cm (6in)

TRILLIUM LUTEUM ♀

Perennial

This clump-forming plant has silver-green mottled leaves with pointed tips. Its yellow, fragrant flowers appear in late spring and are composed of three narrow green sepals and three upright, pale yellow petals. It is a good choice for a woodland garden, and should be grown in a shaded position in moist, well-drained, acid (lime-free) soil. In the autumn, mulch it with well-rotted leaf mould.

◊◊ ☼ ☀ ❀ ❀ ❀

‡ to 40cm (16in) ↔ to 30cm (12in)

TROLLIUS EUROPAEUS

Perennial

The European globeflower is a reliable plant for moist soils. Resembling a large buttercup, the spherical, lemon-yellow flowers appear in late spring and early summer. It also has attractive, glossy, divided foliage. This globeflower can be planted in full sun or partial shade and is suitable for bog gardens, as it does particularly well in fertile soil that never dries out. 'Canary Bird' is one of the best cultivars. European globeflowers can be grown from seed, or divided in the autumn.

◊ ☼ ☀ ❀ ❀ ❀

‡ to 60cm (24in) ↔ to 45cm (18in)

TULIPA
'Golden Apeldoorn'

Perennial bulb

A widely grown single-flowered tulip
with bright golden-yellow flowers. The
base of the inner petals is marked with
a large black patch that disguises the
black stamens. Plant it in well-drained,
fertile soil in a sunny position. Most
tulips look best when grown with a
contrasting colour; this yellow variety
would look good with the cherry-red
'Apeldoorn', or scarlet 'Oxford' in a
bedding scheme.

◊ ☼ ❋ ❋ ❋
‡ to 60cm (24in)

TULIPA
'West Point' ♀

Perennial bulb

This is a striking lily-flowered tulip, the
late spring primrose-yellow flowers of
which have pointed petals that curve
slightly outwards at the tips. It should
be planted in a sunny situation in well-
drained, fertile soil, and looks stunning
when combined with a bright red tulip,
such as the lily-flowered 'Mariette'. It is
particularly suitable for containers.

◊ ☼ ❋ ❋ ❋
‡ to 50cm (20in)

UVULARIA GRANDIFLORA ♀

Perennial

An unusual spreading plant, the large merrybells has erect stems that droop at the tip, and in late spring carry narrow, bell-shaped, yellow flowers. It should be planted in deep, moist, well-drained soil. Merrybells is a hardy plant, and will perform well when grown in a shady border, or in the dappled shade of a woodland garden. It is vulnerable to slug and snail damage and will need to be protected from these pests during the growing season.

◊ ◊ ☼ ❀ ❀ ❀
‡ to 60cm (24in) ↔ to 30cm (12in)

VESTIA FOETIDA ♀

Evergreen shrub

With glossy, dark green, elliptic leaves, and bright tubular flowers, *Vestia* is a valuable asset to the late spring garden. Although reasonably hardy, this shrub can be damaged by a hard frost, and should be planted against a sunny west- or south-facing wall in a well-drained soil. In very cold areas it is better to grow it in a large container and to bring it into a greenhouse or a conservatory during the winter.

◊ ☼ ❀ ❀
‡ to 2m (6ft) ↔ to 1.5m (5ft)

VIOLA BIFLORA

Perennial

A dwarf violet with attractive kidney- or
heart-shaped leaves, this plant spreads
slowly by creeping roots. In the spring
and early summer it produces solitary
or pairs of small, deep lemon-yellow
flowers, the lower petals of which have
purple-brown streaks that radiate out
from the centre. It performs well when
planted in well-drained, moist soil in a
partially shade situation, and is suitable
for a woodland garden.

◊ ◐ ☼ ☀ ❄ ❄ ❄
‡ to 8cm (3in) ↔ to 20cm (8in)

VIOLA
'Jackanapes' ♀

Evergreen perennial

This violet has toothed, bright green
leaves, and spreading stems that bear
bicoloured flowers in late spring and
throughout the summer. The small
blooms are deep maroon purple at the
top, and bright yellow at the base, with
purple streaks radiating from the centre.
'Jackanapes' should be grown in moist,
well-drained soil in full sun or partial
shade. It is short-lived and needs to be
propagated regularly by taking stem-tip
cuttings in late summer.

◊ ◐ ☼ ☀ ❄ ❄ ❄
‡ to 12cm (5in) ↔ to 30cm (12in)

BERBERIS LINEARIFOLIA *'Orange King'*

Evergreen shrub

This attractive barberry has glossy, dark green leaves, and strong, upright, spiny stems. The cup-shaped, bright orange flowers, borne in small clusters, appear in late spring, and are then followed in late summer by waxy black fruit. It will grow well in full sun and deep, moist, well-drained soil. To propagate it, take softwood cuttings in late summer.

○ ◊ ☼ ❀ ❀ ❀
‡↔ to 2.5m (8ft)

PRIMULA × BULLEESIANA

Evergreen perennial

This beautiful candelabra primula is a hybrid between *P. bulleyana* and *P. beesiana.* Plants may have orange, yellow, pink, red and purple flowers, borne in tiers around stout stems. Plant it in a slightly shaded situation in moist, neutral or slightly acid (lime-free) soil. The plant overwinters as a rosette of mid-green leaves, and can be divided, or grown from seed, in the spring.

◊ ☼ ❀ ❀ ❀
‡↔ to 60cm (24in)

PRIMULA BULLEYANA ♀

Perennial

Clusters of crimson flowers that quickly
fade to bright orange are borne on this
striking candelabra primula in the late
spring. The toothed, rounded, lance-
shaped, mid-green leaves form a tight
rosette at the base of the plant. It suits
waterside plantings and bog gardens as
it enjoys partial shade and deep, moist,
fertile, neutral or slightly acid soil that
does not dry out in summer. It can be
propagated by division in spring.

◊ ☼ ✱ ✱ ✱
‡ ↔ to 60cm (24in)

RHODODENDRON
'Frome'

Deciduous shrub

A medium-sized deciduous azalea, this
form has orangy-yellow, frilly, funnel-
shaped flowers with red marks on their
throats. It forms a large, dome-shaped
bush, and is suitable for the middle or
back of a mixed border, or beneath
deciduous trees. It needs a moist, well-
drained, fertile, acid (lime-free) soil in
partial shade. Mulch it annually with
leafmould or chipped bark.

◊ ◊ ☼ ✱ ✱ ✱
‡ ↔ to 1.5m (5ft)

EARLY SUMMER

Not a day goes by without more flowers opening somewhere in the garden. Hanging baskets and containers, brimming with pelargoniums, verbenas and other tender bedding, can be put out now all danger of frost has passed. The herbaceous border reaches a peak of perfection: peonies and delphiniums surround their supports, holding their flowers up against the weather for pure enjoyment, while bearded irises, daylilies, starry alliums and hardy geraniums bloom in profusion and dazzling shades.

In the light shade of trees, making cool leafy ground cover, grow hostas, heucheras and bugle (*Ajuga*). Feathery clumps of goatsbeard (*Aruncus*) and monkshood (*Aconitum*) will thrive in moist conditions, but for permanently wet soil and pond margins the beauty of the Japanese iris is without peer.

Mediterranean shrubs such as genistas, thymes and phlomis revel in the hot dry conditions. More dramatic bursts of colour are provided by sun-loving annuals, especially those sown in autumn, like eschscholzia and cosmos. Half-hardy antirrhinums and salvias can be used for bedding or to fill gaps, perhaps replacing oriental poppies after their flowers have gone. All will flower into autumn if they are deadheaded; the key to extending the display of many annuals and, of course, roses.

SUMMER ROMANCE

Most evocative of summer are the roses, gracing many garden situations with fragrance and colour throughout the season. Modern shrub roses are easier going than hybrid teas, often having the characteristics of old roses but flowering for longer. Ground cover roses are healthy and very versatile; for example, Surrey trails over sunny banks or walls, but is also at home in a large pot or hanging basket, while 'Madame Knorr' makes a spectacular thorny hedge.

ACANTHUS SPINOSUS ♀

Perennial

The distinctive, purple-hooded, white tubular flowers of bear's breeches are held on tall spikes. Its deeply divided leaves are a glossy dark green. Grow it in fertile, well-drained soil, close to a warm wall or in a herbaceous border in full sun. In partial shade it will produce lusher foliage. Divide clumps in spring or autumn. When given plenty of space, this clump-forming perennial makes a striking architectural plant. The flowers dry well when left on the plant or cut.

◊ ☼ ☀ ❋ ❋ ❋

‡ to 1.2m (4ft) ↔ to 60cm (24in)

ACHILLEA PTARMICA
'The Pearl' ♀

Perennial

Sneezewort is a slender perennial with narrow, serrated, dark green leaves. From early to late summer, 'The Pearl' bears abundant small, pompon-shaped flowers with tiny, white petals. It is happiest when planted in a sunny position, in well-drained fertile soil. Propagate it by division in autumn. The flowerheads dry well.

◊ ☼ ❋ ❋ ❋

‡↔ to 75cm (30in)

ACTINIDIA KOLOMIKTA ♥

Climber

This deciduous, woody-stemmed climber, with its green, white and purple-red variegated leaves, is ideal for clothing a pergola or a wall. Fragrant white flowers are borne in clusters in early summer, and are sometimes followed by yellow-green fruits. Plant in fertile, well-drained soil and provide shelter from strong winds. It will grow in partial shade but full sun will give the best leaf colour. Propagate by semi-ripe cuttings in late summer. Prune lightly in early spring to keep it within bounds.

○ ☼ ☀ ❄ ❄ ❄
‡ to 4m (12ft)

ARUNCUS DIOICUS ♥

Perennial

Goatsbeard forms large clumps of fern-like, mid-green foliage. From early to midsummer, tiny, star-shaped, white flowers appear on fluffy plumes up to 50cm (20in) long. An easy-going plant, it is tolerant of sun or shade, and moist or dry, reasonably fertile soil. It suits a sunny border or damp ground by water, or a woodland border. Divide plants in early spring or autumn.

○ ◑ ☼ ☀ ❄ ❄ ❄
‡ to 2m (6ft) ↔ to 1.2m (4ft)

CARDIOCRINUM GIGANTEUM
Perennial bulb

The giant lily is an impressive plant, with up to 20 fragrant, trumpet-shaped blooms on top of a tall, stout stem that does not require staking. It forms a rosette of dark green, glossy leaves at the base. For the best results, give it a shady, sheltered position in moist, humus-rich soil. Although the lily dies after flowering, the bulb forms plenty of small bulblets that can be dug up and replanted immediately. They will be ready to flower in three to five years. Protect new growth over winter with a dry mulch.

◑ ☼ ❄ ❄ ❄
‡ to 4m (12ft) ↔ to 45cm (18in)

CISTUS LADANIFER ♥
Evergreen shrub

This is a substantial, though often short-lived, upright shrub. The branches are covered with aromatic leaves, and from early summer, it bears large quantities of white, saucer-shaped flowers with yellow centres. Each papery petal carries a crimson spot at its base. A native of the Mediterranean, this shrub thrives in full sun and well-drained soil, and suits a gravel garden or a site close to a sunny wall. It also grows well in coastal gardens. Established plants will not tolerate being moved.

◑ ☼ ❄ ❄
‡ to 2m (6ft) ↔ to 1.5m (5ft)

CLEMATIS FLORIDA *VAR.* SIEBOLDIANA

Climber

This clematis is widely grown for its striking early summer flowers, with their creamy-white petals and rich purple stamens. Severe winters may damage early top growth, so plant it in a sheltered spot in humus-rich, well-drained soil, or in a container of loam-based potting compost. In early spring, prune stems back to a strong pair of buds, approximately 20cm (8in) above the ground. Train it along supporting wires, trellis or over a tripod.

◊ ☼ ☀ ✿ ✿
‡ to 2.5m (8ft)

CLEMATIS 'Silver Moon'

Climber

Large, silvery-white flowers, with a hint of mauve, make this among the most attractive of the early summer-flowering clematis. Rarely growing taller than 2m (6ft), it is ideal for a small garden. It needs a sheltered spot in sun or partial shade, with its roots in shade, and well-drained, humus-rich, fertile soil. Provide it with a support or allow it to scramble through shrubs. In early spring, remove dead stems and prune back the other shoots to a couple of strong buds.

◊ ☼ ☀ ✿ ✿
‡ to 2m (6ft)

CORNUS CANADENSIS ♀

Perennial

Spreading by means of underground
stems, the creeping dogwood will
provide a low-growing carpet of lush
greenery beneath shrubs or trees. The
bright green, oval leaves, which grow
in opposite pairs, are a perfect foil
for the creamy white, petal-like bracts
that surround the tiny green-red flowers.
It does best on moist but well-drained,
slightly acid (lime-free) soil in partial
shade. Divide established plants in early
spring or autumn.

◊ ☼ ❄ ❄ ❄
‡ to 15cm (6in) ↔ to 30cm (12in)

CORNUS
'Norman Hadden' ♀

Deciduous tree

'Norman Hadden' bears masses of large,
creamy-white, petal-like bracts in early
summer which, after a few weeks, turn
a deep shade of pink. The blooms are
followed in autumn by strawberry-like
fruits. Yet another of its attractions is
that, with age, its bark will start to peel,
creating a handsome effect. For best
results, plant in a sunny or partially
shaded position, protected from strong
winds, in well-drained, neutral to acid
(lime-free) fertile soil.

◊ ☼ ☼ ❄ ❄ ❄
‡↔ to 8m (25ft)

CRAMBE CORDIFOLIA ♀

Perennial

This extremely vigorous perennial has
large, dark green, crinkled leaves. In
wonderful contrast, small, highly fragrant,
star-shaped flowers are borne in a white
froth on stiffly branching, slender stems.
To accommodate its sprawling habit,
provide it with plenty of space. Although
it will tolerate poor soil, it prefers a
sunny position in well-drained fertile
soil. Plant it in a gravel garden or
herbaceous border.

◊ ☼ ☀ ❄ ❄ ❄
‡ to 2.5m (8ft) ↔ to 1.5m (5ft)

DELPHINIUM
'Butterball'

Perennial

In summer, this vigorous perennial bears
tall spikes of white, semi-double flowers
with deep yellow eyes. For the greatest
impact, plant in groups of up to 10 in
well-drained, fertile soil in full sun. The
stems will need supporting with canes
from a young age to prevent them
snapping in strong winds. Feed the
plants in spring and remove the faded
flowerheads, and you may be rewarded
with a second burst of flowers.

◊ ☼ ❄ ❄ ❄
‡ to 1.5m (5ft) ↔ to 90cm (36in)

DEUTZIA GRACILIS

Deciduous shrub

An upright, spreading shrub, it bears clusters of fragrant, pure white flowers in early summer. Plant it in a sunny site in fertile, well-drained soil, and provide protection from late-spring frosts which can damage the flowers. Prune back the old shoots after flowering has finished. Take softwood cuttings in summer and hardwood cuttings in autumn.

◊ ☼ ❁ ❁ ❁
‡↔ to 1m (3ft)

DIANTHUS
'Haytor White' ♥

Perennial

This white, modern pink is widely grown for cutting, and will fill a room with its delicious clove scent. The double flowers have deeply serrated petals. Pinks do best in a sunny position at the front of a border or by paving, and should be planted in reasonably fertile, well-drained soil. In spring, pinch out the growing tips to promote bushy growth. Dead-heading will help prolong flowering. Take cuttings from non-flowering stems in early spring.

◊ ☼ ❁ ❁ ❁
‡ to 45cm (18in) ↔ to 40cm (16in)

DIGITALIS PURPUREA
F. ALBIFLORA ♟

Biennial

This foxglove will grow easily in most
gardens, provided you give it moist but
well-drained soil and a little shade. In
the first year it produces a large rosette
of oval-shaped, deep green leaves,
followed, in early summer of the next
year, by a tall spire of pure white
flowers. Sow seed in spring, and plant
out the young seedlings in autumn.
Foxgloves look best when planted in
groups in front of a dark background
by shrubs or in a dappled woodland.

◊ ◊ ☀ ❄ ❄ ❄
‡ to 2m (6ft) ↔ to 60cm (24in)

DRYAS OCTOPETALA ♟

Evergreen shrub

The dainty flowers of the mountain
avens belie its tough nature – this plant
can cope with the harsh conditions on
top of windswept, stony slopes and
cliffs. What it lacks in height it more
than makes up for in spread: its glossy,
dark green leaves will quickly fill
crevices between rocks, gaps in dry-
stone walls or form large mats in a
gravel garden. Grow it in well-drained,
gritty soil in sun or partial shade.

◊ ☼ ☀ ❄ ❄ ❄
‡ to 10cm (4in) ↔ to 1m (3ft)

ERICA VAGANS
'Lyonesse' ♆

Evergreen shrub

The Cornish heath forms a nicely rounded, spreading bush, suitable for ground cover, with bright green, needle-like leaves. The long spikes of small white flowers, which appear in summer and continue into early autumn, are a favourite of hoverflies and butterflies. Plant it in full sun, in moist, well-drained, humus-rich, acid (lime-free) soil, although it tolerates slightly alkaline soils. After flowering, clip over the plant to keep it looking neat.

⬦ ◊ ☼ ❀ ❀ ❀
‡ to 25cm (10in) ↔ to 50cm (20in)

GALEGA OFFICINALIS
'Alba' ♆

Perennial

An ideal plant for the back of a sunny border, this goat's rue bears small, pea-like, white flowers in early summer. For the best results, plant it in sun or partial shade in moist, well-drained soil. If the soil is rich the stems will be floppy and the plant will need supporting, either with canes, inserted in late spring, or by allowing it to grow through other open, sturdy shrubs. Propagate by dividing established plants between late autumn and spring.

⬦ ◊ ☼ ☼ ❀ ❀ ❀
‡ to 1.5m (5ft) ↔ to 90cm (36in)

GILLENIA TRIFOLIATA ♀

Perennial

This is an upright, herbaceous perennial with red-tinted, branched stems and small, single, white to pinkish-white flowers which are good for cutting. Plant it in a well-drained, fertile soil. Originally from the woods of North America, it needs the light or dappled shade of a woodland garden or shady border beneath deciduous trees. The tall, wiry stems will need supporting early in the year if the site is exposed. Divide large clumps in spring or autumn.

◊ ◊ ☼ ❄ ❄ ❄
‡ to 1m (3ft) ↔ to 60cm (24in)

GLADIOLUS CALLIANTHUS

Perennial corm

This half-hardy gladiolus may be sold under its former name of acidanthera. The fragrant white flowers, borne on tall, arching stems, have deep red or purple throats, and are good for cutting. Plant the corms in a sunny border, in well-drained, fertile soil. They will rot quickly in wet conditions, and it is advisable to mix grit with heavier soil when planting. They will not survive a cold winter, so dig up the corms in early autumn, dry them and store in a frost-free place until planting in spring.

◊ ☼ ❄ ❄
‡ to 1m (3ft) ↔ to 5cm (2in)

× HALIMIOCISTUS SAHUCII ♀

Evergreen shrub

A spreading shrub with narrow, dark green, downy leaves, this species bears a profusion of saucer-shaped, white flowers from early summer to autumn. It makes a welcome addition to a gravel or rock garden, or a raised bed, where it will enjoy basking in the full heat of the sun. It does well in poor soils and very well-drained conditions are a must. If in doubt, improve drainage by adding grit to the soil.

○ ☼ ✿ ✿ ✿

‡ to 45cm (18in) ↔ to 90cm (36in)

HEBE
'Pewter Dome' ♀

Evergreen shrub

A rounded, spreading shrub, it bears greyish-green leaves and spikes of small, white flowers for several weeks from early summer. Grow in reasonably fertile, well-drained soil in sun or partial shade. Provide some shade from strong sun, which can burn the leaves. It is suitable for a rock garden or a mixed border, and is good for seaside gardens. In mild areas it can be used as a low hedge. It needs no pruning, but hedges can be clipped lightly after flowering.

○ ☼ ✿ ✿

‡ to 40cm (16in) ↔ to 60cm (24in)

HELIANTHEMUM
'Wisley White'

Evergreen shrub

Rock roses are attractive dwarf shrubs
that bear an abundance of small,
saucer shaped flowers all summer. The
papery flowers of 'Wisley White' are
pure white with yellow stamens, offset
by greyish-green leaves. Rock roses
thrive in well-drained soil on sun-baked
banks, cracks in paving and in gravel
gardens. Trim after flowering to keep
the shape of the bush neat. Propagate
by semi-ripe cuttings in early summer

◊ ☼ ❀ ❀ ❀
‡ to 20cm (8in) ↔ to 30cm (12in)

HEMEROCALLIS
'Joan Senior'

Perennial

Most daylilies come within the yellow
spectrum but 'Joan Senior', with its
white flowers tinged green at the throat,
is something quite different. Although
each bloom typically lasts only a day,
flowers continue to be produced from
early to midsummer. It does best in
fertile, moist but well-drained soil in a
sunny situation. If the plants become
too congested, divide large clumps of
the mid-green strappy leaves in late
summer or early spring.

◊ ◊ ☼ ❀ ❀ ❀
‡ to 60cm (24in) ↔ to 75cm (30in)

HESPERIS MATRONALIS *VAR.* ALBIFLORA

Perennial

The tall flower spikes of sweet rocket are a favourite with butterflies. Make the most of the heavenly scent – which, incidentally, grows stronger after dusk – by planting it alongside a path or patio. It is short-lived and best grown as a biennial. Plants are easy to raise from seed sown *in situ* outdoors. Grow in full sun, in fertile, moist, well-drained soil. It is also tolerant of poor soil.

◊ ◊ ☼ ❉ ❉ ❉
‡ to 75cm (30in) ↔ to 60cm (24in)

IBERIS AMARA

Annual

In summer, this fast-growing annual produces masses of white to purplish-white scented flowers which are borne in dense, flattish clusters. Enjoying a sunny site and well-drained soil, it is perfect for edging a path or planting in a gravel garden or raised bed. Sow seed *in situ*, in spring or autumn.

◊ ☼ ❉ ❉ ❉
‡ to 30cm (12in) ↔ to 15cm (6in)

IRIS
'Bold Print'

Perennial

Bearded iris come in a huge range of colours and subtle colour combinations. 'Bold Print' has striking white flowers that are edged and lightly veined with deep purple. Grow it in full sun, in a well-drained, neutral to slightly acid soil. Divide congested clumps in late summer. When planting, make sure that the tops of the rhizomes are exposed to the sun.

◊ ☼ ❀ ❀ ❀
‡ to 55cm (22in) ↔ indefinite

JASMINUM OFFICINALE
'Argenteovariegatum' ♥

Climber

This jasmine is semi-evergreen, with cream-edged, green leaves. The highly fragrant, pure white flowers appear in clusters from early summer to early autumn. Grow it in full sun or partial shade, in fertile, well-drained soil. Once flowering is over, thin old or congested stems. During summer, take semi-ripe cuttings. It is not fully hardy, so plant it in a sheltered position or by a warm wall. It can also be grown in containers of loam-based compost.

◊ ☼ ☀ ❀ ❀
‡ to 12m (40ft)

LAMIUM MACULATUM
'White Nancy' ♀

Perennial

Ideal as ground cover in shady areas, and beneath trees and shrubs, this attractive dead nettle retains its green-edged, silver leaves throughout most winters. In early summer, it produces dainty spikes of hooded, white flowers. Plant it in moist but well-drained soil in full or partial shade. Divide large clumps in autumn or early spring.

○ ◊ ☼ ☀ ❆ ❆ ❆
‡ to 15cm (6in) ↔ to 1m (3ft)

LAVATERA × CLEMENTII
'Barnsley'

Perennial

The tree mallow is a vigorous, free-flowering, semi-evergreen shrub with lobed green leaves. From early summer until the first frosts, 'Barnsley' steadily produces clusters of funnel-shaped, white flowers with distinctive red eyes. Choose a spot for it in full sun, in well-drained, ideally light, fertile soil. Provide shelter from strong winds as the branches are brittle. Propagate by softwood cuttings in summer. It is suitable for gardens in coastal areas.

◊ ☼ ❆ ❆ ❆
‡↔ to 2m (6ft)

LEUCANTHEMUM × SUPERBUM
'Wirral Supreme' ♓

Perennial

A stalwart of the herbaceous border, this vigorous plant produces masses of double, daisy-like flowers on stiff, erect stems held above dark green, lance-shaped leaves. The blooms make good cut flowers. In exposed sites, the tall stems may need support. Happiest in fairly fertile, well-drained but moist soil, in full sun or partial shade, it will eventually spread to form a large clump. Divide established plants in early spring or late summer.

○ ◐ ☼ ☀ ❄ ❄ ❄
‡ to 90cm (36in) ↔ to 75cm (30in)

LEUCOJUM AESTIVUM
'Gravetye Giant' ♓

Perennial bulb

If left undisturbed in a lightly shaded spot in damp, fertile soil, the summer snowflake will quickly spread to form a large clump of glossy, dark green leaves. From spring to early summer, 'Gravetye Giant' produces up to eight slightly pendent, white flowers tipped with green that have a faint chocolate scent. Plant the bulbs in autumn, preferably in a waterside setting.

○ ☀ ❄ ❄ ❄
‡ to 90cm (36in) ↔ to 8cm (3in)

LILIUM
'Mont Blanc'
Perennial bulb

From early to midsummer, this sturdy Asiatic lily produces bunches of ivory-white flowers with brown-spotted throats. Its compact stems make it ideal for growing in containers or in a raised bed. Plant bulbs in full sun, in fertile, well-drained soil from late autumn to early spring. The flowers are good for cutting, but care must be taken because the pollen stains clothing and damages polished surfaces.

◊ ☼ ❄❄❄
‡ to 70cm (28in)

MATTHIOLA
'Hansens Park'
Perennial

Their sweet fragrance makes stocks a popular bedding plant and cut flower. Most have narrow, greyish-green leaves and erect stems. Sow seed in spring in pots of loam-based seed compost, and overwinter young plants in a cold frame before planting out the following spring, in moist but well-drained, slightly fertile soil. There are a few white-flowering forms available. *M. fructiculosa* 'Alba' is a compact form that is ideal for containers.

◊◊◊ ☼ ❄❄❄
‡ to 45cm (18in) ↔ to 30cm (12in)

PAEONIA LACTIFLORA
'Baroness Schröder'

Perennial

This superb Chinese peony produces a
bold clump of dark green leaves and
very large, almost globe-shaped flowers.
The petals are blushed pink when they
first open but turn snow-white as they
mature. Plant in fertile, moist but well
drained soil, in full sun or partial shade.
The blooms are heavy so provide support
for them before they open. The fragrant
flowers are excellent for cutting, although
they are best left undisturbed in a border.

◊ ◊ ☼ ☀ ❀ ❀ ❀
‡↔ to 90cm (36in)

PASSIFLORA CAERULEA
'Constance Elliot'

Climber

This passion flower bears pure white,
lightly scented flowers, followed by
orange-yellow fruit. It is a fast-growing
climber, especially when grown in the
protection of a warm wall. In cold
winters, mulch the root area to protect
the plant from hard frosts, then, come
spring, new shoots should grow again.
Plant it in fertile, moist but well-drained
soil in full sun or light shade.

◊ ◊ ☼ ☀ ❀ ❀
‡ to 10m (30ft) or more

PHILADELPHUS
'Belle Etoile' ♀

Deciduous shrub

Mock orange is a superb free-flowering shrub with sprays of large, white fragrant flowers. When weighted down with blossom, the branches arch over, giving the shrub a graceful spreading outline. Plant it in full sun or partial shade, in reasonably fertile, well-drained soil. Each year, when it has finished flowering, prune some of the older branches down to the ground to encourage new, young shoots.

○ ☼ ☼ ❋ ❋ ❋
‡ to 1.2m (4ft) ↔ to 2.5m (8ft)

PYRACANTHA
'Watereri'

Evergreen shrub

This upright shrub combines glossy, dark green leaves with an abundance of small, white, early-summer flowers. These are followed in autumn and winter by shiny red berries. A good choice for a boundary hedge, its sharp spines will deter intruders; or train it against a wall. Plant it in a sheltered position, in well-drained, fertile soil in full sun or shade. Shorten side shoots to two or three leaves after flowering, and trim hedges in spring and summer.

○ ☼ ☼ ☀ ❋ ❋ ❋
‡↔ to 2.5m (8ft)

RHEUM
'Ace of Hearts'

Perennial

A close relative of edible rhubarb, this
imposing plant has large, heart-shaped,
dark green leaves with red undersides.
In summer it produces tall, branching
stems that are covered in masses of
tiny, star-shaped, white flowers. A lover
of deep, fertile, moist soil, it would suit
the dappled shade of a woodland garden
or the sunny banks of a stream or pond.
Divide large clumps if necessary in
spring, and mulch annually with well-
rotted garden compost.

◊ ☼ ☀ ❄ ❄ ❄
‡ to 1.2m (4ft) ↔ to 90cm (36in)

RODGERSIA AESCULIFOLIA ♀

Perennial

A sizeable, clump-forming plant, with
creeping roots and large, dark, bronzy-
green leaves that are similar in shape
to a horse-chestnut tree. In summer it
produces tall plumes of fragrant, white
or pinkish white flowers. Plant in moist,
fertile soil in full sun. A perfect pond-
side plant, it will also grow well in a
bog garden. If given partial shade it will
tolerate slightly drier soil. Propagate by
dividing established plants in autumn.

◊ ☼ ☀ ❄ ❄ ❄
‡ to 2m (6ft) ↔ to 1m (3ft)

ROMNEYA COULTERI ♥

Deciduous shrub

The Californian tree poppy is a vigorous shrub with large, poppy-like, fragrant flowers, and grey-green leaves. It can be difficult to establish but in the right conditions will spread extensively. Plant it in a sunny situation, in deep, well-drained soil, and provide protection during cold winters – in frost-prone areas, grow plants in the shelter of a sunny wall or fence. It usually dies down each year, but should reshoot in spring. Mature plants resent disturbance and are best left to grow unhindered.

△ ☼ ✿ ✿
‡ to 2.5m (8ft) ↔ indefinite

ROSA
'Blanche Double de Coubert' ♥

Deciduous shrub

This shrub rose flowers from early summer to early autumn, producing semi-double, fragrant, white blooms. Occasionally it will go on to develop bright red hips in autumn. Suitable for a mixed border, it can also be used as a hedge. It tolerates a wide range of conditions but prefers full sun and an open site on fairly fertile, moist but well-drained soil. In early spring, cut out a few of the oldest stems, and lightly trim back flowering shoots.

△ △ ☼ ✿ ✿ ✿
‡ to 1.5m (5ft) ↔ to 1.2m (4ft)

ROSA
'Madame Hardy' ♀

Deciduous shrub

Ideal for a mixed border, this extremely
attractive shrub rose has vibrant green,
leathery foliage and forms a rounded
shape. It flowers only once, producing
rosette-shaped blooms that have a
green button eye and carry a spicy
fragrance. A sunny site and fairly fertile,
moist but well-drained soil is ideal,
although it will tolerate a wide range of
growing conditions. Prune it in early
spring, removing only the old stems, or
lightly trimming it into shape.

◊◊ ☼ ❀❀❀
‡ to 1.5m (5ft) ↔ to 1.2m (4ft)

SISYRINCHIUM STRIATUM
'Aunt May'

Evergreen perennial

A very striking clump-forming plant,
whose sword-shaped variegated leaves
are boldly striped with creamy-yellow.
The cream flowers, lined on the reverse
with purple, are borne on stiff, upright
spikes. After flowering the spikes die
down but are replaced the following
year by new growth. Choose a spot in
full sun, in poor to moderately fertile,
well-drained soil. Protect it from
excessive damp in winter.

◊ ☼ ❀❀❀
‡ to 50cm (20in) ↔ to 25cm (10in)

TANACETUM PARTHENIUM *'Aureum'*

Perennial

In summer, feverfew produces clusters of daisy-like, white flowers with dark yellow centres borne on upright stems above aromatic, golden-yellow leaves. Grow in a sunny border, herb or gravel garden in well-drained soil. Dead-head regularly as it will self-seed liberally around the garden.

◊ ☼ ❋ ❋ ❋
‡↔ to 45cm (18in)

VERATRUM ALBUM

Perennial

A statuesque plant with large, pleated, green leaves, in early summer it throws up a tall spike of small, star-shaped, white flowers lightly tinged with green. Tolerant of shade and happy in humus-rich, moist but well-drained soil, it is ideal for a woodland garden or shady border. Provided the soil never dries out, it will also cope in full sun. Protect it from cold, drying winds, and divide congested clumps in autumn or early spring. All parts of this plant are toxic.

◊ ◑ ☼ ◗ ❋ ❋ ❋
‡ to 2m (6ft) ↔ to 60cm (24in)

ZANTEDESCHIA AETHIOPICA
'Crowborough' ♀

Perennial bulb

The arum lily has shapely flowers held
on stiff stems above luxuriant, dark
green leaves. 'Crowborough' is hardy and
can be planted in shallow water at the
edge of a pond, or in a border in deep,
moist, fertile soil in sun or dappled
shade. In the latter situation, protect the
root area over winter with a thick layer
of mulch. When grown in a container,
move under cover when frost threatens.

◊ ▲ ☼ ☀ ❋ ❋ ❋
‡ to 90cm (36in) ↔ to 60cm (24in)

ZENOBIA PULVERULENTA

Deciduous shrub

From early to midsummer, this attractive
shrub produces aniseed-scented, bell-
shaped, white flowers that are similar to
those of lily of the valley. Its leaves are
glossy green above and waxy beneath.
Give it a sheltered spot and it may
retain some leaves in winter. It prefers
a humus-rich, acid (lime-free), moist
soil, preferably in partial shade. It will
grow in a sunny situation provided the
soil never dries out.

◊ ☼ ☀ ❋ ❋ ❋
‡ to 2m (6ft) ↔ to 1.5m (5ft)

ALLIUM CERNUUM

Perennial bulb

The nodding onion is a graceful plant with erect, strappy, pungently scented leaves. In summer, stiff stems, arching at the top, produce loose clusters of 25–40 deep pink, bell-shaped flowers. A good plant for a gravel garden or the front of a border, it prefers fertile, well-drained soil in full sun. Plant the bulbs in autumn, in groups, at a depth of 5–10cm (2–4in).

◊ ☼ ✿ ✿ ✿
‡ to 60cm (24in) ↔ to 5cm (2in)

ALLIUM SCHOENOPRASUM

Perennial bulb

Chives are widely grown as a kitchen herb but the plant is pretty enough to use in a herbaceous border or edge a bed. In summer, small, dark pink, or occasionally lavender-white flowers appear on the top of narrow stems among the greyish-green leaves. Cut back after flowering to encourage fresh leaves to sprout. Chives prefer full sun and well-drained soil. Large clumps may be divided in spring.

◊ ☼ ✿ ✿ ✿
‡ to 60cm (24in) ↔ to 5cm (2in)

ARGYRANTHEMUM
'Vancouver' ♀

Perennial

With its fern-like foliage and unusual, rose-pink blooms, 'Vancouver' is a particularly striking argyranthemum. It has a long flowering period, from early summer until early autumn, making it excellent for borders, bedding and container displays. Pinching out the growing tips will help maintain a neat, bushy habit. It is not fully hardy and is best planted in a sheltered spot in well drained soil and full sun. If potted up it is easily moved under glass for winter.

◊ ☼ ❀ ❀
‡ to 90cm (36in) ↔ to 80cm (32in)

ASTILBE
'Straussenfeder' ♀

Perennial

The dark green leaves – bronze tinted when young – of this astilbe will provide attractive ground cover for a permanently moist border, by water or in a bog garden. Sprays of coral-pink flowers are produced in summer. Astilbes prefer wet, fertile soil in full sun. Plant in groups of four or five for maximum impact. A fast grower, clumps will need dividing every few years in early spring to maintain vigour. The faded flowerheads remain attractive through to autumn.

◊ ◖ ☼ ☀ ❀ ❀ ❀
‡ to 90cm (36in) ↔ to 60cm (24in)

ASTILBE 'Venus'

Perennial

The limited spread of this astilbe makes
it ideal for a small garden. In early
summer tall sprays of bright pink flowers
are borne above vibrant green foliage.
It grows best in moist, fertile soil in full
sun and is excellent for a bog garden or
damp soil beside a pond. In drier soils,
grow in partial shade. Divide clumps
every few years in early spring to keep
plants strong and to encourage more
flowers. The bleached flowerheads dry
well and continue to look attractive on
the plants through to autumn.

◑ ◐ ☼ ☀ ✽ ✽ ✽
‡ to 1m (3ft) ↔ to 45cm (18in)

ASTRANTIA MAJOR

Perennial

Hattie's pincushion is a clump-forming
plant with toothed, mid-green leaves.
The tiny, early summer flowers are pink
or green and surrounded by a pinkish-
white, papery collar. Astrantias prefer
moist, fertile soil in full sun or light
shade. They are good for a slightly
shaded herbaceous border, a woodland
garden, or damp ground beside a pond
or stream. Dead-head to prevent self-
seeding. Large clumps may be divided
in spring.

◑ ☼ ☀ ✽ ✽ ✽
‡ to 60cm (24in) ↔ to 45cm (18in)

CAMPANULA LACTIFLORA

Perennial

An upright bellflower with thin, mid-green leaves. In summer, tall stems carry clusters of large, pale pink, white, or blue bell-shaped flowers. In exposed sites they may need supporting with canes. Choose a spot in full sun or partial shade, in fertile, moist but well-drained soil. Divide in spring or autumn to keep the plant healthy and vigorous.

◊ ◑ ☼ ☀ ❄ ❄ ❄
‡ to 1.5m (5ft) ↔ to 60cm (24in)

CAMPANULA PUNCTATA

Perennial

This low-growing bellflower thrives in moist but well-drained, fertile, fairly light soil, particularly if it gets plenty of sun. In early summer, dusky- to shell-pink flowers hang from erect stems. Their inner surfaces are freckled red and covered in a fuzz of soft hairs. The dark green, semi-evergreen leaves are heart-shaped at the base. To encourage a second flush of blooms, and prevent self-seeding, cut back after flowering.

◊ ◑ ☼ ☀ ❄ ❄ ❄
‡ to 30cm (12in) ↔ to 40cm (16in)

CENTAUREA HYPOLEUCA
'John Coutts'

Perennial

This upright plant has greyish-green,
wavy-edged leaves. The long-lasting,
fragrant flowers are borne singly on
long stems throughout early summer.
The outer florets are star-shaped, with
bright pink thistle-like centres. Plant
in a border or rock garden, in full
sunshine and well-drained soil. Divide
big clumps in spring or autumn.

◊ ☼ ✿ ✿ ✿
‡↔ to 60cm (24in)

CENTRANTHUS RUBER

Perennial

Red valerian will grow in some of the
most exposed places, on cliffs, walls,
and at the edge of roads. It is also grown
successfully as a border perennial, where
it is valued for its long flowering season.
It has fleshy, bright-green leaves and,
throughout summer, branching stems
covered with small, star-shaped, pink,
red, or white flowers. Plant in poor, well-
drained soil in full sun and dead-head
regularly. Suitable for coastal gardens.

◊ ☼ ✿ ✿ ✿
‡↔ to 1m (3ft)

CISTUS × ARGENTEUS
'Peggy Sammons' ♀

Evergreen shrub

Each bloom on a rock rose lasts for
only one day, but they are produced
constantly from early to late summer.
'Peggy Sammons' has large, purplish-
pink flowers and greyish-green leaves.
It thrives on well-drained soil, even
poor, in full sun and will survive most
winters in a sheltered position. Grow
in containers, around paved areas, on
sunny banks or in a border and in
coastal gardens.

◊ ☼ ✿ ✿
‡↔ to 1m (3ft)

CLEMATIS
'Comtesse de Bouchaud' ♀

Climber

A vigorous, deciduous clematis with pale
green leaves. In summer many pinkish-
mauve flowers are produced, with dark
lines radiating out from their yellow
centres. Grow in well-drained, fertile
soil, in sun or partial shade, with the
roots in shade. Cut back in early spring
to a pair of strong buds 20cm (8in)
above soil level, as this will encourage
flowers. Clematis are often grown
through roses and other shrubs or trees,
or used to clothe trellis, walls or arches.

◊ ☼ ☀ ✿ ✿ ✿
‡ to 3m (10ft)

CLEMATIS
'Nelly Moser' ♀

Climber

In early summer this deciduous clematis
bears large, pinkish-purple flowers, with
a reddish stripe down the centre of
each petal. The foliage is a pretty, pale
green. It is best grown in well-drained
fertile soil, in a slightly shaded position
as the blooms fade in strong sun.
Scramble it through a tree or shrub, or
over a trellis or an arch. To encourage
lots of flowers, remove any dead stems
in early spring and prune remaining
shoots back to a pair of strong buds.

◊ ☼ ❊ ❊ ❊
‡ to 3m (10ft)

CORDYLINE AUSTRALIS
'Torbay Red' ♀

Evergreen tree

The exotic-looking cabbage palm has
an erect stem topped by a crown of
strap-shaped, pink and red striped
leaves. It is not completely hardy, but
will survive in most areas as long as it
is mulched generously and planted in a
position sheltered from cold winds and
penetrating frost. Elsewhere, it makes
a good container plant that can be
brought into a frost-free greenhouse or
conservatory during the winter months.

◊ ☼ ☼ ❊ ❊
‡ to 3m (10ft) ↔ to 1m (3ft)

CORNUS KOUSA
'Satomi' ♀

Deciduous tree

This dramatic dogwood has many attractions, including decorative bark, deep purplish-red leaves in autumn, and a handsome shape. Perhaps most striking, though, is the early summer display of masses of dark pink bracts against the dark green foliage. The bracts surround a cluster of tiny flowers. Plant in a sunny or partially shaded situation, in soil that is neutral or acid (lime free), well drained and humus rich.

◊ ☼ ☀ ❀ ❀ ❀
↑ to 7m (22ft) ↔ to 5m (15ft)

COSMOS BIPINNATUS
Sensation Series

Annual

This elegant hardy annual is perfect for an annual or mixed border where it is valued for its feathery, mid-green leaves and large, showy blooms. The long-stemmed, daisy-like flowers come in a range of pinks and whites and are good for cutting. Prolong flowering with regular dead-heading. It prefers a sunny position in moist but well-drained soil. For early flowering, sow seed in autumn.

◊ ◊ ☼ ❀ ❀ ❀
↕ to 90cm (36in) ↔ to 45cm (18in)

DEUTZIA X ELEGANTISSIMA *'Rosealind'* ♀

Deciduous shrub

Deutzias are stunning when grown in the border or as a specimen plant; choose a position in full sun and fertile, well-drained soil. Thousands of star-shaped, pale pink flowers are borne in early summer. Maintain this shrub's neat shape by pruning out old and flowered shoots when the blooms have faded.

⬦ ☼ ✿ ✿ ✿
‡ to 1.2m (4ft) ↔ to 1.5m (5ft)

DIANTHUS ALPINUS *'Joan's Blood'* ♀

Perennial

Alpine pinks are compact, tuft-forming evergreens with narrow, shiny, dark green leaves. In summer, 'Joan's Blood' is almost completely covered by large, deep pink flowers with toothed petals. This decorative plant is ideal for planting at the front of borders, in raised beds, rock gardens, and between paving slabs. Choose a sunny spot in humus-rich, well-drained soil.

⬦ ☼ ✿ ✿ ✿
‡ to 8cm (3in) ↔ to 10cm (4in)

DIANTHUS
'Houndspool Ruby' ♀

Perennial

This bold pink has double, rose-pink
flowers, with a splash of red at their
centre, and delicately fringed petals.
Modern pinks bloom throughout
summer, are good in a border and
excellent for cutting. They also form
dense mounds of narrow, grey-green,
evergreen leaves. Choose a position in
full sun with well-drained soil.

△ ☼ ✿ ✿ ✿
‡ to 45cm (18in) ↔ to 40cm (16in)

DIANTHUS
'Doris' ♀

Perennial

With its pale pink, wavy-edged petals
and raspberry coloured centre, this is
one of the prettiest pinks. Often two or
three flushes of clove-scented blooms
will be borne from early summer to
autumn, above a mound of grey-green
leaves. The flowers are decorative in
a border and very long lasting when
cut. Pinks thrive in well-drained soil
and full sun.

△ ☼ ✿ ✿ ✿
‡ to 45cm (18in) ↔ to 40cm (16in)

DICTAMNUS ALBUS *VAR.* PURPUREUS ♀

Perennial

The burning bush produces aromatic oils that can, very occasionally, ignite on a hot summer's day. Long spikes of large pink flowers with dark purple veins are produced in early summer. The foliage is lemon-scented, but take care as contact with its leaves may irritate the skin. Plant in well-drained soil, in sun or partial shade, and avoid transplanting as it resents disturbance.

◊ ☼ ☀ ❈ ❈ ❈
↕ to 90cm (36in) ↔ to 60cm (24in)

DIERAMA PULCHERRIMUM

Perennial bulb

Angel's fishing rod is so named because the bright pink, bell-shaped flowers hang from graceful, arching stems in summer. The narrow leaves are greyish-green and grass-like. It is especially pretty grown beside a pond, where the water will reflect its slender form, or in a border. Choose a sunny situation, in reliably moist but well-drained soil, planting the bulbs 5–7cm (2–3in) deep, in spring.

◊ ◐ ☼ ❈ ❈
↕ to 1.5m (5ft) ↔ to 60cm (24in)

DIGITALIS × MERTONENSIS ♀

Perennial

This foxglove has large, strawberry-coloured, funnel-shaped flowers borne on sturdy spikes in early summer. It forms clumps of handsome, glossy green leaves. Foxgloves prefer moist, well-drained soil in partial shade, but will tolerate a wide range of conditions. They are equally happy in a border or naturalized beneath deciduous trees. Allow plants to self-seed or sow seed in late spring.

◊ ◊ ☼ ◊ ✳ ✳ ✳
‡ to 90cm (36in) ↔ to 30cm (12in)

EREMURUS ROBUSTUS ♀

Perennial

From a clump of strappy, bluish-green leaves, this impressive plant produces a tower of pale pink flowers on top of a tall, leafless stem. Foxtail lilies are effective when several are grouped together in a border. Grow in a sunny position, in sandy, very well-drained soil, as the roots will die if they get too wet in winter. The flower spikes may need support, especially in exposed areas. In late winter and spring, if frost threatens, mulch with bracken, straw or fleece to protect emerging shoots.

◊ ☼ ✳ ✳ ✳
‡ to 3m (10ft) ↔ to 1.2m (4ft)

ESCALLONIA
'Apple Blossom' ♀

Evergreen shrub

A bushy shrub with rounded, glossy green leaves, this escallonia bears small, clear pink flowers with white centres in early summer. Grow it in a border, against a wall, or as a hedge or windbreak. If the wind is not too cold, it will also thrive in coastal areas. To help retain a neat shape, trim lightly in mid- to late spring.

◊ ☼ ❀ ❀ ❀
‡↔ to 2.5m (8ft)

FRAGARIA
Pink Panda

Perennial

This vigorous ground-cover plant is related to the strawberry but rarely fruits. Deep pink flowers are produced for a long period during summer. The leaves are bright green, deeply veined, and almost evergreen. It does well in full sun or partial shade and prefers moist but well-drained, fertile soil. Ideal for the front of a herbaceous border, if it threatens to spread out of bounds, control it by removing unwanted runners (the horizontal stems).

◊ ◊ ☼ ☼ ❀ ❀ ❀
‡ to 15cm (6in) ↔ indefinite

GERANIUM ENDRESSII ♥

Perennial

A clump-forming hardy geranium, or
cranesbill, with trumpet-shaped, pale
pink flowers with notched petals. The
evergreen leaves are hairy and wrinkly.
Cranesbills tolerate a wide range of soil
types and growing conditions, coping
well in full sun or partial shade – a
rock garden, the front of a mixed
border, or a wild garden are ideal. Clip
over after flowering to encourage fresh
growth and more flowers. G. endressii
combines well with a blue-flowering
geranium such as G. ibericum.

○ ◐ ☼ ❄ ❄ ❄
‡ to 45cm (18in) ↔ to 60cm (24in)

GERANIUM X
RIVERSLEAIANUM
'Russell Prichard' ♥

Perennial

This hardy geranium, or cranesbill, has
trailing, creeping stems, making it a
good ground-cover plant. In summer it
has deeply divided, slightly hairy, greyish
green leaves and deep magenta flowers.
It prefers to be planted in full sun in
well-drained, slightly fertile soil, but will
tolerate a wide range of conditions. Clip
over after flowering to encourage fresh
growth and more flowers.

○ ☼ ❄ ❄ ❄
‡ to 30cm (12in) ↔ to 1m (3ft)

GLADIOLUS
'Rose Supreme'

Perennial corm

This is one of the largest gladioli available; the tall spikes can hold as many as 24 flowers above a fan of sword-shaped leaves. Each rose-pink bloom has a cream throat and dark pink edges. Plant it in full sun, in fertile, well-drained soil and support with a cane. Gladioli are superb for adding height to a border and make excellent cut flowers. Lift corms in autumn, store dry over winter and replant in spring in soil enriched with organic matter.

◊ ☼ ❉
‡ to 1.7m (5½ft) ↔ to 25cm (10in)

HELIANTHEMUM
'Rhodanthe Carneum' ♀

Evergreen shrub

A wide-spreading rock rose with silver-grey leaves. In summer it produces numerous flat, pale pink flowers marked with yellow in the centre. Grow it at the front of a border, in a raised bed, alongside paving, or in a rock or gravel garden. Choose a position in fertile, well-drained soil and full sun. Prune after flowering to keep the bush neat and tidy and prevent it from becoming leggy.

◊ ☼ ❉ ❉ ❉
‡ to 30cm (12in) ↔ to 45cm (18in)

HEMEROCALLIS
'Joylene Nichole'

Perennial

The daylily is so called because its
flowers open for just one day. 'Joylene
Nichole' is unusual in that it unfurls its
flowers late in the afternoon and they
stay open throughout the night. It has
large, pink flowers with a yellowish-
green throat, lined with deep pink veins.
The flowers are borne above a large
clump of almost evergreen, bluish-green
leaves. Plant in moist but well-drained
soil, in a sunny border near the house
or patio to enjoy its blooms fully.

○ ◊ ☼ ❀ ❀ ❀
‡ to 50cm (20in) ↔ to 1m (3ft)

IMPATIENS WALLERIANA
'Tempo Lavender'

Perennial

With its vivid, lavender-pink, long-
lasting flowers and light green leaves,
'Tempo Lavender' is a particularly pretty
summer-bedding plant. Available in a
wide range of colours, busy lizzies are
tender perennials that are usually
grown as annuals. For the best flowers,
choose a spot in partial shade, in moist
but well-drained soil. They also make
good container plants.

○ ◊ ❁ ❀ ❀
‡↔ to 25cm (10in)

INCARVILLEA DELAVAYI

Perennial

An exotic-looking plant with large flowers held on strong stems above a rosette of lush, mid-green leaves. The flowerhead consists of up to 10 trumpet-shaped, rose-pink or purple blooms. Grow it in fertile, moist, well-drained soil in a bright, sunny position but, preferably, one that avoids direct midday sun. A good choice for a gravel garden or mixed or herbaceous border.

◊ ◊ ☼ ❀ ❀ ❀
‡ to 60cm (24in) ↔ to 30cm (12in)

IRIS
'Carnaby'

Perennial

Bearded irises are mostly grown for their flamboyant flowers that come in a huge range of colours; however, their sword-shaped leaves are attractive, too. This variety has large flowers with peach-pink upper petals and pink-purple lower petals that are furred with an orange 'beard'. Divide congested clumps of iris after flowering, replanting only plump sections of rhizome in a sunny spot in well-drained fertile soil, ensuring their tops are exposed to the sun.

◊ ☼ ❀ ❀ ❀
‡ to 1m (3ft) ↔ indefinite

KALMIA LATIFOLIA ♀

Evergreen shrub

The calico bush is an excellent choice
for slightly acid soil, where your reward
will be large heads of pink or white
flowers. It forms a nicely rounded bush,
with oval, dark green leaves. Kalmias
prefer humus-rich, moist but well-
drained, acid (lime-free) soil in partial
shade, although they will tolerate full
sun where the ground remains damp
in summer. Dead-head regularly and
lightly trim after flowering to maintain
a neat shape. Mulch annually with leaf
mould or chipped bark.

○ ◐ ☼ ☀ ✽ ✽ ✽
‡↔ to 3m (10ft)

LATHYRUS GRANDIFLORUS

Climber

The everlasting pea is a herbaceous
perennial that will climb through
shrubs, over banks, or along a trellis
using clinging tendrils. In the summer
it produces small clusters of red or
purple-pink flowers, and pairs of oval
leaves. It is best grown in a sunny
position, in well-drained, fertile soil.
This pea spreads underground; if
unwanted shoots emerge then remove
them at ground level.

○ ☼ ✽ ✽ ✽
‡ to 1.5m (5ft)

LAVATERA × CLEMENTII *'Bredon Springs'* ♥

Deciduous shrub

Mallows are short-lived plants, grown for their profuse flowers borne throughout the summer months. 'Bredon Springs' is almost evergreen, with grey-green leaves and deep, dusky pink blooms. Position it in full sunshine, in fertile, well-drained soil, sheltered or staked against the wind. When the flowers have finished, prune back hard to a strong bud close to the base of the plant. Suitable for coastal gardens.

◊ ☼ ✿ ✿ ✿

↕↔ to 2m (6ft)

LAVATERA MARITIMA ♥

Shrub

This shrubby perennial has rounded, greyish-green leaves with shallow lobes. In summer it bears solitary, saucer-shaped, pink flowers with deep magenta veins radiating out from the centre. It prefers a spot in full sun, in fertile, well-drained soil, sheltered or staked against the wind. To encourage healthy growth the following year, after flowering cut back to a strong bud close to the base. Mallows tend to be short lived. Well suited to seaside gardens.

◊ ☼ ✿ ✿ ✿

↕ to 1.5m (5ft) ↔ to 1m (3ft)

MATTHIOLA INCANA
Cinderella Series

Perennial

Stocks are extremely fragrant flowers
that, despite being perennial, are
usually grown as a biennial or annual.
The Cinderella Series has double, white,
deep pink, purple, or lavender flowers,
produced from early summer. Plant in a
sunny position, in fertile, well-drained,
neutral or slightly alkaline soil. Stocks
are excellent as annual bedding and as
cut flowers.

◊ ☼ ❀ ❀
↕↔ to 25cm (10in)

MORINA LONGIFOLIA

Perennial

A spiny-toothed, evergreen perennial
with dark-green, aromatic leaves that
overwinter as a thistle-like rosette. In
early summer it produces a spike of
small, dangling, tubular flowers – these
open white, turn pink after they have
been fertilized, then eventually change
to red before falling. Plant in a sunny
position, in poor, very well-drained soil.
The roots will rot if the soil is wet
during the winter months, so mulch
with grit or gravel.

◊ ☼ ❀ ❀ ❀
↕ to 90cm (36in) ↔ to 30cm (12in)

NECTAROSCORDUM SICULUM *SUBSP.* BULGARICUM

Perennial bulb

An elegant perennial with pendulous, pink-flushed, bell-shaped flowers that are borne on tall stems. These emerge from a clump of garlic-smelling, linear leaves. It can be grown in full sun, or partial shade, and prefers a slightly fertile, well-drained soil. This bulb is ideal for a wild garden, where it may freely self-seed. In a herbaceous border, to help control its spread simply dead-head regularly.

◊ ☼ ◑ ❈ ❈ ❈
‡ to 1.2m (4ft) ↔ to 45cm (18in)

NEILLIA THIBETICA

Deciduous shrub

This shrub grows well in a border or beneath deciduous trees, spreading by suckers to form a dense thicket. The arching branches have glossy green leaves and long clusters of bright pink, bell-shaped flowers. Grow in full sun or partial shade, in fertile, well-drained soil. To encourage strong new growth the following year, prune after flowering by cutting branches back to a strong pair of buds, and removing a quarter of the stems right to the base of the plant.

◊ ☼ ❈ ❈ ❈
‡↔ to 2m (6ft)

ONOPORDUM ACANTHIUM

Biennial

The Scotch thistle is an architectural plant that is good for a large border or a wild or gravel garden. In its first year, an impressive rosette of spiny, greyish green leaves is formed. During the second year, a strong, prickly stem, which is covered with white hairs, is produced. The stem is crowned with thistle-like flowerheads, composed of many small deep pink, or occasionally white, flowers. Grow in full sun, in fertile, well-drained, neutral or alkaline soil. It will readily self-seed.

◊ ☼ ❀ ❀ ❀
‡ to 1.8m (6ft) ↔ to 1m (3ft)

OSTEOSPERMUM JUCUNDUM ♀

Perennial

Free-flowering and extremely decorative, this is a superb perennial for any border. It has pretty mauvish pink or magenta, daisy-like blooms that are produced throughout summer above a clump of greyish-green leaves. Grow in well-drained, fertile soil in full sun. Regular dead-heading will help extend the flowering period.

◊ ☼ ❀ ❀ ❀
‡ to 50cm (20in) ↔ to 1m (3ft)

PAEONIA LACTIFLORA
'Monsieur Jules Elie' ♀

Perennial

A large, herbaceous peony, forming
bold clumps of glossy, dark green
leaves. In early summer it produces
deep pink, double flowers that are
good for cutting. Grow in a border,
in sun or partial shade, in deep, fertile,
well-drained soil. For the best blooms,
mulch generously with organic matter
in autumn. The blooms, which reach
over 20cm (8in) across, may need some
support – encircling stakes are ideal.
Clumps are best left undisturbed.

◊ ◊ ☼ ☀ ❈ ❈ ❈
‡↔ to 1m (3ft)

PAPAVER ORIENTALE
'Cedric Morris' ♀

Perennial

The Oriental poppy is a vigorous plant
that will provide a spectacular splash of
colour in any border. It forms a large
clump of lobed, grey-haired leaves and,
in summer, tall stems bear very large,
soft-pink flowers with a black mark
at the base of each petal. After the
decorative seed pods appear, the plant
dies down – make sure it is masked by
other plants during this unattractive
phase. Plant in full sun, in fertile, well-
drained soil; sow seed in spring.

◊ ☼ ❈ ❈ ❈
‡↔ to 90cm (36in)

PAPAVER SOMNIFERUM
'Paeony Flowered'

Annual

Although grown mainly for its beautiful
flowers, the opium poppy also has
handsome blue-green leaves and
decorative pepper-pot seed pods. In
summer, the 'Peony Flowered' type bears
huge, rounded, frilly blooms in shades
of pink or purple. Sow *in situ* in spring
in a sunny situation, in very well-
drained soil in an annual border or in
gaps in a herbaceous or mixed border.

◊ ☼ ❋ ❋ ❋
‡ to 1.2m (4ft) ↔ to 30cm (12in)

PERSICARIA BISTORTA
'Superba' ♀

Perennial

Bistort is a vigorous plant that is often
used in a border or wild garden, or as
ground cover. Numerous flower spikes
are held well above clumps of broad,
mid green leaves in early summer. They
are made up of many tiny, densely
packed, soft-pink flowers. It prefers
moist ground, although it will tolerate
dry soil, in full sun or partial shade.
Divide large clumps in spring or autumn.

◊ ◊ ☼ ☼ ❋ ❋ ❋
‡↔ to 90cm (36in)

PETUNIA
Surfinia Pink Vein

Perennial

The Surfinia Series is well-known for its
large flowers and vigorous growth. Their
trailing habit makes them ideal for
containers and hanging baskets. They
can also be used as bedding but the
flowers may be damaged by heavy rain.
In a border, provide a sunny position
and well-drained soil. Dead-head
regularly and feed container-grown
plants with a tomato feed every 10–14
days to prolong flowering. Petunias are
usually grown as annuals.

◊ ☼ ❄

‡ to 40cm (16in) ↔ to 90cm (36in)

PRIMULA VIALII ♥

Perennial

Grow this unusual-looking primula
beside a pond or in any moist site in
sun or, preferably, partial shade. In
summer, from a rosette of hairy leaves,
it produces a stout stem topped with a
tight spike of small pink flowers that
emerge from crimson buds. *P. vialii* is
happiest in humus-rich, neutral or acid
soil. Although perennial it can be rather
short-lived; sow, or allow to self-seed,
in spring to renew your stock.

◊ ☼ ☼ ❄ ❄ ❄

‡ to 60cm (24in) ↔ to 30cm (12in)

ROSA
'Blessings' ♀

Deciduous shrub

If dead-headed regularly, this hybrid
tea rose will produce many urn-shaped,
pink, scented blooms through to
autumn. Prune the main stems to 25cm
(10in) above ground in early spring,
then apply a balanced fertilizer and
mulch generously with well-rotted
manure to encourage the production of
lots of flowers. Roses should be planted
in a sunny situation, in fertile, humus-
rich, well-drained soil, preferably
slightly acid or neutral.

◊◊☼ ❀❀❀
‡ to 1m (3ft) ↔ to 60cm (24in)

ROSA
'Frühlingsmorgen'

Deciduous shrub

A healthy, upright shrub rose with
dark, greyish green leaves. The single,
blossom-pink, hay-scented flowers are
produced in early summer. It can be
grown up a pillar, in mixed borders or
as hedging and will even tolerate light
shade. It needs less rich conditions than
hybrid teas and other bush roses. To
maintain a neat shape, lightly trim the
bush after flowering.

◊◊☼ ❀❀❀
‡ to 2m (6ft) ↔ to 1.5m (5ft)

ROSA
Gertrude Jekyll ♀

Deciduous shrub

Named after the famous Edwardian
garden designer, this is a slender, large-
flowered shrub rose. It is grown for its
deep pink flowers, which are extremely
fragrant and start to appear in early
summer. With regular dead-heading,
flowering may continue into early
autumn. This disease-resistant rose needs
rich growing conditions, so mulch
deeply in early spring with well-rotted
manure after lightly pruning it to shape
– although this is not essential.

◊◊☼ ✿✿✿

‡ to 1.5m (5ft) ↔ to 1m (3ft)

ROSA
'Madame Knorr' ♀

Deciduous shrub

An old variety of Portland rose with
large, lilac-pink, very fragrant flowers
throughout the summer months. It is an
easy-going rose with mid-green foliage
and thorny stems. It does well on most
well-drained soils, and even in poor
conditions. When used as hedging, trim
it back in late winter or early spring.

◊◊☼ ✿✿✿

‡ to 1.2m (4ft) ↔ to 1m (3ft)

ROSA
Surrey ♥

Deciduous shrub

Ground-cover roses are chosen for their low, spreading habit and abundant, healthy foliage. They can be used in many situations: in a border, trailing down a bank or over a wall, and in a container or large hanging basket. Surrey is disease resistant, grows quickly and is very free flowering, with double, soft-pink blooms. Grow in moist but well-drained, fertile soil in full sun. Trim in late winter or early spring to keep it within bounds.

◊ ◊ ☼ ✿ ✿ ✿
‡ to 80cm (32in) ↔ to 1.2m (4ft)

SALVIA VIRIDIS
'Claryssa Pink'

Annual

Clary is an aromatic plant with upright, branching stems. Seed is available in single shades or in rainbow mixtures. The bracts of 'Claryssa Pink' are a particularly bright, rose-pink hue. Sow seeds *in situ* in mid-spring, in well-drained soil. It can be used as a long-lasting cut or dried flower.

◊ ◊ ☼ ☼ ✿ ✿ ✿
‡ to 40cm (16in) ↔ to 23cm (9in)

SANGUISORBA OBTUSA

Perennial

Burnet is a clump-forming plant with
bold, greyish-green leaves. In summer,
thin wiry stems, tipped with spikes of
tiny pink flowers like bottle-brushes,
are produced. Grow them in a border,
or next to a pond in moist but well-
drained soil, in full sun or partial shade.
Both the flowers and leaves are good
for cutting.

◊ ◑ ☼ ☀ ❉ ❉ ❉
‡ to 1.2m (4ft) ↔ to 60cm (24in)

SAPONARIA OFFICINALIS
'Rosea Plena'

Perennial

Before commercial detergents became
available, soapwort was used as a soap
substitute for washing delicate fabrics.
Today it is still often used in natural
shampoos. A robust plant with rough,
rounded leaves, this form has double,
pale pink flowers. It can spread rapidly
and may need to be kept in check in a
border to prevent it smothering other
plants. It is best in well-drained neutral
to alkaline soils in a sunny position.

◊ ☼ ❉ ❉ ❉
‡ to 60cm (24in) ↔ to 50cm (20in)

SIDALCEA
'Elsie Heugh' ♀

Perennial

This false mallow forms clumps of
rounded, basal leaves. In early summer
upright stems hold purple-pink, fringed
flowers that have the texture of satin.
They are excellent for cutting. Grow in
a sunny border, in well-drained, neutral
to slightly acid, fertile soil.

◊ ◐ ☼ ◑ ✤ ✤ ✤
‡ to 90cm (36in) ↔ to 45cm (18in)

TAMARIX RAMOSISSIMA
'Pink Cascade'

Deciduous shrub

This tamarisk is an attractive small tree
with graceful, arching branches and
feathery foliage. In summer it is covered
with tiny pink flowers. It makes a
superb windbreak or hedge in coastal
areas; in inland areas it will need a
more sheltered position. To prevent
plants becoming straggly, cut back
shrubs and hedges in early spring. It
grows best in sandy, well-drained soil
in full sun.

◊ ☼ ✤ ✤ ✤
‡ to 4m (12ft) ↔ to 3.5m (11ft)

TANACETUM COCCINEUM
'Eileen May Robinson' ♀

Perennial

The painted daisy is a bushy plant with silver-haired, balsam-scented leaves, which can be used as a cut flower and to make pot-pourri. In early summer it produces an abundance of soft-pink flowers. Cut back after flowers fade to encourage a second flush. It will tolerate any light, well-drained soil in full sunshine.

◊ ☼ ❁ ❁ ❁
‡ to 75cm (30in) ↔ to 45cm (18in)

THYMUS SERPYLLUM
'Annie Hall'

Evergreen shrub

This thyme forms a mat of creeping branches covered, in summer, with numerous, tiny, pale pink flowers. Its small, dark green leaves are highly aromatic when crushed, making it ideal for planting in paving crevices where its pungent oils are released each time it is trodden on. Alternatively, plant it in a herb or rock garden, or in containers, choosing a sunny position and very well-drained soil.

◊ ☼ ❁ ❁ ❁
‡ to 25cm (10in) ↔ to 45cm (18in)

VERBASCUM
'Helen Johnson'

Perennial

This mullein produces tall spikes of
pinkish-brown, saucer-shaped flowers
in early to midsummer. They emerge
from an evergreen rosette of downy,
greyish-green leaves. Plant in a border
or gravel garden in a sunny position, in
well-drained soil. 'Helen Johnson' can
be short-lived, so propagate new plants
by division in autumn.

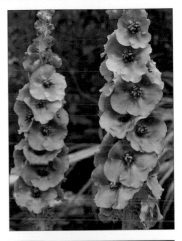

◊ ☼ ❁ ❁ ❁
‡ to 90cm (36in) ↔ to 30cm (12in)

VERBENA
'Sissinghurst' ♀

Perennial

This sprawling verbena is ideal for
containers and especially hanging
baskets. It has dark green leaves and,
during summer and into autumn, large,
round clusters of bright, magenta-pink
flowers. Usually grown as an annual in
cooler countries, it can be potted up
and taken into a greenhouse over
winter. It is easily raised from semi-ripe
cuttings of non-flowering shoots taken
in late summer.

◊ ◊ ☼ ❁ ❁
‡ to 20cm (8in) ↔ to 1m (3ft)

ADONIS ANNUA

Annual

Pheasant's eye is a striking plant, with finely divided leaves and bright scarlet, cup-shaped flowers with a black spot in the centre. It makes a superb addition to an annual border or hot hued herbaceous border, where it will fill the gaps left by early spring bulbs. Very hardy, it likes a sunny situation, in well-drained, preferably alkaline soil. Sow seed *in situ* in autumn or spring.

⬦ ☼ ❋ ❋ ❋
‡ to 45cm (18in) ↔ to 30cm (12in)

ASTILBE × ARENDSII 'Fanal' ♀

Perennial

This dramatic herbaceous plant bears plumes of tiny red flowers in early summer. Its divided, toothed, deep green foliage contrasts well with the blooms and is a feature in its own right. Astilbes flourish in humus-rich, fertile soil, in a permanently damp border, at the edge of a woodland garden, in a bog garden or by water. They prefer a position in partial shade, although they will grow in full sun, as long as the soil never dries out.

⬦ ⬦ ☼ ☼ ❋ ❋ ❋
‡ to 60cm (24in) ↔ to 45cm (18in)

ASTRANTIA
'Hadspen Blood'

Perennial

This plant forms a clump of deeply
lobed green leaves, and bears sprays of
tiny dark red flowers, surrounded by
petal-like bracts, for many months from
early to midsummer. Plant astrantias
beside a stream, in a damp border or
a deciduous woodland garden, in moist,
fertile soil in full sun or partial shade.
Large clumps can be divided in spring.

◊ ☼ ☀ ❋ ❋ ❋
‡ to 90cm (36in) ↔ to 45cm (18in)

CIRSIUM RIVULARE
'Atropurpureum'

Perennial

The thistle-like flowers and informal
habit of this plant make it ideal for
growing in a wild garden, a damp
meadow, or in association with
ornamental grasses. It forms clumps of
narrow, lance-shaped leaves, covered
beneath with soft hairs, and in early
summer produces tall stems of reddish-
purple blooms. It needs to be planted
in a sunny situation, in moist, well-
drained soil. To increase stocks, divide
it in the autumn or early spring.

◊ ◊ ☼ ❋ ❋ ❋
‡ to 1.2m (4ft) ↔ to 60cm (24in)

DIANTHUS BARBATUS
'Dunnet's Dark Crimson'

Biennial

Sweet Williams are valued for their
early summer flowers and wonderful
perfume, and 'Dunnet's Dark Crimson'
is a particularly decorative variety. Its
dark, bronzy-green leaves contrast well
with the dense clusters of deep red
flowers. Sweet Williams will grow well
in a sunny herbaceous border in fertile,
well-drained, neutral to alkaline soil.
Good for cutting.

◊ ☼ ✽ ✽ ✽
‡ to 60cm (24in) ↔ to 30cm (12in)

DIANTHUS
Telstar Series
'Telstar Crimson'

Biennial

In early summer, this bushy, compact
plant bears small, deep red flowers in
clusters on short stems above dark
green leaves. It is much smaller than
the more vigorous Sweet William, and
when planted in groups makes a good
bedding plant. It is also useful for the
front of a herbaceous border. Sow *in
situ* in autumn, in full sun and well-
drained, fertile soil.

◊ ☼ ✽ ✽ ✽
‡ to 25cm (10in) ↔ to 23cm (9in)

ECCREMOCARPUS SCABER

Climber

The Chilean glory flower is a vigorous evergreen, with tubular, bright orange-red flowers, which appear early in summer and continue to autumn.
A short-lived, tender perennial, it will only survive the winter outside if planted in a sunny, sheltered position, such as against a south-facing wall that is protected from hard frosts.
Alternatively, grow it as an annual. Use it to clothe a trellis, or pergola, or train it on wires up a house wall. Plant it in full sun in well-drained, fertile soil.

◊ ☼ ❀
‡ to 4m (12ft)

GAILLARDIA
'Dazzler' ♈

Perennial

As the name suggests, the flowers of this plant will certainly catch the eye in a bed or border. Their petals are deep orange-red, tipped with yellow, while the centres resemble a maroon pincushion. The blooms appear in early summer and continue up until the early autumn. Grow 'Dazzler' in a sunny position, in fertile, well-drained soil, and remove the dead flowers to prolong blooming. Good for cutting.

◊ ☼ ❀ ❀ ❀
‡ to 85cm (34in) ↔ to 45cm (18in)

HELIANTHEMUM
'Fire Dragon' ♥

Evergreen shrub

This rock rose flowers for many months from early summer and quickly spreads to form a dense mound of linear, grey-green leaves, which set off the bright orange-red, cup-shaped blooms. It will inject colour into a sunny bank, rock or gravel garden, or a raised bed. It will flourish in full sun and a well-drained, alkaline soil, and should be trimmed after flowering to maintain its shape.

◊ ☼ ❄ ❄ ❄
‡↔ to 30cm (12in)

HEMEROCALLIS
'Stafford'

Perennial

A beautiful daylily, this form produces deep red flowers with golden-yellow centres, borne above a clump of strap-like, mid-green leaves. It flowers from early to midsummer, and will help to fire up a gravel garden or the front of a border. Alternatively, it can be grown in a large container if well watered in the summer. Plant it in full sun in moist, well-drained soil.

◊ ◊ ☼ ❄ ❄ ❄
‡ to 70cm (28in) ↔ to 1m (3ft)

LEPTOSPERMUM SCOPARIUM 'Kiwi' ♀

Evergreen shrub

This New Zealand tea tree has aromatic, lance-shaped, purple-tinged leaves, and produces masses of dark, crimson-red flowers from the late spring to early summer. It is not hardy and may need to be overwintered in a container in a cool greenhouse. In mild areas, grow it outside in well-drained soil next to a sunny, south-facing wall, ideally on a sheltered patio or terrace where the flowers can be fully appreciated. Suitable for coastal gardens.

◊ ☼ ❀ ❀
‡↔ to 3m (10ft)

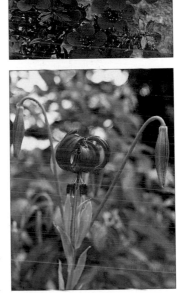

LILIUM CHALCEDONICUM

Perennial bulb

The scarlet turkscap lily is a tall plant with deep green leaves, arranged in a spiral up the stem. It flowers from early to midsummer and has bright scarlet petals, which are strongly swept back, while the long stamens with bright red anthers drop down from the centre of the flower. This unusual lily makes a valuable addition to a sunny or partially shaded herbaceous border, and will grow in almost any well-drained soil

◊ ☼ ❀ ❀ ❀
‡ to 1.5m (5ft)

LONICERA SEMPERVIRENS ♀

Climber

The beautiful trumpet honeysuckle is semi-evergreen in mild winters, and in summer produces clusters of tubular, orange-red flowers with a yellow throat. The oval, paired leaves help to frame the flowers, and highlight their intense colour. In autumn, the plant is covered with bright red berries, giving it a long season of interest. Use it to cover a warm wall, or to brighten up a sheltered position in the garden. Plant it in full sun or partial shade in fertile, well-drained soil.

◊ ☼ ◑ ❋ ❋
‡ to 4m (12ft)

LUPINUS
'Inverewe Red'

Perennial

Bold spikes of deep red flowers appear on this lupin in early summer above clumps of palmate leaves. Planted in groups in a herbaceous border, or as a superb addition to a cottage-style garden. Encourage a second flush of flowers by deadheading. Lupins need a site in full sun or partial shade, and should be planted in well-drained, fertile soil. They usually benefit from staking and the succulent new growth is favoured by slugs and snails.

◊ ☼ ◑ ❋ ❋ ❋
‡ to 1.2m (4ft) ↔ to 45cm (18in)

MECONOPSIS NAPAULENSIS

Perennial

The satin poppy is a very large plant which can take several years to grow to flowering size. When mature, it will produce clusters of large, red, purple or pink bowl-shaped flowers from early to midsummer, after which the plant will die. It is suited to a woodland garden or the back or a wild area. Plant it in semi-shade, in neutral or acid, moist soil. Sow new seed annually in autumn or spring to provide a continual supply of mature plants that will be ready to bloom in the summer.

◊ ◊ ☼ ❈ ❈ ❈
‡ to 2.5m (8ft) ↔ to 90cm (36in)

MONARDA
'Cambridge Scarlet' ♀

Perennial

Bergamot, or bee balm, is a clump-forming herb with aromatic, toothed leaves. 'Cambridge Scarlet' has vivid red, hooded, spidery-looking flowers and, like all bergamot, it is attractive to bees. Perfect for a border or prairie-style garden, it spreads quickly in a moist but well-drained soil that does not dry out in summer, or become waterlogged in winter, and a sunny situation. It can be divided in spring.

◊ ◊ ☼ ❈ ❈ ❈
‡ to 1m (3ft) ↔ to 45cm (18in)

PAEONIA DELAVAYI ♀

Deciduous shrub

The flowers of this tree peony are
borne in early summer, and have dark
red petals and yellow stamens. The
handsome, deeply-dissected, blue-green
foliage provides colour and structure
long after the flowers have faded. It is
perfect for the back of a herbaceous or
mixed border, and prefers a sunny or
partially shaded situation in moist, well-
drained soil. Best left alone, apart from
occasionally cutting out one or two of
the oldest stems in autumn.

◊ ◊ ☼ ☀ ❄ ❄ ❄
↕↔ to 2m (6ft)

PAPAVER COMMUTATUM
'Ladybird' ♀

Annual

A distinctive hardy annual poppy, with
numerous glossy brilliant-red flowers.
Grow it in groups in a gravel garden,
or a border with a fiery colour theme,
in full sun and well-drained soil. It does
not need staking. It will self-seed
naturally, or seed can be collected and
sown in spring where it is to flower.
Alternatively, remove the dead heads
to prevent seed setting and prolong
the flowering season.

◊ ☼ ❄ ❄ ❄
↕ to 45cm (18in) ↔ to 15cm (6in)

PAPAVER ORIENTALE
Goliath Group
'Beauty of Livermere'

Perennial

Large scarlet blooms with black centres
are borne on the long, sturdy stems of
this poppy from early to midsummer.
Its vibrant colours contrast well with
gravel, or plant it in a sunny border,
where it will help to disguise the dying
foliage of spring bulbs. It dies back
early after flowering, and should be
grown close to late-flowering perennials
that will fill the gap later in the year.
Plant it in well-drained soil.

○ ☼ ❈ ❈ ❈
‡ to 1.2m (4ft) ↔ to 90cm (36in)

PELARGONIUM
'Caligula'

Perennial

This miniature zonal pelargonium bears
dark green leaves, and double, bright
scarlet flowers, which are produced
from early summer up to the first frosts,
if they are deadheaded regularly. Its
compact size and long flowering season
combine to make it an excellent plant
for containers, although it can also be
used as bedding in the garden planted
in full sun, in free-draining soil. It is
tender, and must be kept in a frost-free
place in winter.

○ ☼ ❈
‡ to 12cm (5in) ↔ to 10cm (4in)

PERSICARIA AMPLEXICAULIS
'Firetail' ♀

Perennial

This Himalayan bistort is a vigorous
clump-forming plant with decorative,
large, dark green, lance-shaped leaves.
From the beginning of summer to the
autumn 'Firetail' produces tall spikes of
small, bright red flowers. It likes moist
soil conditions and offers a long season
of interest in a damp border, or an area
partially shaded by deciduous trees. Its
foliage also makes good ground cover.

◊ ☼ ☀ ❄ ❄ ❄
‡↔ to 1.2m (4ft)

POTENTILLA
'Gibson's Scarlet' ♀

Perennial

A profusion of single, bright scarlet
flowers appear on this cinquefoil from
early to late summer. The blooms are
produced on long stems above clumps
of soft green, palmate foliage. It is an
excellent plant for the front of a sunny
border, or use it in a raised bed or
gravel garden. It needs a sunny
position, in poor or moderately fertile,
well-drained soil.

◊ ☼ ❄ ❄ ❄
‡ to 45cm (18in) ↔ to 60cm (24in)

POTENTILLA
'Red Ace'

Evergreen shrub

This shrubby cinquefoil bears orange-red, saucer-shaped, single flowers, which contrast well with the small, divided leaves. It blooms from late spring to mid-autumn, and makes a wonderful low informal hedging or gravel garden plant. Grow it in a sunny position, in well-drained, poor to moderately fertile soil, and trim after flowering, removing weak shoots and cutting dead wood back to the base.

◊ ☼ ❀ ❀ ❀
‡ to 1m (3ft) ↔ to 1.5m (5ft)

RHEUM PALMATUM
'Atrosanguineum' ♀

Perennial

Chinese rhubarb is a large, spreading plant with huge, deeply cut, rough-textured, green leaves that are crimson-purple when young. In early summer the spectacular foliage is accompanied by tall stems of feathery, pinky-red flowers that provide a focal point in a damp border, or beneath deciduous trees. This plant is happy in full sun or partial shade, in moist soil. Mulch plants annually in spring with well-rotted compost.

◊ ☼ ◐ ❀ ❀ ❀
‡ to 2.5m (8ft) ↔ to 2m (6ft)

ROSA GALLICA VAR. OFFICINALIS ♀

Deciduous shrub

The crimson damask rose produces lightly scented, pinky-red flowers from early summer. These are followed in autumn by orange-red hips. Plant this compact rose with other old-fashioned roses, or in a shrub or mixed border, alongside hardy geraniums. Alternatively, use it as a low hedge which can be clipped over lightly in early spring. Plant it in full sun in fertile, moist, well-drained soil.

◊◊☼ ❁ ❁ ❁
‡ to 80cm (32in) ↔ to 1m (3ft)

ROSA
L.D. Braithwaite ♀

Deciduous shrub

A superb modern shrub rose, this form is covered from early summer to autumn with crimson flowers. The blooms are slightly scented when they first open, but develop a stronger fragrance as they age. This rose has a compact habit, and is ideally suited to small gardens, where it can be planted as a specimen or in a border. It will do best when grown in full sun in fertile, moist, well-drained soil. Lightly trim to shape in late winter or early spring.

◊◊☼ ❁ ❁ ❁
‡ to 90cm (36in) ↔ to 1.2m (4ft)

ROSA
'Roseraie de l'Haÿ' ♀

Deciduous shrub

A rugosa shrub rose with heavily
scented, purple-red flowers from early
summer through to the autumn. The
blooms are complemented by the light
green, healthy foliage. It makes a
prickly-stemmed hedge, ideal for a
house boundary, or it can be used as
a specimen plant or grown in a mixed
border. It prefers full sun, and a deep,
fertile, moist but well drained soil. Clip
hedges to shape in early spring,
otherwise little pruning is required

○◐☼ ❄ ❄ ❄
‡ to 2.2m (7ft) ↔ to 2m (6ft)

ROSA
Royal William

Deciduous shrub

This hybrid tea rose is very free
flowering, and produces fragrant,
double, deep velvety-crimson blooms
from early summer to autumn. The
flowers contrast well with the dark
green leaves. Grow several of these
compact, upright, bush roses together
in a bed. As a standard it makes a
central focal point for a bedding
scheme. Plant it in full sun, in a deep,
fertile, well-drained soil. Prune and
mulch as for 'Blessings' (see p.195).

○◐☼ ❄ ❄ ❄
‡ to 1m (3ft) ↔ to 75cm (30in)

SALVIA FULGENS ♀

Perennial

This tender plant produces tall, dark red stems that bear scarlet flowers from early to midsummer. It will add colour and height to a bedding scheme or container planting. It can be overwintered in a frost-free greenhouse, or alternatively grow it as an annual; collect the seed in autumn and sow it under glass the following spring to flower the same year. It prefers full sun and a moist, reasonably fertile, well-drained soil or loam-based compost.

◊ ☼ ☀ ❀
‡ to 1m (3ft) ↔ to 90cm (36in)

SEMPERVIVUM TECTORUM ♀

Perennial

Often overlooked as a garden plant, the common houseleek forms rosettes of pointed, bristle-tipped, blue-green leaves, which often turn a rich purpled-red in the summer. The star-shaped, reddish-purple flowers appear in early summer, after which the leafy rosettes die, but are quickly replaced by new growth. Plant houseleeks in a sunny situation in a rock garden or a trough, or on a dry stone wall. Good drainage is also essential, and they should be grown in gritty, well-drained compost.

◊ ☼ ❀ ❀ ❀
‡ to 15cm (6in) ↔ to 50cm (20in)

TROPAEOLUM SPECIOSUM ♀

Climber

The flame nasturtium has beautiful
rounded leaves that resemble flower
petals. Throughout the summer and
into autumn, it bears long-spurred,
vermilion flowers, which are followed
by round, blue fruit. It looks best
grown against a trellis, or through an
evergreen shrub, which has the benefit
of providing some winter protection as
it is not totally hardy. Otherwise use a
thick winter mulch. Plant it in moist,
but well-drained, fertile, neutral to acid
soil in full sun or dappled shade.

◊ ◑ ☼ ※ ❉ ❉
↕ to 3m (10ft)

VERATRUM NIGRUM ♀

Perennial

This large herbaceous plant has highly
decorative pleated, bright green leaves.
In the summer it produces branched
stems, covered with small, star-shaped
red-purple flowers. It forms a
statuesque plant for a wild garden or
woodland setting, and will grow well
when planted in partial shade and a
moist, but well-drained, fertile soil.
Divide congested clumps in spring.
All parts of this plant are toxic.

◊ ◑ ☼ ※ ❉ ❉ ❉
↕ to 1.2m (4ft) ↔ to 60cm (24in)

ALLIUM
'Globemaster' ♛

Perennial bulb

The large flowerheads of this ornamental onion are made up of numerous small, intense-purple flowers grouped together in a huge globe that can reach 20cm (8in) across. The grey basal leaves are slightly hairy and arch over at the tips. For maximum impact, plant the bulbs in the autumn in groups of at least five, in a sunny border, in well-drained, fertile soil. Although good for cutting fresh, the globes look most dramatic when left to dry on the plant.

◊ ☼ ❀ ❀ ❀

‡ to 80cm (32in) ↔ to 20cm (8in)

ALLIUM CRISTOPHII ♛

Perennial bulb

The clusters of pinkish-purple flowers on this ornamental onion look like a collection of shooting stars. When the sun catches them, they take on a metallic sheen. The flowers top a 60cm (24in) stalk which emerges from dark green, strap-shaped leaves. This allium looks best when planted in a group of at least ten bulbs – that may sound extravagant, but the effect is well worth it. Plant the bulbs in autumn in full sun, and fertile, well-drained soil. Leave the flowerheads to dry on the plant before cutting.

◊ ☼ ❀ ❀

‡ to 60cm (24in) ↔ to 19cm (7in)

ALLIUM CYATHOPHORUM
VAR. FARRERI

Perennial bulb

Another beautiful ornamental onion but
daintier in form than the flamboyant
'Globemaster' and *A. cristophii*. Up to
30 small, bell-shaped, violet flowers
dangle from the top of a 30cm (12in)
stem. The slightest breeze will set them
swaying and nodding. In keeping, the
mid-green, grass-like leaves, are delicate,
too. To enjoy its subtle charms, plant
small groups of bulbs in autumn at the
front of a border in fertile, well-drained
soil in full sun.

◊ ☼ ❀ ❀ ❀
‡ to 30cm (12in) ↔ to 5cm (2in)

ANGELICA GIGAS

Perennial

The double pleasures of purple flowers
and burgundy flower stems make this
short-lived perennial well worth growing
in a large border. Closely related to
culinary angelica, be sure to give its
lush, mid-green leaves plenty of room
to spread. It is ideally suitable for an
informal woodland garden and, as a
lover of moist, but well-drained, fertile
soil, it is at home around the margins of
a large pond. It will tolerate sun and
partial shade. Grow from seed because
mature plants resent being moved.

◊ ☼ ☀ ❀ ❀ ❀
‡ to 2m (6ft) ↔ to 1.2m (4ft)

BUDDLEJA ALTERNIFOLIA ♀

Deciduous shrub

Clusters of the sweetly scented, pale lilac flowers wreath the arching branches of this shrub in early summer. So many are produced that they nearly hide the silvery-green, lance-shaped leaves. It flowers on the previous year's wood and should be pruned back to a strong bud after flowering. Cut out around a quarter of the old branches each year to stimulate new growth. It can be also be trained as a standard tree, as shown here. Grow in fertile, well-drained, preferably alkaline soil in full sun.

◊ ☼ ✿ ✿ ✿
‡↔ to 4m (12ft)

BUDDLEJA DAVIDII
'Black Knight' ♀

Deciduous shrub

The butterfly bush is well named for its ability to attract these insects like a magnet. This vigorous shrub has long, arching branches and lance-shaped, mid-green leaves. From early summer to autumn, it produces large conical spikes of tiny, deep purplish-blue, fragrant flowers. In early spring, prune it back hard to a low framework of branches to improve flowering later in the year. Grow it in a sunny position, in well-drained, fertile soil.

◊ ☼ ✿ ✿ ✿
‡ to 3m (10ft) ↔ to 5m (15ft)

CAMPANULA LATILOBA
'Hidcote Amethyst' ♀

Perennial

The pale mauve of this rosette-forming
bellflower is a good mixer in the busy
colour palette of the herbaceous border.
Tall flower stems carry the large, bell-
shaped flowers well above the bed of
broad, lance-shaped leaves. Plant in any
fertile, neutral to alkaline soil, which is
also moist but well drained. Light shade
is preferable, although a spot in full sun
is fine but the flower colour may fade.
Divide large clumps in autumn.

◊ ◊ ☼ ☀ ❀ ❀ ❀
‡ to 90cm (36in) ↔ to 45cm (18in)

CLEMATIS
'The President' ♀

Climber

This free-flowering clematis deserves
a prominent spot on a pergola or
decorative trellis where it can show off
its amazing silver-backed, deep purple-
blue blooms. These can measure up to
15cm (6in) across. It should be planted
in fertile, well-drained soil in full sun
or partial shade. Clematis grow best
when their roots are in the shade.
Remove any dead shoots in early
spring and prune the others back to
a strong pair of buds.

◊ ☼ ☀ ❀ ❀ ❀
‡ to 3m (10ft)

CONVOLVULUS SABATIUS ♀

Perennial

From summer through to autumn, this trailing plant bears an endless supply of lavender-blue, funnel-shaped flowers on a cushion of bright green leaves. It will love the sharply drained conditions of a rock garden or sunny bank. Plant it in full sun, in poor to moderately fertile, very well-drained soil. In cold areas it is best grown in a container and moved into a cool greenhouse for the winter.

◊ ☼ ❀ ❀
‡ to 15cm (6in) ↔ to 50cm (20in)

CYNARA CARDUNCULUS ♀

Evergreen perennial

Closely related to the globe artichoke, the cardoon is a fast-growing, large architectural plant with greyish-green, deeply divided, arching evergreen leaves. The purple, thistle-like flowers are borne on tall, robust stems from summer until autumn. If space allows, for real impact plant it in groups of 3–4 in a sheltered, sunny spot by a wall or fence in fertile, well-drained soil. A useful plant, it is attractive to bees, the flowers dry well and, when blanched, the leaf-stalks and midribs are edible.

◊ ☼ ❀ ❀ ❀
‡ to 1.5m (5ft) ↔ to 1.2m (4ft)

DELPHINIUM
'Bruce' ♀

Perennial

A mixed summer border would be incomplete without delphiniums. 'Bruce' produces deep violet-purple flowers on tall spires in early summer. An autumn flowering can often be encouraged if the faded flowering stems are cut back. Easily damaged by winds and rain, the plants should be staked when young with a strong cane and the tall stems tied in as they grow. Plant in a well-drained, fertile soil in full sun. Protect emerging foliage from slugs and snails.

◊ ☼ ❁ ❁ ❁
‡ to 2.2m (7ft) ↔ to 90cm (36in)

DIPSACUS FULLONUM

Biennial

In its first season, the teasel produces a rosette of spiny, toothed leaves. The following year, it throws up tall stems topped with thistle-like globes composed of tiny, pinky-purple blooms. These make wonderful dried flowers. The stems carry pairs of glossy green leaves that form a natural cup; rainwater collects in them attracting small birds to drink. The teasel is also a favourite food plant of the goldfinch. Sow seed in a wild garden in sun or partial shade, on moderately fertile soil, including clay.

◊ ◊ ☼ ☀ ❁ ❁ ❁
‡ to 2m (6ft) ↔ to 80cm (32in)

ERIGERON
'Dunkelste Aller' ♀

Perennial

Daisy-like flowers always look so
cheerful and the blooms of the fleabane
are no exception. This one has a sunny
yellow centre, fringed with violet, semi-
double petals. A clump-forming plant
with lance-shaped, greyish-green leaves,
it would do well in a mixed herbaceous
border or rock garden. It will also thrive
in a coastal garden but will need staking
on exposed sites. As a cut flower, it also
has great lasting qualities. Plant in fertile
soil that does not dry out in summer.

◊ ☼ ❀ ❀ ❀

‡ to 60cm (24in) ↔ to 45cm (18in)

ERODIUM MANESCAUI

Perennial

The delicate magenta-purple, saucer-
shaped blooms of this clump-forming
plant are very similar to those of the
hardy geranium. Throughout summer,
they are borne on long stalks in profuse
clusters of up to 20. The top two petals
of each flower are darkly freckled. The
leaves are attractive, too, being deeply
divided, lance-shaped and slightly hairy.
Plant it in gritty, very well-drained soil,
in full sun. A rock garden would suit
it well, or plant it at the front of the
herbaceous border. It self-seeds freely.

◊ ☼ ❀ ❀ ❀

‡ to 45cm (18in) ↔ to 20cm (8in)

ERYSIMUM
'Bowles' Mauve' ♀

Evergreen perennial

A long-flowering wallflower, 'Bowles Mauve' produces tall spikes of mauve blooms throughout the year; but early summer is when they are most profuse. The flowers are set off by narrow, grey-green leaves. Plant it in well-drained, poor to moderately fertile, preferably alkaline soil in full sun. A lovely border plant, in cold areas give it the shelter of a warm wall. Trim after flowering and take cuttings to make more plants as it tends to be short lived.

◊ ☼ ❋ ❋ ❋
‡ to 75cm (30in) ↔ to 60cm (24in)

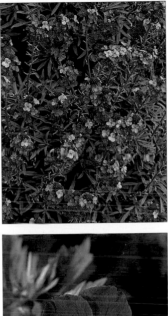

GERANIUM PSILOSTEMON ♀
Perennial

One of the largest hardy geraniums, this fast-growing plant has deep magenta purple flowers with an almost black eye. The toothed, mid-green leaves are infused with crimson in spring and autumn. A useful ground-covering plant to infill around shrubs in a border, it grows well in most well-drained soils, in sun or partial shade. Trim it over after flowering to encourage new growth. In the right conditions it will self seed freely; alternatively divide large clumps in spring.

◊ ☼ ◑ ❋ ❋ ❋
‡ to 1.2m (4ft) ↔ to 60cm (24in)

GERANIUM SYLVATICUM *'Mayflower'* ♀

Perennial

With its white-centred, rich violet-blue, upward-facing flowers, 'Mayflower' is one of the most attractive geraniums available. Its deeply lobed, mid-green leaves form a shapely mound. It is a good naturalizer in open ground or under trees and shrubs. Plant it in moist, but well-drained, soil; although it tolerates shade it would prefer full sun. Trim the plant over after flowering to encourage new growth.

◊ ◊ ☼ ☀ ❄ ❄ ❄
‡ to 75cm (30in) ↔ to 60cm (24in)

GLADIOLUS COMMUNIS *SUBSP.* BYZANTINUS ♀

Perennial corm

The tall flower spikes of this gladiolus carry up to 20 magenta flowers that add zest to an early summer border, and are good for cutting. The rich-green, strappy leaves reach 70cm (28in) long. Unless you want huge swathes of these plants, take care if disturbing the soil around them as small corms will break off and spread. Plant in full sun, in fertile, well-drained soil. Corms do not need to be lifted in winter, but in cold gardens cover the soil with a mulch.

◊ ☼ ❄ ❄ ❄
‡ to 1m (3ft) ↔ to 8cm (3in)

HELIOTROPIUM ARBORESCENS
'Marine'

Evergreen shrub

The heliotrope is a tender, short-lived
shrub often grown as annual bedding.
With its clusters of fragrant, violet-blue
flowers, it looks good in pots and
window boxes or as front-of-the-border
edging. Plant it in full sun in moist, but
well-drained, fertile soil. Take softwood
cuttings in summer and overwinter
them in a cool greenhouse. You can
also grow heliotropes as conservatory
plants. Use a loam-based compost and
provide shading from strong sunlight.

◊ ◊ ⚙ ❀
‡↔ to 45cm (18in)

HEUCHERA MICRANTHA
'Palace Purple'

Evergreen perennial

Heucheras are evergreen, or nearly
evergreen, clump-forming plants, which
are grown primarily for their attractive
foliage. 'Palace Purple' has glossy,
deeply lobed, purplish-red leaves and
airy spikes of tiny greenish-cream
flowers. It makes a sumptuous ground-
cover plant in a herbaceous or shrub
border. Plant in full sun or partial
shade, in moist, but well-drained,
neutral, fertile soil.

◊ ◊ ☼ ☀ ❀ ❀ ❀
‡↔ to 60cm (24in)

IRIS ENSATA
'Hue and Cry' ♀

Perennial

The Japanese iris is a beautiful aquatic marginal plant. The purple 'Hue and Cry' has flat flowers with six large, white-veined, lower petals, each with a yellow stripe down the centre. Short periods of flooding are tolerated but rather than total immersion, this plant prefers permanently moist or wet, acid soil, and is suitable for a bog garden.

♦♦ ☼ ☀ ❄ ❄ ❄
‡ to 90cm (36in)

IRIS VERSICOLOR ♀

Perennial

The richly coloured petals of the blue flag iris have beautiful markings, with heavy purple veining and a large white patch at their base. Together with the vibrant green, sword-shaped leaves, this is an attractive plant for a bog garden, the shallow margins of a natural pond, or a moisture-retentive border. Plant the rhizomes in permanently moist or wet soil, but not underwater.

♦♦ ☼ ☀ ❄ ❄ ❄
‡ to 80cm (32in)

IRIS × ROBUSTA
'Gerald Darby' ♀

Perennial

Another stunning water iris, 'Gerald Darby' has narrow, sword-shaped leaves that are covered at the base with purple spots. Its stems, which are dark violet, produce four bluish-purple flowers, each marked with a patch of yellow. Plant it in a moist border or at the edge of a pond. Given the right conditions, this vigorous clump-former can reach the spectacular height of 1.8m (6ft); however, it usually measures just under half that.

◊ ◐ ☼ ❄ ❄ ❄
‡ to 75cm (30in)

LATHYRUS PUBESCENS

Climber

This is an attractive, perennial sweet pea with pairs of lance-shaped, dark green leaves, and hairy stems. It is a strong growing plant that produces long-stalked clusters of deep, lilac-blue flowers. Using its tendrils for support, it will happily clamber up trellis or through shrubs, or will sprawl over a bank. Plant it in a sunny site, in well-drained, fertile soil. It is not completely hardy and is vulnerable to severe frost unless provided with a deep mulch over winter.

◊ ☼ ❄ ❄
‡ to 3m (10ft)

POLEMONIUM
'Lambrook Mauve' ♀

Perennial

Jacob's ladder is a free-flowering plant
that produces clusters of lilac-blue
flowers on upright, branched stems.
A neat, mound-forming perennial, it is
ideally suited to the front of a mixed
or herbaceous border. It also makes a
lovely feature plant in formal planting,
or among low-growing grasses. Give
it a spot in full sun or partial shade, in
a moist, but well-drained, fertile soil.
Dead-head regularly and divide large
clumps during the spring.

◊ ◑ ☼ ☀ ❄ ❄ ❄
↕↔ to 45cm (18in)

ROSA
Blue Moon

Deciduous shrub

The blooms of this large-flowered rose
are a delicate shade of lilac-mauve, and
held on upright, thorny stems, which
also bear dark green foliage. Its fragrant
flowers are semi-double and good for
cutting; to produce the best colour
grow in full sun. Plant roses in fertile,
well-drained soil, and apply a rose
fertilizer regularly in the growing
season. Prune the main stems to 20cm
(8in) above the ground in late winter
to ensure lots of flowers.

◊ ◊ ☼ ❄ ❄ ❄
↕ to 1m (3ft) ↔ to 70cm (28in)

ROSCOEA HUMEANA ♛

Perennial

This unusual tuberous plant has orchid-like flowers with a prominent, hooded upper petal. The lush, deep-green, rounded leaves set the blooms off perfectly. A sheltered woodland garden would be the ideal home for this plant, as it grows best in damp shade in a cool climate. It is not fully hardy, so where frosts are likely in winter, cover the root area with a deep mulch, such as leaf mould.

◊ ☀ ❋ ❋
‡ to 25cm (10in) ↔ to 15cm (6in)

STACHYS MACRANTHA 'Superba'

Perennial

Erect spikes of pinky-purple, hooded flowers are held above rosettes of wrinkled, dark green, heart-shaped leaves. An easy going plant for the front of a herbaceous border, it flowers over a long period from early summer until early autumn. Plant it in well-drained, fertile soil. It is best in full sun, but will tolerate a certain amount of shade.

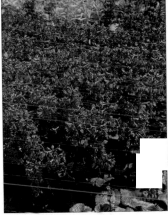

◊ ☀ ☀ ❋ ❋ ❋
‡ to 60cm (24in) ↔ to 30cm (12in)

ACONITUM × CAMMARUM 'Bicolor' ♀

Perennial

This tall, elegant plant forms clumps of deeply lobed, mid-green leaves, and in summer produces spikes of bicoloured blue and white, hooded flowers. It is a woodland plant and suits a similar garden situation beneath deciduous trees or in a partially-shaded border. However, it will tolerate a sunny site as long as the soil is reasonably moist and fertile. All parts of this plant are highly toxic.

○ ☼ ◑ ❀ ❀ ❀
‡ to 1.2m (4ft) ↔ to 30cm (12in)

ADENOPHORA BULLEYANA

Perennial

Reminiscent of a bellflower, this pretty herbaceous plant in summer bears tall spikes of pendent, funnel-shaped, pale blue flowers. For the greatest impact, plant it in large groups in a herbaceous border or summer flower garden. It will do well when grown in moist but well-drained soil in full sun or partial shade. It resents being moved once planted so position it carefully.

○ ○ ☼ ◑ ❀ ❀ ❀
‡ to 1.2m (4ft) ↔ to 30cm (12in)

AGERATUM HOUSTONIANUM *'Adriatic'*

Annual

The floss flower forms a mound of downy, oval, green leaves, above which frothy-looking heads of tiny mid-blue flowers are borne in summer and up to the first frosts. It is widely grown as a bedding plant and complements low-growing annuals with bright yellow flowers, such as calceolarias. It is also suitable for containers and hanging baskets. Plant it in full sun, in a moist, well-drained soil. In containers, keep it well watered when in flower.

◊ ◊ ☼ ❈
‡ to 20cm (8in) ↔ to 30cm (12in)

AGERATUM HOUSTONIANUM *'Bavaria'*

Annual

This decorative bedding or container plant grows quickly in the spring. In the summer and up to the first frosts, it produces branched clusters of pale blue flowers with white centres. It can be used to edge a border or path, or grown in containers, including hanging baskets, within a pastel colour scheme. Plant as for 'Adriatic' (see above).

◊ ◊ ☼ ❈
‡ to 25cm (10in) ↔ to 30cm (12in)

AJUGA REPTANS
'Variegata'

Evergreen perennial

Bugle is a useful, easy going ground-cover plant which forms a carpet of evergreen leaves, borne on spreading stems. 'Variegata' has grey-green leaves with a cream edge and cream markings. From late spring to early summer, bugle produces upright stems of small, dark blue tubular flowers. Plant it in any moist soil in partial shade. It will also tolerate full sun if the soil does not dry out during the summer.

⬥ ☼ ☀ ✽ ✽ ✽
‡ to 15cm (6in) ↔ to 90cm (36in)

ALLIUM CAERULEUM ♛

Perennial bulb

A beautiful onion, this variety produces spherical heads of tiny bright blue, star-shaped flowers in early summer. The blooms are produced after the narrow leaves have died down on triangular, stiff green stems. Plant groups of bulbs in the autumn in a herbaceous border, gravel garden, or a large container, in full sun and well-drained, fertile soil.

⬥ ☼ ✽ ✽
‡ to 60cm (24in) ↔ to 15cm (6in)

ANCHUSA AZUREA
'Loddon Royalist' ♀

Perennial

This beautiful, early summer-flowering
plant forms a clump of lance-shaped
leaves, and robust branched stems of
deep blue flowers. The blooms are
attractive to bees, making it a good
candidate for a wild garden, or a
herbaceous border. Plant it in groups
in full sun and moist, well-drained soil.
Young plants should be cut back after
flowering to promote the growth of
basal leaves. Dead-head mature plants
to encourage a second flush of flowers.

◊ ◊ ☼ ❋ ❋ ❋
‡ to 90cm (36in) ↔ to 60cm (24in)

ANCHUSA AZUREA
'Blue Angel'

Perennial

A compact, bushy plant, 'Blue Angel'
produces a mass of pale blue flowers
that resemble those of forget-me-nots.
The leaves are rough-textured, and
covered with bristles. It is a short-lived
perennial which can be grown as an
annual, and can be used at the front
of a border, in a raised bed or rock
garden, or as a container plant. Plant
it in full sun and moist, well-drained,
fertile soil.

◊ ◊ ☼ ❋ ❋ ❋
‡ to 20cm (8in) ↔ to 15cm (6in)

BAPTISIA AUSTRALIS ♀

Perennial

False indigo is a spreading plant with mid-green leaves divided into three egg-shaped leaflets. In the summer it produces tall spikes of dark-blue pealike flowers, which are often marked with white or cream. The flowers are followed in autumn by large seed pods, suitable for drying. Plant it in an open, sunny site in deep, very free-draining, neutral to acid soil. It is suitable for a herbaceous border, but once planted it is best left undisturbed. Stake tall plants unless the planting site is sheltered.

◊ ☼ ❁ ❁ ❁
‡ to 1.5m (5ft) ↔ to 60cm (24in)

CAMPANULA BARBATA

Perennial

The bearded bellflower is so named because of the unusual hairs that edge the pendent, lavender-blue flowers that appear in early summer. A short-lived perennial, it forms rosettes of hairy, lance-shaped, mid-green leaves beneath the erect flower stems. It is a suitable plant for a rock or gravel garden and should be planted in full sun or partial shade, in moist, but well-drained soil.

◊ ◊ ☼ ☼ ❁ ❁ ❁
‡ to 20cm (8in) ↔ to 12cm (5in)

CAMPANULA PERSICIFOLIA
'Telham Beauty'

Perennial

One of the most vigorous bellflowers, this form bears rosettes of evergreen lance-shaped, bright green leaves. In early summer pale-blue, bell-shaped flowers appear for many weeks on tall stems. Flowering can be prolonged by regular dead-heading. It is best planted in groups in a herbaceous or mixed border, or in a woodland or wild-flower garden. Grow it in full sun or partial shade, in fertile, well-drained, neutral or slightly alkaline soil.

◊ ☼ ☀ ❄ ❄ ❄
‡ to 1m (3ft) ↔ to 30cm (12in)

CEANOTHUS
'Cynthia Postan'

Evergreen shrub

This Californian lilac forms a rounded bush, with toothed, glossy, evergreen leaves. It is very free flowering, and from late spring to early summer bears clusters of deep blue flowers. Plant it in a sheltered, sunny position in fertile, well-drained soil. Grow it in a mixed shrub border, as a specimen plant, or train it against a warm, sunny wall.

◊ ☼ ❄ ❄
‡↔ to 2.5m (8ft)

CEANOTHUS × DELILEANUS
'Gloire de Versailles' ♀

Deciduous shrub

Hardier than many other Californian
lilacs, 'Gloire de Versailles' has oval
dark green leaves, and clusters of tiny
deep sky-blue flowers, held in open
spikes at the end of the stems. It
flowers in early summer and again in
the autumn. A good shrub for a mixed
border or a Mediterranean-style garden,
it prefers a position in full sun and a
well-drained soil. Overgrown specimens
can be cut back hard in spring.

◊ ☼ ❄ ❄ ❄
‡↔ to 1.5m (5ft)

CENTAUREA CYANUS

Annual

Once a common weed of wheat fields
the cornflower is now more often used
in borders, meadows or wild gardens.
It has lance-shaped leaves, and in early
summer produces dark-blue flowers
with violet-blue centres. When grown
in a meadow or wild-garden, combine
it with poppies (*Papaver rhoeas*) and
corn cockles (*Agrostemma githago*). It
is also an excellent cut flower. Sow the
seed *in situ* in autumn or spring in full
sun and a well-drained soil.

◊ ☼ ❄ ❄ ❄
‡ to 80cm (32in) ↔ to 15cm (6in)

CICHORIUM INTYBUS

Perennial

Chicory forms a clump of lance-shaped, toothed leaves, and is often grown as a salad vegetable. However, when left to flower, it is a good decorative plant and in early summer produces branched stems of blue, daisy-like flowers with toothed petals. Plant it in groups in a flower garden or mixed border in full sun and a well-drained, fertile soil.

◊ ☼ ❀ ❀ ❀
↕ to 1.2m (4ft) ↔ to 60cm (24in)

CONSOLIDA AJACIS

Annual

The annual delphiniums, otherwise known as larkspurs, are fast-growing herbaceous plants, with deeply divided, feathery leaves. They look similar to perennial delphiniums but tend to have shorter flowering stems. In the summer they produce spikes of violet-blue, pink or white flowers, with long spurs, and are good for cutting. Ideal for filling gaps left by spring bulbs in a border, they grow best in full sun in light, well-drained soil. Sow the seed *in situ* in spring, or autumn in mild gardens.

◊ ☼ ❀ ❀ ❀
↕ to 1.2m (4ft) ↔ to 30cm (12in)

DELPHINIUM
'Blue Nile' ♀

Perennial

This beautiful delphinium has deeply divided green foliage, and in summer produces tall, elegant spikes of mid-blue flowers with white eyes. The flowerheads should be removed when they fade to leave the side shoots to flower. Stake it with strong canes in spring when the foliage emerges, and tie in the flower stems as it grows. Plant it in groups at the back of a border in full sun, out of strong winds, and in fertile, humus-rich, well-drained soil.

◊ ☼ ✿ ✿ ✿
‡ to 1.5m (5ft)

DELPHINIUM GRANDIFLORUM
'Blue Butterfly'

Perennial

A short-lived plant, this delphinium is often grown as an annual. It has deeply divided leaves, and in summer it bears spikes of bright blue flowers. Grow it in a bedding scheme, or at the front of a herbaceous border. It also makes a good cut flower. Plant this delphinium in well-drained, fertile soil in full sun. It is less demanding than the large-flowered varieties, such as 'Blue Nile'.

◊ ☼ ✿ ✿ ✿
‡↔ to 30cm (12in)

ECHINOPS RITRO
'Veitch's Blue'

Perennial

Grown partly for its architectural, spiny, greyish-green leaves, in summer this vigorous plant also produces spherical dark blue flowerheads on woolly grey stems. The lollipop-shaped flowerheads contrast well with flat-headed blooms, such as those of achillea, in a gravel garden or a herbaceous border. The flowers are frequently used, fresh or dried, in floral arrangements. Plant it in groups of four or five in poor, well-drained soil, in full sunshine.

◊ ☼ ☀ ✽ ✽ ✽
‡ to 90cm (36in) ↔ to 45cm (18in)

ECHIUM VULGARE
'Blue Bedder'

Biennial

The dwarf form of viper's bugloss has an upright habit, and produces bristly, lance-shaped, dark-green leaves. In the early summer it bears an abundance of blue flowers, which turn pink as they age. Plant it in a wild-flower garden or use it as bedding. Viper's bugloss likes a sunny situation and reasonably fertile, well-drained soil.

◊ ☼ ✽ ✽ ✽
‡ to 40cm (16in) ↔ to 30cm (12in)

ERYNGIUM GIGANTEUM ♀

Biennial

Commonly known as 'Miss Wilmott's Ghost', this biennial or short-lived perennial forms a rosette of bluish-green, spiny leaves. The tiny silver-blue flowers are borne in cone-like clusters, and are surrounded by a collar of large silver bracts. It works well in a hot gravel or Mediterranean-style garden, or grow it in a herbaceous border. Its skeletal form can be left to decorate the winter. Plant it in full sun in well-drained soil, and it will self-seed freely.

◊ ☼ ❀ ❀ ❀
‡ to 1.2m (4ft) ↔ to 30cm (12in)

ERYNGIUM × OLIVERIANUM ♀

Perennial

This striking sea holly forms a clump of heart-shaped, mid-green, spiny leaves with distinctive silver veining. In the summer and early autumn, branched stems produce lavender-blue, thistle-like flowers, surrounded by spiny, linear, leaf-like bracts. The whole plant is suffused with a steel-blue colouration. Plant it in a sunny position in well-drained soil, and use it in a herbaceous border or gravel garden. The flower stems make excellent cut flowers, too, or they can be left to stand in winter.

◊ ☼ ❀ ❀ ❀
‡ to 90cm (36in) ↔ to 45cm (18in)

GERANIUM
'Johnson's Blue' ♀

Perennial

This is one of the most widely-grown
geraniums, favoured for its deeply
lobed, mid-green leaves, and long
flowering season in summer. It bears
deep lavender-blue, saucer-shaped
flowers with pink centres. Plant it at the
front of a herbaceous border or use it
as underplanting in a rose bed. It will
grow in most soils, but does best in
well-drained, fertile soil in a sunny or
partially shaded situation. Divide large
clumps in autumn.

◊ ◊ ☼ ☼ ❋ ❋ ❋
‡ to 45cm (18in) ↔ to 75cm (30in)

GERANIUM PRATENSE
'Mrs. Kendall Clark' ♀

Perennial

The meadow cranesbill is a clump-
forming plant, with deeply lobed, mid-
green leaves. The single flowers appear
from early to midsummer and are
bluey-grey flushed with pale pink, or
sometimes violet-blue with delicate
white veining. The meadow cranesbill
is a beautiful plant for the front of a
border, or use it as ground cover. It
grows well in most soils, but prefers
a well-drained, fertile soil in full sun
or partial shade.

◊ ◊ ☼ ☼ ❋ ❋ ❋
‡ to 90cm (36in) ↔ to 60cm (24in)

GERANIUM WALLICHIANUM
'Buxton's Variety' ♀

Perennial

This hardy geranium, or cranesbill, forms a wide-spreading but compact clump of decorative, deeply divided, marbled leaves. In summer it produces single sky-blue flowers with white centres, marked with prominent blue veins. Its carpeting foliage makes good ground cover, and it suits a sunny site at the front of a border or rock garden. For the best results, plant it in a well-drained, fertile soil.

○ ☼ ❀ ❀ ❀
‡ to 30cm (12in) ↔ to 1.2m (4ft)

HEMEROCALLIS
'Prairie Blue Eyes'

Perennial

The majority of daylilies have yellow or orange blooms, but this one has deep lavender-blue flowers, produced from early to midsummer. Semi-evergreen, it forms a clump of narrow mid-green leaves, which add structure and form to a sheltered border throughout the year. It can also be used in a large container or in gravel beds, and prefers a sunny site and fertile, moist, well-drained soil.

○ ◑ ☼ ❀ ❀ ❀
‡ to 70cm (28in) ↔ to 75cm (30in)

HOSTA
'Halcyon' ♥

Perennial

The thick, heart-shaped, blue-green
leaves of this hosta may be slightly less
susceptible to slug damage than some
other varieties. In the summer it bears
spikes of greyish-lavender funnel-
shaped flowers. The colour of the
foliage may fade in bright sun, so it is
advisable to plant it in partial shade,
beneath shrubs or trees, in moist, well-
drained soil. In spring, mulch hostas
with organic matter, such as composted
bark, to conserve moisture in summer.

○ ◐ ☼ ❀ ❀ ❀
‡ to 40cm (16in) ↔ to 70cm (28in)

HYSSOPUS OFFICINALIS

Deciduous shrub

Hyssop is a pretty garden plant, which
can also be used for medicinal and
culinary purposes. It has small, aromatic
leaves, and the flowers vary in colour
from blue to violet, pink and white. It
blooms from early or midsummer to
early autumn, and will add colour and
form to a herb bed or the front of a
border. It can also be grown in a large
container or a gravel garden. Plant it
in a sunny situation in well-drained soil.

○ ☼ ❀ ❀ ❀
‡ to 60cm (2ft) ↔ to 1m (3ft)

IRIS ENSATA
'Flying Tiger' ♀

Perennial

Japanese irises are beautiful plants with striking, large flat blooms. The flowers of 'Flying Tiger' measure up to 30cm (12in) across and have rounded petals, marked with bold violet-blue veins and a splash of yellow radiating from the centre. Although it is an aquatic plant, it will grow in a bog garden or moist border, as long as the roots do not dry out in the summer. When grown in a border, it prefers a rich, moist, acid soil.

◊ ● ☼ ☼ ❄ ❄ ❄
‡ to 90cm (36in) ↔ indefinite

IRIS
'Jane Phillips' ♀

Perennial

An elegant, tall bearded iris, this variety has bluish-green, sword-shaped leaves, and mid-blue, fragrant flowers. To ensure a good show of flowers year after year, plant it in front of a sunny wall, or in a hot border where its rhizomes can enjoy the summer sun. It also grows well in neutral or slightly alkaline, fertile, well-drained soil. Divide large clumps after flowering and replant plump sections so that the top of the rhizomes are exposed to the sun.

◊ ☼ ❄ ❄ ❄
‡ to 90cm (36in) ↔ to 60cm (24in)

IRIS LAEVIGATA ♛

Perennial

The deep purple-blue flowers of this beardless water iris appear in early summer, and make a superb addition to a sunny or partially shaded bog garden, or the margins of a pond in acid (lime-free) soil. The blooms are set off by broad, mid-green, strap-like leaves. This is a vigorous iris and large clumps can be divided in the spring. 'Variegata' is an attractive cultivar with white and green-striped leaves.

◐ ◑ ☼ ☀ ❊ ❊ ❊
‡ to 80cm (32in) ↔ indefinite

IRIS PALLIDA
'Variegata' ♛

Perennial

The dramatic, variegated sword-shaped leaves of this iris provide structure, colour and form in a sunny herbaceous border from spring to autumn. The beautiful bearded, mid-blue flowers, which appear in early summer, are a bonus and magnify this plant's charms. For the best results, plant it in groups in well-drained, neutral or alkaline soil.

◐ ☼ ❊ ❊ ❊
‡ to 1.2m (4ft) ↔ indefinite

LINUM PERENNE

Perennial

The perennial flax is a clump-forming plant, with narrow, bluish-green, lance-shaped leaves and slender flower stems. Although each pale blue flower lasts for just one day and fades before evening, the blooms are produced in succession from early to midsummer. Grow it in groups in full sun and a well-drained, fertile soil, and use it in a flower garden or herbaceous border. It can be raised from seed sown in pots in a cold frame in autumn or early spring.

◊ ☼ ❀❀❀
‡ to 30cm (12in) ↔ to 15cm (6in)

LITHODORA DIFFUSA
'Heavenly Blue' ♥

Evergreen shrub

This prostrate plant produces trailing branches, covered with small, elliptic, deep green leaves. In the summer it bears large numbers of rich azure-blue flowers. It can be planted in a raised bed, or a rock or gravel garden, and to grow well it needs an acid (lime-free), fertile soil and a sunny situation.

◊ ☼ ❀❀❀
‡ to 15cm (6in) ↔ to 60cm (24in)

LOBELIA ERINUS
'Sapphire'

Perennial

This dainty plant is usually treated as an
annual and raised from seed each year.
It is grown for its trailing stems of
small, mid-green, leaves and abundant
bright blue flowers with striking white
eyes. It flowers from summer to mid-
autumn and is an excellent plant for
containers, hanging baskets, and edging
borders. It should be planted in full sun
or partial shade in moist, well-drained
soil. When grown in containers, feed it
every fortnight with a liquid fertilizer.

◊ ◊ ☼ ◐ ❄

‡ to 20cm (8in) ↔ to 15cm (6in)

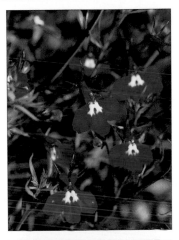

LUPINUS ALBIFRONS

Evergreen shrub

A decorative tree-lupin, this variety has
a rounded habit and attractive foliage
covered with silvery hairs. Throughout
the summer it produces spikes of pea-
like, blue or reddish-purple flowers.
Although reasonably hardy, to survive
the winter it needs to be planted in a
sunny position in very well-drained soil,
such as by a wall, in a sheltered raised
bed or gravel garden. Mulch generously
with gravel.

◊ ◊ ☼ ❄ ❄

‡↔ to 75cm (30in)

NEMOPHILA MENZIESII

Annual

Throughout summer, the aptly-named baby blue-eyes produces bright blue, saucer-shaped flowers with darker veins and paler centres, among downy, grey-green divided foliage. It is suitable for the front of the herbaceous border, or hanging baskets and containers. Baby blue-eyes should be planted in fertile, moist, well-drained soil in full sun or partial shade. It is hardy and will self-seed when planted in a border.

◊ ◊ ☼ ☼ ❋ ❋ ❋
‡ to 20cm (8in) ↔ to 30cm (12in)

NIGELLA DAMASCENA
'Miss Jekyll' ♀

Annual

A widely-grown, self-seeding annual, love-in-a-mist has highly decorative, finely divided green leaves and early summer blooms. 'Miss Jekyll' bears sky-blue flowers, surrounded by a 'ruff' of thread-like leaves, which are followed by attractive seedheads. In spring or autumn, sow the seed *in situ* in bold groups at the front of a mixed border, or with other annuals in a wild-flower meadow. It needs to be grown in full sun and a well-drained soil.

◊ ☼ ❋ ❋ ❋
‡ to 45cm (18in) ↔ to 20cm (8in)

PASSIFLORA CAERULEA ♀

Climber

The blue passion flower has woody
stems and dark green divided foliage.
The exotic-looking flowers have white
petals, which are sometimes tinged with
pink, and a ring of purple-blue banded
strands that radiate out from the centre.
In hot summers the blooms may be
followed by round, yellow fruit. Plant it
in a sunny, sheltered site in moist, well-
drained soil. It is not fully hardy and
may be killed by hard frosts, but young
shoots often appear from the base if the
root area is mulched over winter.

◊ ◊ ☼ ✿ ✿

‡ to 10m (30ft) or more

POLEMONIUM CAERULEUM

Perennial

Jacob's ladder has decorative, divided
foliage, and in early summer bears erect
stems of clear blue, bell-shaped flowers.
It is very adaptable and can be grown
in an informal planting among low-
growing grasses, or at the front of a
herbaceous border, where it can help
to disguise the dying foliage of early
spring bulbs. Plant it in full sunshine
or partial shade, in fertile, moist, well-
drained soil. Dead-head regularly and
divide large clumps in spring.

◊ ◊ ☼ ✿ ✿ ✿ ✿

‡↔ to 45cm (18in)

SALVIA PATENS
'Cambridge Blue' ♀

Perennial

From summer to autumn this form
of sage produces delicate pale blue
flowers. Beneath the flower stems,
it forms a clump of oval, mid-green
leaves. Plant it in a sunny, sheltered
border, or by a wall, in well-drained
soil. Not fully hardy, this salvia is
unlikely to survive a hard frost and
is better treated as an annual in cold
areas. Sow seed under glass in spring,
or overwinter mature plants in a frost-
free greenhouse.

⬤ ☼ ❋ ❋
‡ to 60cm (24in) ↔ to 45cm (18in)

SCABIOSA CAUCASICA
'Clive Greaves' ♀

Perennial

A beautiful scabious, 'Clive Greaves' has
grey-green basal leaves, and violet-blue
flowers with cream-coloured centres,
which attract bees and butterflies. It is
perfect for a wild-flower garden or a
herbaceous border, and needs a sunny
position and well-drained, reasonably
fertile, neutral to alkaline soil to thrive.
Young plants flower most freely, so
divide and replant them every spring
to ensure a good display each summer.
Dead-head the plants regularly, too.

⬤ ☼ ❋ ❋ ❋
‡↔ to 60cm (24in)

SISYRINCHIUM ANGUSTIFOLIUM

Perennial

Blue-eyed grass is a semi-evergreen plant that forms tussocks of grass-like leaves. The purplish-blue flowers with bright yellow eyes are produced in succession throughout the summer. It should be planted in full sun in well-drained soil, and will provide a long season of interest in a rock or gravel garden, or a raised bed.

◊ ☼ ❋ ❋ ❋
‡ to 30cm (12in) ↔ to 15cm (6in)

VERONICA AUSTRIACA
'Crater Lake Blue' ♀

Perennial

This striking mat-forming perennial has hairy greyish-green leaves, and spikes of vivid, deep-blue, saucer-shaped flowers are produced for many weeks in summer. Ideal for a herbaceous or mixed border, or a rock garden, it will perform well when planted in full sun or partial shade in a well-drained, even poor soil.

◊ ☼ ☼ ❋ ❋ ❋
‡↔ to 60cm (24in)

CAREX PENDULA

Perennial

The weeping sedge forms substantial clumps of relatively wide, strap-like, mid-green leaves that are blue-green underneath. In early summer arching, triangular stems bear pendent, catkin-like flower spikes, which look attractive when hanging over water at the edge of a pool, or in a damp border or woodland setting. Grow this sedge in permanently moist or wet soil in partial shade or sun. It can self seed profusely.

◊ ◖ ☼ ☀ ✿ ✿ ✿
‡ to 1.4m (4½ft) ↔ to 1.5m (5ft)

EUPHORBIA CHARACIAS

Evergreen shrub

This impressive spurge creates structure and form throughout the year, with its ascending stems, clothed with greyish-green, narrow leaves. In spring and early summer it produces dome-shaped clusters of small green flowers with maroon eyes. A very variable plant, it is best to grow a named variety, and for good results plant it in a sunny position in a well-drained soil. Remove the old stems when they have flowered.

◊ ☼ ✿ ✿
‡ to 1.2m (4ft) ↔ to 1.2m (4ft)

HOSTA
'Frances Williams' ♀

Perennial

A widely-grown hosta, this variety is
favoured for its large, thick, blue-green,
heart-shaped leaves with yellow-green
margins. It has very pale lavender-grey
flowers, borne in clusters on tall stems
in early summer. It is best to grow it in
moist soil in a partially shaded situation
because the leaves have a tendency to
scorch in bright sun. Plant it to provide
interest beneath deciduous trees, or in
a mixed or herbaceous border. Take
measures to prevent slug damage.

◊ ☼ ✳ ✳ ✳
‡ to 60cm (24in) ↔ to 1m (3ft)

HOSTA PLANTAGINEA
VAR. JAPONICA ♀

Perennial

The large oval, light green leaves of
this hosta have a glossy texture and
distinctive raised veins. It grows well
in sun or partial shade, in moist but
well-drained soil, and it can be used in
a herbaceous or mixed border, or in the
light shade underneath deciduous trees.
The majority of hostas are grown for
their foliage, but this also has attractive,
trumpet-shaped, fragrant white flowers,
borne on long stems in midsummer.
Slugs may cause leaf damage.

◊◊ ☼ ☀ ✳ ✳ ✳
‡ to 60cm (24in) ↔ to 1m (3ft)

HOSTA SIEBOLDIANA *VAR.* ELEGANS ♛

Perennial

Few plants can compete with hostas for foliage effects, and this variety is particularly spectacular, with its large, blue-grey, crinkled leaves and deeply incised veins. Spikes of pale lilac, funnel-shaped flowers appear in late summer, but can only just be seen above the leaves. Plant this hosta in partial shade in moist, fertile, well-drained soil, and propagate by dividing clumps in the spring. Like all hostas, it is prone to slug damage.

○ ◐ ☼ ☀ ❀ ❀ ❀
‡ to 1m (3ft) ↔ to 1.2m (4ft)

HOSTA UNDULATA *VAR.* ALBOMARGINATA

Perennial

The clumps of relatively small, bright green leaves of this hosta are enlivened with creamy-white margins that define their elliptic shape. Lavender, funnel-shaped flowers are borne on long stems from early to midsummer. This hosta will lighten up a partially shaded site in a herbaceous or mixed border or use it in deciduous woodland. It prefers a moist, well-drained soil. Grow it in loam-based compost in a pot to reduce the chance of slug damage.

○ ☼ ☀ ❀ ❀ ❀
‡ to 55cm (22in) ↔ to 60cm (24in)

LIRIODENDRON TULIPIFERA ♀

Deciduous tree

The tulip tree has a conical shape and bears unusual lobed, square leaves, which appear as though they have been chopped off at the tips. The tulip-shaped flowers are yellowish-green with a hint of orange at the base of the petals, but are only produced on mature trees. In the autumn the foliage turns wonderful shades of golden-yellow. Grow the tulip tree in a large garden where it can reach its full size unhindered, in full sun or partial shade, and fertile, moist, well-drained soil.

◊ ◊ ☼ ☀ ✳ ✳ ✳
‡ to 30m (100ft) ↔ to 15m (50ft)

MISCANTHUS SINENSIS *'Zebrinus'*

Perennial

Zebra grass will bring drama and height to a mixed or herbaceous border, or a gravel bed. It bears tall, strap-like foliage marked with yellow horizontal bands. This grass forms a large clump and produces spikes of silky, maroon flowerheads in the autumn. Leave the foliage and flowers to dry to a buff colour during the autumn and winter, and then cut them down in spring to make way for new growth.

◊ ◊ ☼ ☀ ✳ ✳ ✳
‡ to 2.5m (8ft) ↔ to 1.2m (4ft)

ACHILLEA
'Coronation Gold' ♛

Perennial

The bright-yellow flowerheads of yarrow are made up of numerous tiny flowers gathered together in broad, flat clusters. The grey-green, deeply cut leaves provide a perfect foil for them. This vigorous plant tolerates a wide range of growing conditions but does best in a sunny situation, in well-drained, fertile soil. It is a lovely plant for a wildflower garden. When cut and dried, the flowerheads retain their colour well. Propagate by division in autumn.

◊ ◊ ☼ ✿ ✿ ✿
‡ to 90cm (36in) ↔ to 45cm (18in)

ACHILLEA FILIPENDULINA
'Cloth of Gold' ♛

Perennial

Although this plant grows nearly double the height of 'Coronation Gold', it is actually less vigorous. It has attractive, feathery, light green leaves and bears large, golden-yellow flowerheads, up to 12cm (5in) across, from early summer right through until early autumn. It is ideal for growing in a herbaceous border and will thrive in any well-drained soil. By late spring, the tall stems will need supporting with canes. Good for cutting fresh or for drying.

◊ ◊ ☼ ✿ ✿ ✿
‡↔ to 1.5m (5ft)

ALCHEMILLA MOLLIS ♥

Perennial

After rain or heavy dew, the downy
leaves of lady's mantle glisten with
water droplets captured in the hairs on
their surface. From early summer to
early autumn large, airy sprays of tiny
yellow-green flowers are produced,
which are good for cutting. Fairly
drought resistant, it is tolerant of most
soil conditions, and although it prefers
full sun it will also grow in partial
shade. Plant it along the edge of a path
or in a wildflower border, where it will
self-seed freely.

○ ◐ ☼ ☀ ❉ ❉ ❉
‡ to 60cm (24in) ↔ to 75cm (30in)

ALLIUM FLAVUM ♥

Perennial bulb

A large clump of these alliums would
look wonderful at the front of a border.
A satisfyingly fast-growing bulb, it
produces stems topped with up to
60 delicately scented, bright yellow
flowers. These dangle on slender stalks
but turn upwards when the seed is
developing. The bluey-green leaves are
waxy and cylindrical. Plant bulbs in
autumn in a sunny position, in well-
drained soil.

○ ☼ ❉ ❉ ❉
‡ to 35cm (14in) ↔ to 5cm (2in)

ALLIUM MOLY

Perennial bulb

The golden garlic produces clusters of up to 30 golden-yellow, star-shaped flowers on slender stems. Its waxy, lance-shaped leaves are usually produced in pairs. Plant in a sunny situation, in fertile, well-drained soil. It often self-seeds freely and can become invasive, which, if grown in a wild garden or naturalized in woodland, is more of an asset than a problem. Plant bulbs and, if necessary, divide large clumps in autumn.

◊ ☼ ✽ ✽ ✽
‡ to 25cm (10in) ↔ to 5cm (2in)

ANTHEMIS TINCTORIA
'E.C. Buxton'

Perennial

Filigree foliage and a long-flowering season make the golden marguerite a great-value border plant. A clump-forming evergreen, it produces masses of lemon-yellow, daisy-like flowers with deep yellow centres. The leaves are mid-green above and a soft downy-grey on the reverse. Cut back hard after flowering to reinvigorate the plant and encourage it to produce a neat clump of leaves for next spring. Plant it in a sunny position, in well-drained soil.

◊ ☼ ✽ ✽ ✽
‡ to 70cm (28in) ↔ to 60cm (24in)

ARGYRANTHEMUM
'Jamaica Primrose' ♥

Perennial

In frost-free areas, this plant will just
keep on flowering; elsewhere it is
usually grown as summer bedding or in
containers. Beautiful, soft-yellow, daisy-
like flowers and deeply divided, fern-
like, mid-green leaves are a winning
combination. Grow in moderately fertile,
well-drained soil in full sun. Pot up the
whole plant and move under glass for
winter, or take stem cuttings in early
autumn and grow on undercover for
next year. Easy to train as a standard.

◊ ☼ ❉

‡ to 1.1m (3½ft) ↔ to 1m (3ft)

ASPHODELINE LUTEA

Perennial

An unusual, clump-forming plant that
produces a fountain of greyish-green,
grass-like foliage. The tall flower spikes
appear in early summer and are covered
with yellow, star-shaped flowers. After
flowering the plant dies down but new
leaves start to push through in autumn.
It needs a well-drained, not too rich,
soil in full sun – a sunny bank would
be ideal. Propagate by division, but
take care not to damage the fleshy
roots. It can also be grown from seed
sown in autumn or spring.

◊ ☼ ❉ ❉ ❉

‡ to 1.5m (5ft) ↔ to 30cm (12in)

BIDENS FERULIFOLIA ♀

Perennial

The trailing stems of this plant can be best appreciated when tumbling over the edges of a window box or used to plump up the planting in a hanging basket. It has large, daisy-like, golden-yellow flowers and bright green, filigree foliage and stems. A short-lived perennial, it is usually grown as an annual and is best propagated by taking cuttings at the end of the year. It needs moist, but well-drained, fertile soil. Plants grown in a conservatory or heated greenhouse may flower until winter.

○ ☼ ❀ ❀

‡ to 30cm (12in) ↔ indefinite

BRACHYGLOTTIS 'Sunshine' ♀

Evergreen shrub

A free-flowering habit and attractive silvery-grey, slightly woolly foliage make this mound-forming plant a useful addition to any shrub border. From early to midsummer it produces a profusion of bright yellow, daisy-like flowers. Plant it in a sunny situation, in well-drained fertile soil. It does well in coastal areas but needs to be protected from strong cold winds inland. Prune in the early spring to keep the bush tidy and well shaped.

○ ☼ ❀ ❀ ❀

‡ to 1.5m (5ft) ↔ to 2m (6ft)

BUPHTHALMUM SALICIFOLIUM

Perennial

Yellow ox-eye has dark green, narrow leaves and deep yellow, daisy-like flowers held on long, willowy stems In late spring, insert supports so they are in place before the flowers open. When cut, the flowers are long lasting. It is best grown in full sun in well-drained, poor soil. If given richer soil it may become invasive, in which case, divide plants regularly to keep them in check. In certain situations, however, its spreading habit would be useful, such as on a bank or in a wild garden.

◊ ☼ ❊ ❊ ❊
‡ to 60cm (24in) ↔ to 45cm (18in)

CALCEOLARIA
'John Innes'

Perennial

Curiously pouch-shaped and often beautifully marked, the flowers of the slipper flower are a delight. 'John Innes' has intense yellow flowers with red brown spots. It is a vigorous, clump-forming plant that needs a well-drained, moderately fertile, acid soil in sun or partial shade. It is not fully hardy, so pot up and take under glass in winter, or take softwood cuttings in summer and keep the plants in a cold frame during winter as an insurance policy.

◊ ☼ ❊ ❊
‡ to 20cm (8in) ↔ to 30cm (12in)

CALLISTEMON PALLIDUS

Evergreen shrub

Aptly named, the yellow bottle brush
bristles with stiff-stemmed, greenish-
yellow flowers. Its graceful arching
branches are covered with greyish-
green leaves that are tinged with pink
when they are young. Plant in full sun,
in well-drained, neutral to acid soil. Not
entirely hardy, it needs a sheltered spot
against a south- or west-facing wall.
Alternatively, plant it in a container
of loam-based compost and overwinter
in a cool greenhouse.

◊ ☼ ❋
‡↔ to 4m (12ft)

CAREX ELATA
'Aurea' ♀

Perennial

A vibrantly coloured, ornamental
sedge-like plant, Bowles' golden sedge
is an evergreen that is grown for its
gently arching, green-margined, bright
yellow leaves. In early summer, it may
throw up long, brown, male flower
spikes. It requires a site in full sun, in
a fertile, moist, but well-drained, soil.
To keep the tufts neat and tidy, cut
out dead leaves in summer. Plant in a
container, or in groups near water or a
in mixed border.

◊ ◐ ☼ ☀ ❋ ❋ ❋
‡ to 70cm (28in) ↔ to 45cm (18in)

CENTAUREA MACROCEPHALA
Perennial

An imposing ornamental for the back of
a herbaceous border, this thistle-like
plant has deeply cut, lance-shaped,
slightly hairy leaves. The rounded
flowerheads, which are good for cutting
and drying, are enclosed in papery
bracts that split open to reveal a sunny
burst of bright yellow petals. Grow in
moist, but well-drained, soil in full sun
or light shade.

○ ◑ ☼ ☀ ✳ ✳ ✳
‡ to 1.5m (5ft) ↔ to 80cm (24in))

COREOPSIS GRANDIFLORA
'Badengold'
Perennial

Bees love the daisy-like flowers of
tickseeds, as do flower arrangers who
value them for their long life after
cutting. 'Badengold', is a short-lived
perennial that is most often grown as
an annual. Sow seed *in situ* from early
spring to early summer. Its orange-
centred, yellow blooms are held aloft
on tall stems above bright green, lance-
shaped leaves. It needs a sunny spot, in
well-drained, fertile soil. Dead-heading
helps prolong flowering.

○ ☼ ✳ ✳ ✳
‡ to 75cm (30in) ↔ to 60cm (24in)

COREOPSIS VERTICILLATA
'Grandiflora' ♀

Perennial

A good choice for a sunny herbaceous border, this cheerful tickseed bears masses of single, yellow flowers in early summer. Dead-heading helps prolong the flowering period. Plants raised from seed sown in early to mid-spring in a prepared seedbed will go on to flower the same year, while the feathery, mid-green leaves quickly knit together to form a good-sized clump. Plant in fertile, well-drained soil in full sun or light shade. A good cut flower and bee plant.

◊ ☼ ❄ ❄ ❄
‡ to 60cm (24in) ↔ to 30cm (12in)

CYTISUS BATTANDIERI ♀

Deciduous shrub

In early summer, the pineapple broom produces tight clusters of fruit-scented, bright yellow, lupin-like flowers. Its silvery-green leaves are carried on arching, spreading branches, giving the bush an open shape. Although not fully hardy, it should overwinter successfully if it is planted in a sunny, sheltered spot by a wall, in well-drained, sandy, moderately fertile soil. Other than to remove shoots that spoil the symmetry of the bush – do this in early spring – it does not really need pruning.

◊ ☼ ❄ ❄
‡ ↔ to 5m (15ft)

DELPHINIUM
'Sungleam' ♀

Perennial

In early summer, this stunning
delphinium sends up tall, tapering
spires of creamy-yellow flowers with
strong yellow eyes. A second flush of
flowers can be encouraged by cutting
down the flower spikes as soon as they
fade. Plant it in groups in a sunny
position in well-drained, humus-rich,
fertile soil. To prevent wind damage,
especially on exposed sites, insert
strong canes when planting and tie
in the flower stems as they grow.

◊ ☼ ✿ ✿ ✿
‡ to 1.5m (5ft) ↔ to 90cm (36in)

DIGITALIS GRANDIFLORA ♀

Perennial

Overwintering as a rosette of deep
green leaves, the yellow foxglove is an
upright, short-lived, perennial that
produces its spikes of pale lemon,
tubular flowers in early summer. It
prefers a semi-shaded situation and
damp, well-drained soil, where it will
happily self-seed. Deadheading after
flowering will check its spread. Grow
the slightly smaller *D. lutea* if you have
an alkaline soil. Both varieties would
suit a wild garden or a less formal
mixed border.

◊ ◊ ☼ ✿ ✿ ✿
‡ to 1m (3ft) ↔ to 45cm (18in)

EREMURUS STENOPHYLLUS ♀

Perennial

The foxtail lily produces canary-yellow flowers, fading to copper, on spikes that soar above other early summer border plants. Although fairly hardy, they start to grow early in the year and the young buds are prone to frost damage. Cover the crowns in winter and spring with fleece, straw or bracken to protect the emerging shoots. The bent, strappy leaves will die down when the flower spike starts to emerge. Plant in very well-drained, sandy soil in full sun. An excellent cut flower.

○ ☼ ❁ ❁ ❁
‡ to 1m (3ft) ↔ to 60cm (24in)

ERIOPHYLLUM LANATUM

Perennial

The woolly sunflower has silvery-green, slightly furry, deeply divided leaves that knit together to form a dense mat. The deep yellow, daisy-like flowers are produced right through summer. Plant in full sun, in well-drained, light soil. Fairly drought tolerant, it is a good plant for rock gardens and crevices in walls and paving. To keep it compact, trim back after flowering has finished. Divide plants in spring.

○ ☼ ❁ ❁ ❁
‡↔ to 60cm (24in)

EUPHORBIA PALUSTRIS ♈

Perennial

Needing soil that is permanently moist, this spurge would make an unusual waterside plant for an informal pond. The strong stems are covered with narrow, lime-green leaves topped, in early summer, by clusters of greeny-yellow flowers. In autumn, the leaves turn various shades of yellow and orange. Choose a site in full sun. Avoid skin contact with the milky sap.

◊ ☼ ❁ ❁ ❁
‡↔ to 90cm (36in)

GAZANIA
'Talent Yellow'

Perennial

A superb plant for providing a splash of colour in patio containers and as summer bedding, this tender perennial is usually grown as an annual because it rarely survives a cold winter. It has greyish-green, felted leaves and open, yellow flowers, which are produced over a long period. It must be planted in full sun because a quirk of gazanias is that the flowers close on dull or cool days. Best planted in light, sandy, well-drained soil. Tolerant of coastal conditions.

◊ ☼ ❁
‡↔ to 25cm (10in)

GENISTA AETNENSIS ♀

Deciduous tree

The Mount Etna broom forms a large shrub or medium-sized tree with green, arching, almost leafless branches. In summer it explodes into colour, producing masses of fragrant, yellow, pea-like flowers. It makes a spectacular specimen tree for a sunny situation, with a canopy that is light enough to allow underplanting. Pruning is unnecessary, except to remove damaged stems. Plant in well-drained, light, poor to moderately fertile soil.

△ ☼ ✿ ✿
↕↔ to 8m (25ft)

GENISTA LYDIA ♀

Deciduous shrub

Ideally suited to the well-drained conditions of a rock garden or raised bed, this dome-shaped, low-growing shrub will trail over sunny walls and rocks. In early summer, its prickle-tipped, grey-green, arching branches are covered in bright yellow, pea-like flowers. It prefers hot sites in poor, light soils that have not been enriched. Take semi-ripe cuttings in summer or sow seed in autumn. Pruning is unnecessary and straggly plants are best replaced.

△ ☼ ✿ ✿ ✿
↕ to 60cm (24in) ↔ to 1m (3ft)

GEUM
'Lady Stratheden' ♀
Perennial

Geums are especially suitable for the
front of a herbaceous border. They
form clumps of arching, kidney-shaped
leaves that have a covering of fine
hairs. The cup-shaped, semi-double,
golden-yellow flowers are carried on
branching stems. Plant in full sun, in
moist but well-drained soil. Divide
large clumps in autumn. Unlike many
geums, 'Lady Stratheden' will come
true from seed.

○ ◑ ☼ ❀ ❀ ❀
↕ ↔ to 60cm (24in)

HELIANTHUS ANNUUS
Annual

A fast-growing, unfussy flower that is a
favourite with children. The growth
spurt of some of the giant sunflowers is
spectacular – in one season they can
reach 3m (10ft). The large daisy-like
flowers have long yellow petals and a
dark purply-brown centre. If left to dry,
the seedhead will provide valuable food
for the bird table over winter. Sunflowers
need a sunny position, in well-drained,
fertile soil. Grow them from seed each
year. Tall growing plants will need
staking and a sheltered site.

○ ☼ ❀ ❀ ❀
↕ to 3m (10ft) ↔ to 60cm (24in)

HELICHRYSUM ITALICUM *SUBSP.* SEROTINUM

Perennial

The curry plant is grown for its aromatic, evergreen, sage-green foliage and clusters of yellow flowers. Despite its common name, the leaves of this plant are not used in curry powder, however, they are edible and their savoury tang can be used to enliven cream cheese, egg or chicken dishes. It can suffer during wet winters and should be planted in a raised bed or open, sunny situation in very well-drained soil.

○ ☼ ❀ ❀
‡ to 40cm (16in) ↔ to 75cm (30in)

HEMEROCALLIS LILIOASPHODELUS ♀

Perennial

There are thousands of cultivated daylilies to choose from but this species is up there with the best of them. It is vigorous and easy to grow, with funnel-shaped, fragrant flowers that only last for a day or two, but are soon replaced. They open in the afternoon and last through the night, so plant a clump close to the patio or other area in the garden that you use in the evening. Plant in full sun, in moist, but well-drained, soil. Divide large clumps in spring.

○ ◐ ☼ ❀ ❀ ❀
‡↔ to 1m (3ft)

HEMEROCALLIS
'Stella de Oro'

Perennial

Daylilies are perfect herbaceous border plants. Their narrow, arching leaves quickly form an attractive clump; and while their colourful flowers may only last a day or so, they appear in rapid succession over several weeks. Happiest in full sun, in moist, but well-drained, soil, daylilies will tolerate the damp margins of a pond. 'Stella de Oro' is a compact form that is very free-flowering and powerfully fragrant. Propagate by division in spring.

◊ ◊ ☼ ❄ ❄ ❄
‡ to 30cm (12in) ↔ to 45cm (18in)

HUMULUS LUPULUS
'Aureus' ♀

Climber

A herbaceous climber that will quickly clothe a pergola or fence. Male and female flowers grow on separate plants, with the female producing the hops. The yellow colour of 'Aureus' – which is far less vigorous than commercially grown hops – is transitory because the leaves turn green later in the year. Grow in moist, but well-drained, soil. Full sun will enhance leaf colour. Remove remains of old growth in early spring. Dry hops for decoration.

◊ ◊ ☼ ❄ ❄ ❄
‡ to 6m (20ft)

IRIS
'Brown Lasso' ♀

Perennial

Bearded irises come in a wide range
of colours. 'Brown Lasso' is a lovely
combination of yellow upper petals
and lilac lower petals edged with
butterscotch. Each stem carries 6–12
of these three-toned flowers. Plant in
fertile, well-drained, neutral to acid soil,
in full sun. Divide clumps when they
become congested, usually after 3–5
years. The upright, sword-shaped leaves
remain after the flowers have faded to
add form to the herbaceous border.

○ ☼ ✽ ✽ ✽
‡ to 55cm (22in) ↔ indefinite

IRIS INNOMINATA

Perennial

This attractive Pacific Coast iris
originates from the West coast of the
United States. It has pale yellow to
cream flowers with bold brown veining.
Other colours include purple and pale
lavender. It is quite a small plant, rarely
exceeding a height of 25cm (10in), with
narrow, dark green, evergreen leaves
that flush to purple at their base. Easily
swamped in a border, it is best
appreciated in a raised bed or trough.
Plant in full sun or partial shade, in
neutral or slightly acid soil.

○ ☼ ☀ ✽ ✽ ✽
‡ to 25cm (10in) ↔ to 30cm (12in)

KNIPHOFIA
'Wrexham Buttercup'

Perennial

A yellow red hot poker, 'Wrexham Buttercup' bears tapering spikes of tubular flowers, lightly tipped with orange. It is similar to, but rather larger than, 'Buttercup' (see below). Grow in full sun or light shade, in fertile, moist, but well-drained soil. Red hot pokers are classic herbaceous border plants and a favourite of bees. Leave remains of old foliage in place over winter for protection and remove in spring, when large clumps can also be divided.

○ ◐ ☼ ☀ ❀ ❀ ❀
‡ to 1.2m (4ft) ↔ to 60cm (24in)

KNIPHOFIA
'Buttercup' ♀

Perennial

A robust red hot poker, 'Buttercup' will hold its own in a busy herbaceous border. It forms a large clump of narrow, strappy leaves and, in early summer, produces several tall spikes of clear yellow flowers that open from green buds. They are very attractive to bees. For best results, plant in full sun or light shade, in fertile, moist but well-drained soil. Old foliage offers protection over winter; remove it in spring and divide large clumps.

○ ◐ ☼ ☀ ❀ ❀ ❀
‡↔ to 75cm (30in)

LIGULARIA PRZEWALSKII ♥

Perennial

Tall, narrow spikes of yellow flowers on purple-green stems rise in stately fashion above a robust clump of deeply divided leaves. A lover of deep, moist soil, this plant would look wonderful beside a large pond. Another situation it would suit is tucked towards the back of a permanently moist, mixed or herbaceous border where, sheltered among other plants, it is less vulnerable to strong, gusting winds. Although it is happy in full sun, light shade during the middle of the day would be ideal.

🌢 🌢 ☼ ☼ ❀ ❀ ❀
‡ to 2m (6ft) ↔ to 1m (3ft)

LIMNANTHES DOUGLASII ♥

Annual

The two-tone petals of this fast-growing, hardy annual inspired its common name of poached-egg plant. It has deeply divided, slightly succulent, glossy green leaves, and stays in flower over a long period right through summer. Sow seed *in situ* during spring or late summer in moist, but well-drained, fertile soil. Use it to edge a path or dot it among rows of vegetables where it will attract hoverflies which help control aphids.

🌢 ☼ ❀ ❀ ❀
‡↔ to 15cm (6in)

LONICERA PERICLYMENUM
'Graham Thomas' ♀

Climber

A vigorous climber with white flowers
that turn yellow with age and are
followed by glossy, red berries. Grow
it through trees and over pergolas or
trellis, or it can be used as ground cover
and over banks. The flowers are highly
fragrant and attract night-flying moths
and insects. Bear this in mind if you are
considering planting it near the house.
Plant in sun or partial shade in any
reasonable soil. Cut established plants
back by up to a third after flowering

◊ ◊ ☼ ※ ✿ ✿ ✿
‡ to 7m (22ft)

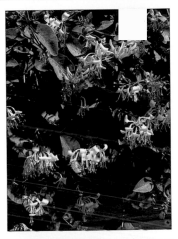

LUPINUS ARBOREUS ♀

Evergreen shrub

Tree lupins are strong shrubs, often
evergreen in mild winters, with
sprawling branches of greyish-green
leaves. They make wonderful specimen
plants in a hot, dry border. The species
has fragrant, sulphur-yellow flowers,
but there are also lavender or white
forms. The tree lupin is not fully hardy
and may be damaged by hard frost, so
plant it in a sunny position, in sandy,
well-drained soil, preferably by the
coast where it grows very well.
Propagate by seed in spring.

◊ ☼ ✿ ✿ ✿
‡↔ to 2m (6ft)

MIMULUS GUTTATUS

Perennial

The monkey flower is at home in the deep, moist soil beside a stream or pond where it forms a spreading mat of toothed, mid-green leaves. Through summer until autumn it produces tall, narrow spikes of deep yellow flowers, which are often freckled with reddish brown spots. Their shape resembles the intricate flowers of the snapdragon (*Antirrhinum*). Plant in full sun or in dappled shade. Monkey flowers tend to be shortlived, so propagate plants by dividing them in spring.

◊ ◖ ☼ ☀ ✻ ✻ ✻
‡ to 30cm (12in) ↔ to 60cm (24in)

OENOTHERA FRUTICOSA
'*Fyrverkeri*' ♀

Perennial

The scented, deep yellow flowers of the evening primrose open at dusk and are pollinated by night-flying insects. While they may last only a day or so, the flowers are produced in abundance all summer long. The plant has striking red stems and, when young, the lance-shaped leaves are flushed red, too. It is a good plant for a raised bed, gravel garden, or the front of a herbaceous border. Grow it in full sun or partial shade, in well-drained, sandy soil.

◊ ☼ ☀ ✻ ✻ ✻
‡ to 1m (3ft) ↔ to 30cm (12in)

PHLOMIS FRUTICOSA ♀

Evergreen shrub

Jerusalem sage forms a mound of aromatic, felted, grey-green leaves. From early to midsummer, short stems of golden-yellow, hooded flowers are produced in bunches. A massed planting would suit a sunny border or a gravel garden with well-drained, light soil. Although generally hardy, there is a risk it may be killed by particularly cold, damp winters – in cold areas, give it the shelter of a warm wall. Propagate by taking cuttings in summer.

△ ☼ ❀ ❀ ❀
‡ to 1m (3ft) ↔ to 1.5m (5ft)

PRIMULA FLORINDAE ♀

Perennial

The giant Himalayan cowslip is one of the largest primulas, with a handsome basal rosette of mid-green, toothed leaves. The freshly fragrant, sulphur-yellow, bell-shaped flowers are borne on tall stems up to 1.2m (4ft) high. It should be planted in full sun or partial shade in moist, humus-rich, neutral or slightly acid soil. Plant in swathes along a stream bank, or in large groups in a bog or woodland garden, or around the margins of a natural pond.

♦ ☼ ☼ ❀ ❀ ❀
‡ to 1.2m (4ft) ↔ to 90cm (36in)

RANUNCULUS CONSTANTINOPOLITANUS *'Plenus'*

Perennial

This cultivated buttercup has neat, double, yellow-green pompon flowers in early summer. It has deeply divided leaves, which are often dotted with greyish-white spots. It is a well-behaved plant that would suit a rock garden or mixed border. Plant it in full sun in moist, but well-drained, soil. Propagate by dividing the woody roots after flowering has finished.

◊ ◊ ☀ ❀ ❀ ❀
↕ to 50cm (20in) ↔ to 30cm (12in)

RHODIOLA ROSEA

Perennial

The waxy-covered, triangular-shaped leaves of roseroot clump together to form a neat mound of stiffly erect stems. In early summer it produces large heads of pink buds that open to greenish-yellow, star-shaped flowers. Give it a sunny spot in well-drained, moderately fertile soil in a rock garden, dry walls, or at the front of a raised bed or herbaceous border.

◊ ☀ ❀ ❀ ❀
↕↔ to 30cm (12in)

ROSA
Graham Thomas   ♀

Deciduous shrub

This superb modern shrub rose forms
a nicely rounded bush. It never gets out
of hand and is one of the best yellow
roses available. All through summer
until autumn, it has deep golden-
yellow, cup shaped, fragrant flowers.
If space allows, plant in a group of 4–5,
in full sun in well-drained, humus-rich,
fertile soil. Shrub roses are suitable for
growing in mixed borders and need
less rich growing conditions than bush
roses such as Mountbatten.

◊ ☼ ❄ ❄ ❄
‡ to 1.2m (4ft) ↔ to 1.5m (5ft)

ROSA
Mountbatten   ♀

Deciduous shrub

A very vigorous, repeat-flowering
floribunda rose, with double, fragrant,
deep yellow flowers. It forms a nice
bush with plenty of glossy green
foliage. Plant it in a sunny position in
well-drained soil, enriched with plenty
of organic matter. Remove dead flowers
to encourage the production of new
buds. Prune main stems to about 30cm
(12in) above the ground in early spring,
then apply a balanced fertilizer and a
thick mulch of well-rotted manure.

◊ ☼ ❄ ❄ ❄
‡ to 1.2m (4ft) ↔ to 75cm (30in)

ROSA XANTHINA
'Canary Bird' ♀

Deciduous shrub

This is a very decorative, but rather large, shrub rose suitable for a wild garden, as it needs a lot of space to develop well. It produces long, arching branches covered in early summer with single, saucer-shaped, lightly fragrant, deep-yellow flowers. A smattering of flowers may appear until autumn. In exposed areas it is vulnerable to severe frost and the young buds may be damaged by cold winds. Grow in moist, but well-drained, fertile soil, in full sun.

◊ ☼ ❀ ❀ ❀
‡ to 3m (10ft) ↔ to 4m (12ft)

SEDUM ACRE
'Aureum'

Perennial

A mat-forming plant, with upright or sprawling stems that are covered with small fleshy, green leaves with yellow variegated tips. The bright yellow, star-shaped flowers are borne throughout the summer. Given the right conditions – full sun and a very well-drained soil – it may become invasive, but it is easily controlled. It makes a colourful plant for a trough filled with gritty compost, a raised bed, or a rock garden. Take cuttings in spring or late summer.

◊ ☼ ❀ ❀ ❀
‡ to 5cm (2in) ↔ to 60cm (24in)

THERMOPSIS RHOMBIFOLIA VAR. MONTANA

Perennial

An upright plant with divided leaves and tall spikes of bright yellow, pea-like flowers that are attractive to bees. Although tolerant of a wide range of conditions, it prefers a sunny spot in fertile, light, sandy soil. Often used to provide vertical accent in a herbaceous border, it is perhaps best suited to an informal wildlife garden where its invasive tendencies are more easily accommodated. Propagate by division in spring or sow seed in autumn.

◊ ◊ ☼ ☀ ✻ ✻ ✻
‡ to 90cm (36in) ↔ to 60cm (24in)

VERBASCUM 'Gainsborough' ♀

Perennial

This mullein is one of the Cotswold hybrids and overwinters as a large rosette of downy, greyish-green leaves. In early summer it springs into action and produces a stately spire of saucer-shaped, pale yellow flowers. Further flowers often appear on side branches. A long-flowering plant for a herbaceous border, it is, sadly, rather short-lived. Plant in a sunny position, in well-drained fertile soil.

◊ ☼ ✻ ✻ ✻
‡ to 1.2m (4ft) ↔ to 30cm (12in)

BEGONIA
'City of Ballarat'
Perennial

Bright orange flowers, up to 18cm (7in)
across, adorn this tuberous begonia.
Grow it in containers of loam-based
compost as a houseplant, and move it
outside in summer. It can be used as
bedding if the tubers are lifted in
autumn before the first frost and stored
in trays of dry sand in a cool place. In
early spring, moisten the trays of tubers
and move them to a warm place before
planting out in late spring, in moist but
well drained soil in partial shade.

◊ ☼ ❋

‡ to 60cm (24in) ↔ to 45cm (18in)

BUDDLEJA GLOBOSA ♀
Deciduous shrub

The orange ball tree forms a large
shrub or small tree, with spherical
clusters of dark orange or yellow,
fragrant flowers It has lance-shaped
leaves, which may be semi-evergreen
in sheltered areas. It can be used in
a shrub border or makes a good
specimen plant, although it tends to get
leggy with age. It prefers a sunny site
in well-drained, preferably chalky soil.
Pruning is unecessary.

◊ ☼ ❋ ❋ ❋

‡↔ to 5m (15ft)

EREMURUS × ISABELLINUS
'Cleopatra'

Perennial

This is a dramatic foxtail lily, with tall,
stately spikes of deep orange flowers,
held above mid-green, lance-shaped
leaves. It needs to be grown in very
well-drained, fertile, sandy soil in full
sun. The fleshy roots will quickly rot if
the soil becomes too wet, so it is
advisable to plant it in a raised bed,
where any excess water will quickly
drain away. Mulch them over in winter
with straw, bracken or fleece to protect
the emerging shoots.

◊ ☼ ✿ ✿ ✿
‡ to 1.5m (5ft) ↔ to 90cm (36in)

ESCHSCHOLZIA CALIFORNICA

Annual

Perfect for a sun-drenched situation in
a Mediterranean-style or gravel garden,
the Californian poppy has decorative
finely-divided, feathery, blue-green
foliage, and bright yellow-orange cup-
shaped flowers. The blooms open in
full sun and close as the light dims at
the end of the day, and appear from
early to midsummer. Sow them *in situ*
in spring, or autumn where winters are
mild in poor, free-draining soil, and
deadhead them regularly to stimulate
new flowers to develop.

◊ ☼ ✿ ✿ ✿
‡ to 30cm (12in) ↔ to 15cm (6in)

GLADIOLUS
'Peter Pears'

Perennial corm

The green, sword-shaped leaves of this gladiolus set off beautifully the spikes of apricot flowers. In a border, plant corms in spring, in groups of 5–10. The flower stems will need to be supported early to prevent them blowing over. Like other gladioli, it makes a good cut flower. Grow it in full sun in fertile, well-drained soil, with added organic matter. In autumn, lift the corms, dry them, and then overwinter in a frost-free place. until mid- to late spring.

◊ ☼ ❀

‡ to 1.7m (5½ft) ↔ to 35cm (14in)

HEMEROCALLIS FULVA
'Flore Pleno'

Perennial

This is a vigorous daylily, which forms large clumps of mid-green, strap-shaped foliage. In summer, it bears a constant succession of double, brownish-orange flowers with darker stripes inside. It needs to be planted in full sun in moist, well-drained soil. Shade or very dry conditions will reduce the number of flowers produced. Use this daylily in a mixed or herbaceous border, or in a gravel bed. It could also be planted in a container if kept well watered.

◊ ◑ ☼ ☼ ❀ ❀ ❀

‡ to 75cm (30in) ↔ to 90cm (36in)

IRIS
'Blue Eyed Brunette'

Perennial

The name of this bearded iris accurately brings to mind the colour of its distinctive flowers. The petals are tinted orange-brown, with the lower set highlighted with a bright lilac spot, surmounted by a golden-yellow 'beard'. Use it in a mixed or herbaceous border and combine it with bronze grasses, such as *Carex flagellifera*, to create an unusual colour theme. Plant in a sunny situation in well-drained, fertile, neutral to acid soil (see 'Bold Print' p 159).

◊ ☼ ❄ ❄ ❄
‡ to 90cm (36in) ↔ indefinite

KNIPHOFIA
'Bees' Sunset' ♀

Perennial

A beautiful red hot poker, 'Bees' Sunset' produces tall spikes of pale orange, tubular flowers over a long period from early summer. Grow it in groups in a fiery colour-themed border or gravel garden. It complements pale yellow and bright red flowers, such as dahlias. Plant it in moist, well drained soil in full sun or partial shade. Leave the remains of the old foliage over winter for protection and remove it in spring, when large clumps can also be divided.

◊ ◊ ☼ ☼ ❄ ❄ ❄
‡ to 90cm (36in) ↔ to 60cm (24in)

PAPAVER
'Fireball'

Perennial

This low-growing poppy has cheerful, bright orange flowers which open from bristly buds in early summer. The foliage is very hairy, and provides good ground cover. Grow it towards the front of a border or in a gravel garden; it spreads by running stems but is not difficult to keep within bounds. Choose a position in full sun in any reasonably fertile, well-drained soil. Deadhead regularly to keep the flowers coming. Large clumps can be divided in spring.

⬦ ☼ ❋ ❋ ❋
‡ to 40cm (16in) ↔ to 30cm (12in) or more

ROSA
'Just Joey' ♥

Deciduous shrub

A hybrid tea rose, with large, pinkish-orange, slightly fragrant blooms that will appear throughout summer with regular deadheading. It grows to form a medium-sized bush with dark green leaves. It can be used in a border, but it is best grown *en masse* in a rose bed, and is very good for cutting. Plant it in sun, in fertile, moist, well-drained soil, perferably neutral or slightly acid and enriched with organic matter. For further care see *Rosa* 'Blessings' (p.195).

⬦◐ ☼ ❋ ❋ ❋
‡ to 75cm (30in) ↔ to 70cm (28in)

TAGETES
'Tangerine Gem'

Annual

An upright Signet marigold with ferny,
dark green leaves. It is very free
flowering, producing vast numbers of
single, orange flowers throughout the
summer. These marigolds make
excellent edging and bedding plants, or
use them in hanging baskets and
containers. Plant them in full sun, in
fertile, well-drained soil and deadhead
regularly. They are easily raised from
seed sown in early spring in pots on a
windowsill or under glass.

◊ ☼ ❄

‡ to 20cm (8in) ↔ to 30cm (12in)

TROPAEOLUM MAJUS

Climber

Nasturtiums are colourful annuals with
rounded, pale green leaves, held on
climbing or scrambling stems. They are
very free flowering and bear orange,
yellow and red long-spurred flowers.
Plant nasturtiums in containers, hanging
baskets or use them in an annual or
herbaceous border trained up a tripod.
They prefer a sunny situation and
moist, well-drained soil. Check plants
regularly for caterpillars and black fly,
and remove them before the plants
become infested.

◊ ◐ ☼ ❄

‡ to 30cm (12in)

LATE SUMMER

Many of the plants that bless the hottest and driest time of year are annuals. Sweet peas, sunflowers, marigolds, clarkia and nasturtiums are just a few that can make a cheerful show in a border. Other plants, used as annuals, can join them, like salvias and *Ricinus communis* 'Carmencita'. Unlike most annuals, which are sun-lovers, tobacco plants (*Nicotiana*) also thrive in shade where their pastels and lime-greens glow alluringly. As with sweet peas, not all are scented, so check the variety if fragrance is required.

Fuchsias bloom continuously; the large frilly flowers of many are favourites for hanging baskets and pots, along with pelargoniums. As temperatures soar, water containers on a daily basis. It is also vital to water new plants in dry periods. Give priority to trees, shrubs and climbers planted less than a year ago and water generously so moisture penetrates deep below the soil surface.

Borders and gravel gardens are aglow with coneflowers (*Echinacea* and *Rudbeckia*) and red-hot pokers (*Kniphofia*), but for sheer elegance a white colour theme is hard to beat. Combine *Anemone* × *hybrida* 'Honorine Jobert', *Epilobium angustifolium* var. *album,* and tall white dahlias, hollyhocks and lilies for a display that takes on a luminous quality at dusk. To extend the show into autumn, keep deadheading and fill any gaps with fast growers like penstemon.

HOT TROPICAL STYLE
Mirror the heat of summer days with combinations of red and orange flowers. *Phygelius* × *rectus* 'African Queen' and dahlias like 'Bishop of Llandaff' and 'Wootton Impact' will set the garden alight. Punctuate them with red-hot pokers, and choose *Ensete ventricosum*, cannas, agaves and yuccas to increase the tropical flavour with their flamboyant foliage.

ABELIA X GRANDIFLORA ♥

Evergreen shrub

This large rounded plant has arching branches, and glossy dark green leaves. It flowers from mid- to late summer and produces fragrant, funnel-shaped, pink-flushed white flowers. Plant in a sunny site in a sheltered position, or against a west-facing wall, where it will be protected from cold, damaging winds. Grow it in fertile, well-drained soil, and to rejuvenate established plants, cut out some of the older stems after flowering.

○ ☼ ❋ ❋
‡ to 3m (10ft) ↔ to 4m (12ft)

ACTAEA ALBA

Perennial

The white baneberry forms a clump of toothed leaves, divided into egg-shaped leaflets. In late spring or early summer it produces spikes of small white flowers, followed in late summer by shiny, round, white toxic berries held on red stems. It grows best in a shady situation in deep, moist soil, which should be watered during the summer to prevent it from drying out.

◕ ☼ ❋ ❋ ❋
‡ to 1m (3ft) ↔ to 50cm (20in)

AESCULUS PARVIFLORA ♀

Deciduous shrub

A close relative of the horse chestnut, the bottlebrush buckeye has similar leaves, which are divided into several long, slightly waxy, bronze green leaflets. In midsummer, it produces tall spikes of white flowers. In the autumn the leaves turn bright yellow. It is a very tolerant plant, and can be grown in full sun or partial shade, preferring fertile, slightly moist but well-drained soil. The bush spreads by suckers, which can be separated and replanted, or removed to control the spread.

◊ ◊ ☼ ☼ ✽ ✽ ✽
‡ to 3m (10ft) ↔ to 5m (15ft)

ANEMONE × HYBRIDA
'Honorine Jobert' ♀

Perennial

The Japanese anemone is a popular late-flowering plant, perfect for growing in a summer or autumn herbaceous border. It is also good for cutting. This is one of the prettiest varieties, bearing single, pure white flowers, with bright green centres surrounded by golden-yellow stamens. Plant it in sun or light shade in moist, fertile, well-drained soil. It spreads quickly to form large clumps and can be invasive. Divide the plants in early spring.

◊ ◊ ☼ ☼ ✽ ✽ ✽
‡ to 1.5m (5ft) ↔ indefinito

CAMPANULA ALLIARIIFOLIA

Perennial

Ivory bells is an elegant, herbaceous plant which forms clumps of greyish-green, hairy, heart-shaped leaves. The white, bell-shaped, pendent flowers are held on branched, wiry stems. It prefers a slightly shaded situation, and is ideal for planting beneath a light canopy of deciduous trees or shrubs in a mixed border. It blooms from summer to early autumn, and can be cut to the ground after flowering to prevent self-seeding. Grow it in moist, well-drained, fertile, neutral or alkaline soil.

◊ ◊ ◐ ☼ ❄ ❄ ❄
‡ to 60cm (24in) ↔ to 50cm (20in)

CLERODENDRUM TRICHOTOMUM *VAR.* FARGESII ♛

Deciduous shrub

This upright large shrub or small tree in late summer produces clusters of very fragrant, white flowers with persistent green sepals. The flowers are followed later in the year by bright blue berries. The young leaves are also a feature, opening bronze before turning green. In cold areas, plant it against a west- or south-facing wall in moist, well-drained, fertile soil. Pruning is rarely required, except to remove crossing branches.

◊ ◊ ☼ ❄ ❄ ❄
‡ to 6m (20ft) ↔ to 6m (20ft)

DAHLIA
'Angora'

Perennial

This dahlia has double, white flowers, and creates a stunning display when planted in front of a dark background, or in a white border. The blooms also make excellent cut flowers. Dahlias need a sunny position in fertile, moist, well-drained soil. Plant it in spring and insert a supporting cane when planting. Lift the tubers after the first frost, allow them to dry, and then store them in boxes of dry sand or compost in a frost-free, cool place.

⬤ ⬤ ☼ ❄ ❄
‡ to 1m (36in) ↔ to 60cm (24in)

ECHINACEA PURPUREA
'White Swan'

Perennial

Coneflowers originate from the prairies of North America, and have daisy-like flowers with raised cone-like centres. The flowers of 'White Swan' are borne on tall, erect stems above lance-shaped leaves, and are composed of white petals, with an orange-brown cone. Plant it in a sunny site in a herbaceous border, in deep, well-drained soil. It will also tolerate a little shade. Cut the stems back after flowering to encourage a second flush of blooms.

⬤ ☼ ❄ ❄ ❄
‡ to 60cm (24in) ↔ to 45cm (18in)

EPILOBIUM ANGUSTIFOLIUM *VAR.* ALBUM

Perennial

The common rosebay willow herb is an invasive thug of a plant, and is not suitable for growing in the garden. However, this beautiful white form is less aggressive and perfect for a wild area of the garden or the herbaceous border. Narrow, lance-shaped leaves provide a foil for the tall spikes of white summer flowers. It is not fussy about soil conditions, and will grow in full sun or partial shade. It self-seeds, so deadhead it after flowering.

○ ◑ ● ☼ ☼ ✽ ✽ ✽
‡ to 1.5m (5ft) ↔ to 1m (3ft)

ERICA TETRALIX 'Alba Mollis' ♀

Evergreen shrub

The cross-leaved heath is a spreading bush, with small, silvery-grey leaves, which are arranged in the shape of a cross. In late summer, it is covered with small, bell-shaped, white flowers. It grows naturally on wet moorland, and needs damper soil conditions than other species of heather. It also requires an acid soil, and should be grown in full sun for the best results. Clip over the plant in spring to keep it neat.

● ☼ ✽ ✽ ✽
‡ to 20cm (8in) ↔ to 30cm (12in)

EUCOMIS BICOLOR ♛

Perennial bulb

An exotic-looking bulb, the pineapple
lily has large, strap-like, light green
leaves, and purple-spotted flower stems.
In late summer it bears dense spikes of
purple-edged white flowers, topped by
a rosette of small leaves that inspired its
common name. Plant bulbs about 15cm
(6in) deep, in full sun in fertile, well-
drained soil. The bulbs may survive
the winter in mild areas, but in cold
climates, lift them and store in a frost-
free place, then replant them in spring.
Alternatively, grow them in pots.

○ ☼ ❄❄
‡ to 50cm (20in) ↔ to 20cm (8in)

FALLOPIA BALDSCHUANICA

Climber

The 'mile-a-minute plant', or Russian
vine, is a rampant climber which grows
rapidly up to a height of 12m (40ft). It
has woody, twining stems, covered with
heart-shaped, pale green leaves. In late
summer, it bears masses of small, pink-
flushed, creamy-white flowers. Although
unsuitable for a small garden, it is
useful for covering an ugly wall or a
dead tree. Grow it in full sun or partial
shade, in poor or slightly fertile, well-
drained soil. Don't be afraid to cut it
back hard in the spring.

○ ☼ ◑ ❄❄❄
‡ to 12m (40ft)

FUCHSIA
'Annabel' ♀

Evergreen shrub

'Annabel' is a free-flowering, trailing fuchsia that produces delicate white flowers, and is well suited to hanging baskets and tall containers. It can also be trained as a standard, if provided with a permanent supporting stake. Feed it regularly throughout its growing season. This fuchsia is not hardy, so move it indoors for the winter into a frost-free greenhouse. To propagate it, take softwood cuttings in the spring.

◊ ◊ ☼ ☀ ✻

‡ to 60cm (24in) ↔ to 60cm (24in)

GALTONIA CANDICANS ♀

Perennial bulb

Valued for its late summer blooms, this bulbous plant has long greyish-green, strap-like leaves, and white, pendent, slightly fragrant, tubular flowers, which are produced on tall spikes. It is quite hardy, but in areas that experience very cold winters, the bulbs should be dug up in autumn and stored in a frost-free place, or covered with a deep mulch. Plant the bulbs in spring in full sun and fertile, moist soil that never dries out.

◊ ☼ ✻ ✻

‡ to 1.2m (4ft) ↔ to 23cm (9in)

HELIANTHUS DEBILIS
'Italian White'

Annual

The flowerheads of this pale sunflower
can measure up to 10cm (4in) across.
It also has slightly hairy leaves, and the
tall stems may need support in exposed
gardens. Plant it in full sun in slightly
fertile, well-drained soil. Raise this
annual from seed under glass in late
winter or sow *in situ* in the spring.

○ ☼ ❁ ❁ ❁
‡ to 1.2m (4ft) ↔ to 60cm (24in)

HYDRANGEA MACROPHYLLA
'Veitchii' ♀

Deciduous shrub

Lacecap hydrangeas have flat-topped
flowerheads composed of a cluster of
small fertile blooms, surrounded by
larger sterile flowers 'Veitchii' has white
sterile flowers that become pink as they
age, and forms a mound of dark green
foliage. The flowerheads can be cut
and dried, or left over the winter and
removed in spring, when a few of the
oldest stems can also be pruned to the
ground. Plant in sun or partial shade,
in moist, well-drained, fertile soil.

○ ◑ ☼ ❁ ❁ ❁
‡ to 2m (6ft) ↔ to 2.5m (8ft)

HYDRANGEA PANICULATA
'Grandiflora' ♥

Deciduous shrub

This is a large beautiful plant, perfect for a mixed border or a specimen. In late summer it produces large, conical clusters of creamy-white, sterile flowers, which turn a delicate shade of pink as they age. Plant it in a sheltered area, in moist, well-drained, fertile soil in sun or partial shade. Pruning is not essential, but for the best display of flowers, cut it back annually in early spring to a pair of buds above a low framework of permanent branches.

○ ◗ ☼ ☀ ❋ ❋ ❋
‡ to 7m (22ft) ↔ to 2.5m (8ft)

LATHYRUS LATIFOLIUS
'Albus' ♥

Climber

The everlasting pea is a herbaceous perennial, which can be used to climb up a support or as ground cover. 'Albus' produces white to creamy-white flowers that appear from summer to early autumn. It grows well in full sun or light shade in well-drained, fertile soil, which has been enriched with well-rotted manure. Cut back any dead stems in the spring, but otherwise leave it undisturbed.

○ ☼ ☀ ❋ ❋ ❋
‡ to 2m (6ft) or more

LILIUM AURATUM *VAR.* PLATYPHYLLUM

Perennial bulb

The golden-rayed lily originates from Japan, and bears lance-shaped, dark green leaves, and 12 or more sweetly-scented, white flowers with yellow stripes down the centre of the petals, are borne on stiff stems. This lily is short-lived, and requires an acid, well-drained soil. Plant the bulbs in autumn or spring in full sun, and mulch well with leaf mould. They are more usually grown in pots of ericaceous compost, with canes to support the stems.

◊ ☼ ❋ ❋ ❋
‡ to 1.5m (5ft)

LILIUM REGALE ♀

Perennial bulb

One of the best lilies for perfume, the regal lily is a vigorous plant with erect or arching stems, clothed with shiny, greyish-green leaves. In midsummer it produces up to 25, intensely fragrant, trumpet-shaped, white flowers. The petals have purple streaks on the back and golden-yellow throats. Regal lilies grow well in containers, although they need the support of tall canes. Plant them in well-drained, fertile soil in full sun, with the lower part of the plant shaded by other planting.

◊ ☼ ❋ ❋ ❋
‡ to 2m (6ft) ↔ to 2m (6ft)

LOBULARIA MARITIMA
'Little Dorrit'

Annual

Also known as *Alyssum maritimum*, this pretty plant is usually grown as an annual, although it can also be a short-lived perennial. It forms a mound of narrow, greyish-green leaves, and bears rounded clusters of tiny, scented, white flowers in midsummer. For the best effect, plant 'Little Dorrit' in groups to form a carpet at the front of a border, or use it in bedding displays or in containers. Plant it in well-drained soil in full sun.

◊ ☼ ✿ ✿

‡ to 10cm (4in) ↔ to 10cm (4in)

MAGNOLIA GRANDIFLORA

Evergreen tree

Given a warm, sheltered position, the bull bay eventually makes a large tree, with glossy, leathery, dark green leaves. In late summer it bears large, creamy-white flowers, up to 25cm (10in) across. Flowers may also appear sporadically at other times of the year. It is not fully hardy, and in cold areas it should be grown against a west- or south-facing wall in moist, well-drained soil. Grow it in full sun or partial shade. 'Exmouth' is one of the hardiest cultivars, and will flower at an earlier age.

◊ ◊ ☼ ✿ ✿ ✿

‡ to 18m (60ft) ↔ to 15m (50ft)

MYRTUS COMMUNIS ♀

Evergreen shrub

Myrtle has an upright habit and bears
rounded, glossy, dark green, aromatic
leaves. The attractive, fragrant white
flowers have frothy centres, created by
long white stamens. It blooms from the
middle of the summer to the beginning
of the autumn. A Mediterranean plant,
myrtle is not completely hardy and is
more likely to survive cold winters if
planted against a sunny wall. Grow it in
slightly fertile, moist, well-drained soil.

◊◊ ☼ ❄❄
‡ to 3m (10ft) ↔ to 3m (10ft)

NICOTIANA SYLVESTRIS ♀

Perennial

A vigorous, short-lived perennial, the
tobacco plant is frequently grown as an
annual in cool climates. The flowers of
this species are borne on long stems
above a rosette of elliptic, dark green,
sticky leaves. The long, white, highly
fragrant flowers resemble shooting stars
and are produced from midsummer. It
is easily damaged by frost, but may
survive a mild winter if protected by a
thick layer of mulch. Plant it in a sunny
or partially shaded site in moist, well-
drained soil.

◊◊ ☼ ☼ ❄
‡ to 1.5m (5ft) ↔ to 60cm (2ft)

RESEDA ODORATA

Annual

The common mignonette is an erect
or slightly spreading plant, with ribbed
stems and lance-shaped leaves. In the
summer and early autumn it produces
rounded heads of small, star-shaped,
white or greenish-white flowers with a
sweet perfume. It has been grown for
centuries because the flowers keep their
fragrance even when they have been
cut and dried. Plant it in well-drained
soil in full sun or partial shade.

○ ☼ ☀ ❄ ❄ ❄
‡ to 60cm (24in) ↔ to 30cm (12in)

SCHIZOPHRAGMA
INTEGRIFOLIUM ♀

Climber

This is a vigorous self-clinging climber.
It bears flat-topped clusters of small,
lightly-scented, creamy-white flowers
surrounded by large sterile bract-like
flowers, which appear among the dark
green leaves from midsummer. Grow it
against a wall, or up a large tree, in
deep, fertile, moist but well-drained
soil. Happy in full sun or partial shade,
it can grow to a height of 12m (40ft),
but is slow to get started.

○ ◑ ☼ ❄ ❄
‡ to 12m (40ft)

SENECIO CINERARIA
'Silver Dust' ♀

Evergreen shrub

This attractive shrub has deeply divided leaves, which are covered with greyish-white felt. It produces mustard-yellow, daisy-like flowers in summer, although these these should be removed before they open to maintain its foliage effect. Plant it in full sun and slightly fertile, well-drained soil. It is reasonably hardy, but dislikes winter wet, and semi-ripe cuttings should be taken at the end of the summer to guarantee new plants the following year.

◊ ☼ ❈ ❈
‡ to 30cm (12in) ↔ to 30cm (12in)

YUCCA FILAMENTOSA ♀
Evergreen shrub

The Spanish dagger is an architectural plant, and bears stiff, lance-shaped, spiky leaves with razor-sharp points. Cut off these points if growing yuccas in gardens used by children. In late summer it produces a tall spike of bell-shaped, creamy-white flowers. Plant it in well-drained soil in a sunny position, such as in a gravel garden, where it has space to grow to its full size. Protect young plants during cold, wet winters with a straw mulch or fleece.

◊ ☼ ❈ ❈
‡ to 2m (6ft) ↔ to 1.5m (5ft)

AGROSTEMMA GITHAGO 'Milas'

Annual

Corn cockle used to be a cornfield annual weed, but the widespread use of herbicides has made it a rare plant in the wild. It has lance-shaped, greyish-green leaves, and in the summer 'Milas' has vibrant plum-pink flowers with white centres. Plant corn cockles in full sun in poor, well-drained soil. They can be grown in a cottage-style garden, in containers, or planted in a summer flower meadow. The species self-seeds freely.

◊ ☼ ❀ ❀ ❀
‡ to 90cm (36in) ↔ to 30cm (12in)

ALCEA ROSEA

Perennial

Hollyhocks are tall, vigorous plants, with rounded, slightly hairy leaves. In summer they produce a long spike of funnel-shaped pink, white, purple or creamy-yellow flowers. 'Chater's Double' is a beautiful double form. Hollyhocks need a sunny position and well-drained, fertile soil. They look good grown by a wall. Rust can be a problem, so look out for resistant types; they are often grown as biennials to reduce the effects of this disease. They may need staking in open positions.

◊ ☼ ❀ ❀ ❀
‡ to 2m (6ft) ↔ to 60cm (24in)

ANEMONE HUPEHENSIS
'Hadspen Abundance' ♀

Perennial

This late-flowering anemone produces deep pink flowers over a long period that are good for cutting. The edges of the petals fade to white as the flower ages. The long-stalked leaves have three leaflets. This anemone enjoys a sunny or partially shaded site. Plant it in moist soil in a herbaceous border. In cold areas, mulch it well in the autumn.

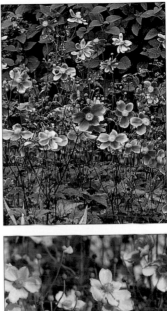

◊ ☼ ☀ ❋ ❋ ❋
‡ to 90cm (36in) ↔ to 40cm (00in)

ANEMONE X HYBRIDA
'Max Vogel'

Perennial

The Japanese anemone is a vigorous late-flowering plant with upright, branched stems. From late summer to mid-autumn, 'Max Vogel' produces masses of beautiful single, light pink flowers, which become darker as they age. It looks superb in a herbaceous border, and is good for cutting. It does best in a moist, fertile soil in full sunshine or partial shade. 'Margarete' has double, pale pink flowers.

◊ ◊ ☼ ☀ ❋ ❋ ❋
‡ to 1.5m (5ft) ↔ indefinite

BEGONIA
'Roy Hartley'

Perennial

The glossy leaves provide the perfect foil for this tuberous begonia's large, salmon-pink flowers, which are borne from midsummer. Its upright growth makes it an excellent bedding plant. Tubers can be planted in the garden when all risk of frost has passed; it flowers better in a partially shaded site and moist, well-drained soil. For an indoor display, plant 'Roy Hartley' in a large container of loam-based compost in bright light, away from direct sun.

○ ◐ ☼
‡ to 60cm (24in) ↔ to 45cm (18in)

CALLISTEPHUS CHINENSIS
Ostrich Plume Series

Annual

China aster flowers resemble chrysanthemums with double blooms. The Ostrich Plume Series are tall plants, with flowers in shades of pink, purple and red. They bloom from late summer until the middle of autumn, and can be deadheaded to prolong flowering. Plant them in a sunny, sheltered site in moist, well-drained soil. China asters make good bedding plants and cut flowers.

○ ◐ ☼ ❄
‡ to 60cm (24in) ↔ to 30cm (12in)

CALLUNA VULGARIS
'County Wicklow' ♀

Evergreen shrub

There are over 500 different cultivars
of ling, or heather. All are evergreen
shrubs and can be used in heather
gardens or as ground cover. 'County
Wicklow' is compact, with slightly
prostrate stems and mid-green foliage.
It bears spikes of small, double shell-
pink flowers, and blooms from late
summer to late autumn. Plant it in full
sun in well-drained, acid (lime-free)
soil. Clip it over in spring to keep it
neat and bushy.

◊ ☼ ❄ ❄ ❄
‡ to 30cm (12in) ↔ to 35cm (14in)

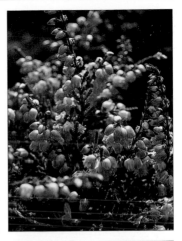

CAMPANULA LACTIFLORA
'Loddon Anna' ♀

Perennial

The milky bellflower is a tall
herbaceous plant, which in late summer
bears large clusters of bell-shaped, lilac-
pink flowers. They may need staking as
they are inclined to fall over in strong
winds. It enjoys full sun, or dappled
shade, in a fertile, neutral to alkaline,
moist, well-drained soil. It self-seeds,
and can be divided in spring or
autumn. 'Prichard's Variety' is not as
tall and has violet-blue flowers.

◊ ◊ ☼ ☀ ❄ ❄ ❄
‡ to 1.5m (5ft) ↔ to 60cm (24in)

CHELONE OBLIQUA

Perennial

The turtlehead plant bears stiff stems sparsely covered with lance-shaped, mid-green leaves. From late summer to mid-autumn it produces clusters of pink flowers with turtle mouth-like openings, which explain its common name. It will perform well planted in a sunny border or partial shade in deep, fertile, moist soil. To propagate it, divide clumps in spring.

◑ ☼ ☀ ✿ ✿ ✿
‡ to 60cm (24in) ↔ to 30cm (12in)

CHRYSANTHEMUM
'Clara Curtis'

Perennial

Unlike many chrysanthemums, this variety has simple, single daisy-like flowers, with pale pink petals and greeny-yellow centres. Their perfume comes as something of a surprise, because many chrysanthemums are unscented. Plant it in well-drained soil that has previously been enriched with well-rotted manure. It is hardy, but in cold, wet areas it should be dug up and overwintered in a frost-free place.

◑ ☼ ✿ ✿ ✿
‡ to 75cm (30in) ↔ to 45cm (18in)

CLARKIA UNGUICULATA

Annual

This is a tall, elegant, slender-stemmed hardy annual, which from midsummer produces funnel-shaped, often frilly flowers in shades of salmon, lavender-pink, purple and reddish-purple. It makes a superb cut flower, and should be grown in full sun or partial shade in moist, well-drained, slightly acid (lime-free) soil. Plant the seed in autumn or early spring.

◊ ◊ ☼ ✽ ✽ ✽
‡ to 1m (39in) ↔ to 20cm (8in)

CLEOME HASSLERIANA
Rose Queen

Annual

Spider flowers are tall, handsome plants with hand-like leaves. They flower in late summer, producing large clusters of spidery, pink, white or purple blooms that are good for cutting. They are ideal for the back of a herbaceous border as they do not need staking, and for filling spaces created when spring flowering perennials are over. Sow seed in spring, in a heated propagator, and plant out after all risk of frost has passed, in full sun and fertile, well-drained soil.

◊ ☼ ✽
‡ to 1.5m (5ft) ↔ to 45cm (18in)

CRINUM × POWELLII ♀

Perennial bulb

From late summer to autumn, tall stems of large, slightly fragrant, funnel-shaped, pale pink flowers appear on this vigorous, clump-forming perennial. The strap-like leaves can measure up to 1.5m (5ft) in length. Crinums are not completely hardy, and in cold areas protect them with a thick mulch during the winter. They should be planted with the neck of the bulb just above the ground, preferably in the shelter of a sunny wall, in fertile, moist, well-drained soil.

◊◊◑ ☼ ❊❊
↕ to 1m (3ft) ↔ to 60cm (2ft)

DAHLIA
'Fascination' ♀

Perennial

Dahlias provide a late burst of colour after early-flowering perennials are past their best. 'Fascination' is a dwarf form, with bronze-tinged leaves, and purple-pink flowers. It can be used as a bedding plant at the front of a border, and makes a good cut flower. Grow it in full sun in fertile, well-drained soil. Dig up the tubers after the first frost, pack them in boxes of dry sand, or compost, and overwinter them in a frost-free place. Plant out in late spring.

◊ ☼ ❊❊
↕ to 45cm (18in) ↔ to 30cm (12in)

DIANTHUS
GRATIANOPOLITANUS ♥

Perennial

The Cheddar pink is a compact, low-growing evergreen that forms a carpet of waxy, narrow, grey-green leaves. In late summer solitary, very fragrant, pink or red flowers with toothed petals are borne on short stems. It will flourish in a rock garden, raised bed or trough, and should be planted in well-drained, gritty soil in full sun

○ ☼ ❀ ❀ ❀
‡ to 15cm (6in) ↔ to 30cm (12in)

DIASCIA BARBERAE
'Blackthorn Apricot' ♥

Perennial

This mat-forming plant produces masses of apricot-pink flowers in summer and autumn and is ideal for the front of a herbaceous border, a rock garden, or a container. Diascias grow well in full sun, in moist, well-drained, fertile soil, and need protection in cold, wet winters. Other excellent forms include 'Salmon Supreme', with larger, pale apricot flowers, and 'Ruby Field', which produces deep salmon-pink flowers.

○ ◐ ☼ ❀ ❀
‡ to 25cm (10in) ↔ to 50cm (20in)

ECHINACEA PURPUREA
Perennial

The coneflower has tall, erect stems that bear slightly hairy, lance-shaped leaves. In the late summer and early autumn it produces large, purplish-pink, daisy-like flowerheads, with cone-shaped centres comprised of tiny golden-brown flowers. It is ideal for the middle or back of a border, and to grow well, needs full sun and a deep, well-drained soil. Good for cutting.

◊ ☼ ❄ ❄ ❄
‡ to 1.5m (5ft) ↔ to 45cm (18in)

ERICA CILIARIS
'Corfe Castle'
Evergreen shrub

The Dorset heath 'Corfe Castle' bears rose-pink flowers from midsummer to the middle of autumn. In winter the mid-green foliage has a bronze tone, and its spreading stems make good ground cover. *Erica ciliaris* and its cultivars should be planted in an open, sunny situation in acid (lime-free), well-drained soil. Although hardy, it may suffer during very cold winters. Clip over the plants in spring to keep them neat, and remove dead flowers.

◊ ☼ ❄ ❄ ❄
‡ to 22cm (9in) ↔ to 35cm (14in)

ERICA CINEREA
'C.D. Eason' ♀

Evergreen shrub

The bell-heathers are grown for their needle-like, evergreen leaves and small urn-shaped flowers. There are many attractive forms, but 'C.D. Eason' is one of the best, bearing masses of bright magenta flowers from the middle of summer to the early autumn. It is very hardy, and should be planted in full sun and well drained, acid (lime-free) soil. Clip over the plants in spring to keep them compact and remove faded flowers.

◊ ☼ ❊ ❊ ❊
‡ to 25cm (10in) ↔ to 50cm (20in)

ERIGERON KARVINSKIANUS ♀

Perennial

This carpeting plant produces spreading stems and greyish-green, lance-shaped leaves. The pretty, daisy-like flowers, which appear in summer, are solitary or produced in groups of up to five white or pink blooms, which darken to reddish-purple as they age. It should be planted in full sun, in moist but well-drained soil. The blooms will liven up a rock garden or the front of a border, and it is ideal for planting in cracks and crevices in walls and paving. Once established it spreads freely.

◊ ☼ ❊ ❊
‡ to 30cm (12in) ↔ to 1m (3ft)

EUPATORIUM PURPUREUM
'Atropurpureum' ♀

Perennial

Joe Pye weed is tall, with very strong,
reddish-purple stems, and pointed,
lance-shaped, purple-tinged green
leaves. The large heads of pinkish-
purple flowers appear from midsummer
to early autumn. It is a useful plant for
the back of a large, late summer border
and blends well with grasses such as
Miscanthus. It enjoys damp, slightly
alkaline soil, in full sun or partial shade.

◑ ☼ ☀ ❀ ❀ ❀
‡ to 2.2m (7ft) ↔ to 1m (3ft)

FILIPENDULA RUBRA
'Venusta' ♀

Perennial

Queen of the prairies is a spreading
perennial with architectural, deeply-cut,
mid-green foliage. In summer it
produces branched stems bearing
clusters of tiny, fragrant, deep rose-pink
flowers. It is a bog plant and needs to
be sited in partial shade, although it
tolerates full sun in permanently moist
soil. Grow close to a pond margin, or
in damp ground beneath deciduous
trees; it will only thrive in a herbaceous
border if the soil never dries out.

◑◑ ☼ ☀ ❀ ❀ ❀
‡ to 2.5m (8ft) ↔ to 1.2m (4ft)

FUCHSIA
'Leonora'

Deciduous shrub

A free-flowering, upright fuchsia that
has bell-shaped, soft pink flowers with
reflexed outer sepals. It is a good
choice for a patio container; use loam-
based potting compost and position it
in full sun or light shade. In summer,
water well, and feed regularly with a
balanced fertilizer, or use a slow-release
fertilizer when planting. Keep it frost-
free over winter, moving it outside after
frosts are over. New plants are easy to
raise from softwood cuttings in spring.

◊ ◑ ☼ ☀ ❄
‡ to 75cm (30in) ↔ to 60cm (24in)

GAURA LINDHEIMERI
'Siskiyou Pink'

Perennial

This robust plant has branched stems
and forms a clump of narrow lance- or
spoon-shaped leaves. The flowers of
'Siskiyou Pink' are white, but heavily
flushed with deep pink. They first
appear in late spring, but reach their
peak in late summer, and continue into
the early autumn. This long-flowering
plant is perfect for the front of a sunny
border and needs a fertile, moist, well-
drained soil. It will tolerate partial
shade and dry soil during the summer.

◊ ◑ ☼ ☀ ❄ ❄
‡ to 1.2m (4ft) ↔ to 1m (3ft)

HEBE
'Great Orme' ♀

Evergreen shrub

There are over 75 species of hebe, all suitable for coastal gardens. This one forms a rounded bush, with purple shoots and glossy leaves. From midsummer to mid-autumn it produces spikes of pink flowers, which fade to white as they age. It is a medium-sized shrub, and will add year-round interest to a mixed border. Plant it in a sunny or partially shaded position, sheltered from cold winds and frost, in well-drained soil. No pruning is necessary.

◊ ◊ ☼ ☀ ❈ ❈
‡↔ to 1.2m (4ft)

HYDRANGEA PANICULATA
Pink Diamond ♀

Deciduous shrub

In late summer and early autumn this spreading hydrangea bears large, cone-shaped flowerheads, that open creamy-white but then turn deep pink as they age. It should be planted in a moist, well-drained, fertile soil in sun or partial shade. It will also benefit from some protection against cold, drying winds. No pruning is necessary, but flowering is improved by cutting back stems in early spring to a permanent framework of branches.

◊ ◊ ☼ ☀ ❈ ❈ ❈
‡ to 7m (22ft) ↔ to 2.5m (8ft)

HYDRANGEA VILLOSA ♀

Deciduous shrub

This delightful spreading plant is much loved by garden designers for its lance-shaped, velvety, mid-green leaves, and large, flat flowerheads. In summer, masses of tiny, bluish-purple fertile flowers are borne, surrounded by larger, lilac-pink sterile blooms. It can be grown as a specimen plant, or in a mixed border. This hydrangea will thrive when grown in sun or partial shade, and moist, well-drained soil. Little pruning is needed apart from deadheading in spring.

◊ ◊ ☼ ◐ ❀ ❀ ❀
↔ to 3m (10ft)

INDIGOFERA DIELSIANA

Deciduous shrub

The dark green leaves of this medium-sized bush are composed of many small opposite leaflets, and contrast well with the pea-like, pale reddish-pink flowers that are produced from summer to early autumn. *Indigofera* is not completely hardy and should be grown in full sun in a sheltered shrub border, or against a warm, south- or west-facing wall. It will do well when planted in fertile, moist, well-drained soil. The stems produce an orangy-yellow latex when they are cut which may irritate the skin.

◊ ☼ ❀ ❀
↕↔ to 1.5m (5ft)

LATHYRUS LATIFOLIUS ♥

Climber

The everlasting pea is a herbaceous
climber with branched stems and pairs
of blue-green leaflets. The leaves
terminate in tendrils, which allows
it to scramble or climb over banks or
through shrubs. In late summer and
early autumn, it bears clusters of pea-
like, magenta-purple flowers. Plant it
in fertile, well-drained soil in full sun
or partial shade, and prune it to the
ground in spring to encourage new
stems, otherwise leave undisturbed.
Sow seed in the autumn.

◊ ☼ ☀ ❀ ❀ ❀
‡ to 2m (6ft)

LATHYRUS ODORATUS
'Jayne Amanda'

Climber

'Jayne Amanda' is a superb sweet pea,
which can be trained up canes or over
tripods. The branched stems bear pairs
of leaves and delicate tendrils. In the
summer it produces an abundance of
highly perfumed, deep pink flowers.
Plant it in full sun or dappled shade in
fertile, well-drained soil. Cut flowers
regularly to prolong flowering and
deadhead if necessary. Seed can be
sown under glass in autumn or spring.
Plant out young plants in late spring.

◊ ◊ ☼ ☀ ❀ ❀ ❀
‡ to 3m (10ft)

LILIUM
Pink Perfection Group ♀

Perennial bulb

These Asiatic lilies have large, slightly nodding, trumpet-shaped flowers, held on tall, robust stems. The blooms are fragrant, and have deep pinkish purple petals with swept-back tips. Plant Asiatic lilies in well-drained, fertile soil which has been enriched with leaf mould or well-rotted garden compost. They need a sunny position to thrive, with the base of the plant to shade. If using them as cut flowers, snip off the orange anthers as the pollen stains.

◊ ☼ ❋ ❋ ❋

‡ to 2m (6ft)

LONICERA PERCLYMENUM
'Serotina' ♀

Climber

The late Dutch honeysuckle has woody, twining stems, and greyish-green leaves. In mid- to late summer it produces clusters of pink buds opening to display highly perfumed, creamy-white and purple-pink flowers. It is very hardy and can be grown over fences and pergolas, or through trees and shrubs, or as ground cover over a bank. Plant it in full sun or partial shade, in fertile, moist, but well drained soil. Prune back after flowering to keep within bounds.

◊ ◊ ☼ ❋ ❋ ❋ ❋

‡ to 7m (22ft)

LYCHNIS CORONARIA ♀

Biennial

The rose campion has lance-shaped, soft, downy, silver-grey leaves and stems, which in mid- to late summer contrast beautifully with the bright magenta, rounded, flat-topped flowers. It self-seeds with abandon, and is a welcome addition to any garden bed or border. Plant rose campion in full sun in slightly fertile, well-drained soil. Sow the seed in spring to flower the following year.

◊ ☼ ✿ ✿ ✿
‡ to 80cm (32in) ↔ to 45cm (18in)

LYCHNIS FLOS-JOVIS ♀

Perennial

The upright stems of the flower of Jove are covered with white hairs, giving them a silvery appearance, while the spoon-shaped, soft basal leaves are also silver-grey. From mid- to late summer clusters of pink, scarlet or white flowers with deeply divided petals appear. This species is a good choice for the front of a sunny border or a gravel garden. Plant it in well-drained, slightly fertile soil, and sow seed in spring.

◊ ☼ ✿ ✿ ✿
‡ to 60cm (24in) ↔ to 45cm (18in)

MACLEAYA MICROCARPA
'Kelway's Coral Plume' ♀
Perennial

This unusual member of the poppy family is a spreading perennial with deeply-lobed, greyish-green leaves, the undersides of which are covered with a white felt. In late summer greyish-green stems carry tall plumes of pinkish-beige, feathery flowers. Plant it in the flower border or among shrubs, in slightly fertile, moist, well-drained soil in full sun or light shade. Provide it with some protection from cold winds.

◊ ◊ ☼ ◐ ✿ ✿ ✿
‡ to 2.2m (7ft) ↔ to 1m (3ft)

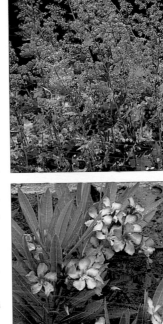

NERIUM OLEANDER
Evergreen shrub

The rose bay forms an upright or rounded bush of narrow, greyish evergreen leaves. In summer it produces loose clusters of clear pink flowers. It is often grown in a container and moved to frost-free conditions under glass during the winter, although it can survive outside in sheltered urban gardens and in mild areas. Water it frequently during the warmer months, but keep the soil drier in winter. All parts of the plant are very toxic.

◊ ☼ ✿
‡↔ to 6m (20ft)

NICOTIANA
'Domino Salmon-pink'

Annual

This tobacco plant is grown as an annual in cooler climates. It has large, sticky basal leaves and narrow, lance-shaped stem leaves. In mid- to late summer, 'Domino Salmon-pink' is clothed with star-shaped, salmon-pink flowers that open up in the early evening and emit a delicate scent. Grow tobacco plants in full sun or partial shade in fertile, moist, well-drained soil, near a window or path where the fragrance can be enjoyed.

◊◊ ☼ ☀ ☀ ❊

‡ to 45cm (18in) ↔ to 40cm (16in)

ORIGANUM
'Kent Beauty'

Deciduous shrub

A semi-evergreen herb with creeping roots and a prostrate habit, with aromatic, rounded, bright green leaves. From midsummer it produces masses of small, tubular, pale-pink or mauve flowers, surrounded by deep pink bracts. Oregano is perfect for a herb or gravel garden, patio pot, or the front of a herbaceous border. Plant it in full sun in slightly fertile, well-drained soil.

◊ ☼ ❊ ❊ ❊

‡ to 10cm (4in) ↔ to 20cm (8in)

PELARGONIUM
'Bird Dancer' ♀

Perennial

This frost-tender plant bears decorative rounded green leaves, with wavy edges and a darker zone in the centre. The flowers are pale salmon-pink and borne on long stems in ball-headed clusters from summer to autumn. Its compact, neat habit makes it ideal for a patio container or a sunny window box. Plant it in fertile, well-drained potting compost or bed out in free-draining garden soil. Move under cover for the winter and keep fairly dry.

◊ ☼ ☀ ♦

‡ to 20cm (8in) ↔ to 15cm (6in)

PELARGONIUM
'Clorinda'

Perennial

This vigorous scented-leaved pelargonium has crinkled evergreen foliage that smells of cedar. Rounded clusters of deep rose-pink flowers appear from summer to autumn. Grow it in containers in well-drained potting compost, in a position in sun or light shade. A tender plant, this pelargonium must be overwintered in a frost-free greenhouse or indoors. Alternatively, take softwood cuttings of non-flowering shoots from spring to autumn.

◊ ☼ ☀ ❀

‡ to 50cm (20in) ↔ to 25cm (10in)

PENNISETUM SETACEUM
'Rubrum'

Perennial

This beautiful grass has red leaves and feathery, purplish-pink flowerheads which appear from midsummer. Plant it in a sunny border, gravel garden, or in a large container in full sun or partial shade in slightly fertile, well-drained soil. It is not reliably hardy and is best grown as an annual; raise it from seed sown in spring in a heated propagator. Otherwise overwinter in a conservatory or greenhouse. 'Burgundy Giant' is a larger variety, and has purplish flowers.

◊ ☼ ❋ ❋
‡ to 1m (3ft) ↔ to 45cm (18in)

PENSTEMON
'Apple Blossom' ♀

Perennial

This penstemon bears spikes of elegant, tubular, light pink flowers with white throats from midsummer right through to autumn, if the blooms are deadheaded regularly. It prefers a moist but free-draining soil in full sun or light shade, and is perfect for a border with a pastel colour theme. Although it may survive the winter in a sheltered site, it is not fully frost hardy. As a precaution, take softwood cuttings from the middle of summer.

◊ ☼ ☼ ❋ ❋
‡ to 60cm (24in) ↔ to 60cm (24in)

PHLOX PANICULATA
'Windsor' ♥

Perennial

The dense, conical heads of carmine-rose flowers with distinctive, deep red eyes are borne on this phlox in late summer above oval, mid-green leaves. Grow it in full sun or partial shade in well-drained, moist soil, and stake where necessary. Plant groups of this tall phlox in a herbaceous border or behind shorter plants in a gravel garden. Deadhead regularly in summer, and thin out weak shoots in spring for improved flowering.

◊ ☼ ◐ ❀ ❀ ❀
‡ to 1.2m (4ft) ↔ to 1m (36in)

PHYSOSTEGIA VIRGINIANA
'Variegata'

Perennial

The obedient plant is unusual because its flower stalks are hinged, so that when the blooms are moved they stay in position. In summer, tall spikes bear small, mauve-pink, tubular flowers, which will brighten up a border and are also good for cutting. The leaves are lance-shaped and mid-green, edged with white. Plant in sun or partial shade in a moist soil.

◊ ☼ ◐ ❀ ❀ ❀
‡ to 60cm (24in) ↔ to 30cm (12in)

RHODANTHE MANGLESII

Annual

The strawflower is a fast growing, half-hardy annual, ideal for cutting and drying. It has pink, daisy-like summer flowers with papery petals and yellow centres, and greyish-green leaves. Grow it in a sunny annual or mixed border, in a poor, well-drained soil. Sow the seed outdoors *in situ* in mid-spring. To dry the flowers, cut them as soon as the buds begin to open and hang them upside down in bunches in a cool dry place out of the sun.

○ ☼ ❀
‡ to 30cm (12in) ↔ to 15cm (6in)

SCHIZOSTYLIS COCCINEA *'Sunrise'* ♀

Perennial

The kaffir lily produces tall spikes of delicate, cup-shaped, soft pink flowers in late summer and autumn. The mid-green, narrow, leaves are sword-shaped, and both flowers and foliage are excellent for indoor arrangements. In the garden, it is suited to sunny borders, waterside plantings, or it can be planted against sunny wall. Grow in fertile, moist, well-drained soil in full sun. Divide regularly in the spring to maintain the plant's vigour.

◐ ☼ ❀ ❀ ❀
‡ to 60cm (24in) ↔ to 30cm (12in)

SEDUM SPECTABILE
'Brilliant' ♀

Perennial

Excellent for the front of a sunny
border, the ice plant is invaluable from
late summer to autumn when its flat
heads of pink flowers open from green
buds. They are attractive to bees and
butterflies. The fleshy leaves are borne
on upright stems and are a feature in
their own right. Plant in any well-
drained soil in sun. The flowerheads
can be cut and dried, or left to stand
over winter. Clear them in early spring,
when large clumps can be divided.

△ ☼ ❋ ❋ ❋
↕↔ to 45cm (18in)

SPIRAEA JAPONICA
'Anthony Waterer'

Deciduous shrub

This medium-sized, twiggy shrub has
small, lance-shaped leaves that emerge
red and gradually turn dark green as
they age. The foliage is occasionally
tinged with cream or pink, too. The
flat heads of purple buds open to
frothy, dark pink flowers from mid-
to late summer. Grow this spiraea in a
shrub or mixed border in full sun and
any moderately fertile soil that does not
completely dry out. Cut back lightly
after flowering.

△ ◑ ☼ ❋ ❋ ❋
↕↔ to 1.5m (5ft)

ASTER NOVAE-ANGLIAE
'Andenken an Alma Pötschke'
Perennial

New England asters are clump-forming perennials, with erect, woody stems covered with mid-green, narrow, lance-shaped leaves. This variety bears dense sprays of salmon-red, daisy-like flowers and is a superb plant for a late summer border. It is also good for cutting. Plant New England asters in full sun or light shade and fertile, moist, well-drained soil. They also benefit from support with twiggy sticks, or canes and string. Divide clumps regularly in the spring.

◊ ◊ ☼ ☼ ✱ ✱ ✱
↕ to 1.2m (4ft) ↔ to 60cm (24in)

BEGONIA
Nonstop Series ♀
Perennial

These compact tuberous begonias have heart-shaped, mid-green leaves and double flowers, measuring up to 8cm (3in) across. They are available in a wide range of bright colours, including red, pink, yellow, and orange. Use them as bedding plants or in pots, and grow them in full sun in fertile, moist, well-drained soil. They are not hardy and the tubers must be dug up before the first frosts. Store them in dry sand in a cool room indoors.

◊ ◊ ☼ ✱
↕ to 30cm (12in) ↔ to 30cm (12in)

BRACTEANTHA BRACTEATA

Annual

The golden everlasting flower has greyish-green, lance-shaped leaves, and flowers over a long period from late spring to mid-autumn. There are many good varieties available, but the Bright Bikini Series is among the best, with double flowers in a wide range of colours, including red, orange and pink. This everlasting flower is a useful filler in a herbaceous border, and is excellent for cutting or drying (cut before the flowers are fully open). Plant it in full sun and moist, but well-drained soil.

⬤ ◐ ☼ ❋ ❋
‡ to 30cm (12in) ↔ to 30cm (12in)

CAMPSIS RADICANS

Climber

The common trumpet creeper has dark green leaves, divided into many leaflets, and in late summer produces clusters of orange-red, trumpet-shaped flowers. It is not fully hardy and is best planted in full sun against a warm wall, to which it will cling with aerial roots. Plant it in fertile, moist, well-drained soil. In warm areas it will grow vigorously to cover a large area within a few seasons, and it suits a tropical-style garden. Keep it clear of roofs and gutters, and hard prune it in winter to keep it in check.

⬤ ◐ ☼ ❋ ❋
‡ to 10m (30ft)

CANNA
'Assaut'

Perennial

The Indian shot plant is grown for its large, broad leaves and exotic-looking flowers. 'Assaut' has impressive purple-brown foliage, and spikes of scarlet blooms. Cannas grow quickly and make a dramatic addition to a late summer border, tropical-style garden, or they can be grown in pots. Plant them in late spring in full sun and moist, well-drained soil. They are not hardy and the rhizomes should be overwintered in just-moist compost in a frost-free place.

○ ◐ ☼ ❄
↕ to 1.2m (4ft) ↔ to 60cm (2ft)

CHRYSANTHEMUM
'Cherry Chintz'

Perennial

'Cherry Chintz' produces huge double blooms, composed of many red petals, in late summer. Plant it in a sheltered site in fertile, moist, well-drained soil, with well-rotted manure incorporated into it before planting. It is mostly grown for cutting and needs staking. Often grown in pots of loam-based compost under glass, it is also suitable for a sheltered, sunny patio or terrace. Remove all but the terminal bud for the largest flowers for exhibition.

○ ◐ ☼ ❄ ❄
↕ to 1.3m (4½ft) ↔ to 75cm (30in)

CLEMATIS
'Niobe' ♀

Climber

Possibly the best of all the red clematis, 'Niobe' has single, velvety, deep ruby-red flowers with yellow stamens, and blooms for a long period in summer. It will brighten up a trellis, or train it over an arch, or up a post. Plant 'Niobe' in a fertile, well-drained soil in sun or partial shade, with the roots in shade. It does particularly well in alkaline soil. In early spring remove any dead or damaged growth, and cut the rest of the stems back to a strong pair of buds.

◊ ☼ ☼ ✿ ✿ ✿
‡ to 3m (10ft)

COSMOS
ATROSANGUINEUS

Perennial

This Mexican plant has green, deeply-lobed leaves, and from midsummer to early autumn produces masses of dark red, chocolate-scented, single flowers on reddish-brown stems. While it is not completely hardy, it should survive most winters if covered with a thick layer of mulch. In very cold locations, dig up the tubers in the autumn and store them during the winter in trays of slightly damp sand or compost. Plant it in full sun in moist, well-drained soil.

◊◊ ☼ ✿ ✿
‡ to 75cm (30in) ↔ to 45cm (18in)

CROCOSMIA
'Lucifer' ♀

Perennial

This widely-grown plant has dramatic mid-green leaves, and from mid- to late summer produces arching stems bearing clusters of bright-red flowers. For maximum effect, plant it in groups in a gravel garden or herbaceous border. It prefers full sun or partial shade and a moist, well-drained soil. When clumps become congested after a few years divide them in the autumn and replant the corms elsewhere. In cold gardens, apply a protective mulch in winter.

◊ ◊ ☼ ☀ ❄ ❄
‡ to 1m (3ft) ↔ to 25cm (10in)

DAHLIA
'Bishop of Llandaff' ♀

Perennial

This superb dahlia is grown as much for its reddish-black foliage as for its bright red, semi-double flowers, which appear from midsummer to the early autumn. Plant it in full sun in fertile, moist, well-drained soil, and deadhead regularly. Dig up dahlia tubers after the first frost, and store them during the winter in dry sand in a frost-free place. Plant them out in mid- to late spring, with the top of the tuber about 8cm (3in) below the surface.

◊ ◊ ☼ ❄ ❄
‡ to 1m (3ft) ↔ to 45cm (18in)

DAHLIA
'Hillcrest Royal' ♀

Perennial

The red-purple, cactus-type flowers of
this striking dahlia are held on strong
stems, and make a dramatic statement
in the middle of a herbaceous border.
It needs a sunny site and fertile, moist,
well-drained soil. Deadhead it regularly
to promote the development of more
flowers, and in summer feed it with a
general-purpose fertilizer. Lift the tubers
and store them over winter in a frost-
free place. Plant in mid- to late spring,
and insert a stake at the same time.

◊ ◊ ☼ ❄ ❄
‡ to 1.2m (4ft) ↔ to 60cm (24in)

DAHLIA
'Whale's Rhonda'

Perennial

A dark purple-red pompon dahlia, the
petals of 'Whales Rhonda' have silver
undersides, giving them a two-tone
appearance. It is often grown for cut
flower arrangements or for exhibitions,
and should be planted in full sun in a
moist, well-drained soil. It can also be
planted in a large container. Lift and
store the tubers as described for the
'Bishop of Llandaff' (see left).

◊ ☼ ❄ ❄
‡ to 1m (3ft) ↔ to 60cm (24in)

FUCHSIA
'Celia Smedley' ♀

Deciduous shrub

This upright fuchsia produces flowers
with currant-red petals and pink sepals
from the middle of summer. It can be
grown outside in sun or partial shade
after the risk of frost has passed, in a
container of loam-based compost. Feed
it every month with a balanced liquid
fertilizer, or use a slow-release fertilizer
when planting. It is also suitable for
training as a standard. Overwinter it in
a frost-free greenhouse or conservatory.

○ ◐ ☼ ◑ ❋
‡ to 75cm (30in) ↔ to 75cm (30in)

FUCHSIA
'Golden Marinka' ♀

Deciduous shrub

From midsummer to early autumn this
trailing fuchsia produces bright red
flowers, set off by variegated green and
yellow foliage. Grow it in full sun or
partial shade. It can be used as ground
cover, or planted in hanging baskets in
soil-less potting compost, or containers
of loam-based compost. In the garden,
grow it in moist, well-drained soil. Feed
fuchsias in containers every fortnight
with a balanced liquid fertilizer, or mix
in slow-release fertilizer when planting.

○ ◐ ☼ ◑ ❋
‡ to 30cm (12in) ↔ 45cm (18in)

FUCHSIA MAGELLANICA
'Thompsonii'

Deciduous shrub

A hardy fuchsia with small red flowers
that appear in midsummer, this plant
can be grown as a hedge, or a shrubby
specimen in a border. In cold areas,
mulch it over winter, as the top growth
may be damaged by frost. Cut out dead
stems in spring, and pinch out the soft
tips of the stems to encourage bushy
growth. It is suitable for training as a
standard, or grow it in a large pot. Plant
it in a sheltered position in moist, free-
draining soil, in sun or partial shade.

○ ◐ ☼ ✷ ❉ ❉
‡ to 3m (10ft) ↔ to 2m (6ft)

GREVILLEA
ROSMARINIFOLIA ♥

Evergreen shrub

This shrub from Australia has ascending
or arching stems, covered with clusters
of narrow, dark green leaves with silky
hairs on the undersides. In summer it
produces clusters of spider-like, red,
pink, or creamy-white flowers. It is not
fully hardy, so plant it in a sheltered,
sunny spot, such as by a wall, in free-
draining neutral to acid soil, and mulch
it over winter. Alternatively, grow it in
containers of gritty, ericaceous compost,
and bring it inside in winter.

○ ☼ ❉ ❉
‡ to 2m (6ft) ↔ to 2m (6ft)

KNAUTIA MACEDONICA

Perennial

This clump-forming, often short-lived plant forms a rosette of hairy, lobed, basal leaves, and in summer produces branched stems that bear deeply divided leaves, and small, pincushion-shaped heads of tiny dark red flowers. Attractive to bees, it is perfect for a wild garden, herbaceous border, or cottage garden. It will flourish in full sun, in a well-drained, preferably alkaline soil.

◊ ☼ ❋ ❋ ❋

‡ to 75cm (30in) ↔ to 60cm (24in)

LATHYRUS ODORATUS
'Red Ensign'

Climber

This sweet pea carries sweetly scented, scarlet-red flowers from the summer to late autumn. It can be grown up a cane pyramid in a border for instant height, or train it against trellis. Cut the flowers regularly for the home and to stimulate more to develop. Grow sweet peas in full sun in moist, well-drained soil with well-rotted manure incorporated into it. Sow the seeds in pots in autumn to overwinter in a cold frame for planting out in spring, or sow *in situ* in spring.

◊ ☼ ❋ ❋ ❋

‡ to 2m (6ft)

LILIUM SPECIOSUM *VAR.* RUBRUM

Perennial bulb

This tall lily has erect, purple-flushed stems, and lance-shaped, dark green leaves. In late summer it produces up to a dozen fragrant, slightly pendent, turk's-cap flowers with swept-back petals. The deep carmine-red blooms are marked with darker red spots, and have very long stamens. This lily grows well in moist, well-drained slightly acid soil in partial shade, and will thrive in a woodland garden.

○ ○ ◑ ☼ ❋ ❋ ❋
‡ to 1.7m (5½ft)

LOBELIA *'Cherry Ripe'*

Perennial

'Cherry Ripe' has narrow, deep green leaves, and in summer, spikes of bright, cherry-red flowers. It will bring a splash of colour to a damp herbaceous border, woodland or the margins of a pool. For a spectacular effect, plant a group of five or more, in moist soil and full sun. Lobelias are very vulnerable to damage by slugs and snails in spring – sharp grit around the new shoots may deter these pests.

◑ ☼ ❋ ❋
‡ to 1m (3ft) ↔ to 23cm (9in)

LYCHNIS CHALCEDONICA ♛

Perennial

The Jerusalem cross forms a clump of
evergreen basal leaves, above which
domed heads of small, scarlet flowers
appear in summer, borne on tall, hairy
flower stems. The stems of this hardy
plant are rather weak and will need to
be staked if it is grown in an exposed
site. It is ideal for a herbaceous border,
or a gravel or wild garden, and should
be planted in moist, well-drained soil,
in full sun or dappled shade.

◊ ◊ ☼ ☀ ❁ ❁ ❁
‡ to 1.2m (4ft) ↔ to 30cm (12in)

PELARGONIUM
'Brockbury Scarlet'

Perennial

This erect pelargonium has rounded
leaves zoned with darker green. In the
summer, it produces clusters of spiky,
single, scarlet flowers, which should be
deadheaded regularly to keep the show
going. Pelargoniums are not hardy, and
are best grown in containers, or used as
bedding. When grown in the garden,
plant them in full sun in well-drained,
fertile soil, and then discard them or
pot them up to overwinter in a frost-
free greenhouse, or on a windowsill.

☼ ◊ ❁
‡ to 30cm (12in) ↔ to 20cm (8in)

PELARGONIUM
'Voodoo' ♀

Perennial

This tall, shrubby pelargonium produces clusters of single, bright red flowers with purplish-black centres in the summer and early autumn. Plant it in a container and place it in a sheltered, sunny location, on a patio or terrace. Deadhead regularly, and feed it occasionally in summer when it is in flower with a tomato fertilizer

◊ ☼ ❄
‡ to 60cm (24in) ↔ to 25cm (10in)

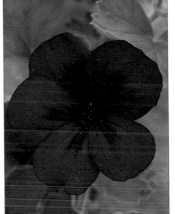

PENSTEMON
'Chester Scarlet' ♀

Perennial

In late summer and up to the first frosts this beautiful penstemon produces tall spikes of bell-shaped, scarlet flowers. It should be planted in full sun or partial shade in fertile, well-drained soil, and is suitable for a warm herbaceous border. Deadhead it regularly to prolong the flowering period. As this plant is not reliably hardy, protect it during winter with a thick layer of mulch. It is easy to propagate from softwood cuttings taken in early summer.

◊ ☼ ☼ ❄ ❄
‡ to 90cm (36in) ↔ to 75cm (30in)

PHYGELIUS × RECTUS
'African Queen' ♀

Evergreen shrub

In late summer, this upright plant bears
tall spires of pendent, pale red flowers
above lance-shaped, dark green leaves.
It should be planted in fertile, free-
draining soil in a border among hardy
shrubs, or against a sunny wall. In cold
locations, it is best to treat this frost
tender shrub as a herbaceous perennial.
To protect it in the winter, cover with
a thick mulch in autumn, and cut the
stems down to the ground in spring.

◊ ◊ ☼ ❄ ❄

‡ to 1m (3ft) ↔ to 1.2m (4ft)

RICINUS COMMUNIS
'Carmencita' ♀

Annual

The castor oil plant is usually grown
for its large, architectural, palm-shaped
leaves. This variety has dark bronzy-
red foliage, and in late summer it may
produce tall spikes of small, bright red
flowers. It should be planted in full sun
in fertile, well-drained soil, and is useful
in bedding schemes and tropical-style
gardens. It can also be grown in a large
container. All parts of this plant are
highly toxic.

◊ ☼ ❄

‡ to 1.5m (5ft) ↔ to 90cm (3ft)

SALVIA COCCINEA
'Lady in Red' ♀

Perennial

This tender South American perennial is
usually treated as an annual in colder
countries. It has erect stems and oval or
heart-shaped dark green leaves, and in
the summer and autumn it produces
spikes of bright red flowers. Plant it in a
sunny position in light, well-drained soil.
This bushy salvia works well at the front
of a herbaceous border, or use it as a
bedding or container plant. The seeds
should be sown in spring for flowers
the same year.

○ ☼ ❋ ❋
‡ to 60cm (24in) ↔ to 30cm (12in)

SALVIA SPLENDENS
'Scarlet King'

Perennial

Scarlet sage is a perennial, but is widely
grown as an annual bedding plant.
'Scarlet King' has a compact habit and
produces dense spikes of bright red
flowers, above slightly hairy, oval, dark
green leaves. Grow it in groups in a
sunny position in moist, well-drained
soil, or in containers. Plant out young
plants in early summer after all risk of
frost has passed.

○ ◐ ☼ ❋
‡ to 25cm (10in) ↔ to 35cm (14in)

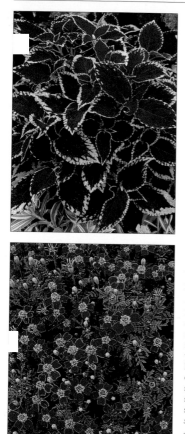

SOLENOSTEMON SCUTELLARIOIDES

Perennial

Better known as coleus, the flame nettle is a tender plant, grown primarily for its foliage. The most decorative varieties have toothed, hairy variegated leaves in a range of bright colours, including red, yellow, burgundy and green. They bear spikes of small blue or white flowers, which should be removed before they open to retain the foliage effect. Plant them in light shade, in pots of loam-based compost, or as part of a bedding scheme in moist, well-drained soil.

◊ ◊ ☼ ❈
‡ to 45cm (18in) ↔ to 30cm (12in)

TAGETES
'Cinnabar'

Annual

One of many varieties of fast-growing French marigold, this has feathery, deeply-divided, dark green leaves. From midsummer to early autumn it bears rusty-red, single flowers with bright yellow eyes. Usually grown as a half-hardy annual bedding plant or for containers, it should be planted in a sunny location in fertile, well-drained soil. Easy to raise from seed, it can be sown under glass in early spring, or *in situ* in late spring.

◊ ☼ ❈
‡ to 30cm (12in) ↔ to 30cm (12in)

ZAUSCHNERIA CALIFORNICA
'Dublin' ♀

Perennial

The Californian fuchsia forms a clump of
slightly hairy, greyish-green, lance-shaped
leaves, and in late summer bears large
numbers of bright red, tubular flowers on
slightly arching stems. Plant it in a gravel
or rock garden, at the front of a mixed
border, or in the gaps of a dry stone
wall, in full sun and reasonably fertile,
well-drained soil. It is quite hardy, but
needs a protected site, out of cold winds.

◊ ☼ ❋ ❋
‡ to 30cm (12in) ↔ to 45cm (18in)

ZINNIA ELEGANS
'Ruffles'

Annual

A striking, upright, bushy plant with
egg- or lance-shaped, mid-green leaves,
'Ruffles' lives up to its name, bearing
frilly, pompon, fully double flowers in
a wide range of colours, including red.
Plant it in sun, in any well-drained soil.
Use it as bedding, or plant it in groups
in a herbaceous border. Zinnias are also
good for cutting for use in the home.

◊ ☼ ❋
‡ to 60cm (24in) ↔ to 30cm (12in)

ACONITUM
'Bressingham Spire' ♀

Perennial

Monkshood is a tall, striking plant that
thrives in woodland gardens and in
herbaceous borders. It has glossy, dark
green, deeply-lobed leaves, and in late
summer and early autumn produces
large spikes of deep violet-blue flowers.
It can be grown in full sun, but will
perform better in partial shade and
moist soil. To maintain its vigour, dig it
up and divide it after 3-4 years. All
parts of this plant are very toxic.

◊ ☼ ☀ ❉ ❉ ❉
‡ to 1m (3ft) ↔ to 50cm (20in)

ASTER × FRIKARTII
'Mönch' ♀

Perennial

Considered by many people to be one
of the best of the perennial asters, this
form has bright lavender-blue, daisy-
like flowers, held on tall sturdy stems
that rarely need staking. It flowers over
a very long period from midsummer
until the first frosts. An excellent
addition to a herbaceous border, this
aster needs a sunny site and well-
drained, fertile soil. It can be
propagated by division in spring.

◊ ☼ ❉ ❉ ❉
‡ to 70cm (28in) ↔ to 40cm (16in)

ASTER NOVI-BELGII
'Chequers'

Perennial

Also known as 'Queen Charlotte', this
vigorous plant will spread rapidly. The
erect, branched stems bear dark green
leaves, and purple, daisy-like flowers
with yellow eyes appear from late
summer to early autumn. Plant this
Michaelmas daisy in rich, moist soil in
full sun or partial shade in a border or
gravel garden and provide support from
early summer with twiggy sticks which
will soon be covered by the foliage.

◐ ☼ ❀ ❀ ❀
‡ to 90cm (36in) ↔ to 75cm (30in)

BUDDLEJA DAVIDII
'Dartmoor' ♀

Deciduous shrub

This butterfly bush has long, arching
branches and grey-green leaves. From
mid- to late summer, it produces large
conical clusters of small, magenta-
purple, fragrant flowers. Its flowers
attract butterflies, and it is ideal for a
wildlife garden. Alternatively, plant it
close to a path or the house where the
butterflies can be seen. It prefers full
sun and a well-drained soil. Prune it
hard in the spring, to the ground or to
a low permanent framework.

◐ ☼ ❀ ❀ ❀
‡ to 3m (10ft) ↔ to 5m (15ft)

CLEMATIS
'Jackmanii' ♀

Climber

From midsummer to the middle of
autumn, this widely grown clematis
bears an abundance of large, single,
velvety, purple-violet flowers. Team it
with roses on a pergola or arch, or train
it up trellis for late summer colour. It
will flourish in full sun or partial shade,
in fertile, moist, well-drained soil, with
the roots in shade. Flowering on the
current year's stems, it should be
pruned back to about 20cm (8in) from
the ground in early spring.

◊ ◊ ☼ ☀ ❄ ❄ ❄
‡ to 3m (10ft)

CLEMATIS VITICELLA
'Purpurea Plena Elegans' ♀

Climber

This variety of clematis has leathery,
lobed leaves. In late summer, it
produces double, purplish-mauve
flowers with unusual ruffled petals.
Plant it in full sun or partial shade in
fertile, moist, well-drained soil, and
train it over a pergola or arch, or grow
it through a large shrub. It flowers on the
current year's stems and should be
cut back to just above the ground in
early spring.

◊ ◊ ☼ ☀ ❄ ❄ ❄
‡ to 4m (12ft)

DABOECIA CANTABRICA
'Bicolor' ♀

Evergreen shrub

The leaves of the Cantabrian heath are larger than other heathers. The urn-shaped flowers are borne over a long period from summer to mid-autumn, and 'Bicolor' produces blooms in purple-pink, white or striped on the same flower spike. Plant it in full sun or light shade, in neutral or acid, well-drained soil. It is suitable for a rock or heather garden, and forms a colourful carpet when used as ground cover.

◊ ☼ ☀ ❄❄❄
↕ to 45cm (18in) ↔ to 60cm (24in)

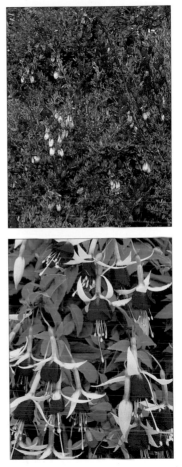

FUCHSIA
'Auntie Jinks'

Deciduous shrub

From midsummer to mid-autumn this trailing plant produces flowers with deep pink tubes, pink-edged white sepals and purple petals. For hanging baskets, use a soil-less compost, while plants in containers are better grown in loam-based compost. Feed fortnightly with a balanced fertilizer. It is happy in full sun or partial shade, but it is not hardy and should be overwintered in a light, frost-free place. Easy to raise from softwood cuttings in spring.

◊ ◊ ☼ ☀ ❄
↕ to 20cm (8in) ↔ to 40cm (16in)

FUCHSIA
'La Campanella' ♀

Deciduous shrub

The trailing branches of this fuchsia
bear mid-green leaves and masses of
blooms from midsummer up to the first
frosts. The semi-double flowers are pale
pink and deep purple. In summer, plant
it outside in full sun or partial shade,
in hanging baskets filled with soil-less
compost. It can also be grown in
a container filled with a loam-based
compost. Feed fortnightly with a
balanced fertilizer. It should be
overwintered in a cool greenhouse.

◊ ◊ ☼ ☼ ❄
‡ to 30cm (12in) ↔ 45cm (18in)

LAVANDULA ANGUSTIFOLIA
'Hidcote' ♀

Evergreen shrub

This English lavender has narrow,
silver-grey, aromatic leaves, and in mid-
to late summer it produces spikes of
highly fragrant, small purple flowers,
loved by bees. 'Hidcote' makes a good
low hedge, or is suitable for planting in
a gravel garden. It needs a site in full
sun, and a slightly fertile, well-drained
soil. Lavenders are easily propagated by
taking semi-ripe cuttings in summer.
Trim hedges in spring and lightly after
flowering to remove the dead heads.

◊ ☼ ❄ ❄ ❄
‡ to 60cm (24in) ↔ to 75cm (30in)

LAVANDULA STOECHAS ♥

Evergreen

French lavender forms an attractive
rounded shrub, with branching stems
covered with narrow greyish-green,
slightly fragrant leaves. It is smaller and
flowers slightly earlier than English
lavender, but the blooms are not as
fragrant. The small purple flowers, each
topped by a tuft of pinky-mauve, petal-
like bracts, are produced throughout
the summer. It is not completely hardy,
and should be grown in a warm,
sheltered position in slightly fertile,
well-drained soil, or in containers..

◊ ☼ ❋ ❋
‡ to 60cm (74in) ↔ to 60cm (24in)

LIATRIS SPICATA

Perennial

Gayfeather is an attractive plant from
the prairies of North America. It forms a
tuft of narrow leaves, measuring up to
40cm (16in) in length, and in late
summer and early autumn it produces
tall spikes of feathery, pinkish-purple
flowers that are attractive to bees. The
flower buds at the top of the spike
open before those further down. Plant
it in full sun and very well-drained,
reasonably fertile soil. It is not suitable
for heavy clay soils, as the roots will rot
if they get too wet.

◊ ☼ ❋ ❋ ❋
‡ to 60cm (74in) ↔ to 30cm (12in)

LIMONIUM PLATYPHYLLUM

Perennial

Sea lavender forms a rosette of large, elliptic- or spoon-shaped, dark green leaves, and in late summer it produces dense, wiry, branched stems, covered with clusters of tiny, tubular, lavender-blue flowers. It grows well in coastal areas, but the frothy sprays of flowers are a valuable addition to any mixed or herbaceous border. Plant four or five plants together for maximum impact, and grow them in full sun and sandy, well-drained soil. The cultivar 'Violetta' has deep violet flowers.

◊ ☼ ❊ ❊ ❊
‡ to 60cm (24in) ↔ to 45cm (18in)

LOBELIA ERINUS
'Cascade Blue' ♀

Perennial

This small, trailing lobelia flowers from summer to the middle of autumn. It is grown as an annual. It produces hundreds of tiny, two-lipped, dark blue flowers, although similar plants with white, pink, red, purple, and violet flowers are available. All lobelias make superb plants for hanging baskets and trailing over the edges of containers or window boxes. Plant them in full sun, or in partial shade, which they last longer in, and do not let them dry out.

◊ ☼ ◐ ❊
‡ ↔ to 15cm (6in)

LOBELIA × GERARDII
'Vedrariensis'
Perennial

This tall, stately plant forms a rosette
of elliptic- or lance-shaped deep green
leaves. The flower spikes appear in late
summer and bear small, violet-purple,
tubular flowers. Position four or five
plants together in a group to maximize
their impact, and plant them in moist,
fertile soil that does not dry out, in full
sun or partial shade. This lobelia is
perfect for a late-summer border, or for
the margins of a water garden.

◊ ☼ ❀ ❀ ❀
‡ to 1m (3ft) ↔ to 30cm (12in)

LYTHRUM SALICARIA
Perennial

Purple loosestrife is a vigorous, clump
forming plant with lance-shaped, soft
green leaves. In late summer a large
number of tall flower spikes appear,
composed of small, star-shaped, reddish-
purple flowers. It needs permanently
moist soil and a sunny situation to do
well, and will flourish in a bog garden,
damp border, or beside water.

◊ ☼ ❀ ❀ ❀
‡ to 1m (36in) ↔ to 45cm (18in)

PASSIFLORA
'Amethyst' ♀

Climber

This fast-growing passion flower bears
distinctive purple-blue flowers in late
summer, followed by large, oval, orange
fruits. It is not hardy, and in cold areas,
it is best to grow this climber in a warm
greenhouse or a conservatory where it
will form a leafy canopy when trained
on wires or support. Plant it in a
container filled with loam-based
compost, and water well in summer.
Prune back the vigorous growth in
spring to keep within bounds.

○ ◐ ☼ ❄
‡ to 4m (12ft)

PENSTEMON
'Stapleford Gem' ♀

Perennial

The bell-shaped flowers of this lilac-
purple penstemon are suffused with
shades of mauve, pink and purple,
giving a multi-coloured effect. It blooms
from midsummer to early autumn, and
needs full sun and a well-drained soil.
Penstemons are wonderful plants for a
herbaceous border, and this one works
well as part of a pastel colour scheme.
'Stapleford Gem' is one of the hardiest
penstemons, but will need a sheltered
spot and winter mulch in cold areas.

○ ☼ ☀ ❄ ❄
‡ to 60cm (24n) ↔ to 45cm (18in)

STACHYS OFFICINALIS

Perennial

Wood betony is an attractive perennial which produces ground covering rosettes of deeply veined leaves with scalloped edges. From early summer to early autumn it is adorned with spikes of tubular, reddish-purple flowers. Its long flowering season makes it an ideal candidate for the front of a herbaceous border, or use it in a wild garden. Easy to grow, this betony prefers a sunny or lightly shaded position in well-drained, slightly fertile soil. Divide in autumn or spring.

◊ ☼ ◑ ✿ ✿ ✿
‡ to 60cm (24in) ↔ to 45cm (18in)

THALICTRUM AQUILEGIIFOLIUM 'Thundercloud' ♀

Perennial

Meadow rues are clump-forming plants with fern-like foliage composed of small, rounded leaflets. 'Thundercloud' has erect, waxy stems, and clusters of tiny flowers are borne in the summer. The outer part of the flower quickly falls away to leave the colourful, dark purple stamens that give the blooms a frothy appearance. It may take some time to become established, and prefers partial shade and deep, moist soil.

◊ ◑ ✿ ✿ ✿
‡ to 1m (3ft) ↔ to 45cm (18in)

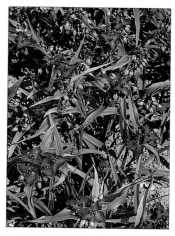

TRADESCANTIA
'Purple Dome'

Perennial

This clump-forming, hardy plant belongs to the Andersoniana group of tradescantias, and has branching stems and narrow, strappy leaves. In summer to early autumn, it produces clusters of small, deep purple flowers with three triangular petals and fluffy purple stamens. Plant it *en masse* in a mixed or herbaceous border, in full sun or partial shade, and a moist, fertile soil. Divide large clumps in autumn or spring.

◊ ☼ ◑ ❄ ❄ ❄
‡ to 60cm (24in) ↔ to 45cm (18in)

TULBAGHIA VIOLACEA

Perennial bulb

This South African plant forms clumps of narrow, greyish-green leaves, and from midsummer to early autumn it produces stout stems that bear clusters of fragrant, star-shaped, lilac-blue flowers. In mild areas it can be grown outside in a sunny position in slightly fertile, well-drained soil. In cold countries where temperatures dip well below freezing for long periods, pot it up in a container filled with loam-based compost, and overwinter it in a cool greenhouse or conservatory.

◊ ☼ ❄ ❄
‡ to 60cm (24in) ↔ to 30cm (12in)

VERBENA BONARIENSIS ♛

Perennial

The tall, airy, branched stems of this
verbena hold aloft small, domed
clusters of tiny, lilac-purple, scented
flowers, which appear from midsummer
to early autumn. Individual plants come
into their own when planted in a
group, and can be positioned at the
front, as well as the back, of the border
or in a gravel garden. They need full
sun and fertile, well-drained soil, and a
sheltered position. In cold gardens
mulch with bracken or garden compost
for winter protection.

◊ ☼ ❀ ❀
‡ to 1.5m (5ft) ↔ to 60cm (2ft)

VIOLA
'Bowles' Black'

Perennial

This short-lived, clump-forming pansy is
more often grown as a biennial. It is
quite vigorous, and produces a mat of
short stems, covered with lobed, oval
leaves. The flowers open from spring to
autumn and are a very deep shade of
violet, which can appear almost black.
A good plant for a rock garden, gravel
garden, sunny bank or terracotta pot,
this viola needs a sunny position and a
well-drained, reasonably fertile soil.

◊ ☼ ❀ ❀ ❀
‡ to 15cm (6in) ↔ to 8cm (3in)

AGAPANTHUS
'Blue Giant'

Perennial

The African blue lily is impossible to overlook in the late summer garden. It forms a clump of arching, deep green, strap-shaped leaves, and large spherical flowerheads, held on tall, stiff stems. 'Blue Giant' is exceptionally large, with huge balls of deep blue, bell-shaped flowers. It should be grown in a sunny, sheltered position, in fertile, moist, well-drained soil. It is borderline hardy, so in cold areas, protect it with a thick layer of mulch in winter.

◊ ◊ ☼ ❁ ❁ ❁
‡ to 1.2m (4ft) ↔ to 60cm (24in)

ASTER AMELLUS
'King George' ♥

Perennial

This species prefers drier conditions than the popular New England and New York asters, and thrives in alkaline soil. It has small, mid-green leaves, and from late summer to late autumn produces loose clusters of light violet-blue, daisy-like flowers. Plant it in groups in a sunny herbaceous or mixed border, in reasonably fertile, well drained soil. Divide clumps every three to four years in spring to rejuvenate and to keep plants growing vigorously.

◊ ☼ ❁ ❁ ❁
‡ ↔ to 45cm (18in)

BRACHYSCOME IBERIDIFOLIA
Annual

The Swan River daisy is a bushy, sprawling plant, with deeply divided, greyish-green, ferny foliage. From mid- to late summer it produces blue, violet or white, slightly scented, daisy-like flowers. An excellent plant for edging summer containers, including hanging baskets, it will also bring colour to the front of a herbaceous border. The seed should be sown under glass in the spring, and young plants moved out after the last frost, in a sunny position and well-drained, fertile soil.

◊◊ ☼ ❋

‡ to 45cm (18in) ↔ to 35cm (14in)

CAMPANULA COCHLEARIIFOLIA 🏆
Perennial

Known as fairies' thimbles, this dwarf campanula forms rosettes of toothed, bright green leaves, and in summer produces masses of slightly pendent, pale blue or white flowers. It will add colour and interest to a rock garden, or the gaps in paving or a dry-stone wall, flourishing in the well-drained soil both these sites afford. It can be grown in full sun or partial shade, and although it may become rather invasive, it is easy to control by pulling up surplus growth.

♨ ᛭ ᛭ ⚛ ⚛ ⚛

‡ to 8cm (3in) ↔ to 30cm (12in)

CARYOPTERIS X CLANDONENSIS *'Heavenly Blue'*

Deciduous shrub

This free-flowering plant with aromatic, greyish-green foliage forms clusters of deep blue flowers in late summer. It provides colour and form in a mixed border or gravel garden, and needs full sun and a sheltered site in well-drained soil. In cold gardens, plant by a sunny wall to give some extra protection during winter. Prune it back hard in spring, taking care not to cut into old wood, from which it may not regrow.

◊ ☼ ✿ ✿
‡ to 1m (3ft) ↔ to 1m (3ft)

CATANANCHE CAERULEA *'Major'* ♀

Perennial

Cupid's dart is a short-lived perennial, which is often grown as biennial. It looks rather like a cornflower, with oblong, lilac-blue petals with serrated tips and a dark blue centre. Plant it in a sunny position in well-drained soil at the front or in the middle of a flower or herbaceous border. It does not grow very well in heavy soils, and may die at the end of the year.

◊ ☼ ✿ ✿ ✿
‡ to 60cm (24in) ↔ to 30cm (24in)

CEANOTHUS
'Autumnal Blue' ♀

Evergreen shrub

Although many *Ceanothus* are spring-
flowering, some perform later in the
year. 'Autumnal Blue' bears bright blue
flowers from late summer until the
autumn. It is probably the hardiest
evergreen ceanothus and forms a round
bush, but can also be wall trained, a
particularly suitable way of growing it
in colder gardens. It grows best in well-
drained, fertile soil and sunny position,
sheltered from cold winter winds. Prune
in spring to keep in shape.

○ ☼ ❊ ❊
↕ ↔ to 3m (10ft)

CEANOTHUS
'Burkwoodii' ♀

Evergreen shrub

Compact clusters of tiny, bright blue
flowers, are borne on this medium-
sized bush from late summer to early
autumn. It also produces attractive oval,
glossy, dark evergreen foliage. Although
reasonably hardy, this ceanothus will
thrive and grow larger than indicated
when planted against a west- or south-
facing wall, sheltered from cold winds.
It prefers a well-drained, fertile soil, and
should be pruned lightly in spring to
help maintain its shape.

○ ☼ ❊ ❊
↕ to 1.5m (5ft) ↔ to 2m (6ft)

EICHHORNIA CRASSIPES
Perennial

The water hyacinth is a floating aquatic plant, which forms rosettes of glossy green leaves. In late summer in warm areas it will produce a spike of pale blue or violet flowers. It has become a nuisance in many parts of the world but because it is not hardy it is safe to introduce it into ponds in colder countries. Overwinter in an aquarium of moist compost, at a minimum temperature of 15°C (59°F) in a good light, such as a windowsill. Alternatively, buy new plants each year in late spring.

⬤ ☼ ❄
↕ ↔ to 18cm (45in)

FELICIA AMELLOIDES
'Santa Anita' ♀
Evergreen shrub

The tender blue daisy is often grown as an annual in cooler climates. It is bushy and compact, with oval, deep green leaves. From the middle of summer to autumn, it bears bright blue, daisy-like flowers with yellow centres. It can be grown in containers or is mostly used as bedding, although it may survive in mild, sheltered areas in the garden. Plant it in full sun in any well-drained soil. Pinch out the shoot tips in the spring to promote side shoots.

◊ ☼ ❄
↕ ↔ to 60cm (12in)

FELICIA BERGERIANA
Annual

The kingfisher daisy looks rather like a small aster, with single, blue flowers with bright yellow eyes, and greyish-green, lance-shaped leaves. It is an excellent plant for summer containers or hanging baskets, or for the front of a raised bed. Plant it outside in a sunny position in any well-drained soil, or in containers filled with loam-based potting compost.

◊ ☼ ❊
↕↔ to 15cm (6in)

GENTIANA ASCLEPIADEA ♀
Perennial

An erect herbaceous plant, the willow gentian forms a clump of lance-shaped leaves, and from late summer to early autumn produces clusters of beautiful deep blue, funnel-shaped flowers. A good plant for a lightly shaded border, it prefers permanently moist, but well-drained soil rich in organic matter. There is also an attractive white form called 'Alba'. To propagate it, divide the clumps in spring.

◊ ☼ ❊ ❊ ❊
↕ to 90cm (36in) ↔ to 45cm (18in)

HIBISCUS SYRIACUS
'Oiseau Bleu' ♀
Deciduous shrub

This hardy hibiscus makes an exotic-looking addition to a shrub or mixed border. It has upright branches and toothed, lobed, mid-green leaves that appear late in the spring. In late summer it produces large, deep blue, trumpet-shaped flowers. Plant it in full sun and moist, well-drained, fertile soil. It will survive most winters, but in very cold areas plant it against a warm wall, and cover the root area with a thick mulch during the winter.

◊ ◊ ☼ ❄ ❄ ❄
‡ to 3m (10ft) ↔ to 2m (6ft)

HYDRANGEA MACROPHYLLA
'Blue Wave'
Deciduous shrub

This lacecap hydrangea makes a rounded shrub with large green leaves, and flat flowerheads that appear from mid- to late summer. The blooms are made up of small, dark blue fertile flowers, surrounded by large pale blue sterile flowers. In acid soil the flowers turn a rich shade of gentian-blue but in alkaline soil they are mauve-pink. Plant it in full sun or partial shade in moist, well-drained, fertile soil, rich in organic matter. Suitable for coastal gardens.

◊ ◊ ☼ ☀ ❄ ❄ ❄
‡ to 2m (6ft) ↔ to 2.5m (8ft)

HYDRANGEA SERRATA
'Bluebird' ♥

Deciduous shrub

This compact hydrangea has bright
green leaves. From late summer to early
autumn it bears large flat flowerheads
of tiny, deep blue fertile flowers,
surrounded by larger, pale-blue, infertile
flowers, which may become pink in
alkaline soil. Ideal for a shrub or mixed
border in a small garden, it grows well
in full sun or partial shade and moist,
but well drained, fertile soil, preferably
neutral, or slightly acid for the best
flower colour.

◊ ◊ ☼ ☀ ❋ ❋
‡↔ to 1.2m (4ft)

HYSSOPUS OFFICINALIS

Evergreen shrub

Hyssop is a small, bushy herb, with
narrow, mid-green, aromatic leaves, and
deep blue flowers arranged on a spike,
which appear from late summer to early
autumn. Hyssop makes a superb plant
for a herb, gravel, rock or wild garden,
where it will attract bees and other
nectar-seeking insects. It thrives in full
sun and fertile, well-drained neutral or
alkaline soil. Prune it lightly after
flowering to keep it neat. There are
also forms with white or pink flowers.

◊ ☼ ❋ ❋ ❋
‡ to 60cm (2ft) ↔ to 1m (3ft)

IPOMOEA
'Heavenly Blue' ♛

Climber

Morning glory, grown as an annual, has fast-growing twining stems and heart-shaped, light green leaves. In late summer it produces large sky-blue, funnel-shaped flowers with white throats. Plant this eye-catching climber outside in late spring or early summer, in full sun and well-drained soil. Provide support in the form of a tripod or use it to clothe arches, a trellis or a container.

○ ☼ ❋ ❋
‡ to 4m (12ft)

LATHYRUS NERVOSUS

Climber

Lord Anson's blue pea, a perennial, is often grown as an annual. In late summer it bears fragrant, indigo-blue flowers. Each leaf is split into a pair of greyish-green leaflets. It will quickly ascend a support when grown in full sun and a well-drained, fertile soil. This pea is not fully hardy and will be killed by winter wet and hard frosts unless protected with a cloche and a deep dry mulch. Grow it from seed in early spring and plant it out in late spring or early in the summer.

○ ☼ ❋ ❋
‡ to 5m (15ft)

LATHYRUS ODORATUS
'Noel Sutton' ♀

Annual

'Noel Sutton' is a vigorous sweet pea,
which can be grown up supporting
canes or a trellis. If shoot tips are
pinched out while the plant is young, it
will form a much smaller bush suitable
for a container. In summer the stems
are covered with sweetly perfumed,
mauve-blue flowers, which should be
picked regularly for the home to
promote new blooms. Plant it in sun or
light shade in moist, well-drained soil,
rich in organic matter.

◊ ◗ ☼ ☀ ❋ ❋ ❋
‡ to 2.5m (8ft)

LOBELIA SIPHILITICA

Perennial

The blue cardinal flower forms a rosette
of egg-shaped, light green leaves. In
summer it produces tall stems that bear
tubular, bright blue blooms with double
lips. It needs permanently moist, fertile
soil, and is happy in full sun or partial
shade. It adds grace and elegance to
a damp border, or an area beneath
deciduous trees, or plant it beside a
pool. To propagate this lobelia, divide
it in spring.

◗ ☼ ☀ ❋ ❋ ❋
‡ to 120cm (48in) ↔ to 30cm (12in)

NEMESIA STRUMOSA
'Blue Gem'

Annual

This vigorous, compact, bushy annual
has spoon- or lance-shaped, toothed,
and slightly hairy leaves. In late
summer it bears vast numbers of small,
bright blue flowers, and makes a
colourful bedding or container plant.
It needs a site in full sun and moist,
well-drained soil. It must be watered
regularly during the summer if it is to
produce a good display of flowers.
Nemesias come in other colours
including red, yellow and pink.

◊ ◊ ☼ ❄

‡ to 30cm (12in) ↔ to 15cm (6in)

NEPETA SIBIRICA

Perennial

This relative of catmint is a vigorous
plant, with branched, upright stems
and dark green, lance-shaped,
toothed, aromatic foliage. In late
summer lavender-blue flowers appear
on tall spikes, and make a bold
statement in a gravel garden or a
herbaceous bed. As its name suggests,
this plant comes from Siberia and is
very hardy. It should be planted and
divided in spring in a sunny position,
in well-drained soil.

◊ ☼ ❄ ❄ ❄

‡ to 90cm (36in) ↔ to 45cm (18in)

PEROVSKIA
'Blue Spire' ♀

Deciduous shrub

This is an attractive, late flowering
shrub with tall stems and silver, deeply
dissected, aromatic foliage. In the late
summer it produces branched spikes of
small lavender-blue flowers. It prefers a
sunny position and should be planted
in very well drained soil in a gravel bed
or a herbaceous border, or use it in a
low hedge to edge a path. To keep it
bushy, cut back stems in spring. It will
tolerate chalk soil and coastal conditions.

◊ ☼ ❄ ❄ ❄
‡ to 1.2m (4ft) ↔ to 1m (3ft)

PLATYCODON
GRANDIFLORUS ♀

Perennial

The balloon flower is often mistaken
for a campanula, to which it is related.
The leaves appear late in the spring,
but eventually grow to form a clump
of toothed, blue green foliage. In late
summer, bell-shaped, purplish-blue
flowers open from balloon-shaped
buds. Ideal for a rock garden or the
front of a border, it does not like to be
disturbed and should not be divided.
Plant it in full sun or partial shade in
moist, well-drained soil.

◊ ◊ ☼ ❄ ❄ ❄
‡ to 60cm (24in) ↔ to 30cm (12in)

SALVIA FARINACEA
'Victoria' ♀

Perennial

Although mealy sage is perennial, it is
usually grown as an annual bedding
plant. This erect, bushy plant has
glossy, lance-shaped leaves that are
white beneath, and attractive stems
dusted white. It blooms from summer
to autumn, and bears spikes of deep
blue flowers. Plant after danger of frost
is past in a sunny border, or use as
bedding, in well-drained, moist soil. A
tender plant, mealy sage should be
grown from seed each year.

◊ ◊ ☼ ❋
‡ to 45cm (18in) ↔ to 30cm (12in

SALVIA GUARANITICA
'Blue Enigma' ♀

Perennial

Sage is commonly grown as a tender
perennial, but may survive mild winters
and grow to form a substantial clump
of broad, lance-shaped leaves that smell
of anise if crushed. From late summer
the tall stems of 'Blue Enigma' bear
spikes of tubular, deep blue flowers.
When grown in large groups, it makes
a spectacular display at the back of a
border. Plant it in moist, well-drained
soil in sun or light shade and protect
over winter with a deep mulch.

◊ ◊ ☼ ☼ ❋
‡ to 1.5m (5ft) ↔ to 90cm (36in)

SALVIA ULIGINOSA ♥

Perennial

The bog sage prefers damp conditions.
It forms a clump of lance-shaped mid-
green leaves, above which tall flower
spikes bear clusters of pale blue
flowers. A good source of colour for
the back of a damp late summer
border, it should be planted in full sun
and moist soil. The bog sage is not
totally hardy, but it can survive winters
in mild areas if protected with a thick
layer of mulch or grown in a pot and
moved under glass.

◊ ☼ ❈ ❈
↕ to 2m (6ft) ↔ to 90cm (36in)

SOLANUM RANTONNETII
'Royal Robe'

Evergreen shrub

The blue potato bush has wavy-edged,
deep green leaves, and in late summer
produces clusters of large, violet-blue
flowers with a bright yellow star in the
centre. The blooms are followed by red
fruits in autumn. It is a tender plant, but
offers late summer colour when grown
in a large container and moved out on
to the patio. Plant it in loam-based
compost, and position it in bright,
indirect light, under glass, as strong
sunshine will scorch it.

◊ ☼ ❈
↕ to 2m (6ft) ↔ to 2m (6ft)

STOKESIA LAEVIS

Evergreen perennial

Stokes' aster is an evergreen, clump-forming plant, with long, lance-shaped leaves with a distinctive pale green midrib. From midsummer to early autumn, it bears solitary cornflower-like blooms on stout stems. The outer petals are purplish-blue, pink or white – the pale varieties exhibit a darker centre, while the dark forms have pale centres. 'Blue Star' has deep blue petals and a pale blue eye. Plant Stokes' asters in a sunny border in well-drained soil.

◊ ☼ ❋ ❋ ❋
↕ ↔ to 45cm (18in)

TRADESCANTIA
'J. C. Weguelin' ♀

Perennial

This clump-forming, hardy plant has narrow, lance-shaped, mid-green leaves, held on branching stems. The blooms appear in late summer, and are composed of pale blue petals that surround fluffy stamens. It can be used at the front of a mixed or herbaceous border, and should be planted in full sun or partial shade in moist, well-drained, fertile soil. It can be divided in the spring or autumn.

◊ ☼ ☼ ❋ ❋ ❋
↕ to 60cm (24in) ↔ to 45cm (18in)

VERONICA PROSTRATA ♀

Perennial

The prostrate speedwell forms a low-growing mat of small, toothed leaves, and in late summer short, upright stems are clothed with tiny pale or deep blue blooms. It is ideally suited to a rock garden or raised bed, but will also add interest to a gravel garden or a dry stone wall. Plant it in full sun in slightly fertile, well-drained soil. To propagate it, divide it in the autumn or spring.

△ ☼ ❊ ❊ ❊
‡ to 15cm (6in) ↔ 40cm (16in)

VERONICA SPICATA

Perennial

This mat-forming plant has spreading stems, which root when they touch the soil. It soon makes a dense clump of linear, toothed leaves, and in late summer bears upright stems of small bright blue flowers with purple stamens. Plant this veronica at the front of a herbaceous border or in a gravel garden in full sun or partial shade, and slightly fertile, moist, well-drained soil. 'Rotfuchs' has spikes of deep pink flowers.

△ ◑ ☼ ☼ ❊ ❊ ❊
‡ to 40cm (14in) ↔ to 45cm (10in)

AGAVE AMERICANA 'Variegata' ♀

Perennial

This plant, ideal for a patio or tropical-style garden, forms a basal rosette of fleshy, lance-shaped, cream-edged leaves, with spiny margins and pointed tips. The leaves grow upright, then arch over and finally lie flat on the ground. Plant in a large container of loam-based compost. Place it outside in summer, and move it indoors in winter. It may survive outside in mild, very well-drained, sheltered conditions provided it is protected when young.

◊ ☼ ❋
↕ ↔ to 1.5m (5ft))

DESCHAMPSIA CESPITOSA 'Goldtau'

Perennial grass

Tussock grass is a robust, evergreen plant with rigid, rough-edged green leaves. In late summer 'Goldtau' bears arching stems of yellow-green that turn golden-brown as they age. This form is much more compact than other tussock grasses, and is perfect for a herbaceous or wildflower garden. It is happy in full sun or partial shade, and a moist or well-drained soil. Leave the dried flowerheads to decorate a winter garden, but remove them in spring.

◊ ◗ ☼ ☼ ❋ ❋ ❋
↕ ↔ to 75cm (30in)

ENSETE VENTRICOSUM ♛

Perennial

The Ethiopian banana is a tender plant, and bears huge, paddle-shaped leaves. Grow it in a large pot of loam-based compost. It will inject an exotic look when moved outside and plunged in a late summer border or tropical-style garden, placed in full sun or light shade. It also needs to be fed and watered regularly when in growth. At the end of the summer it must be moved indoors and overwintered in a heated greenhouse or conservatory with a minimum temperature of 7°C (45°F).

◊ ◊ ☼ ☀ ❈
‡ to 6m (20ft) ↔ to 3m (10ft)

MELIANTHUS MAJOR ♛

Evergreen shrub

The honey bush is usually treated as a herbaceous perennial. Grown for its foliage, it has beautiful, bluish-green, feather-like leaves, which are divided into several sharply-toothed leaflets. The brown flowers are rather uninspiring. Plant it in a sunny position, sheltered from cold winds, in moist, well drained, fertile soil. Frost destroys the upper growth, but if it is protected during the winter with a thick mulch it should resprout again in spring.

◊ ◊ ☼ ❈ ❈
‡ ↔ to 3m (10ft)

MOLUCCELLA LAEVIS

Annual

Bells of Ireland bears deeply-veined, rounded, pale green leaves, and in summer and autumn it produces stems of tiny white flowers, surrounded by large, pale green cups. Its architectural flower spikes make a dramatic statement in a herbaceous border, and are very useful in flower arrangements, fresh or dried. Plant it in full sunshine, in fertile, moist, well-drained soil. It is easy to grow from a spring sowing of the seed.

◊◊ ☼ ❄

‡ to 90cm (36in) ↔ to 23cm (9in)

NICOTIANA LANGSDORFFII ♥

Annual

This tobacco plant forms a rosette of large egg-shaped leaves at the base, and in summer produces apple-green flowers that dangle like slender bells from the tall, branched, sticky stems. It adds interest to the middle of a herbaceous border and is ideal for disguising the space left by spring bulbs. Plant it in a sunny or lightly shaded position in fertile, moist, well-drained soil, and stake if necessary.

◊ ◊ ☼ ☼ ❄

‡ to 1.5m (5ft) ↔ to 60cm (24in)

OSMANTHUS HETEROPHYLLUS 'Aureomarginatus'

Evergreen shrub

This plant has spiny, toothed leaves that resemble those on a holly bush, and in mild areas it makes a good hedging plant. 'Aureomarginatus' has glossy, bright green, mottled, foliage, edged in golden-yellow. In late summer it bears small clusters of highly fragrant, small, white, tubular flowers. It is not totally hardy, and should be grown in full sun or partial shade in a sheltered position, and planted in fertile, well-drained soil.

△ ☼ ◐ ❄ ❄
‡ to 5m (15ft) ↔ to 5m (15ft)

ZINNIA ELEGANS 'Envy'

Annual

Most zinnias stand out because of their brightly coloured flowers, but 'Envy' is more subtle, with semi-double, yellow-green blooms. It makes a good bedding or container plant, and will perform well when grown in a sunny or lightly shaded position and fertile, moist, well drained soil. The seed should be sown indoors in early spring, or *in situ* outside in late spring. Useful in flower arrangements because of its unusual colour.

△ ☼ ◐ ❄
‡ to 60cm (24in) ↔ to 30cm (12in)

ARGEMONE MEXICANA
Annual

The prickly poppy is a tall, architectural annual, with beautiful thistle-like, spiky, lobed foliage with silver veins. In late summer and early autumn pale or deep yellow poppy-like flowers appear, their delicate petals contrasting well with the thorny leaves. The flowers are followed by attractive prickly seedheads, which hold the highly toxic seeds. Grow this annual from seed in spring, and plant it in a sunny location in poor, dry soil. This poppy will add interest to a hot, dry gravel garden or herbaceous border.

◊ ☼ ❀
‡ to 1m (36in) ↔ to 40cm (16in)

CANNA
'King Midas'
Perennial

Cannas hint at the exotic in a tropical-style garden or late summer border with their huge, paddle-shaped leaves and gladiolus-like flowers. 'King Midas' has dark green foliage which provides a foil for the clusters of large golden-yellow blooms. Plant out the rhizomes in late spring or early summer in full sun and moist, well-drained soil. In the autumn, cut off the stems, dig up the rhizomes and store them in trays of slightly damp compost or sand in a frost-free place.

◊ ◊ ☼ ❀
‡ to 1.5m (5ft) ↔ to 50cm (20in)

CATALPA BIGNONIOIDES
'Aurea' ♀

Deciduous tree

The golden form of the Indian bean
tree has spreading branches, and large,
heart-shaped leaves. The young foliage
is bronze in spring, but turns golden-
yellow by the time the flowers appear
in midsummer. The candle-shaped
spikes of fragrant, white flowers with
yellow and purple marks are followed
by dangling pods that last through
winter and give this tree its name. Plant
it in full sun, away from strong winds,
in deep, fertile, moist, well-drained soil.

◊◊ ☼ ❄ ❄ ❄
‡ to 10m (30ft) ↔ to 10m (30ft)

CEPHALARIA GIGANTEA

Perennial

The giant scabious is a clump-forming
perennial with large green leaves,
divided into many small lance-shaped
leaflets. In the summer it produces tall,
branched, erect stems that hold large
primrose-yellow flowers, the outer
petals of which surround a pincushion
of smaller blooms. Plant this scabious in
full sun and fertile, moist, well-drained
soil. It makes a superb plant for the
back of a herbaceous border, but unlike
other scabious it needs plenty of space
to grow to its full potential.

◊◊ ☼ ❄ ❄ ❄
‡ to 2.5m (8ft) ↔ to 60cm (24in)

CHRYSANTHEMUM
'Mary Stoker'

Perennial

In late summer and early autumn this hardy chrysanthemum bears single, apricot-yellow, daisy-like flowers, with green centres that turn yellow as they mature. The flowers are set off by the lobed, deep green leaves that have a slight silvery sheen. Plant it in a sunny, sheltered herbaceous or mixed border, in well-drained soil. It will benefit from a protective, thick mulch in the winter.

○ ☼ ❀ ❀ ❀
‡ to 1.2m (4ft) ↔ to 75cm (30in)

CROCOSMIA
'Citronella'

Perennial corm

The clumps of sword-shaped leaves and arching spikes of lemon-yellow flowers, make this crocosmia a perfect plant for a late summer border or gravel garden. It prefers a sunny or partially shaded situation, and fertile, moist, well-drained soil. It is not completely hardy and in cold areas it should be protected over winter with a thick layer of mulch. To maintain the plant's vigour, every three or four years lift the corms in spring and divide them.

○ ◑ ☼ ◐ ❀ ❀
‡ to 75cm (30in) ↔ to 8cm (3in)

CROCOSMIA ×
CROCOSMIIFLORA
'Solfatare' ♀

Perennial corm

The bronzy-green leaves and clusters of apricot-yellow flowers that appear on slender, arching stems make this a very desirable plant for a border or gravel garden. It will grow well in full sun or partial shade, and prefers moist, well-drained soil. The individual plants are quite small and are best planted in groups of three or five. It is not fully hardy and needs a sheltered site and thick mulch to survive a harsh winter.

◊ ◊ ☼ ◐ ❄ ❄ ❄
↕ to 70cm (28in) ↔ to 8cm (3in)

DAHLIA
'Yellow Hammer' ♀

Perennial

This tender perennial is usually grown as an annual bedding plant, and has bronze-green leaves and clear yellow flowers. For a dazzling bedding display, plant it with other dwarf dahlias, such as the scarlet-flowered 'Preston Park', or use it in a herbaceous border, or in containers. Providing it is deadheaded regularly, 'Yellow Hammer' will flower continuously up to the first frosts. Plant it in full sun in fertile, well-drained soil, or loam-based compost.

◊ ☼ ❄
↕ to 60cm (24in) ↔ to 45cm (18in)

GENTIANA LUTEA

Perennial

As implausible as it may seem, the dainty blue gentian is a relative of this tall, imposing plant. The yellow gentian is a herbaceous, clump-forming perennial with pleated, elliptic, bluish-green leaves. Yellow, starry flowers are borne in clusters on a tall, sturdy stem. Found growing wild in the dappled shade of deciduous woodland or beside a stream, this gentian needs a light soil that is moist but well-drained, and neutral to acid (lime-free). In a partially shaded border it mixes well with ferns.

◊ ◐ ☼ ❋ ❋ ❋
‡ to 1.5m (5ft) ↔ to 60cm (24in)

HEDYCHIUM GARDNERIANUM ♀

Perennial

From the imposing spikes of fragrant flowers with their long red stamens, to the lance-shaped, bluish-green leaves, the Kahili ginger is every inch an exotic. It could be the star turn in a 'hot' border, or the main focus of planting around an ornamental pool. For best effect, grow it in groups. It needs the protection of a warm greenhouse during the winter, and should not be planted out until all danger of frost is past. Choose a sunny spot in moist but well-drained soil, or plant it in pots of loam-based compost.

◊ ◐ ☼ ❋
‡ to 2.2m (7ft) ↔ to 1m (3ft)

HELENIUM
'Butterpat' ♀

Perennial

Unlike many heleniums, which tend to
have muddy-coloured flowers, those of
'Butterpat' are a clear, bright yellow.
Very free flowering, it is a good clump-
forming plant for a herbaceous border.
The blooms, which are usually crowded
with bees, are held on tall stems and
make excellent cut flowers. Remove the
dead heads to encourage more blooms.
Grow it in sun, in moist, well drained,
fertile soil, and divide it in early spring
every 2–3 years to maintain its vigour.

◊ ◊ ☼ ❄ ❄ ❄
‡ to 90cm (36in)) ↔ to 60cm (24in)

HELIANTHUS
'Lemon Queen'

Perennial

In late summer 'Lemon Queen' bears
large quantities of acid yellow, daisy-
like flowers with darker centres. This is
a vigorous, herbaceous perennial with
erect stems and slightly hairy, lance-
shaped, dark green leaves. Plant it in
a sunny position in fertile, moist, but
well-drained, neutral or alkaline soil. A
good plant for cutting, it also combines
well with other plants in a herbaceous
border. To maintain its vigour, divide
plants in early spring every 2–4 years.

◊ ◊ ☼ ❄ ❄ ❄
‡ to 1.7m (5½ft) ↔ to 1.2m (4ft)

HELIANTHUS
'Monarch' ♀
Perennial

In late summer the dark-eyed sunflower bears large, semi-double, daisy-like flowers with golden-yellow petals and yellowish-brown centres. If the side buds are removed in spring, the flowers will grow to 15cm (6in) across, and are good for cutting. The leaves are toothed and lance shaped. It is a tall plant, ideal for the back of the border, but it will need supporting, so insert canes early in summer. Give it a spot in full sun, in well-drained, fertile soil.

◊ ☼ ❀ ❀
‡ to 2m (6ft) ↔ to 1.2m (4ft)

HELICHRYSUM
'Schwefellicht'
Perennial

Clusters of small, fluffy, sulphur-yellow flowers that turn orange-yellow as summer progresses, make this an interesting plant for a well-drained rock, gravel or scree garden. Its spreading stems, which are covered with white hairs and narrow, silvery white leaves, form an attractive, weed-suppressing mound. Plant it in a sunny situation, in reasonably fertile, well-drained, neutral to acid soil.

◊ ☼ ❀ ❀ ❀
‡ to 40cm (16in) ↔ to 30cm (12in)

HELIOPSIS HELIANTHOIDES
'Sommersonne'

Perennial

A superb plant for the herbaceous
border, the ox eye is a clump-forming
perennial with erect, branched stems
and egg- or lance-shaped, mid-green
leaves. In late summer it produces
semi-double flowerheads, which look
rather like small sunflowers, with deep-
golden petals and a brownish centre.
Grow it in full sun, in fertile, moist, but
well-drained soil. Established clumps
need dividing in early spring every 2–3
years to maintain vigour.

○ ◑ ☼ ❄ ❄ ❄
‡ to 90cm (36in) ↔ to 60cm (24in)

HEMEROCALLIS
'Corky' ♀

Perennial

One of the more compact daylilies,
'Corky' is suitable for planting in a
small garden or in containers. Clusters
of reddish-brown buds appear on long,
erect stems among the evergreen, mid-
green leaves. These buds open one or
two at a time to reveal bright yellow
flowers. Although each flower lasts only
for one day, they are quickly replaced.
Plant it in full sun, in fertile, moist, but
well-drained soil. Propagate daylilies by
dividing large clumps in the spring.

○ ◑ ☼ ☼ ❄ ❄ ❄
‡ to 70cm (28in) ↔ to 40cm (16in)

HYPERICUM CALYCINUM

Evergreen shrub

Through summer to mid-autumn, the rose of Sharon produces yellow, cup-shaped flowers with showy stamens. It is a low-growing shrub that quickly spreads by means of trailing stems. It is unfussy, and not surprisingly, it makes excellent ground cover for a bank or area where little else will grow. It can become invasive; to keep it neat and bushy, cut it back to the ground in spring. Plant in full sun, or partial shade, any well-drained soil. It is easily propagated by division in spring.

◊ ◊ ☼ ❄ ❄ ❄

‡ to 60cm (24in) ↔ indefinite

HYPERICUM
'Hidcote' ♥

Evergreen shrub

The arching, spreading branches of 'Hidcote' are covered with handsome, lance-shaped, dark green leaves. Through summer to early autumn clusters of bright golden-yellow flowers, up to 6cm (2½in) across, are produced in profusion. Plant in a reasonably fertile, moist, but well-drained soil, in full sun. This is a good choice for a shrub or mixed border.

◊ ◊ ☼ ❄ ❄ ❄

‡ to 1.2m (4ft) ↔ to 1.5m (5ft)

INULA HOOKERI

Perennial

A superb plant for a shady border, this perennial from the Himalayas will soon form large clumps where conditions suit. It has slender, erect, softly hairy stems, and lance-shaped, mid-green leaves. From late summer to autumn, it produces clusters of pale yellow flowers with a darker, brownish-yellow centre. Plant it in partial shade, in fertile, moist, but well-drained, soil. To propagate, divide established clumps in spring or autumn.

◊ ◐ ☼ ✿ ✿ ✿
‡ to 75cm (30in) ↔ to 60cm (24in)

IRIS PSEUDACORUS ♥

Perennial

The yellow flag is a vigorous aquatic plant, ideal for a large wildlife pool, but in a small pond you will need to thin it out unless you contain it in a planting basket. It has upright, sword-shaped leaves that are a soft grey-green colour. Choose 'Variegata' for yellowish-white striped foliage. Full sun and wet soil is the yellow flag's first choice but it is unfussy and adaptable. In early spring, propagate by division, or sow seed in pots, and keep the soil wet. 'Golden Fleece' has deeper yellow blooms.

◊ ◐ ☼ ☼ ✿ ✿ ✿
‡ to 2m (6ft) ↔ indefinite

KNIPHOFIA
'Royal Standard' ♀

Perennial

Although 'Royal Standard' has been around for a long time, it is still one of the best red hot pokers for the herbaceous border. Green, strappy leaves form a large clump from which rise tall, robust, flower spikes. These are studded with scarlet-red buds that open to bright yellow, tubular flowers. Kniphofias are a favourite of bees. Plant them in fertile, moist but well-drained soil in sun.

◊ ◑ ☼ ❋ ❋ ❋
‡ to 1m (3ft) ↔ to 60cm (24in)

KOELREUTERIA
PANICULATA ♀

Deciduous tree

The golden-rain tree deserves a rest over winter because for the other three seasons it puts on an amazing show. In late summer, this wonderful specimen tree produces spikes of small yellow flowers followed, in autumn, by pink or red seed capsules. Early spring foliage is a bright pinkish-red, turning through mid-green to a rich, buttery yellow in late summer and early autumn. Plant it in full sun, in fertile, well-drained soil. No pruning is needed.

◊ ☼ ❋ ❋ ❋
‡ ↔ to 10m (30ft)

LIGULARIA
'Gregynog Gold' ♀
Perennial

In late summer, from a base of large, heart-shaped leaves, 'Gregynog Gold' throws up pyramids of daisy-like golden flowers on very tall, stiff stems. Each flower is delicately flecked with chocolate brown filaments. Choose a site where the soil is moderately fertile and permanently damp – around the margins of a natural pond would be ideal – in full sun or partial shade.

◊ ● ☼ ☀ ❄ ❄ ❄
‡ to 1.8m (6ft) ↔ to 1m (3ft)

LILIUM PYRENAICUM
Perennial bulb

In summer this clump-forming lily produces a dozen or so yellow to greenish-yellow blooms with maroon throats. They are produced on stiff stems clothed with lance-shaped dark green leaves. However, these stylish flowers are best enjoyed in the border rather than a vase, because they have a rather unpleasant smell. Plant preferably in early autumn or spring, in neutral or slightly alkaline, well-drained soil, in full sunshine or partial shade.

◊ ☼ ☀ ❄ ❄ ❄
‡ to 100cm (39in)

LINARIA DALMATICA

Perennial

The bright yellow, spurred flowers of this toadflax bear more than a passing resemblance to those of the snapdragon (*Antirrhinum*). The slightly erect, lance-shaped, waxy, green leaves grow up to 18cm (7in) long. Plant it in full sun, in a light, preferably sandy, fertile, well-drained soil. Its upright stature will ensure it stands out in the middle of a busy herbaceous border; it would also do well in a gravel garden.

◊ ☼ ❀ ❀ ❀
‡ to 1m (3ft) ↔ to 60cm (24in)

LYSIMACHIA NUMMULARIA
'Aurea' ♀

Perennial

The golden form of creeping Jenny is a vigorous evergreen that readily roots when its stems touch the soil. It can become rampant and may need to be controlled by weeding. The leaves are a bright yellow, lime green in shade, and during summer it has small, yellow, upright, cup-shaped flowers. Choose a spot in full sun or partial shade, in a moist, well-drained soil that won't dry out during summer. Propagate by division in spring or autumn.

◊ ☼ ☼ ❀ ❀ ❀
‡ to 5cm (2in) ↔ indefinite

LYSIMACHIA PUNCTATA

Perennial

This is an extremely vigorous perennial
which quickly spreads by means of
underground rhizomes. The upright
stems have tiers of lance-shaped leaves
and numerous bright yellow, cup-
shaped flowers. It makes an attractive
plant for a damp border; but take care,
because it can become invasive. It
grows best in partial shade, but will
tolerate full sun. Plant it in fertile, moist,
but well-drained soil.

∧ ◑ ☼ ✳ ❋ ❋ ❋
↕ to 1m (3ft) ↔ to 60cm (24in)

OSTEOSPERMUM
'Buttermilk'

Perennial

This tender subshrub starts flowering in
spring it keeps on going right through
late summer to autumn. The single
flowers are primrose-yellow with a dark
mauve centre. An upright, perky plant
for a gravel garden, a border, or in a
container. It has handsome toothed,
mid-green leaves. The plant does not
usually survive outdoors over winter, so
overwinter in pots under glass or take
semi-ripe cuttings in late summer. Plant
in full sun, in very well-drained soil.

◊ ☼ ❋ ❋
↕ ↔ to 60cm (24in)

ROBINIA PSEUDOACACIA
'Frisia' ♥

Deciduous tree

Dramatic leaf colour is what makes this
fast-growing, spreading tree so special.
In spring, the leaves are bright yellow,
in early summer they take on a dash of
lime, then, in late summer, they turn a
rich orange-yellow. The tree has
fragrant, white flowers in spring and
spiny branches. A wonderful specimen
tree, with a canopy light enough for
underplanting. Give it a spot in full sun,
in fertile, moist, but well-drained, soil.
No pruning is required.

◊ ◊ ☼ ❋ ❋ ❋
‡ to 15m (50ft) ↔ to 8m (25ft)

RUDBECKIA
'Herbstsonne'

Perennial

The cheerful coneflower is one of the
mainstays of the late-summer garden.
'Herbstsonne' has yellow, daisy-like
flowers with conical greeny-brown
centres that are carried aloft on tall,
upright stems. The rich, glossy green
leaves are deeply veined. It does best
in fertile, moist, but well-drained, soil,
including clay. This clump-forming plant
is perfect for the back of a herbaceous
border where it will act as a foil for
smaller plants. Good for cutting.

◊ ◊ ☼ ☀ ❋ ❋ ❋
‡ to 2m (6ft) ↔ to 90cm (36in)

RUDBECKIA FULGIDA
'Goldsturm' ♀

Perennial

The dark-centred flowers of the black-eyed Susan are produced in abundance from late summer to mid-autumn. The deep green leaves are lance-shaped. It will grow in any reasonably fertile, well-drained soil as long as it does not dry out in the summer; it also suits clay soil. A good mixer in a herbaceous or woodland border, it is also perfect for naturalistic plantings with ornamental grasses.

○ ◑ ☼ ☀ ✽ ✽ ✽
‡ to 60cm (24in) ↔ to 45cm (18in)

SILPHIUM PERFOLIATUM

Perennial

From summer through to early autumn, the upright, branching stems of the cup plant are crowned with sunny-yellow, daisy-like flowers. Its deeply toothed leaves are attractive too, if a little bristly to touch. This clump-forming herbaceous perennial prefers a rather heavy, neutral or alkaline soil, including clay, that is moist but well-drained. It would be at home in a partially shaded wild or woodland garden.

○ ◑ ☼ ☀ ✽ ✽ ✽
‡ to 2.5m (8ft) ↔ to 1m (3ft)

SOLIDAGO 'Goldenmosa' ♥

Perennial

With its upright, yellow-stalked golden flowerheads and wrinkled, mid-green leaves, this is a select form of golden rod. Compact and bushy, it is much less invasive than the species. Plant it in a late-summer border, in full sunshine, in well-drained, slightly fertile, sandy soil. It is an ideal plant for a wild garden and is also good for cutting.

◊ ☼ ❀ ❀ ❀
‡ to 75cm (30in) ↔ to 45cm (18in)

SPARTIUM JUNCEUM ♥

Deciduous shrub

When broom comes into bloom, the profusion of fragrant, golden-yellow, pea-shaped flowers really brightens up a garden. In autumn, long brown seed pods are borne. Its green, upright stems are sparsely covered in narrow leaves. Originally from the Mediterranean, it will grow in any well-drained soil in full sun. Grow it against a warm wall or in a shrub border. It will also thrive on chalky soils and by the coast. Trim back after flowering, but do not cut back into the old wood; it will not re-shoot.

◊ ☼ ❀ ❀
‡ ↔ to 3m (4ft)

TROPAEOLUM PEREGRINUM

Climber

The Canary creeper is a vigorous annual climber with deeply lobed, grey-green leaves. In summer it produces clusters of bright yellow flowers. These have three small lower petals and two larger, deeply fringed, upper petals, which give it a bird-like appearance. Plant it in a sunny position, in moist, but well-drained, slightly fertile soil. Canary creeper is ideal for growing against a trellis, over a fence or pergola, or through a deciduous tree. Sow seed *in situ* in early spring.

△ ◐ ☼ ❀
‡ to 4m (12ft)

VERBASCUM NIGRUM

Perennial

The elegant dark mullein bears 50cm (20in) tall flower spikes dotted with yellow, saucer-shaped blooms that have purple filament hairs. The heart-shaped leaves are fuzzy and grey beneath, and form a rosette at the base, gradually becoming smaller as they grow up the stem. Grow in poor, well-drained, alkaline soils; in richer soils the plant grows larger and needs staking. Ideal for planting in gravel or naturalizing in a wild garden, this mullein also mixes well in a sunny herbaceous border.

△ ☼ ❀❀❀
‡ to 90cm (36in) ↔ to 60cm (24in)

ANTIRRHINUM MAJUS
'Trumpet Serenade'

Perennial

In a range of jolly colours, including this rich gold, the freesia-like blooms of 'Trumpet Serenade' are very different to the usual 'squeeze-open, snap-shut' flowers of most snapdragons. As short-lived, tender perennials, they are usually grown as annual bedding plants, filling gaps at the front of a herbaceous border or used as a cut flower. Plant in full sun, in fertile, preferably sandy soil. Avoid wet soil as it encourages rust, although this is a resistant variety.

○ ☼ ❄
↕ ↔ to 30cm (12in)

ARCTOTIS FASTUOSA

Perennial

The deeply lobed leaves of the African daisy are silvery white and covered with hairs. In late summer, it bears orange, daisy-like flowers with a black or dark maroon centre. It is a tender perennial, and it is usually treated as a half-hardy annual used in bedding schemes, gravel gardens, and containers. Outside it needs a moist but very well-drained soil, in an open, sunny site. It can be kept from year to year in a pot of gritty, well-drained compost and overwintered under glass.

○ ☼ ❄
↕ to 60cm (24in) ↔ to 30cm (12in)

CALENDULA OFFICINALIS

Annual

An old favourite, the pot marigold is a
vigorous, erect plant with hairy, aromatic,
spoon-shaped leaves. The bright orange-
yellow, daisy-like flowers are produced
from summer to autumn. Superb as
bedding, it can also be used in pots, or
as a cut flower. Plant it in sun or partial
shade, in well-drained, fertile soil. Sow
seed *in situ* in spring. For strong orange
shades, choose 'Fiesta Gitana' (a dwarf
cultivar), 'Orange King' (double blooms)
or 'Indian Prince' (reddish flowers).
Deadhead to keep the show going.

○ ☼ ✿ ✿ ✿
↕ to 75cm (30in) ↔ to 45cm (18in)

CAMPSIS × TAGLIABUANA
'Madame Galen' ♀

Climber

The trumpet creeper is a vigorous, self
clinging climber with long, divided
leaves. From late summer to autumn
it produces clusters of orange-red,
trumpet-shaped flowers. It can quickly
cover a trellis or clamber through an
old tree. Keep it clear of the roof and
gutters and hard prune in winter to
keep within bounds. Vulnerable to frost
damage, in colder areas grow the vine
against a sunny wall. The soil should
be fertile and moist but well drained.

○ ○ ☼ ✿ ✿
↕ to 10m (30ft)

CANNA
'Striata'

Perennial

In late summer, this striking plant pushes up tall spikes of gladiolus-like orange flowers. The real scene-stealer, though, is the flamboyant foliage, marked with green and yellow stripes. It makes a superb plant for a border among other red or orange flowers, or can be grown in pots. Plant out in late spring in sun and well-drained soil. It is tender, so lift rhizomes before the first frosts, place in a tray of moist compost, and overwinter under glass.

◊ ☼ ❊
‡ to 1.5m (5ft) ↔ to 50cm (20in)

CROCOSMIA
'Star of the East' ♀

Perennial corm

With its large, orange flowers, 'Star of the East' is a particularly attractive crocosmia. A vigorous plant with erect, sword-shaped, deep green leaves, it looks wonderful planted among shrubs or with other late-flowering perennials. If the corms become overcrowded they will lose their vigour, so dig them up in spring, and replant them on a fresh site. Crocosmia prefer a spot in full sun, in fertile, moist but well-drained soil.

◊ ◊ ☼ ❊❊
‡ to 70cm (28in) ↔ to 8cm (3in)

DAHLIA
'Hamari Gold' ♛

Perennial

Golden-yellow blooms and deeply
divided, dark green leaves make this an
attractive border plant. Dahlias are not
hardy, so when the foliage has been
blackened by the first frosts, dig up the
tubers and store them in dry compost
over winter. Wait until all risk of frost
has past before replanting in full sun, in
well-drained soil. It benefits from a
stake, best inserted at planting time to
avoid damaging the tubers. Feed
regularly in the growing season.

◊ ☼ ❀
‡ to 1.2m (4ft) ↔ to 60cm (24in)

DAHLIA
'Woolton Impact' ♛

Perennial

This attractive, semi-cactus dahlia is
ideal for a sunny border where space is
limited. Strong stems of medium-sized,
bronze coloured flowers, which are
good for cutting, are held well above
the main bulk of the plant. They need
early staking. Like all dahlias, it requires
a sunny spot in fertile, well-drained
soil, while in winter the tubers need
to be lifted and stored (see 'Hamari
Gold', above).

◊ ☼ ❀
‡ to 1.2m (4ft) ↔ to 60cm (24in)

FUCHSIA
'Coralle'

Deciduous shrub

The tubular bells of 'Coralle', which are borne in tight clusters, will appeal to those who prefer less artificial-looking fuchsias. Upright in habit, this shrub has strong stems with velvety, olive-green leaves. It is superb for growing in a container, use a loam-based compost and choose a spot in full sun or light shade. Feed regularly throughout the summer with a balanced fertilizer, and move under glass during the winter as it is not hardy.

◊ ◊ ☼ ☼ ❄
‡ to 90cm (36in) ↔ to 60cm (24in)

HELENIUM
'Septemberfuchs'

Perennial

Heleniums are invaluable for providing areas of warm colour in the late-summer border. This particularly tall variety benefits from early staking with canes or hazel twigs. It has dark green leaves and burnt-orange flowers streaked with yellow. Bees find the domed centres irresistible. For best effect, plant them in groups of three or more in a sunny position, in moist but well-drained fertile soil. Established clumps need dividing every couple of years.

◊ ◊ ☼ ❄ ❄ ❄
‡ to 1.5m (5ft) ↔ to 60cm (24in)

HELIANTHUS ANNUUS
'Music Box'

Annual

From late summer this small sunflower
produces an abundance of bright
orange, yellow or red flowers, each
bloom measuring up to 12cm (5in)
across. The markings on the petals
subtly darken towards the black central
disc. Wonderful as cut flowers, and
short enough to grow in a pot, they
also blend well among other plants in
a sunny herbaceous or annual border.
Sow the seed *in situ* in spring, in fertile,
moist but well-drained soil.

◊ ◊ ☼ ❀ ❀ ❀
‡ to 70cm (28in) ↔ to 60cm (24in)

KNIPHOFIA ROOPERI

Perennial

Living up to its common name of red
hot poker and torch lily, this dazzling
plant is guaranteed to brighten up the
herbaceous border or gravel garden. Its
globe-shaped spikes of reddish-orange
flowers turn a golden colour as they
mature. It is a very robust, clump-
forming plant with shapely, pointed,
evergreen leaves. Plant it in late spring,
in full sun or partial shade, in fertile,
well-drained, preferably sandy soil.
Mulch over winter in the first year.
Divide large clumps in spring.

◊ ☼ ☀ ❀ ❀ ❀
‡ to 1.2m (4ft) ↔ to 60cm (2ft)

LILIUM HENRYI ♀

Perennial bulb

Vigorous and clump-forming, this tall lily has erect stems and narrow, dark green, lance-shaped leaves. In late summer, its develops clusters of ten or more delicately scented flowers, with black-spotted, swept-back petals. It is happiest in partial shade, in neutral or slightly alkaline, well-drained soil. Tall lilies, like this one, are ideal for brightening up the back of a shrub or herbaceous border.

◊ ☀ ❊ ❊ ❊
‡ to 3m (10ft)

LONICERA × HECKROTTII

Climber

The twining stems of this pretty hybrid honeysuckle make it ideal for growing through a small tree or against a wall or trellis. Its fragrant, orange-yellow, tubular flowers are followed in autumn by bright red berries. The lush, dark green leaves are deciduous or semi-evergreen, depending on conditions. Look out for the cultivar 'Gold Flame' which is more vigorous and has even brighter flowers. Honeysuckles need moist but well-drained, fertile soil. They grow well in sun or light shade.

◊ ◊ ☀ ☀ ❊ ❊ ❊
‡ to 5m (15ft)

MIMULUS AURANTIACUS ♀

Evergreen shrub

The shrubby musk is an attractive, small plant for a warm, sunny border. The dark green, sticky, lance-shaped leaves are the perfect foil for the orange, trumpet-shaped flowers, which appear from late summer through to autumn. Plant it in fertile, well-drained soil and, as it is not completely hardy, somewhere sheltered in full sunshine. In cold areas it is best grown in a conservatory.

◊ ☼ ❋ ❋
‡ ↔ to 1m (3ft)

XEROCHRYSUM BRACTEATUM
Monstrosum Series

Annual

Everlasting flowers are erect annuals with greyish green, lance-shaped leaves. The Monstrosum Series has vibrant orange, double flowers that measure 8cm (3in) across. Other colours are available, including yellows and reds. Use it as a bedding plant, to fill spaces in a herbaceous border or in containers. Plant in full sunshine, in slightly fertile, moist, but well-drained soil. Everlasting flowers dry well and retain their colour for a long time.

◊ ◊ ☼ ❋
‡ to 90cm (36in) ↔ to 30cm (12in)

AUTUMN

As THE DAYS BEGIN to shorten and night temperatures fall, many plants have completed their annual cycles and will retreat underground. The end of the growing season is signalled by the brilliant colour displays of deciduous trees before they drop their leaves and enter their dormancy. The vibrance of the show varies each year but most of the maples (*Acer*) give rich, reliable autumnal tints. In gardens that are too small for large trees, there are plenty of shrubs, such as *Euonymus alatus* and the stag's horn sumach (*Rhus typhina*), that can provide dramatic foliage displays of crimson, scarlet and gold.

Ornamental vines *Vitis* 'Brant' and *V. coignetiae* are among the climbers with bright red foliage in autumn, and vigorous Boston ivy, *Parthenocissus tricuspidata*, transforms the appearance of walls as it turns from green and becomes a glowing sheet of scarlet.

FRUIT AND FLOWERS

Decorative fruits are much in evidence now and some of the best crops are carried on cotoneasters, rowans (*Sorbus*) and crab apples (*Malus*). And there are shrub roses, such as *Rosa rugosa*, which produce masses of shining scarlet hips.

Although the annual border has been cleared and many perennials have begun to die down, some flowering plants come into their own at this time, notably autumn crocuses and colchicums. Monkshood (*Aconitum*), Michaelmas daisies (*Aster*) and chrysanthemums of every colour will continue to flower as long as the weather permits. Do not be in too much of a hurry to clear away all remnants of summer; decorative seedheads can stay until they collapse, and allow the graceful flowerheads and foliage of ornamental grasses to stand through winter, not only so you can enjoy them, but for the protection it offers the plant.

ANAPHALIS TRIPLINERVIS ♀

Perennial

Pearl everlasting is a hardy, easily grown perennial from the Himalayas and SW China. It is a good ground-cover plant, forming dense clumps of soft, silvery green, spear-shaped leaves. From midsummer well until into autumn, the clumps are topped by clusters of papery, white, daisy-like flowers. The flowers can be dried for indoor display by hanging them upside down in bunches in a light, airy place. Grow in well-drained, moisture-retentive soil, in sun or partial shade.

△ ◊ ☼ ◑ ✿ ✿ ✿
‡ to 90cm (36in) ↔ to 60cm (24in)

ARALIA ELATA
'Variegata' ♀

Deciduous tree

The Japanese angelica tree is upright in habit with stout, spreading, thorny branches arranged in tiers. In mild areas it forms a small tree, but elsewhere may only be a large shrub up to 3m (10ft) tall. The leaflets, which are edged with creamy-white, turn gold in autumn. Abundant clusters of small white flowers are borne in late summer and early autumn. It prefers fertile, moist but well-drained soil in sun but tolerates light, dappled shade.

△ ◊ ☼ ◑ ✿ ✿ ✿
‡↔ to 10m (30ft)

ARBUTUS X ANDRACHNOIDES ♥

Evergreen tree

The Grecian strawberry tree is a shrubby, spreading evergreen with peeling, red-brown bark and oval, glossy, dark green leaves. From autumn through to spring, it bears hanging clusters of small, almost spherical, white flowers; occasionally it produces small, bright red fruits at the same time. Grow in a site sheltered from cold winds, in full sun in humus-rich, well-drained soil. It tolerates alkaline soils so long as they are deep and rich in leafy organic matter.

◊ ☼ ❀ ❀
‡↔ to 0m (25ft)

ASTER ERICOIDES
'White Heather'

Perennial

Asters are invaluable for autumn colour in herbaceous and mixed borders. This bushy perennial has wiry, upright stems smothered in tiny, long-lasting, white daisies from late summer to late autumn. The slender stems need staking. Grow in sun or partial shade in fertile, well-drained soil that does not dry out during the growing season; moisture helps reduce the risk of mildew, although this variety shows some resistance to the disease.

◊ ◊ ☼ ☼ ❀ ❀ ❀
‡ to 1m (3ft) ↔ to 30cm (12in)

CIMICIFUGA SIMPLEX

Perennial

The tiny, star-shaped autumn flowers of this herbaceous perennial, also known as *Actea simplex*, appear brilliant white against their dark stems. The tall, arching flower spikes are seen at their best if the stems are supported by an unobtrusive, grow-through support, positioned in spring. The leaves are glossy, finely divided and fresh green. Good for late colour in a woodland garden or shady border. Grow in moist, humus-rich soil in light shade to prevent the sun scorching the delicate leaves.

◊ ☼ ❋ ❋ ❋

↕ to 1.2m (4ft) ↔ to 60cm (24in)

CORTADERIA RICHARDII ♀

Perennial

Commonly known as toe toe, *Cortaderia richardii* is native to New Zealand. The arching, fluffy flowerheads, up to 60cm (2ft) long, first appear in summer, high above the tussocks of long, narrow, olive-green leaves. If left on the plant, the slender creamy-white plumes will persist through autumn and winter. They can also be cut for fresh or dried-flower arrangements. Grow in well-drained soil in sun. Cut out the dead foliage and flowerheads in early spring – protect your hands with gloves.

◊ ☼ ❋ ❋

↕ to 2.5m (9ft) ↔ to 1.8m (6ft)

CORTADERIA SELLOANA 'Sunningdale Silver' ♥

Perennial

Large, dense, evergreen tussocks of sharp-edged, deep greyish-green leaves are topped by tall upright stems of long-lasting, silvery-white flowerheads in late summer and autumn. It makes an impressive specimen plant where space is available. Leave dead foliage in place over winter to protect the crown from frosts then, wearing stout gloves, cut and comb it out in spring. Grow in sun in well-drained soil. Cut back every two or three years in spring to rejuvenate.

◊ ☼ ❋ ❋

‡ to 3m (10ft) or more ↔ to 2.5m (8ft)

CROCUS OCHROLEUCUS ♥

Perennial corm

This crocus bears slender, creamy-white flowers with yellow throats in late autumn, when most other autumn-flowering crocus are over. The leaves usually emerge with or just after the flowers, and are green with a central white stripe. It is very easy to grow in well-drained soil in sun, and will naturalize if planted in drifts in short grass. Overcrowded clumps can be divided after flowering. Plant corms in late summer.

◊ ☼ ❋ ❋ ❋

‡ to 5cm (2in) ↔ to 2.5cm (1in)

GALANTHUS REGINAE-OLGAE

Perennial bulb

This snowdrop flowers from mid-autumn to early winter, with petals up to 2.5cm (1in) long. The narrow leaves appear after flowering and are dark green with a central grey stripe. Grow in sun or light dappled shade in well-drained, neutral to alkaline soil. It prefers drier soils and more sun than other snowdrops. Overcrowded clumps can be divided as the leaves start to wither. Plant bulbs in autumn.

◊ ☼ ☀ ✽ ✽
‡ to 20cm (8in) ↔ to 5cm (2in))

JASMINUM POLYANTHUM ♀

Climber

Grown for its beautiful and abundant, highly scented flowers, this vigorous climber bears large clusters of white, tubular blooms that open from pink buds between late summer and winter. The foliage is evergreen, or almost so, and the dark green leaves are made up of several leaflets. It is not frost hardy and requires a warm, sheltered site or the protection of a greenhouse or conservatory in cold areas. Best in full sun, in well-drained, fertile soil, although it tolerates light shade.

◊ ☼ ☀ ✽
‡ to 3m (10ft)

LEUCOJUM AUTUMNALE ♥

Perennial bulb

The autumn snowflake is a beautiful
plant with narrow, dark green, grass-
like leaves. The nodding white flowers,
tinged with pink at the base, are borne
on slender stems in late summer and
early autumn. A native of the stony
slopes of the western Mediterranean, it
prefers a warm, sunny spot in light,
free-draining soil. It is ideal for rock
gardens, sunny banks and terraces.
Plant bulbs in late summer.

◊ ☼ ❀ ❀
‡ to 15cm (6in) ↔ to 5cm (2in)

SORBUS CASHMIRIANA ♥

Deciduous tree

The Kashmir rowan forms a spreading,
open-branched small tree. The white or
blush-pink flowers open in late spring
or early summer. The finely divided,
rich green leaves turn gold and russet
in autumn, forming a backcloth to the
clusters of white, marble-sized berries
that appear from late summer and early
autumn onwards. Grow in sun or light
dappled shade, in fertile, well-drained
but moisture-retentive soil. It is most
easily propagated by seed, sown as
soon as it is ripe in autumn.

◊ ◊ ☼ ☼ ❀ ❀ ❀
‡ to 8m (25ft) ↔ to 7m (22ft)

AMARYLLIS BELLADONNA ♀

Perennial bulb

This South African bulb is grown for its late-summer and early-autumn flowers. The fragrant, trumpet-shaped, pink blooms are borne in clusters on long, purple-tinted stems. The dark green, strap-like leaves appear after the flowers and last until the following summer. In cold areas, protect the leaves from frost by using a cloche. Grow in a warm, sheltered, sunny site in very well-drained soil enriched with organic matter. Plant in summer, with the tip of the bulb just below the soil surface.

◊ ☼ ❊ ❊
‡ to 80cm (32in) ↔ to 45cm (18in)

ANDROSACE LANUGINOSA ♀

Perennial

The fine, silky hairs that clothe the evergreen leaves of this low-growing perennial give the plant a soft-textured appearance. The primrose-like, pink flowers appear in mid- to late summer or early autumn. Rosettes of tiny, deep grey-green leaves are arranged along the length of the trailing stems. It needs a sunny position and very well-drained soil. Add plenty of grit to heavy clay soils to improve drainage. Good for a rock garden, trough or along the top of a dry-stone wall.

◊ ☼ ❊ ❊ ❊
‡ to 10cm (4in) ↔ to 30cm (12in)

CHRYSANTHEMUM
'Rose Yvonne Arnaud'

Perennial

The fully double flowers of this florist's
chrysanthemum are produced in
abundance in late summer and autumn.
The deep rose-pink petals are neatly
backswept. The plant should be lifted
in autumn after flowering and overwintered in frost-free conditions. New
shoots can be planted out after the last
frost or used for basal cuttings in early
spring to produce new plants. Grow in
fertile, well-drained soil, in full sun.

○ ☼ ✿ ✿
‡ to 1.2m (4ft) ↔ to 75cm (30in)

CLERODENDRUM BUNGEI

Deciduous shrub

This suckering shrub is not fully frost-
hardy, but if the woody stems die back
in cold winters, they often grow again
from the base in spring if given a deep
winter mulch. The fragrant flowers are
deep pink and, although tiny, are borne
in large clusters throughout late summer
and early autumn. The large, heart-
shaped, serrated-edged leaves emit a
pungent odour when brushed against.
Grow in a warm, sunny, sheltered site,
in a humus rich, well-drained soil.

○ ☼ ✿ ✿
‡ ↔ to 2m (6ft)

COLCHICUM BYZANTINUM ♀

Perennial corm

C. byzantinum produces up to 20 large, funnel-shaped, pale mauve-pink flowers in autumn. The broad leaves, which are ribbed or pleated, appear in spring and last until early summer. As they fade they can look rather untidy, so hide the foliage by growing them among other plants. Plant the corms, which resemble a tiny clenched fist, in late summer, in a sunny position in soil that is moist but free draining. This colchicum establishes quickly and will spread where the conditions suit it.

△ ◊ ☼ ❀ ❀ ❀
↕ to 12cm (5in) ↔ to 10cm (4in)

COLCHICUM 'The Giant'

Perennial corm

The flowers of this autumn-flowering corm are very large. Mauve-pink with white throats, they are lightly chequered and crocus-like. This is one of the easiest colchicums to grow, and it will increase rapidly. Broad leaves appear in winter and die back in summer. The corms are best grown among other plants to conceal the leaves. Plant the corms in late summer in fertile, free-draining soil in sun. Plants tolerate light or partial shade.

◊ ☼ ❀ ❀ ❀
↕↔ to 20cm (8in)

CROCUS KOTSCHYANUS ♀

Perennial corm

In autumn, this fully hardy crocus bears delicate, lilac-pink flowers with yellow centres and white stamens. The flowers open out fully in sun to display the glossy surface of the petals. They are followed, in winter through to spring, by narrow, semi-erect leaves with white lines along the centre. It is ideal for naturalizing in drifts in well-drained soil in a warm, sunny position. Overcrowded clumps can be divided after flowering. Plant corms in late summer.

◊ ☼ ❉ ❉ ❉
‡ to 8cm (3in) ↔ to 5cm (2in)

CYCLAMEN HEDERIFOLIUM ♀

Perennial

This small cyclamen has ivy-shaped leaves that are intricately patterned in shades of grey-green. Appearing after the flowers in autumn, they can provide a foil for other winter-flowering bulbs until they fade by early summer. The pink flowers appear from late summer to autumn. Grow in light shade in a well-drained soil that is rich in leafy organic matter. Plant tubers in late summer about 2.5cm (1in) deep. Clumps are best left undisturbed, but self-sown seedlings can be lifted and moved.

◊ ☼ ◑ ❉ ❉ ❉
‡ to 13cm (5in) ↔ to 15cm (6in)

HYDRANGEA MACROPHYLLA
'Hamburg'

Deciduous shrub

Long-lasting 'mopheads' of flowers
appear on this vigorous, deciduous
shrub from summer and into autumn.
They are a deep rose-pink on neutral
to alkaline soils and deep blue on acid
(lime-free) soils. The leaves are deep
green, oval and pointed. Position in
full sun, or light, dappled shade, in a
fertile, moist but well-drained soil. The
flowerheads can be cut and dried for
winter arrangements.

◊ ◊ ☼ ◐ ❀ ❀ ❀
‡ to 1m (3ft) ↔ to 1.5m (5ft)

NERINE BOWDENII ♀

Perennial bulb

Stout stems bear umbrella-like clusters
of rose-pink flowers with wavy-edged
petals from early to mid-autumn. The
strap-shaped leaves appear with, or just
after, the flowers. Grow in sun in very
free-draining soil; they are best at the
foot of a warm, sunny wall and left to
multiply undisturbed. Plant in spring
with the tip of the bulb at, or just
below, the soil surface. In winter in
colder areas, cover over with a mulch
of leaf mould or bracken.

◊ ☼ ❀ ❀
‡ to 45cm (18in) ↔ to 15cm (6in)

PHYSOSTEGIA VIRGINIANA
'Vivid' ♀

Perennial

Commonly known as the obedient plant
because the flowers will remain in
position after they are moved on their
stalks. Tall spikes of small, tubular,
vivid purple-pink flowers appear from
midsummer to autumn and are ideal for
cutting. The mid-green leaves are lance-
shaped and toothed and form dense
clumps. Grow in full sun in well-drained,
moisture-retentive soil. Overcrowded
clumps can be divided in spring.

○ ◑ ☼ ✿ ✿ ✿
‡ to 60cm (24in) ↔ to 30cm (12in)

SCHIZOSTYLIS COCCINEA
'Viscountess Byng'

Perennial

Kaffir lilies originate from South Africa,
where they grow beside streams and
in damp meadows. They have narrow,
bright green leaves and spread gradually
to form clumps. 'Viscountess Byng' is a
delicate variety and its flowers can be
damaged by frost. However, it is good
for cutting and in late autumn produces
masses of pink flowers, measuring up
to 3cm (1¼in) across. Plant it in full sun,
in moist soil and mulch over winter.

◑ ☼ ✿ ✿
‡ to 60cm (24in) ↔ to 30cm (12in)

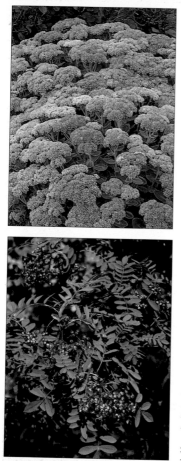

SEDUM SPECTABILE ♛

Perennial

The ice plant is deservedly popular and flowers over long periods from late summer to autumn. It is ideal for the front of a sunny border, where its densely packed, flat heads of tiny star-shaped, soft-pink flowers will attract butterflies and bees. The leaves are fleshy and pale grey-green. Grow in any well-drained soil in full sun. The flowerheads can be cut and dried or left to stand until winter, adding interest to the border.

○ ☼ ❊ ❊ ❊
‡↔ to 45cm (18in)

SORBUS HUPEHENSIS *VAR.* OBTUSA ♛

Deciduous tree

This rowan has a narrow, compact habit. The young foliage is followed by trusses of white flowers in late spring and early summer. Pink berries form during late summer and become deeper pink as they mature. The leaves are divided into many leaflets that turn fiery orange and red in autumn. The berries remain long after the leaves have fallen. Grow in moisture-retentive, well-drained neutral or slightly acid (lime-free) soil in sun or light dappled shade.

○ ◐ ☼ ☀ ❊ ❊ ❊
‡ to 12m (40ft) ↔ to 8m (25ft)

SORBUS VILMORINII ♀

Deciduous tree

The delicate-looking, fern-like leaves of
Vilmorin's rowan are dark green, turning
shades of orange to bronze-red in the
autumn. This large shrub or small tree
has a rounded crown with slender,
arching branches and is suitable for a
small garden. White flowers in late spring
are followed by fruits in autumn, which
ripen through shades of deep red-pink
to white flushed with pink. Plant in
moisture retentive but well-drained
neutral or slightly acid (lime-free) soil
in full sun or light dappled shade.

△ ◐ ☼ ☀ ✿ ✿ ✿
‡↔ to 5m (15ft)

ZEPHYRANTHES
GRANDIFLORA ♀

Perennial bulb

Soft pink, funnel-shaped flowers open
to a starry shape between late summer
and early autumn above clumps of very
slender leaves. Plant bulbs 10cm (4in)
deep in spring in a sheltered, sunny
site, in well-drained, moisture retentive
soil. In cold areas, lift after flowering
and overwinter in a frost-free place. It
can also be grown in containers of
gritty compost and moved under glass
in winter, or grown permanently in the
greenhouse or conservatory.

△ ◐ ☼ ✿
‡ to 30cm (12in) ↔ to 10cm (4in)

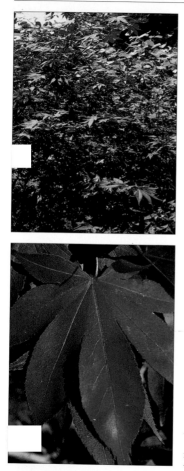

ACER PALMATUM *Dissectum Atropurpureum Group*

Deciduous tree

This small tree is one of the most popular forms of Japanese maple. It has wide-spreading branches clothed with ferny, deeply divided, red-purple leaves that turn red in autumn. Grow in full sun or partial shade, in fertile, moist, but well-drained soil, in a sheltered position; the leaves may be damaged by frosts and cold or dry winds. Grow it with other Japanese maples, or in a large container of loam-based compost (John Innes No. 3).

◊ ◊ ☼ ☀ ❋ ❋ ❋
‡ to 1.5m (5ft) ↔ to 1m (3ft)

ACER PALMATUM 'Ōsakazuki' ♀

Deciduous tree

This Japanese maple has large, bright green leaves that are divided into seven lobes, each drawn out into a finely tapered tip. In autumn they turn a vivid scarlet. Plant it in full sun or partial shade, in fertile, moist but well-drained soil, with shelter from hard frosts and cold, dry winds. To fully appreciate its autumn foliage, it is best grown as a specimen tree.

◊ ◊ ☼ ☀ ❋ ❋ ❋
‡↔ to 6m (20ft)

ACER RUBRUM
'October Glory' ♀

Deciduous tree

The red maple dons its bright red
autumn colours early in the season and
retains its leaves for several weeks,
even in windy weather. The dark green
summer leaves will develop their most
vibrant colours if the tree is grown in
acid (lime-free) soil. Plant it in full sun
or partial shade, in fertile, moist but
well-drained soil. This tree has a
spreading habit.

◊ ◊ ☼ ◑ ❋ ❋ ❋
‡ to 20m (70ft) ↔ to 10m (30ft)

ACER RUBRUM
'Scanlon'

Deciduous tree

There are few trees that colour up as
vividly in autumn as this one – the dark
green leaves turn a vivid shade of deep
reddish orange. Plant it in full sunshine,
in moist but well-drained, fertile soil.
The best autumn colours appear when
grown in acid (lime-tree) soil. This tree
has a narrow columnar form, making it
more suitable for smaller gardens than
'October Glory'.

◊ ◊ ☼ ❋ ❋ ❋
‡ to 15m (50ft) ↔ to 5m (15ft)

AMELANCHIER LAMARCKII ♥

Deciduous tree

Often shrubby, this attractive small tree has upright branches and downy young shoots. It bears hanging clusters of white flowers in mid-spring, which are followed by edible, purplish-black fruit in summer. The leaves are flushed bronze as they emerge in spring, then turn dark green, before becoming orange and finally red in autumn. Plant it full sun or partial shade, in acid (lime-free), fertile, moist but well-drained soil. Thin out main stems if necessary to improve the appearance.

◊ ◊ ☼ ☀ ❋ ❋ ❋
‡ to 10m (30ft) ↔ to 12m (40ft)

ARBUTUS UNEDO ♥

Evergreen tree

The strawberry tree has a bushy, spreading habit and attractive, peeling, reddish-brown bark. The oval leaves are dark green and glossy. From late autumn to spring, it bears hanging sprays of small, waxy-textured white flowers which are accompanied by small, strawberry-like red fruits – these result from the previous year's flowers. Grow in full sun, in a fertile, well-drained soil enriched with leafy organic matter. It is best in a sheltered spot with some protection from strong, cold winds.

◊ ☼ ❋ ❋ ❋
‡↔ to 8m (25ft)

BERBERIS THUNBERGII
'Rose Glow' ♥

Deciduous shrub

This is a vigorous, dense, spiny shrub
with small, rounded, reddish purple
leaves. Later in autumn, white and pink
flecks appear on the leaves, spreading
so the outer leaves become variegated.
In late spring it bears small clusters of
red-tinged, yellow flowers. In autumn
the leaves turn orange and red. It makes
a dense hedge that grows to medium
height, pruning should be delayed until
after flowering. Plant in full sun or
partial shade in well-drained soil.

○ ☼ ☀ ❄ ❄ ❄
↕↔ to 2m (6ft)

BERBERIS WILSONIAE

Deciduous shrub

This is a very dense shrub with spiny,
spreading, gracefully arching branches.
It has glossy, greyish-green leaves that
turn intense shades of bright orange
and red in autumn. In summer, it
produces small clusters of pale yellow
flowers that are followed by tight
bunches of gleaming coral-red fruit in
autumn. Plant it in full sun or partial
shade, in any well-drained soil. Good
for a shrub border or as a specimen.

○ ☼ ☀ ❄ ❄ ❄
↕ to 1m (3ft) ↔ to 2m (6ft)

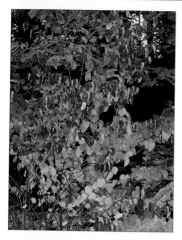

CERCIDIPHYLLUM JAPONICUM ♀

Deciduous tree

The Katsura tree is pyramid-shaped when young, becoming more rounded with maturity. It has rounded, fresh green leaves that turn yellow, orange and red in autumn, with a scent like burnt sugar when they fall. It makes a beautiful specimen tree. Plant it in full sun or dappled shade, in humus-rich, moist but well-drained, neutral to acid (lime-free) soil. The best autumn colour is obtained when it is planted in acid soil.

◊ ◑ ☼ ☀ ✻ ✻ ✻
‡ to 20m (70ft) ↔ to 15m (50ft)

CHRYSANTHEMUM 'George Griffiths' ♀

Perennial

Chrysanthemums should be planted in in a sheltered position in full sun. They need a fertile, moist but well-drained soil that is enriched with well-rotted manure. The flowerheads of 'George Griffiths' are heavy and the stems should be tied in to a cane for support. Lift plants after flowering and overwinter in frost-free conditions. Plant out in spring after the final frost, or raise new plants from basal cuttings. This chrysanthemum is often grown for exhibition.

◊ ◑ ☼ ✻ ✻
‡ to 1.5m (5ft) ↔ to 75cm (30in)

COTINUS
'Grace'

Deciduous shrub

This is an extremely beautiful form of
smoke bush, with rich purple, oval
leaves. In summer, it bears plumes of
small flowers that are followed by sprays
of tiny purplish-pink fruits. In autumn,
the leaves turn a vivid shade of scarlet.
Plant it in full sun or light shade, in
moisture-retentive but well-drained soil.
To obtain the best autumn colour, do
not plant it in too rich a soil and choose
a sunny position; it does not colour as
well in shade.

⬦ ⬦ ☼ ☀ ✽ ✽ ✽
‡ to 6m (20ft) ↔ to 5m (15ft)

COTONEASTER FRIGIDUS
'Cornubia' ♀

Semi-evergreen shrub

This vigorous shrub or small tree has
arching branches clothed in dark green
leaves; some of them turn bronze in
autumn. It is one of the tallest of the
cotoneasters. The clusters of small,
white spring flowers produce an
abundance of bright red fruits in
autumn. Plant it in full sunshine or
partial shade, in moisture-retentive but
well-drained soil. It can be planted as a
screen, in a large shrub border or can
be trained to form a standard tree.

⬦ ⬦ ☼ ☀ ✽ ✽ ✽
‡ ↔ to 10m (30ft)

COTONEASTER HORIZONTALIS ♀

Deciduous shrub

A low-growing shrub, with flattened, wide-spreading branches covered with small, oval, dark green leaves. The branches are arranged in a distinctive herringbone pattern. Small white, pink-flushed flowers appear in spring and are followed, in autumn, by bright scarlet-red fruit. The leaves also turn red in autumn, creating an outstanding display. Grow it against a wall or use it as ground cover. Plant it in full sun in any moderately fertile, well-drained soil.

◊ ☼ ❋ ❋ ❋
↕↔ to 1m (3ft)

EUONYMUS ALATUS ♀

Deciduous shrub

There are few plants that can compete with the winged spindle for dramatic autumn colour. It has dark green leaves that are borne on curious, corky-winged shoots. In autumn the leaves turn a brilliant crimson-red. The purple-red autumn fruits open to reveal seeds with bright orange coats. Plant it in full sun or light shade, in any well-drained soil. It can be grown in a shrub border, but it also makes a beautiful specimen, planted alone so that its beauty can be fully appreciated.

◊ ☼ ☼ ❋ ❋ ❋
↕ to 2m (6ft) ↔ to 3m (10ft)

EUPHORBIA DULCIS
Perennial

This spreading perennial has upright
stems with oblong-shaped green leaves.
The upper part of the stem is branched
and covered with triangular leaves.
In autumn, the stems turn purple and
the leaves take on various shades of
red, yellow and orange. Yellow-green
flowerheads are produced in early
summer. It is best in a moist, humus-
rich soil in light shade, but it does
tolerate drier soils. It self-seeds freely.
Good for a shady border and excellent
for a woodland garden.

◊ ◊ ☼ ❄ ❄ ❄
‡↔ to 30cm (12in)

FOTHERGILLA GARDENII
Deciduous shrub

The witch alder is a small, bushy shrub,
with dark green, oval leaves. In the
summer, it produces cylindrical spikes
of small white flowers. It is mainly
grown for its autumn colour, when the
leaves become infused with intense
shades of red, yellow and orange. It
should be grown in a sunny position,
in moisture-retentive but well-drained,
humus-rich, acid (lime-free) soil. It can
be grown in partial shade but the
colour of the autumn foliage will be
less vibrant.

◊ ◊ ☼ ❄ ❄ ❄
‡↔ to 1m (3ft)

GAULTHERIA TASMANICA

Evergreen shrub

Originating in Tasmania, this is a dwarf, mat-forming shrub, with small, glossy, dark green leaves. In spring, it produces bell-shaped, white flowers that are followed, in autumn, by bright red fruits. It is best planted in partial shade, in moist, neutral or acid (lime-free) soil, but it will tolerate some sun if the soil does not dry out. It is suitable for the front of a shady border or a woodland garden. It can also be planted in containers; use ericaceous compost and do not let it dry out.

◐ ☼ ✽✽✽
‡ to 7cm (3in) ↔ to 25cm (10in)

HAKONECHLOA MACRA
'Aureola' ♥

Perennial

This clump-forming Japanese grass has arching, slender, bright yellow leaves which are narrowly striped with green. They become red tinted in autumn. In late summer and early autumn, it bears spiky flowerheads. Plant it in partial shade, in fertile, moist but well-drained, humus-rich soil. It is ideal for a woodland garden or for planting at the front of a mixed or herbaceous border. It also looks good in containers.

◊ ◊ ☼ ✽✽✽
‡ to 35cm (14in) ↔ to 40cm (16in)

HELENIUM
'Bruno'

Perennial

This upright perennial forms dense clumps of mid-green leaves. From late summer to autumn, it produces abundant heads of deep red-crimson, daisy-like flowers with chocolate-brown centres. Although the flower stems are sturdy, they may need staking on exposed sites. Grow it in a sunny border, in any moisture-retentive but well-drained fertile soil. To keep clumps vigorous and productive, divide them every two or three years.

◊ ◊ ☼ ❋ ❋ ❋
‡ to 1.2m (4ft) ↔ to 60cm (24in)

HYDRANGEA
QUERCIFOLIA ☯

Deciduous shrub

The oak-leaved hydrangea is a mound-forming shrub with deeply lobed green leaves that flush to deep red and bronze-purple in autumn. From late summer to autumn, it bears tall, cone-shaped spikes of white flowers that become flushed with pink as they age. It should be planted in full sun or partial shade, in moist but well-drained, humus-rich, moderately fertile soil. It is suitable for a shrub border or a woodland garden.

◊ ◊ ☼ ☼ ❋ ❋ ❋
‡ to 2m (6ft) ↔ to 2.5m (8ft)

IMPERATA CYLINDRICA *'Rubra'*

Perennial

Japanese blood grass forms clumps of narrow green leaves that turn wine-red as the season progresses. By autumn, when fluffy, silvery flowerheads appear, the leaves have become crimson-scarlet. Grow in full sun or light shade, in humus-rich, moist but well-drained soil. Protect young plants with a winter mulch. Overcrowded clumps can be divided in early spring. It is a good plant for woodland gardens, herbaceous borders or containers.

◊ ◊ ☼ ☀ ❀ ❀
‡ to 40cm (16in) ↔ to 30cm (12in)

LONICERA PERICLYMENUM *'Belgica'*

Climber

Early Dutch honeysuckle is a vigorous climber with bright red berries for autumn interest. It has mid-green leaves and flowers in spring and again in late summer. The tubular flowers, white on the inside and red outside, are highly scented. It is ideal for growing through a tree or over a trellis; if given space to scramble, it seldom needs pruning. Grow it in full sun or partial shade, in humus-rich, moist but well-drained soil.

◊ ◊ ☼ ☀ ❀ ❀ ❀
‡ to 7m (22ft)

MALUS × SCHIEDECKERI
'Red Jade'

Deciduous tree

An attractive small tree with weeping branches, 'Red Jade' has bright pink buds that open in the spring to semi-double, pink-flushed white flowers. These are followed, in autumn, by a profusion of bright red, cherry-sized fruit. The leaves are bright green and glossy. Grow it in full sun, in moist but well-drained, moderately fertile soil. It makes a beautiful specimen tree that is suitable for small gardens.

◊ ◊ ☼ ❋ ❋ ❋
‡ to 4m (12ft) ↔ to 6m (20ft)

NYSSA SYLVATICA ♓

Deciduous tree

The tupelo is a broad, cone-shaped tree, with slightly drooping lower branches, an interesting textured bark, and exuberant autumn colour. The dark green leaves turn vibrant yellow, orange and finally red-crimson shades in mid- to late autumn. Plant it in a sheltered site in full sun or partial shade, in neutral to slightly acid (lime free) soil that is fertile and moisture retentive but well drained. It makes a glorious specimen tree.

◊ ◊ ☼ ☼ ❋ ❋ ❋
‡ to 20m (70ft) ↔ to 10m (30ft)

PARROTIA PERSICA ♀

Deciduous tree

The Persian ironwood is a shrubby tree with peeling, grey and brown bark. The large glossy leaves put on a glorious autumn display in shades of red, orange and yellow. In late winter or early spring, small, spidery red flowers appear on the bare branches. Plant in full sun or partial shade, in a good depth of fertile, moist but well-drained soil. The best autumn colour occurs on acid (lime-free) soil, but it also tolerates alkaline conditions. A fine specimen tree, it develops great character with age.

◊ ◊ ☼ ☀ ❄ ❄ ❄
‡ to 8m (25ft) ↔ to 10m (30ft)

PARTHENOCISSUS TRICUSPIDATA ♀

Climber

Boston ivy is a vigorous woody climber, with glossy, dark green leaves that are toothed and divided into three lobes. In autumn, these turn gold, brilliant red and purple before falling. It is superb for covering a large, unattractive or featureless wall, or for growing through a tall, sturdy tree. Grow it in full sun or shade, in fertile, well-drained soil that is rich in humus. Provide young plants with support until they are established.

◊ ◊ ☼ ☀ ❄ ❄ ❄
‡ to 20m (70ft)

PRUNUS AVIUM ♀

Deciduous tree

The wild cherry, or gean, is a large,
spreading tree with dark green leaves
that are tinted bronze in spring and
turn red and gold in autumn. In the
middle of spring it bears clusters of
white flowers, followed, in late summer
and autumn, by small, dark red fruit,
which the birds love to eat. Plant it in
full sunshine or partial shade, in fertile,
moist but well-drained soil. It is a fine
specimen tree and is also useful in a
larger garden for attracting wildlife.

◊ ◊ ☼ ☀ ❋ ❋ ❋
‡ to 20m (70ft) ↔ to 10m (30ft)

RHUS TYPHINA
'Dissecta' ♀

Deciduous tree

The stag's horn sumach gets its common
name from the upright, velvet-covered
branch tips that resemble antlers. In
summer, upright spikes of small, yellow-
green flowers turn dark crimson as they
fruit. The ferny leaves turn shades of
brilliant red, gold and orange in autumn.
Plant in full sun, in fertile, moist but
well-drained soil. If its spreading suckers
are a nuisance, they can be dug out
over winter when the plant is dormant.

◊ ◊ ☼ ❋ ❋ ❋
‡ to 2m (6ft) ↔ to 3m (10ft)

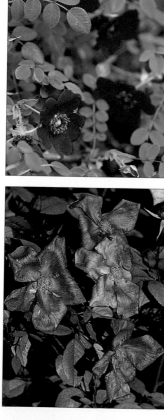

ROSA MOYESII
'Geranium'

Deciduous shrub

'Geranium' is a more compact form of a rather vigorous species. It has strong, arching stems and delicately divided green leaves. In summer, it bears single, cup-shaped, sealing-wax-red flowers, that are followed by spectacular bright orange-red, flask-shaped hips in autumn. It is good for a sunny mixed border or wild garden. Plant it in fertile, humus-rich, moist but well-drained soil. To keep it compact, shorten the main stems by up to a third after flowering.

⬦ ◊ ☼ ❁ ❁ ❁
‡ to 4m (12ft) ↔ to 3m (10ft)

ROSA × ODORATA
'Mutabilis' ♀

Deciduous shrub

This slender shrub has purple-red stems and purple flushed, dark green leaves. The single, cup-shaped flowers open pale yellow, turning first pink and then carmine-red; they are borne over a long period from summer to autumn and have a wonderful fragrance. Plant it in a sheltered position in fertile, humus-rich, moist but well-drained soil. It is normally grown as a shrub rose but will climb if it is provided with some support.

◊◊ ☼ ❁ ❁ ❁
‡↔ to 2m (6ft)

ROSA RUGOSA

Deciduous shrub

Easy-going and vigorous, this repeat-flowering rose has robust, prickly stems and wrinkled, bright green leaves that turn yellow in autumn. The single, fragrant, carmine red flowers are borne from early summer to autumn. From late summer they are accompanied by large, spherical, orange-red hips. Tolerant of a wide range of conditions, it prefers full sun or light shade and a moist but well-drained soil. It makes a superb, intruder-proof hedge. Trim or prune to shape in late winter or early spring.

○ ◑ ☼ ☀ ✻ ✻ ✻
‡↔ to 2m (6ft)

RUSCUS ACULEATUS

Evergreen shrub

Butcher's broom is a clump-forming plant with upright stems that bear very tough, spine-tipped, leaf-like modified stems. From late summer to winter, female plants produce small, round, bright red berries. Male and female or hermaphrodite plants are needed to ensure fruiting. It grows in sun, deep shade and in any but waterlogged soil; it also tolerates dry soil. The cut stems can be used in flower arrangements.

○ ◑ ☼ ☀ ✻ ✻ ✻
‡ to 75cm (2½ft) ↔ to 1m (3ft)

SCHIZOSTYLIS COCCINEA

Perennial

From late summer to autumn, the Kaffir lily produces shiny, bright red flowers on strong but slender stems, which are held above green, strap-shaped, almost evergreen leaves. Remove flowers as they fade. Grow in a sunny, sheltered position in fertile, moist soil and protect the crowns with a mulch in winter in cold or exposed gardens. It spreads freely; divide overcrowded clumps in spring. Plant it in a herbaceous border or beside water. It is also good for cutting.

◐ ☼ ❋ ❋ ❋
‡ to 50cm (20in) ↔ to 30cm (12in)

SORBUS AUCUPARIA

Deciduous tree

The rowan is a small or medium-sized tree, with mid-green leaves divided into small leaflets. In spring, it bears clusters of creamy-white flowers that are followed by bright red berries in autumn. They are very attractive to birds. The foliage turns red or yellow in autumn. Plant in full sun or dappled shade, in moderately fertile, humus-rich, well-drained soil. It is tolerant of a wide range of conditions and will grow happily on both acid (lime-free) and slightly alkaline soils.

◐ ☼ ◑ ❋ ❋ ❋
‡ to 15m (50ft) ↔ to 7m (22ft)

SORBUS COMMIXTA

Deciduous tree

Slightly smaller than *Sorbus aucuparia*, this tree has dark green leaves divided into many small, lance-shaped leaflets. The autumn colour is outstanding as the leaves become infused with brilliant shades of vivid red, yellow and purple. In late spring, it bears clusters of white flowers that are followed by bright orange-red or red autumn fruits. It should be planted in full sunshine or dappled shade, in moderately fertile, humus-rich, moist but well-drained soil.

◊ ◊ ☼ ☀ ✱ ✱ ✱
‡ to 10m (30ft) ↔ to 7m (22ft)

SORBUS SARGENTIANA ♀

Deciduous tree

The large leaves of this slow-growing tree are divided into lance-shaped green leaflets that take on brilliant shades of red and orange in autumn. In winter, distinctive, bright red, sticky buds form. In early summer, it produces clusters of white flowers, followed by broad sprays of small, scarlet autumn fruits. Plant it in a sunny position, in humus-rich, fertile, moist but well-drained soil. It makes a beautiful specimen tree and, like other sorbus, has several seasons of interest.

◊ ◊ ☼ ✱ ✱ ✱
‡ ↔ to 10m (30ft)

TIGRIDIA PAVONIA

Perennial bulb

The tiger flower bears unusual flowers in succession during late summer to early autumn. The flowers, up to 15cm (6in) across, are bright red and marked at the base with dark red or brown spots. Pink, white or yellow varieties are also available. It can be grown in sunny borders in light sandy soil, but in frost-prone areas, must be lifted before autumn frosts. Store bulbs dry in a frost-free place in winter and replant in spring, or grow in deep pots of sandy, loam-based compost.

◊ ☼ ❄

‡ to 1.5m (5ft) ↔ to 10cm (4in)

TITHONIA ROTUNDIFOLIA 'Torch'

Annual

The Mexican sunflower is a robust annual with large, three-lobed leaves. It flowers from late summer to early autumn and has large, dahlia-like flowers on tall, sturdy stems. The petals are bright red or orange-red and surround a raised yellow centre. Plant out after the last frosts. Grow in full sun in fertile, well-drained soil. Provide a spot that is sheltered from strong winds and support the tall stems by tying them in to stout canes as they grow.

◊ ☼ ❄ ❄

‡ to 2m (6ft) ↔ to 30cm (12in)

VITIS
'Brant' ♀

Climber

This vigorous, woody-stemmed vine is grown for its autumn colour and edible, blue-black grapes that ripen in autumn. The deeply lobed leaves are green throughout summer, but in autumn, take on vibrant shades of deep red and purple, with yellow veins. It can be trained against a wall on supporting wires, and is excellent on a pergola. Grow it in a warm, sheltered spot in full sun, in well-drained, preferably neutral to alkaline soil.

◊ ☼ ❄ ❄ ❄
↕ to 7m (22ft)

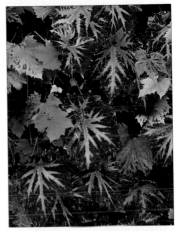

VITIS COIGNETIAE ♀

Climber

Possibly one of the best vines for autumn colour. This rampant climber has large, heart-shaped green leaves that turn vivid shades of bright red and crimson in autumn. It is ideal for clothing a pergola, growing through a big tree, or for disguising a large featureless wall. Plant it in full sun or partial shade, in well drained, neutral to alkaline soil. If it gets too large, prune it back to strong buds in winter, to within 5cm (2in) of the previous year's growth.

◊ ☼ ☼ ❄ ❄ ❄
↕ to 15m (50ft)

ASTER NOVI-BELGII
'Peace'

Perennial

This vigorous Michaelmas daisy produces large, mauve-purple flowerheads from late summer to autumn. It is best planted at the back or middle of the herbaceous border, in full sunshine and in very fertile, moist soil. It has strong stems so supports are not essential. It should be cut back to the ground after flowering and covered with a layer of mulch for the winter. Divide every three years in spring.

💧 ☼ ❋ ❋ ❋
‡ to 90cm (36in) ↔ to 75cm (30in)

ASTER NOVI-BELGII
'Jenny'

Perennial

Late-flowering Michaelmas daisies come in shades of pink, purple or blue. 'Jenny' has yellow-centred, double, red-purple, daisy-like flowerheads. It is best planted in a herbaceous border, in full sunshine or light shade and in very fertile, moist soil with twiggy sticks or canes for support. Cut back to the ground after flowering. Cover with a layer of mulch and divide every third year in spring to maintain vigour.

💧 ☼ ◑ ❋ ❋ ❋
‡ to 1.5m (5ft) ↔ to 60cm (24in)

BILLARDIERA LONGIFLORA 🏆

Climber

The climbing blueberry has rather wiry
stems that will climb over any suitable
support. It has narrow, lance-shaped
dark green leaves. The green, bell-
shaped flowers of summer are followed
by purplish-blue, egg-shaped fruit in
autumn; some plants bear pink, red or
white fruit. Grow in a warm, sheltered
site in full sun or light shade, in humus-
rich, neutral to acid (lime-free) soil. In
very cold areas, grow in a conservatory
in containers of ericaceous compost.

◊ ☼ ☀ ❄ ❄
‡ to 3m (10ft)

BUDDLEJA CRISPA

Deciduous shrub

The arching stems of this attractive, late-
flowering shrub are clothed in toothed,
white-felted leaves. From midsummer to
early autumn, it produces large, fragrant,
clustered spikes of lilac flowers. It is
very attractive to beneficial insects and
butterflies. Grow in a mixed border or
in a shrub border. It is not completely
hardy and is sometimes damaged by
hard frosts, so plant in a sheltered
position in cold or exposed gardens.
Plant it in full sunshine, in fertile, well
drained soil.

◊ ☼ ❄ ❄ ❄
‡↔ to 3m (10ft)

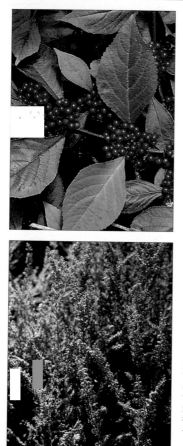

CALLICARPA BODINIERI
'Profusion' ♀

Deciduous shrub

The beauty berry is a striking shrub with upright branches and large, pale green leaves that are tinted bronze in spring. It produces pale pink flowers in midsummer, but is grown mainly for its colourful fruit that look just like clusters of shining, bright violet beads. These are retained on the bare branches after leaf fall. Grow in full sunshine or light, dappled shade, in well-drained, fertile soil. Planting in groups will maximize fruiting.

○ ☼ ☀ ❄ ❄
‡ to 3m (10ft) ↔ to 2.5m (8ft)

CALLUNA VULGARIS
'Silver Queen' ♀

Evergreen shrub

Heathers are invaluable for providing colour at the end of the summer. 'Silver Queen' is grown for the year-round interest of its attractive downy, silver-grey leaves and for the display of tiny, bell-shaped, mauve flowers from midsummer to autumn. The flowers are very attractive to bees. Plant it in full sun, in an open site in humus-rich, well-drained, acid (lime-free) soil. Trim plants in spring to keep them compact and bushy.

○ ☼ ❄ ❄ ❄
‡ to 40cm (16in) ↔ to 55cm (22in)

COLCHICUM AGRIPPINUM ♀

Perennial corm

This autumn-flowering colchicum has funnel-shaped, purplish-pink flowers that are marked with a conspicuous chequerboard pattern. It has upright, slightly wavy, strap-shaped leaves that appear in early spring but disappear by summer. The corms should be planted 10cm (4in) deep in summer or early autumn. Grow in an open situation in full sun, in deep, fertile, well-drained soil. It is suitable for a rock garden, a trough or can be grown in a container.

◊ ☼ ❋ ❋ ❋
‡ to 10cm (4in) ↔ to 8cm (3in)

CROCUS MEDIUS ♀

Perennial corm

This is an attractive dwarf crocus, with funnel-shaped, bright purple flowers in late autumn. The narrow leaves, which are green with a silvery-white line down the centre, appear with or just after the flowers. It is suitable for naturalizing in grass, or for planting on a rock garden. Grow it in full sunshine, in gritty, very well-drained, poor to moderately fertile soil. It prefers dry conditions during the summer when it is dormant.

◊ ☼ ❋ ❋ ❋
‡ to 8cm (3in) ↔ to 2.5cm (1in)

GAULTHERIA MUCRONATA
'Mulberry Wine' ♛

Evergreen shrub

This bushy shrub has shining, spine-tipped, dark green leaves. In late spring and summer, it bears small white flowers that are followed, in autumn, by glossy fruits that ripen to dark purple. Grow in partial shade, in acid (lime-free), humus-rich, moist soil. Grow male and female plants together to ensure fruiting. Gaultherias associate well with heathers and are suitable for woodland gardens. There are also varieties with pink, red or white fruits.

◑ ☼ ❄ ❄ ❄
‡ ↔ to 1.2m (4ft)

LIRIOPE MUSCARI ♛

Perennial

Lilyturf is a densely clump-forming, evergreen perennial, with narrow, strap-shaped, dark green leaves. In late summer and early autumn, it produces long, slender spikes of small violet-mauve flowers. Plant it in partial or full shade, in acid to neutral, preferably moist but well-drained soil. It will tolerate dry, shady conditions. Use it as ground cover, in a woodland garden, or for planting towards the front of a border. Overcrowded clumps can be divided in spring.

◊ ◊ ◑ ☼ ❄ ❄ ❄
‡ to 30cm (12in) ↔ to 45cm (18in)

SORBUS REDUCTA ♀

Deciduous shrub

The upright, suckering stems of this unusual shrubby rowan spread to form a dense, low thicket. The finely divided leaves turn red and purple in autumn. In spring, it bears clusters of small white flowers, followed by pink-flushed white berries. Plant in an open site in full sun, in humus-rich, moderately fertile, well-drained soil. It is good for small town gardens and roadside situations as it tolerates pollution. Pull out unwanted stems when still young and soft.

△ ☼ ❄ ❄ ❄
‡ to 1.5m (5ft) ↔ to 2m (6ft)

TRICYRTIS FORMOSANA ♀

Perennial

This vigorous perennial spreads by means of underground stems. In autumn, it produces small pinkish-purple flowers, patterned with purple spots. It has slightly hairy, branched stems and glossy, dark green leaves. Plant it in a sheltered, shady situation, in moist but well-drained, humus-rich soil. In cold gardens, it needs a deep mulch of straw, leaf mould or dry bracken to protect it from hard frost. It is an excellent plant for a damp woodland garden or a shady border.

△ ♦ ☼ ☀ ❄ ❄ ❄
‡ to 80cm (32in) ↔ to 45cm (18in)

ACONITUM CARMICHAELII *'Arendsii'*

Perennial

This monkshood makes a striking display with its tall spikes of deep blue flowers that appear from early to mid-autumn. An upright plant with deeply lobed, dark green leaves, it is suitable for a woodland garden, and is also successful in a shaded mixed or herbaceous border. Plant in partial shade and in moist, fertile soil. It is best in a site sheltered from strong winds; support the stems with canes. All parts are toxic.

○ ◐ ☼ ❋ ❋ ❋
↕ to 1.5m (5ft) ↔ to 30cm (12in)

AMPELOPSIS GLANDULOSA *VAR.* BREVIPEDUNCULATA

Climber

The leaves of this vigorous vine are divided into three or five lobes and colour well in autumn. It is grown for its attractive fruit, which change colour from pinkish-purple to greenish-blue and deep blue. It needs a warm, sheltered site for the fruit to develop properly. Plant it against a wall, fence or on a pergola. Choose a position in full sun with fertile, moist but well-drained soil. It tolerates partial shade but fruits more freely in sun.

○ ◐ ☼ ☼ ❋ ❋ ❋
↕ to 5m (15ft)

ASTER NOVI-BELGII
'Professor Anton Kippenburg'
Perennial

This is one of the best Michaelmas
daisies for the small garden. From late
summer to mid-autumn, it bears pale,
clear blue, daisy-like flowerheads with
yellow centres. The leaves are dark
green and lance shaped. It is very
vigorous but because it is relatively
short growing it does not require
staking. Plant it in full sun or partial
shade, in fertile, moist soil. Cut back
and mulch after flowering. It should be
divided every three years in spring.

◊ ☼ ◐ ❄ ❄ ❄
‡ to 35cm (14in) ↔ to 45cm (18in)

ASTER × FRIKARTII
'Wunder von Stäfa' ♀
Perennial

A superb plant for the middle of a
border, this tall aster has dark green
leaves and stiffly upright stems. Bright
blue flowers with yellow centres are
produced from late summer until early
autumn. Plant in moderately fertile, well-
drained, preferably alkaline soil, in full
sun. After flowering, cut stems back to
the ground and apply a layer of mulch.
It can be increased quickly by division
in spring.

◊ ☼ ❄ ❄ ❄
‡ to 70cm (28in) ↔ to 40cm (16in)

CEANOTHUS
'Autumnal Blue' ♥

Evergreen shrub

The majority of Californian lilacs flower during spring or early summer, but this one produces clusters of small, vivid blue flowers in late summer to early autumn. It has broadly oval, glossy, dark green leaves. Plant it in full sun, with some protection from cold winds, in fertile, well-drained soil. It rarely needs pruning, but if wayward shoots spoil the symmetry of the shrub, they should be removed when it has finished flowering.

◊ ☼ ❄ ❄
‡↔ to 3m (10ft)

CERATOSTIGMA
WILLMOTTIANUM ♥

Deciduous shrub

This is an attractive, spreading shrub with small, lance-shaped, green leaves. In late summer and early autumn, it bears pale blue flowers – the later ones among red-tinted autumn leaves. Grow in full sun, in moderately fertile, moist but well-drained soil. It is not completely hardy and is best in a sheltered position. In cold winters, the shoots may be killed by hard frosts, but it often produces new shoots from the base in spring.

◊ ◊ ☼ ❄ ❄
‡ to 1m (3ft) ↔ to 1.5m (5ft)

GENTIANA SINO-ORNATA ♀
Perennial

The beautiful autumn gentian
overwinters as a rosette of glossy, dark
green leaves. Low, spreading shoots
appear in spring, each developing at its
tip an upward-pointing, deep blue
flower in autumn. The base of the
flower's throat is greenish white, marked
with distinct purplish-blue lines radiating
from the centre. Plant it in humus-rich,
moist but well-drained, acid (lime-free)
or neutral soil with some shade from
strong summer sunshine. It is suitable
for a rock garden or trough.

◊ ◊ ☀ ❋ ❋ ❋
‡ to 7cm (3in) ↔ to 30cm (12in)

HEBE
'Autumn Glory'
Evergreen shrub

Among the prettiest of the autumn-
flowering hebes, this shrub forms a
spreading mound of purple-tinted, dark
green, broadly oval leaves. The spikes
of small, violet-blue flowers open in the
middle of summer and continue to be
produced until the first frosts. Plant in
full sun or light shade, in moist but
well-drained, fertile, neutral to slightly
alkaline soil. Provide a sheltered site to
protect from cold, drying winter winds
and hard frosts.

◊ ◊ ◊ ☼ ☀ ❋ ❋
‡ to 60cm (24in) ↔ to 90cm (36in)

HORDEUM JUBATUM

Perennial

The squirrel-tail grass is a tufted grass with arching, narrow, green leaves. The attractive, nodding flowerheads, with their long, feathery bristles, appear in summer. They are green when young, turning pale buff-beige in autumn. Plant in full sun, in well-drained, moderately fertile soil in a herbaceous border or wild garden. It is also grown for cutting, which should be done before the flowerheads have set seed.

◊ ☼ ✻ ✻ ✻
‡ to 60cm (24in) ↔ to 30cm (12in)

KNIPHOFIA
'Percy's Pride'

Perennial

This red-hot poker forms clumps of tough, slender, arching leaves and produces stout-stemmed heads of tubular flowers in late summer and early autumn. Green in bud, the flowers open greenish yellow and become cream with age. Grow in a sunny or partially shaded site, in deep, fertile, moist but well-drained soil. Cover young plants with a protective mulch in their first winter, and cut back old growth in spring.

◊ ◊ ☼ ☀ ✻ ✻ ✻
‡ to 1.2m (4ft) ↔ to 60cm (24in)

MATTEUCCIA STRUTHIOPTERIS ♛

Perennial

In spring, the shuttlecock fern produces
a cluster of brilliant green fronds
arranged in a tight funnel. In late
summer, dark brown, fertile fronds
appear at the centre of the shuttlecock.
Plant in partial shade, in moist, neutral
to acid (lime-free), humus-rich soil,
particularly in woodland or near water.
It spreads by underground stems to
form large colonies. It can be increased
by lifting and separating young plants
from the parent plant in spring.

◊ ☀ ❀ ❀ ❀
‡ to 1.5m (5ft) ↔ to 75cm (30in)

MISCANTHUS SINENSIS
'*Silberfeder*'

Perennial

This tall grass forms a large clump of
arching, mid-green leaves and, in early
and mid-autumn, upright stems bearing
silvery buff flowerheads. Suitable for
most soils, it grows best in full sun, in
moderately fertile, moist but well-drained
soil. The flowerheads can be left in place
during winter but should be cut down
to the ground, together with any dead
growth, in early spring. This grass is
easily increased by dividing established
clumps in spring.

◊ ◊ ☀ ❀ ❀ ❀
‡ to 2.5m (8ft) ↔ to 1.2m (4ft)

OSMUNDA REGALIS ♀

Perennial

The elegant royal fern forms a substantial clump of upright, finely divided, bright green fronds that turn shades of apricot-yellow before they die down. In summer, distinctive rusty brown, tassel-like fronds rise from the centre of the clump. Grow in partial shade, in moist, humus-rich, preferably acid (lime-free) soil. It can be planted in full sun in permanently damp soils. The royal fern makes a beautiful specimen in damp woodland or beside a stream or pond.

◐ ◆ ☀ ❄ ❄ ❄
‡ to 2m (6ft) ↔ to 4m (12ft)

PANICUM VIRGATUM *'Heavy Metal'*

Perennial

This is a particularly upright-growing switch grass. In late summer it produces beautiful, nodding spikes of small, purple-green flowers. The metallic, bluish-green leaves turn golden yellow in late autumn and finally light brown in winter. It has a beautiful winter presence in the garden, especially when the flowerheads are left in place. Grow in a sunny site, in well-drained, moderately fertile soil. Cut back before growth begins in early spring.

○ ☀ ❄ ❄ ❄
‡ to 1m (3ft) ↔ to 75cm (30in)

PENNISETUM ALOPECUROIDES 'Hameln'

Perennial

Fountain grass is a clump-forming plant with flat, pointed, dark evergreen leaves. 'Hameln' is compact and, in summer and early autumn, it bears long, arching spikes of pale green flowers. The leaves turn yellow before they die down and the flowers age to a warm, pale grey-brown. Grow in full sun, in moderately fertile, well-drained soil. Provide a protective winter mulch in cold areas or grow in containers. Cut back in spring before growth begins.

◊ ☼ ❋ ❋

‡ to 1.5m (5ft) ↔ to 1.2m (4ft)

THELYPTERIS PALUSTRIS

Perennial

The marsh fern has attractive, long-stalked, lacy, pale green fronds. It is suitable for growing in a damp border and is perfectly at home on the damp banks of a stream or pool, especially in a wild garden. Grow it in full sun or partial shade, in permanently moist, moderately fertile soil. Spreading by means of creeping, underground stems, it can become rather invasive; chop out unwanted clumps with a sharp spade.

◊ ◖ ☼ ◑ ❋ ❋ ❋

‡ to 60cm (24in) ↔ to 1m (3ft)

ASTER LINOSYRIS

Perennial

Goldilocks is an upright, slender, herbaceous perennial with stems clothed in narrow, mid-green leaves. In late summer and early autumn, it produces dense heads of many tiny, fluffy, bright yellow flowers. Grow in well-drained, moderately fertile, preferably alkaline soil in a sunny site. It can be grown on a rock garden, at the front of a border, or in a wild garden. It is attractive to late-flying, beneficial insects.

○ ☼ ❋ ❋ ❋

‡ to 60cm (24in) ↔ to 30cm (12in)

BETULA PENDULA
'Tristis' ♀

Deciduous tree

This elegant, fast-growing tree has white bark and cascading branches bearing diamond-shaped, dark green leaves that turn bright golden-yellow in autumn. It bears long, hanging yellow catkins in early spring. With its narrow crown, it is ideal for a small garden and casts little shade. Plant it as a specimen tree or in a group, in full sun or light, dappled shade. It tolerates a range of soils but prefers it when moist but well drained and moderately fertile.

○ ◗ ☼ ☀ ❋ ❋ ❋

‡ to 25m (80ft) ↔ to 10m (30ft)

CALLUNA VULGARIS
'Robert Chapman' ♀

Evergreen shrub

This heather has dense, golden-yellow
foliage and bears spikes of purple-pink
flowers in late summer. In winter, the
leaves take on orange and red shades,
retaining the colour until the new
growth emerges the following spring.
Plant in a group to maximize its effect;
it associates well with other heathers
with different foliage tints. Grow in sun,
in well-drained, acid (lime-free) soil that
is humus rich. Shear off flowered
shoots in spring to keep it compact.

◊ ☼ ❀ ❀
‡ to 25cm (10in) ↔ to 65cm (26in)

CHRYSANTHEMUM
'Pennine Alfie' ♀

Perennial

In early autumn, this chrysanthemum
has bright yellow, semi double flowers,
with spoon-shaped petals and bright
red bases. Plant it in a sunny border,
in fertile, moist but well-drained soil.
Support the stems with canes. Lift plants
after flowering and overwinter in frost-
free conditions. Plant out in spring after
the final frost and raise new plants from
basal cuttings.

◊ ◊ ☼ ❀ ❀
‡ to 1.2m (4ft) ↔ to 75cm (30in)

CHRYSANTHEMUM
'Wendy' ♀

Perennial

A spray chrysanthemum with light
bronze, double flowers in early autumn.
The outer petals point downwards,
rather like an umbrella. For extra large
flowers, remove all but four of the buds.
Support stems with canes. Lift plants
after flowering and overwinter in frost-
free conditions. Plant out in spring once
frosts are finished, or raise new plants
from basal cuttings taken in winter.
Grow in reasonably fertile, moist but
well-drained soil in a sunny position.

○ ◐ ☼ ❄ ❄
‡ to 1.2m (4ft) ↔ to 75cm (30in)

CLEMATIS
'Bill MacKenzie' ♀

Climber

In late summer and early autumn, this
vigorous climber produces hanging, bell-
shaped flowers up to 8cm (3in) across.
The blooms are yellow with red anthers
and are followed by feathery, silvery
seedheads. Plant in fertile, humus-rich,
moist but well-drained soil, with the
plant's base in shade and the upper
growth in sun or light shade. Provide
support. In spring, cut back the previous
year's growth to a pair of strong buds,
about 20cm (8in) from the base.

○ ◐ ☼ ◑ ❄ ❄ ❄
‡ to 7m (22in)

CLEMATIS TANGUTICA

Climber

This late-flowering clematis has bluish
green, divided leaves and from
midsummer to autumn, produces large
numbers of hanging, bell-shaped, bright
yellow flowers. They are followed by
silky seedheads that last into winter.
Grow it up a trellis, through a small
tree, or allow it to scramble over a
bank as ground cover. Plant in fertile,
humus-rich, moist but well-drained soil,
in full sun or partial shade with the
roots in cool shade. Cut back hard in
spring to within 20cm (8in) of the base.

◊ ◑ ☼ ☀ ❋ ❋ ❋
‡ to 15m (20ft)

CLEMATIS REHDERIANA ♀

Climber

One of the more unusual species of
clematis, with clusters of small, nodding,
primrose-yellow flowers that smell like
cowslips. It flowers from the middle
of summer to autumn. Plant in fertile,
humus-rich, moist but well-drained soil,
in full sun or partial shade, but with
the roots shaded and kept cool with a
gravel mulch. Grow it on supports
against a fence or wall, over a pergola
or into a tree. Cut back hard in spring
and trim each shoot to a pair of strong
buds, 20cm (8in) from the base.

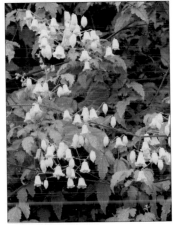

◊ ◑ ☼ ❋ ❋ ❋ ❋
‡ to 7m (22ft)

COTONEASTER FRIGIDUS
'Fructu Luteo'

Deciduous shrub

The upright stems of this shrubby or tree-like cotoneaster arch gracefully as it matures. The narrow leaves are dull green but develop golden tints in autumn. In summer, the branches are wreathed with white flowers that give rise to creamy-yellow fruit in autumn. Grow in sun or light dappled shade, in any well-drained, moderately fertile soil. Use as an ornamental screen, for the back of a shrub border, or as a specimen.

◊ ☼ ☀ ❀ ❀ ❀
‡↔ to 10m (30ft)

COTONEASTER SALICIFOLIUS
'Rothschildianus' ♀

Evergreen shrub

This vigorous, spreading shrub has narrow, pale green leaves and clusters of white flowers along the arching branches in early summer. In autumn, it produces clusters of attractive golden-yellow fruit. It is an extremely beautiful shrub for the back of a mixed or shrub border and, where there is room, makes an attractive specimen. Plant it in full sun or partial shade, in any moderately fertile, well-drained soil.

◊ ◊ ☼ ☀ ❀ ❀ ❀
‡↔ to 5m (15ft)

CREPIS AUREA

Perennial

A pretty late-flowering plant for the rock garden, with a low rosette of rounded, toothed, light green leaves. In late summer and early autumn, it produces hairy, wiry stems bearing yellow-orange, dandelion like flowerheads that are attractive to late-flying, beneficial insects. It is easy to grow in full sun and in any well-drained soil. It has a long taproot that enables it to survive dry summers.

◊ ☼ ❄ ❄ ❄
‡ to 30cm (12in) ↔ to 15cm (6in)

GLADIOLUS PAPILIO

Perennial corm

This is an attractive species of gladiolus that will add valuable late colour to a mixed or herbaceous border. It blooms in late summer and early autumn, producing spikes of funnel-shaped flowers. These are pale yellow to greenish or golden yellow, often with soft purple blotches at the throat and purple-tinged outsides. The leaves are sword shaped. Plant corms in spring in full sun, in light, moderately fertile, well-drained soil. Mulch in winter in cold areas.

△ ☼ ❄ ❄
‡ to 1m (3ft) ↔ to 15cm (6in)

GLEDITSIA TRIACANTHOS *'Sunburst'* ♛

Deciduous tree

This golden-leaved honey locust is a conical tree with an open tracery of spreading branches. The delicate, ferny leaves are golden yellow in spring, later turning green, then brilliant yellow in autumn. 'Sunburst' is less vigorous and thorny than the species and makes a beautiful specimen for smaller gardens, especially in urban situations as it tolerates pollution. Plant it in full sun, in any well-drained, fertile soil.

○ ☼ ❄ ❄ ❄
‡ to 12m (40ft) ↔ to 10m (30ft)

HAMAMELIS VIRGINIANA

Deciduous shrub

The Virginian witch hazel is an upright shrub with oval green leaves that turn bright yellow in autumn. As they begin to fall, small clusters of spidery yellow flowers are produced. Plant it in full sunshine or partial shade, in moderately fertile, moist but well-drained, neutral to acid (lime-free) soil. It will grow in deep soils over chalk. It prefers an open site but with some shelter from strong wind. Grow it as a specimen, at the back of a shrub border or in a woodland garden.

○ ◐ ☼ ◑ ❄ ❄ ❄
‡↔ to 4m (12ft)

HELICHRYSUM SPLENDIDUM ♀

Evergreen shrub

This clump-forming shrub has white-woolly stems and masses of tiny, silver-grey leaves. The deep yellow flowerheads appear at the tips of upright stems from late summer to autumn. They can be cut and dried for winter arrangements. It is drought tolerant and excellent for a hot, sunny bank or a mixed or herbaceous border. Grow in full sun, in very well-drained, poor to moderately fertile soil. Trim each year in spring to keep it compact. It may not survive cold wet winters.

◊ ☼ ❋ ❋ ❋
↕↔ to 1.2m (4ft)

KIRENGESHOMA PALMATA ♀

Perennial

This is a clump-forming perennial with dark stems bearing deeply lobed, slightly hairy, pale green leaves. In late summer and early autumn, it produces nodding, tubular, pale yellow flowers that have a waxy texture. Plant it in a shady situation, in moist, acid (lime-free) soil enriched with leaf mould. It is an elegant plant for a shady border or woodland garden and looks especially beautiful at the sides of streams or pools.

◐ ☼ ❋ ❋ ❋
↕ to 1.2m (4ft) ↔ to 75cm (30in)

LIQUIDAMBAR STYRACIFLUA
'Golden Treasure'

Deciduous tree

A slow-growing tree, the variegated sweet gum is grown mainly for its foliage. The deeply lobed, maple-like leaves are margined with rich yellow, and in late autumn, they take on dramatic tints as they turn red and purple with golden margins. It tolerates partial shade but the best autumn colour develops in full sun. Plant in neutral to acid (lime-free), moderately fertile soil that is moist but well drained.

○ ◑ ☼ ☀ ❋ ❋ ❋
‡ to 10m (30ft) ↔ to 6m (20ft)

MALUS × ZUMI
'Golden Hornet' ♀

Deciduous tree

An attractive crab apple, 'Golden Hornet' is valued for its spherical golden-yellow fruits that appear in autumn and remain on the bare branches well into winter. In spring, it bears masses of white flowers that open from pink buds. Plant it in full sun, in fertile, moist but well-drained soil. It is best grown as a specimen tree, sited where its pretty fruit can be fully appreciated. The slightly smaller variety, *calocarpa*, has bright red fruits.

○ ◑ ☼ ❋ ❋ ❋
‡ to 10m (30ft) ↔ to 8m (25ft)

PHYGELIUS × RECTUS
'Moonraker'

Evergreen shrub

This is a long-flowering, small shrub with glossy, dark green leaves and long, upright spikes of hanging, creamy yellow flowers from midsummer to autumn. Plant in full sun, in fertile, moist but well-drained soil. Dead-head regularly to prolong flowering. Excellent in a mixed or herbaceous border and also good against a warm, sunny wall. In cold areas, it may lose its leaves and die back, but usually grows from the base in spring.

○ ◑ ☼ ❀ ❀ ❀
‡ to 1m (3ft) ↔ to 1.2m (4ft)

SAMBUCUS RACEMOSA
'Plumosa Aurea'

Deciduous shrub

The deeply cut, yellow leaves of this red-berried elder flush bronze when young. The creamy flowers are borne in clusters in spring and are followed by red fruits in summer. Plant this bushy shrub in a lightly shaded site as the foliage may scorch in bright sun. Grow in moderately fertile, moist but well-drained soil. For the best foliage effects, prune it hard in spring to within a few buds of the base, then feed and mulch.

○ ◑ ◐ ❀ ❀ ❀
‡ to 3m (10ft) ↔ to 3m (10ft)

SOLIDAGO
'Golden Wings'

Perennial

Tall, upright golden rod has stems with narrow green leaves that are topped in late summer and early autumn by large, spreading clusters of tiny golden yellow flowers. It is one of the most vigorous forms of golden rod and is good for the back of a large border or a wild garden; it attracts late-flying, beneficial insects. Plant it in full sun in poor to moderately fertile, very well-drained soil. The flowerheads are good for cutting.

◊ ☼ ❀ ❀ ❀
↕ to 2m (6ft) ↔ to 1m (3ft)

SORBUS
'Joseph Rock'

Deciduous tree

Suitable for the smaller garden, 'Joseph Rock' grows quickly once established, forming a crown of upright branches. The finely divided, bright green leaves turn brilliant shades of orange, red and purple during autumn, when it also bears crops of particularly attractive, creamy-yellow berries that age to golden yellow. There are clusters of white flowers in spring. Plant it in full sunshine or partial shade, in fertile, moist but well-drained, humus-rich soil.

◊ ◊ ☼ ◐ ❀ ❀ ❀
↕ to 10m (30ft) ↔ to 7m (22ft)

STERNBERGIA LUTEA

Perennial bulb

The autumn daffodil bears deep yellow, goblet-shaped flowers in autumn. The narrow, dark green leaves appear with, or just after, the flowers. Plant bulbs in late summer, in a warm, sunny site, in gritty, moderately fertile, very well-drained soil. It is a beautiful plant for a rock garden, but is also suitable for a container or a trough filled with gritty compost. If conditions are suitable, it will spread to form clumps; leave bulbs undisturbed and do not divide unless overcrowding impairs flowering.

◊ ☼ ❀ ❀

‡ to 15cm (6in) ↔ to 8cm (3in)

TRICYRTIS OHSUMIENSIS

Perennial

The toad lily is a clump-forming perennial with arching, slightly hairy stems and pale green leaves. In early autumn, it produces star-shaped, primrose-yellow flowers, covered with numerous tiny brown spots. Plant in a sheltered position in deep or partial shade and in moist, leafy, humus-rich, well drained soil. It is excellent for damp woodland or a shady border. In cold areas, mulch with leaf mould, straw or dried bracken in winter.

◊ ◊ ☀ ☀ ❀ ❀ ❀

‡ to 50cm (20in) ↔ to 23cm (9in)

ACER CAMPESTRE ♥

Deciduous tree

The field maple is a very underused tree that is ideal for planting in medium-sized gardens. It has a rounded crown of lobed, dark green leaves that take on autumn tints of apricot yellow and, in frosty autumns, shades of orange and red. It is very hardy and tolerates pollution, clay and shallow, chalky soils. It can also be included in mixed hedges and wildlife gardens. Plant it in full sun or partial shade, in any fertile, moist but well-drained soil.

◊ ◊ ☼ ☀ ❋ ❋ ❋
‡ to 8m (25ft) ↔ to 4m (12ft)

ACER PLATANOIDES *'Palmatifidum'*

Deciduous tree

An attractive form of Norway maple, this tree has five-lobed leaves, with the lobes drawn out into fine points. In autumn, the leaves turn brilliant shades of orange and red. The conspicuous clusters of small flowers emerge in spring before the leaves. It is a large tree and needs plenty of space. Plant it in larger gardens, in an open situation in full sunshine or partial shade, in any fertile, moist but well-drained soil.

◊ ◊ ☼ ☀ ❋ ❋ ❋
‡ to 20m (70ft) ↔ to 10m (30ft)

CHRYSANTHEMUM
'Amber Enbee Wedding' ♀

Perennial

From late summer to mid-autumn, this
upright chrysanthemum produces warm
golden-amber flowers with yellow-green
centres. It is excellent for late colour in
a mixed or herbaceous border. Grow
in full sun in moist but well-drained,
neutral to slightly acid soil that has
been enriched with well-rotted organic
matter. Support the stems with stakes to
prevent them falling over in wind and
heavy rain.

○ ◑ ☼ ❀ ❀
‡ to 1.2m (4ft) ↔ to 75cm (30in)

COTINUS
'Flame' ♀

Deciduous shrub

Primarily grown for its stunning autumn
colour, this bushy shrub or small tree
has oval, light green leaves that turn a
brilliant orange-red. In hot summers, its
sprays of tiny flowers hover like a smoky
haze above the foliage. Grow in a
shrub border or as a specimen in sun
or light shade, in moist but well-drained,
moderately fertile soil. Cut back hard in
spring for the best foliage effects, and
feed and mulch after pruning.

○ ◑ ☼ ☀ ❀ ❀ ❀
‡ to 6m (20ft) ↔ to 5m (15ft)

EUPHORBIA GRIFFITHII
'Fireglow'

Perennial

The upright stems of this spurge are red when young and clothed with dark green, red-veined leaves. In early summer, it produces clusters of yellow flowerheads surrounded by orange-red bracts. The leaves turn fiery orange and red in autumn. Plant in light dappled shade, in moist, humus-rich soil. It is good for woodland gardens or large shady borders. It can become invasive. The milky sap may cause an allergic skin reaction.

⬤ ☀ ✳ ✳ ✳
↕ to 75cm (30in) ↔ to 1m (3ft)

HAMAMELIS VERNALIS
'Sandra' ♀

Deciduous shrub

This Ozark witch hazel has young purple leaves that gradually turn green as spring progresses, then, in autumn, they assume glorious shades of orange and red. The spidery yellow or reddish-yellow flowers appear on the bare shoots during late winter and early spring. Plant it in full sun or partial shade, in neutral to acid (lime-free), moist but well-drained soil. Best in a site that is not exposed to strong winds. It will grow on deep soils over chalk.

○ ⬤ ☀ ✳ ✳ ✳ ✳
↕↔ to 5m (15ft)

HIPPOPHAE RHAMNOIDES ♛

Deciduous shrub

Sea buckthorn is a vigorous shrub with narrow, silvery grey-green leaves and spiny branches. Inconspicuous spring flowers are followed in autumn, on female plants, by clusters of shining orange fruit. Grow male and female plants together to ensure fruiting. Grow in a mixed border or as an intruder-proof hedge. Plant in full sun, in moist but well-drained soil. It thrives by the sea and tolerates exposed sites. If it becomes too large, it can be pruned hard back in late summer or when dormant.

◊ ◊ ☼ ❄ ❄ ❄
‡↔ to 6m (20ft)

LEONOTIS LEONURUS

Deciduous shrub

This frost-tender shrub with upright stems and lance-shaped leaves produces tiers of soft orange-red to scarlet flowers from autumn into early winter. Plant in full sun in moderately fertile, well-drained soil. In cold climates, it needs greenhouse protection in winter, but if container grown, it can be moved on to a sunny patio during the warmer summer months. Cut pot-grown plants back hard in early spring to stimulate new growth. Outdoors, it may lose its leaves in winter.

◊ ☼ ▦
‡ to 2m (6ft) ↔ to 1m (3ft)

MALUS TSCHONOSKII ♥

Deciduous tree

Prized for its autumn colour, this vigorous tree has a flame-shaped crown of rounded, glossy green leaves. It flowers in spring, bearing pink-flushed white flowers, followed by red-tinged, yellow-green fruit. In autumn, the leaves take on spectacular shades of orange, scarlet and purple. Plant it in full sun, in moderately fertile, moist but well-drained soil. It makes a beautiful specimen tree for small to medium-sized gardens.

◊ ◊ ☼ ☀ ❋ ❋ ❋
‡ to 12m (40ft) ↔ to 7m (22ft)

PHYSALIS ALKEKENGI ♥

Perennial

The Chinese lantern is a vigorously spreading perennial with triangular to diamond-shaped green leaves on upright stems. The nodding, creamy-white flowers appear in midsummer and are followed by orange-red, papery pods that enclose orange fruits. Plant it in full sun or partial shade in fertile, well-drained soil. It can be grown in a potager – the fruits are edible when ripe – or a border and cut for dried arrangements. It can be invasive.

◊ ☼ ☀ ❋ ❋
‡ to 75cm (30in) ↔ to 90cm (36in)

STIPA ARUNDINACEA

Perennial

Pheasant's tail grass is an evergreen that forms a loose tussock of arching, rather leathery, dark green leaves. As the season progresses, the leaves begin to exhibit orange streaks and by winter, the whole clump has turned russet-brown. In summer, arching spikes of purplish-green flowers appear that also turn golden orange as they mature. Plant in full sun or partial shade, in moderately fertile, well-drained soil. Cut back dead foliage and flowerheads in spring.

⬠ ☼ ⛅ ❄ ❄ ❄
‡ to 1.5m (5ft) ↔ to 1.2m (4ft)

ZELKOVA SERRATA ♀

Deciduous tree

The Japanese zelkova is an elegant tree with wide-spreading branches that makes a fine specimen for a large garden. At maturity, the grey bark peels to reveal paler orange bark beneath. The coarsely toothed, dark green leaves rustle in the breeze and have wonderful autumn colour in shades of yellow, orange and red. Plant it in full sun or partial shade, in deep, fertile, moist but well-drained soil. Choose a site that will lend some protection from cold, dry winds when young.

◊ ◑ ☼ ⛅ ❄ ❄ ❄
‡ to 30m (100ft) ↔ to 25m (80ft)

WINTER

The dark, cold months of winter need not be without cheer. Many plants flower in winter, and while few have large and exuberant blooms, several are unsurpassed for scent – the witch hazels (*Hamamelis*), wintersweet (*Chimonanthus*) and shrubby honeysuckles are among them. Mahonias produce large sprays of highly fragrant flowers in the very depths of winter and the scented white flowers of *Viburnum farreri* appear in all but the coldest spells.

Consider too the many brightly foliaged evergreens that bring living colour to the winter garden, such as the variegated hollies, *Euonymus fortunei* and skimmias bedecked with buds and berries. Some, such as the heaths and heathers (*Erica* and *Calluna*), assume the most vivid shades of orange, gold and red in winter, often prompted or enhanced by periods of very intense cold.

BARK AND SEEDHEADS

It is now that the branch structure of deciduous trees can be appreciated and the colour and texture of the bark enjoyed, so often overlooked when trees are in full leaf. The snake bark maples, such as *Acer grosseri var. hersii*, are striped green and white and the peeling papery bark of *A. griseum* glows coppery red in low winter light. Young stems of dogwoods also look dramatic at this time: vibrant red in *Cornus sanguinea* 'Winter Beauty' and *C. alba* 'Sibirica', while those of *C. alba* 'Kesselringii' are purple.

The dried seedheads of many plants have their part to play, most notably the silvery heads of pampas grass (*Cortaderia*). Leave them to stand after the autumn clear up, they can look stunning when rimmed with winter frost. Any seeds will be appreciated by the birds, which will also be lured into the garden by berries lingering on pyracanthas and cotoneasters.

ABELIOPHYLLUM DISTICHUM

Deciduous shrub

The white forsythia has spreading branches clothed with oval, dark green leaves in summer. In late winter and early spring, on bare branches, it carries clusters of small, white flowers that are invaluable for bringing fragrance into the winter garden. It performs best if trained against a sunny wall in a sheltered site, but it can also be planted in a mixed border or as a free-standing shrub. Grow it in full sun, in fertile, well-drained soil.

○ ☼ ❄ ❄ ❄
‡↔ to 1.5m (5ft)

BETULA PAPYRIFERA

Deciduous tree

The paper birch has pure white bark that peels off in large sheets to expose the new, pale orange-brown bark beneath. Yellow, hanging catkins appear in spring and the oval, dark green leaves turn attractive shades of yellow and orange in autumn. Plant it as a specimen tree; the white bark is seen at its best against a warm red brick wall or a dark background of evergreen shrubs. Grow in full sun or light shade, in moderately fertile, moist but well-drained soil.

○ ◐ ☼ ◑ ❄ ❄ ❄
‡ to 20m (70ft) ↔ to 10m (30ft)

GALANTHUS ELWESII ♀

Perennial bulb

This is bigger than the common
snowdrop in all its parts. It bears large,
honey-scented white flowers, with green
blotches, in late winter. It is a robust
plant with broad, slightly twisted, waxy,
bluish green leaves. Plant bulbs in early
autumn in partial shade, in humus-rich,
moist but well-drained soil. It does
particularly well on alkaline soil. Grow
in a woodland garden, naturalized in
grass or at the front of a mixed or
herbaceous border. Divide large clumps
after flowering while still in leaf.

◊◊ ☼ ❄ ❄ ❄
‡ to 15cm (6in) ↔ to 8cm (3in)

GALANTHUS NIVALIS ♀

Perennial bulb

The common snowdrop is a small plant
with narrow, waxy leaves and hanging,
sweetly scented flowers in winter. Plant
the bulbs in early autumn. It can
be used beneath trees or shrubs,
naturalized in grass, or on a rock
garden. It grows best in partial shade,
in humus-rich, moist but well-drained
soil, including alkaline soil. In suitable
conditions, it will self-seed freely to
form extensive colonies. Divide large
clumps after flowering while still in leaf.

◊◊ ☼ ❄ ❄ ❄
‡ to 15cm (6in) ↔ to 8cm (3in)

HELLEBORUS NIGER ♀

Perennial

The Christmas rose is a clump-forming perennial with thick, leathery, dark green leaves that remain green over winter. The large, white, saucer-shaped flowers appear in early winter and remain until early spring; they have green centres and yellow stamens, and turn pink as they age. Plant in heavy, neutral to alkaline soil, in dappled or partial shade. It suits a woodland garden and can be appreciated fully in a container placed close to the house. Slugs and snails can be a problem.

◊ ☼ ❋ ❋ ❋
‡ to 30cm (12in) ↔ to 45cm (18in)

LONICERA FRAGRANTISSIMA

Deciduous shrub

This honeysuckle is a bushy, spreading shrub. In late winter and early spring, it produces clusters of fragrant, creamy-white flowers on bare branches, followed by dull red berries. In mild gardens the oval leaves may be held through winter. Plant it in full sun or partial shade, in any well-drained soil. It is suitable for planting in a shrub border and can be grown as a screen or in a mixed hedge. It is also effective flanking a frequently used entrance to make the most of its winter scent.

◊ ☼ ◑ ❋ ❋ ❋
‡ to 2m (6ft) ↔ to 3m (10ft)

NARCISSUS CANTABRICUS

Perennial bulb

The white hoop-petticoat is one of the
earliest flowering narcissus. The blooms
have a white, funnel-shaped trumpet
surrounded by smaller outer petals.
The leaves are narrow, dark green
and almost cylindrical. It needs sharp
drainage, and dry conditions for its
summer dormancy. Grow it in a raised
bed or rock garden in very gritty soil,
or in pots of one part grit to two parts
loam-based compost and keep it in a
cold frame during the summer months.

◊ ☼ ❋ ❋ ❋
‡ to 20cm (8in) ↔ to 5cm (2in)

RUBUS COCKBURNIANUS

Deciduous shrub

This is an outstanding ornamental ghost
bramble with prickly, deep purple
stems that are covered with a striking,
waxy white bloom. The dark green
leaves are covered beneath with greyish
white hairs. Plant it in full sun, in well-
drained, fertile soil. It can be grown in
a wild garden or mixed border; the
winter stems stand out best against a
dark background. Cut canes to the
ground each year in spring to ensure
plenty of new young stems. Feed and
mulch after pruning.

◊ ☼ ❋ ❋ ❋
‡↔ to 2.5m (8ft)

SARCOCOCCA HOOKERIANA
'Purple Stem'

Evergreen shrub

The modest white flowers, tinted pink in this variety of Christmas box, emit a rich honey-like scent. The glossy, dark green leaves grow from purple shoots. The flowers are followed by blue-black fruit. It thrives in deep or partial shade, in humus-rich, moist but well-drained soil; it tolerates sun in reliably moist soil. Excellent in a woodland garden or in a sheltered niche where the fragrance intensifies in the still air.

○◐☼☀ ❄ ❄ ❄
‡ to 1.5m (5ft) ↔ to 2m (6ft)

SKIMMIA JAPONICA
'Wakehurst White'

Evergreen shrub

An attractive shrub with oval, glossy, dark green leaves. Clusters of small, fragrant white flowers open in spring. They are followed by spherical white fruit that persist into winter. Grow in a mixed border or woodland garden and plant a male form nearby to ensure fruit, as male and female flowers are usually borne on separate plants. It prefers some shade, but tolerates sun. Grow in moderately fertile, humus-rich, moist but well-drained soil.

○◐☼ ❄ ❄ ❄
‡↔ to 6m (20ft)

VIBURNUM FARRERI ♀

Deciduous shrub

This upright shrub has highly fragrant,
white or pink-tinged flowers, which
appear on bare branches in late autumn
and winter. The leaves emerge bronze-
green, turn dark green as the season
progresses, then colour in shades of
red-purple in autumn before they fall.
Plant this viburnum in full sun or partial
shade, in fertile, moist but well-drained
soil. Use it in a mixed or shrub border
or as a specimen, for its shape
improves with age.

◊ ◑ ☼ ☀ ❀ ❀ ❀
↕ to 3m (10ft) ↔ to 2.5m (8ft)

VIBURNUM TINUS
'Eve Price' ♀

Evergreen shrub

This is a justifiably popular shrub with
large, oval, dark green leaves. It has
dense clusters of pink buds, deep pink
in 'Eve Price', which open in winter
and early spring to white flowers.
During summer, it bears small bluish
black fruit. Plant in fertile, moist but
well-drained soil, in sun or light shade.
Use it as a flowering hedge or screen,
in a woodland garden or in a mixed
border. Trim hedges after flowering.

◊ ◑ ☼ ☀ ❀ ❀ ❀
↕↔ to 3m (10ft)

CLEMATIS CIRRHOSA
'Freckles' ♀

Climber

This interesting evergreen climber has
deeply divided leaves that turn bronze-
green during winter. In winter and early
spring, it bears pale pink flowers that
are heavily spotted and streaked with
red within. They are followed by silky
seedheads. Grow in full sun, with the
roots in shade, in humus-rich, fertile,
moist but well-drained soil. It is ideal
for training over a pergola or wall, or
through an old tree. Cut back after
flowering to keep within bounds.

⬦ ⬤ ☼ ☀ ❋ ❋
‡ to 3m (10ft)

CYCLAMEN COUM
Pewter Group ♀

Perennial

This tuberous perennial has dark green
leaves with a pewter-silver sheen that
covers almost the entire surface. The
flowers appear from winter to early
spring, they range in colour from pure
white to pink and carmine. Plant tubers
5cm (2in) deep, in sun or partial shade
in humus-rich, rather gritty, moderately
fertile, well-drained soil with added
leafmould. Excellent when grown
beneath deciduous trees or shrubs.

⬦ ☼ ☀ ❋ ❋ ❋
‡ to 8cm (3in) ↔ to 10cm (4in)

DAPHNE MEZEREUM

Deciduous shrub

Mezereon is a compact, upright shrub, bearing masses of small, purplish pink, fragrant flowers at the stem tips in late winter and early spring, before the narrow bluish-green leaves. They are followed by bright red, rather fleshy, toxic fruits. Plant it in full sun or partial shade, in moderately fertile, humus-rich, neutral to alkaline soil. Mezereon thrives in chalky soil. Grow it in a woodland garden, in a mixed or shrub border, or on a sunny bank.

◊ ☼ ☀ ❀ ❀ ❀
‡ to 1.2m (4ft) ↔ to 1m (3ft)

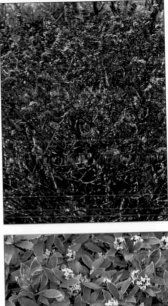

DAPHNE ODORA
'Aureomarginata' ♀

Evergreen shrub

This is an extremely attractive, rounded shrub with rather leathery, dark green leaves, set off by an irregular yellow margin. In late winter and early spring, it produces small clusters of highly fragrant white flowers that are deep pinkish purple on the outside. It is not completely hardy, so plant in a site with shelter from cold winds. It grows best in partial shade, in neutral to slightly alkaline soil that is moist but well-drained and rich in organic matter.

◊ ◗ ❀ ❀ ❀
‡↔ to 1.5m (5ft)

ERICA CARNEA
'Vivellii' ♀

Evergreen shrub

An attractive heather with dark bronze-green leaves that become completely bronzed in winter. It is very free flowering – the spikes of deep purplish pink flowers age to magenta and appear from the middle of winter to mid-spring. Plant it in full sun or partial shade, in peaty, well-drained soil. It will tolerate atmospheric pollution and also grows in alkaline soil. Clip over after flowering to keep compact.

◊ ☼ ☀ ❄ ❄ ❄
‡ to 15cm (6in) ↔ to 35cm (14in)

PRUNUS × SUBHIRTELLA
'Autumnalis Rosea' ♀

Deciduous tree

This is a superb flowering cherry for the winter garden. Clusters of delicate, semi-double, blush-pink flowers appear on a skeleton of bare, spreading branches during periods of mild weather from autumn and throughout the winter until spring. The foliage is bronze-green when new in spring and turns yellow in the autumn. Plant it as a specimen tree in full sun, in fertile, moist but well-drained soil.

◊ ◊ ☼ ❄ ❄ ❄
‡↔ to 8m (25ft)

RHODODENDRON
'Christmas Cheer'

Evergreen shrub

This is a compact rhododendron with clusters of pink buds that open to pale pink flowers. It flowers in mild weather in winter, but it will bloom in early spring if it is cold. It is an old cultivar that was often pot-grown and forced under glass for flowers at Christmas, hence its name. Plant it in humus-rich, acid (lime-free), moist but well-drained soil in a sheltered niche in light dappled shade. Mulch annually with leafmould or chipped bark.

◊ ◊ ☼ ✳ ✳ ✳
↕↔ to 2m (6ft)

VIBURNUM × BODNANTENSE
'Dawn' ♥

Deciduous shrub

This is one of the most reliable of all winter-flowering shrubs. The fragrant, deep pink flowers are produced on bare branches from late autumn to early spring. The oval, toothed leaves are bronze as they emerge in spring, gradually turning to dark green, then red-bronze in autumn. Plant in full sun or partial shade, in moderately fertile, moist but well-drained soil. It is ideal as a specimen or in a mixed border.

◊ ◊ ☼ ☼ ✳ ✳ ✳
↕ to 3m (10ft) ↔ to 2m (6ft)

ACER GRISEUM ♀

Deciduous tree

The paper-bark maple is an elegant tree with a spreading crown of dark green leaves that turn to vivid shades of crimson, gold and scarlet during autumn. When leafless in winter, it reveals the beauty of its attractive bark – a rich mahogany red, peeling away on older trees to reveal the orange-red younger bark beneath. Plant it as a specimen tree or at the back of a mixed border, in full sun or partial shade, in fertile, moist, but well-drained soil.

○ ◑ ☼ ☀ ❋ ❋ ❋
‡↔ to 10m (30ft)

ACER PENSYLVANICUM 'Erythrocladum'

Deciduous tree

The snake-bark maple is a beautiful tree with greenish, white-striped bark that becomes a vivid salmon-pink in winter; the young shoots are an especially bright red-pink. It has three-lobed, green leaves that turn to a warm shade of clear butter-yellow in autumn. Plant it in full sun or dappled shade, in fertile, moist but well-drained soil. It makes a wonderful specimen tree and its beautiful bark is a highly distinctive winter feature.

○ ◑ ☼ ☀ ❋ ❋ ❋
‡ to 12m (40ft) ↔ to 10m (30ft)

ARBUTUS MENZIESII ♀

Evergreen tree

The madroño is a broad, spreading tree
with glossy, dark green, long-oval
leaves. Its main attraction during the
winter months is the bright reddish-
brown bark, which peels away to reveal
the younger, smooth olive-green bark
beneath. In early summer, it bears
upright clusters of waxy, creamy white
flowers, which are sometimes followed
in autumn by orange-red fruit. Plant it
in full sun or dappled shade, in a
sheltered position on acid (lime-free),
humus-rich, moist but well-drained soil.

◊ ◊ ☼ ☀ ❄ ❄ ❄
‡‣ to 15m (50ft)

BERBERIS × OTTAWENSIS
'Superba' ♀

Deciduous shrub

A large shrub with gracefully arching,
spiny branches bearing red berries. The
rounded leaves open purplish red and
turn a brilliant crimson-red in autumn.
In spring, it bears clusters of pale
yellow flowers. It is a tough shrub that
can be planted in almost any well-
drained soil and will grow happily
in full sun or partial shade. Use it in
a shrub or mixed border or as an
intruder-proof hedge. Prune hard
for the best foliage effects.

◊ ☼ ☀ ❄ ❄ ❄
‡↔ to 2.5m (8ft)

BERGENIA
'Ballawley' ♛

Perennial

This vigorous evergreen has large,
leathery, dark green leaves, flushed
with red and bronze-purple in winter.
In spring, upright stems bearing clusters
of bright crimson flowers appear. Plant
in a sheltered site, in full sun or partial
shade, in humus-rich, moist but well-
drained soil. It is a superb ground cover
plant for a woodland garden, or for the
front of a herbaceous border. Remove
tatty leaves in spring. Divide clumps
every 4-5 years to maintain vigour.

◊ ◊ ☼ ☀ ❋ ❋ ❋
‡↔ to 60cm (24in)

BRASSICA OLERACEA *VAR.*
ACEPHALA

Biennial

The ornamental cabbages are grown
for their attractive foliage, with different
combinations of green, red, pink and
white leaves. Extremely useful as a
winter bedding plant, they attain their
deepest colouration during the cold
winter months. Plant in a sunny site,
preferably in lime-rich, fertile, well-
drained soil, or in containers. Sow seed
in spring or buy in as young plants.

◊ ☼ ❋ ❋ ❋
‡↔ to 45cm (18in)

CAMELLIA SASANQUA
'Crimson King' ♀

Evergreen shrub

One of the earliest camellias to flower,
'Crimson King' has glossy, dark green
leaves and single, crimson-red flowers
from late autumn through winter; it is
often in bloom at Christmas. Grow in a
sheltered spot, in dappled shade or sun,
but away from early morning sun, in
humus-rich, acid (lime-free), moist but
well-drained soil. In cold areas, grow in
containers of ericaceous compost and
flower under glass.

◊ ◊ ☼ ☼ ❀ ❀
‡ to 6m (20ft) ↔ to 3m (10ft)

CORNUS ALBA
'Sibirica' ♀

Deciduous shrub

The red-barked dogwood is an upright
shrub, usually grown for its striking red
winter stems, but the dark green leaves
also turn bright red before falling in
autumn. Plant it in full sun, in any
reasonably fertile soil. It is the new
young growth that produces the
brightest and longest lasting winter stem
colour. Cut all stems back in the early
spring, just before growth begins, to
within two or three buds from the
ground. Feed and mulch after pruning.

◊ ◊ ☼ ❀ ❀ ❀
‡↔ to 3m (10ft)

CORNUS SANGUINEA
'Winter Beauty'

Deciduous shrub

The oval green leaves of this vigorous shrub turn bright red in the autumn and, as they fall, they reveal the vivid red and orange winter shoots. Prune hard in early spring to stimulate new growth, which has the best colour. Cut back to within 2-3 buds from the base of the plant, then feed and mulch. The colour develops fully when the shrub grows in full sun. It thrives in any reasonably fertile, well-drained soil.

◊ ☼ ❄❄❄
‡ to 3m (10ft) ↔ to 2.5m (8ft)

COTONEASTER
CASHMIRIENSIS ♥

Evergreen shrub

A low, mound-forming shrub with glossy, dark green leaves. Pink buds open in the summer to small white flowers. They are followed by spherical, deep red berries that persist into winter. It is one of the smaller prostrate cotoneasters, and makes a compact ground cover plant for a rock garden or sunny bank. Plant it in full sun or partial shade, in any moderately fertile, well-drained soil, including chalk. This plant is often sold as *C. cochleatus*.

◊ ☼ ◐ ❄❄❄
‡ to 30cm (12in) ↔ to 2m (6ft)

COTONEASTER CONSPICUUS
'Decorus' ♀

Evergreen shrub

This is an attractive, low-growing,
spreading shrub with small, narrow,
dark green leaves. The tiny white
flowers appear in early summer and are
followed by large quantities of
conspicuous, spherical, bright red
berries that last for most of the winter.
Plant it in full sun or partial shade, in
moderately fertile, well-drained soil. It
is ideal for planting on a dry, sunny
bank, where it will provide colour
throughout the winter.

◊ ☼ ◑ ❋ ❋ ❋
‡ to 1.5m (5ft) ↔ to 2.5m (8ft)

COTONEASTER LACTEUS ♀

Evergreen shrub

This is a substantial shrub with large,
deeply veined, oval, dark green leaves
with a yellowish white, woolly
undersurface. The milky white flowers
appear in large clusters in summer and
are followed in autumn by large
bunches of bright red berries that last
well into winter. It makes a dense,
ornamental hedge, or can be grown
in a mixed border. Trim lightly in late
summer to keep in shape. Plant it in
full sun or partial shade, in any well-
drained, moderately fertile soil.

◊ ☼ ◑ ❋ ❋ ❋
‡↔ to 4m (12ft)

GAULTHERIA PROCUMBENS ♀

Evergreen shrub

Wintergreen is a creeping shrub with underground stems and glossy, dark green leaves that smell strongly of wintergreen when crushed. The white or pink, urn-shaped flowers appear in summer and are followed in autumn by bright red, aromatic fruit. It prefers partial shade, but will grow in full sun if provided with soil that is reliably moist. Grow in neutral to acid (lime-free), peaty soil. It is an excellent plant for providing ground cover in damp woodland or shady borders.

◊ ☼ ✳✳✳
‡ to 15cm (6in) ↔ to 1m (3ft)

HAMAMELIS × INTERMEDIA 'Diane' ♀

Deciduous shrub

This elegant shrub is grown for its clusters of fragrant flowers that appear on bare branches in late winter. They have thread-like, dark red petals. The rounded, bright green leaves turn red and yellow in autumn. Plant in full sun or partial shade, in moderately fertile, neutral to acid (lime-free) moist but well-drained soils rich in leafy organic matter. Grow in a shrub border or use as a specimen.

◊◊ ☼ ☀ ✳✳✳
‡↔ to 4m (12ft)

ILEX AQUIFOLIUM
'J.C. van Tol' ♀

Evergreen tree

This is a form of common holly without
any prickles. The leaves are dark green
and very glossy and are carried on
purple stems. It is a self fertile female
plant that produces its bright red berries
through the winter without the need for
a male plant nearby. Plant it in full sun
or partial shade, in fertile, moist but
well-drained soil. It grows happily in a
woodland garden and can be used as a
hedge or a specimen tree. Clip hedges
in summer.

○ ◐ ☼ ☀ ✽ ✽ ✽
‡ to 6m (20ft) ↔ to 4m (12ft)

ILEX × MESERVEAE
'Blue Princess'

Evergreen shrub

An attractive hybrid holly, with spiny,
bluish green leaves and tiny white or
pink flowers in late spring. It needs
a male plant nearby to produce the
glossy red fruit of autumn and winter.
Grown in a woodland garden or use it
to make an impenetrable hedge. Plant
it in full sun or partial shade, in fertile,
humus-rich, moist but well-drained soil.
If it is grown as a hedge, it should be
trimmed annually in summer.

○ ◐ ☼ ☀ ✽ ✽ ✽
‡↔ 3m (10ft)

LEUCOTHOE
Scarletta

Evergreen shrub

This small to medium-sized, upright shrub has lance-shaped, rather leathery leaves. They are dark red-purple in the spring, becoming dark green in summer before finally assuming red and bronze tints in the winter. In spring, it has clusters of tiny, white, narrowly pitcher-shaped flowers. It should be grown in a shady position, in acid (lime-free), humus-rich, moist soil. It is ideal for planting in a woodland garden or shady border.

◗ ☼ ☀ ❄ ❄ ❄
‡ to 2m (6ft) ↔ to 3m (10ft)

PRUNUS SERRULA ♥

Deciduous tree

This attractive flowering cherry is grown mainly for its tactile, rich coppery red bark. This is very shiny and particularly striking on a sunny winter's day. It has narrow, dark green leaves that turn yellow in autumn and small, single, bowl-shaped white flowers in spring. It should be planted in full sun, in moderately fertile, moist but well-drained soil. It looks particularly dramatic when grown as an avenue tree, but it also makes a handsome specimen in a smaller garden.

◗ ◗ ☼ ❄ ❄ ❄
‡↔ to 10m (30ft)

SKIMMIA JAPONICA 'Rubella' ♀

Evergreen shrub

This skimmia is a compact, dome-shaped shrub with red-edged, dark green leaves. It is a male plant that produces dense clusters of deep red buds from autumn to winter. In early spring, the buds open to reveal small, fragrant white flowers. It is a good pollinator for female skimmias. Grow it in partial to deep shade, in moderately fertile, moist but well-drained soil. Plant in a shrub border or woodland garden. Also good in containers.

○ ◐ ☼ ☀ ✿ ✿ ✿
‡ ↔ to 6m (20ft)

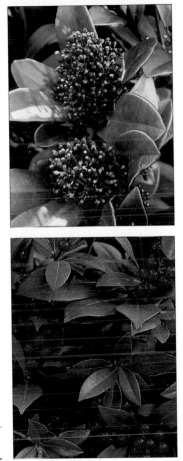

SKIMMIA JAPONICA 'Nymans' ♀

Evergreen shrub

This low-spreading shrub with dark green leaves is a female plant noted for its large, red winter fruits that are borne very freely if the plant is grown with a male plant nearby. They arise from the dense clusters of white spring flowers. Grow it in partial to deep shade, in moderately fertile, moist but well-drained soil. Plant in a shrub border or woodland garden. Like most skimmias, it is good in coastal and urban gardens and tolerates most soils.

○ ◐ ☼ ☀ ✿ ✿ ✿
‡ to 1m (3ft) ↔ to 2m (6ft)

BERGENIA CORDIFOLIA
'Purpurea' ♀

Perennial

During late winter this evergreen produces dark, stout stems of deep magenta-purple flowers. It has substantial, leathery, mid-green leaves that turn reddish purple during the winter; the colour is most intense in very cold weather. Plant it in full sun or partial shade, in humus-rich, moist but well-drained soil. It is suitable for the front of a herbaceous border or for a woodland garden. Remove tatty leaves in spring.

◊ ◊ ☼ ☼ ❋ ❋ ❋
↕↔ to 50cm (20in)

CORNUS ALBA
'Kesselringii'

Deciduous shrub

This striking shrub is especially valuable for its dramatic, purplish black winter stems. Bronzed leaves open in spring, turning green and then reddish purple in autumn. In spring, it bears clusters of white flowers that are followed in autumn by white fruit. Cut back in early spring to within a few buds from the ground to stimulate the growth of new, more deeply coloured shoots, then feed and mulch. Plant in sun in any well-drained, reasonably fertile soil.

◊ ☼ ❋ ❋ ❋
↕↔ to 3m (10ft)

CORYLUS MAXIMA
'Purpurea' ♀

Deciduous shrub

This filbert forms a large, upright shrub
or small tree, with dangling purple
catkins in winter. In spring the dark
purple leaves appear. Later, in summer
and early autumn there are edible,
purple-husked nuts. It makes an
attractive specimen tree. Grow in full sun
for good foliage colour and abundant
nuts. It is best in fertile, well-drained
soil and grows well in chalk soil.

◊ ☼ ❁ ❁ ❁
‡ to 6m (20ft) ↔ to 5m (15ft)

IRIS UNGUICULARIS ♀

Perennial

A wonderful winter flowering iris with
large, fragrant, pale lavender-purple or
deep violet-blue blooms, marked by
a large patch of yellow on the lower
petals. It has upright stems and tough,
grass-like evergreen leaves. Grow it in
a rock garden, raised bed, on a terrace,
or at the foot of a warm, sunny wall.
Plant it in full sun, in gritty, very well-
drained, neutral to alkaline soil.
Good for cutting.

◊ ☼ ❁ ❁ ❁
‡ to 30cm (12in) ↔ indefinite

ACER GROSSERI *VAR.* HERSII ♀

Deciduous tree

The snake-bark maple is an extremely attractive tree with upright, green-barked branches heavily marked with white striations with an appearance reminiscent of snake's skin. The mid-green leaves are shallowly lobed and turn yellow and orange in autumn. Clusters of pale yellow flowers hang beneath the shoots in spring, followed by pink-brown autumn fruit. Plant it as a specimen, in sun or partial shade, in fertile, moist but well-drained soil.

◊ ◊ ☼ ☀ ❈ ❈ ❈
‡↔ to 15m (50ft)

ACER PENSYLVANICUM ♀

Deciduous tree

The moosewood maple looks equally attractive in winter and summer. In spring, it produces long clusters of small, yellow-green flowers. The lobed, bright green leaves turn clear butter-yellow in autumn, revealing the white striped, jade-green bark when they fall. Plant it in full sun or partial shade, in moist but well-drained, fertile soil. Plant close to a footpath, where the bark can be fully appreciated during the winter.

◊ ◊ ☼ ☀ ❈ ❈ ❈
‡ to 12m (40ft) ↔ to 10m (30ft)

ARUM ITALICUM
'Marmoratum' ♀

Perennial

The upright, dark green, arrow-shaped
leaves, heavily mottled with paler green
markings, last through the winter. In
early summer, greenish-white hooded
flowers appear, followed by spikes of
bright orange-red berries. Grow in light
shade or in sun with some shade from
the hottest summer sunshine. Plant
tubers in spring or autumn, in humus-
rich, well-drained soil. It makes good
ground cover beneath deciduous
shrubs, or in a woodland garden.

◊ ☼ ❀ ❀
‡ to 25cm (10in) ↔ to 30cm (12in)

GARRYA ELLIPTICA
Evergreen shrub

The silk-tassel bush is a dense shrub
with wavy-edged, leathery, greyish
green leaves. Male and female flowers
are borne on separate plants; the
male plants are more attractive with
longer, dangling, grey-green catkins,
measuring 20cm (8in) or more, that
are borne in mid-winter and early
spring. Plant it in full sun or partial
shade, in fertile, well-drained soil.
Excellent on a shady wall or shrub
border and good as a specimen or
as hedging in coastal gardens.

◊ ☼ ☼ ❀ ❀ ❀
‡↔ to 4m (12ft)

HELLEBORUS VIRIDIS

Perennial

The green hellebore is a deciduous, clump-forming hellebore with very deeply divided, rather leathery, dark green leaves. In late winter and early spring, it produces tall stems adorned with nodding, bright green flowers. It looks best when planted against a dark background and will grow in deep shade. Plant it in a woodland garden or a shrub border. It grows best in rather heavy, neutral or alkaline soil, in dappled shade. It often self-seeds.

◐ ☼ ☀ ✳ ✳ ✳
‡↔ to 30cm (12in)

RIBES LAURIFOLIUM

Evergreen shrub

This is a low-growing shrub, with spreading branches bearing leathery, dark green leaves. In late winter and early spring, it produces substantial, hanging clusters of greenish yellow flowers. Male and female flowers are borne on separate plants; if grown together, females produce black fruits. Plant it in a shrub border in full sun or partial shade, in moderately fertile, well-drained soil. In cold areas, plant in a sheltered spot away from cold, dry winter winds.

◊ ☼ ☀ ✳ ✳ ✳
‡ to 1m (3ft) ↔ to 1.5m (5ft)

STACHYURUS PRAECOX ⚱

Deciduous shrub

The gracefully arching branches of
this spreading shrub produce hanging
chains of small, pale yellow flowers in
late winter and early spring. The similar
S. chinensis flowers about two weeks
later. Plant in full sun or partial shade,
in fertile, humus-rich, acid (lime-free),
well-drained soil, ideally against a wall
or in a woodland garden. When
mature, cut out the oldest flowered
shoots at the base after flowering; this
ensures the production of strong, new
flowering stems.

◊ ☼ ☀ ❋ ❋ ❋
‡ to 4m (12ft) ↔ to 3m (10ft)

THUJA OCCIDENTALIS
'Hetz Midget'

Evergreen shrub

This dwarf conifer is a slow-growing
selection of the white cedar that forms
a dense, rounded mound of golden
green foliage that smells of apples
when crushed. It is ideal as a specimen
in a rock garden and associates
particularly well with heathers. Grow
in full sun in deep, moisture-retentive
but well-drained, fertile soil. In cool
gardens, plant in a sheltered place,
away from cold, dry winds.

◊ ◑ ☼ ❋ ❋ ❋
‡↔ to 50cm (20in)

Azara microphylla ♀

Evergreen tree

An upright, often shrubby small tree
with oval, glossy, dark green leaves.
In late winter and early spring, it bears
clusters of small, vanilla-scented, yellow
flowers. Plant it in full sun or partial
shade, in humus-rich, well-drained,
fertile soil. It can be grown in a shrub
border but flowers best against a
sheltered, sunny wall. When grown on
a wall, train in the shoots when young
to ensure good coverage. Then prune
back after flowering to within 2-4 buds
of the woody framework of main stems.

◊ ☼ ◐ ❀ ❀
‡ to 10m (30ft) ↔ to 4m (12ft)

Chimonanthus praecox
'Grandiflorus' ♀

Deciduous shrub

The wintersweet is an upright shrub
with lance-shaped green leaves. It is
especially valuable for the highly
fragrant, nodding, deep yellow flowers
that are stained red within. They appear
on bare stems in winter and are
excellent for cutting for winter posies.
Plant it in full sun, in fertile, well-
drained soil in a warm, sheltered place.
Grow as a specimen or train it against a
sunny wall. If wall-trained, shorten any
outward-growing shoots after flowering.

◊ ☼ ❀ ❀ ❀
‡ to 4m (12ft) ↔ to 3m (10ft)

CORNUS MAS

Deciduous shrub

The cornelian cherry is a vigorous
shrub or small tree with spreading
branches and mid-green leaves that turn
red-purple in the autumn. It is most
dramatic in the winter when it produces
an abundance of small, yellow flowers
in clusters on bare branches. Bright red
fruit ripen in late summer or early
autumn, often as the foliage assumes its
autumn tints. Grow as a specimen, in a
shrub border or woodland garden. Plant
in full sun or partial shade, in any
moderately fertile, well-drained soil.

△ ☼ ☀ ❄ ❄ ❄
‡↔ to 5m (15ft)

CORNUS STOLONIFERA
'Flaviramea' ♀

Deciduous shrub

This vigorous dogwood forms a thicket
of bright yellow stems that create a
brilliant winter display. In summer,
small white flowers are followed by
white fruit in autumn, when the leaves
turn vivid orange and red before falling.
It looks beautiful at the side of pools or
streams, especially if planted with the
red-stemmed *C. sanguinea*. Grow in
wet or moist soil in full sun. Cut back
to the base each year in early spring,
and then feed and mulch.

◐ ☼ ❄ ❄ ❄
‡ to 2m (6ft) ↔ to 4m (12ft)

CORONILLA VALENTINA
SUBSP. GLAUCA ♀

Evergreen shrub

A dense, bushy plant with divided, blue-green leaves. In late winter, early spring, and often again in late summer, it produces clusters of bright yellow, pea-like flowers. It is suitable in a shrub border or on a sheltered wall, as it is not completely hardy and needs protection from cold winds. Plant it in full sun in sandy, moderately fertile, well-drained soil. In very cold areas, grow in a container as a conservatory plant and move outdoors in summer.

◊ ☼ ❄ ❄

‡↔ to 80cm (32in)

HACQUETIA EPIPACTIS ♀

Perennial

This is a low-growing spreading perennial that produces tiny yellow flowers, surrounded by a collar of bright emerald-green, leaf-like bracts, in late winter and early spring. The brilliant green leaves only develop fully after flowering. It is suitable for planting in moist, shady situations, such as by poolsides or in a damp woodland garden. Plant it in humus-rich, moist but well-drained, acid or neutral soil. It is easily increased by dividing the clumps in the spring.

◊ ◊ ☀ ❄ ❄ ❄

‡ to 15cm (6in) ↔ to 30cm (12in)

HAMAMELIS
'Arnold Promise' ♀

Deciduous shrub

This attractive winter-flowering shrub
produces a profusion of spidery,
bright yellow flowers on bare, upright
branches. It is excellent in a shrub
border or as a specimen, as the vivid
green leaves turn red and gold in
autumn. Plant in full sun or partial
shade, in fertile, neutral to acid
(lime-free), moist but well-drained soil.

△ ◐ ☼ ◑ ❀ ❀ ❀
‡↔ to 4m (12ft)

HAMAMELIS JAPONICA
'Sulphurea'

Deciduous shrub

The Japanese witch hazel is an upright,
branched shrub with rounded, glossy
green leaves that turn gold in autumn.
In the middle of the winter, the bare
branches are studded with small,
sulphur-yellow flowers with very
narrow petals. Plant it in full sun or
partial shade, in fertile, neutral to acid
(lime-free), moist, but well-drained soil.
Plant it in groups in a woodland garden
or as a specimen. It can also be grown
on deep, humus-rich soil over chalk.

△ ◐ ☼ ◑ ❀ ❀ ❀
‡↔ to 4m (12ft)

ILEX AQUIFOLIUM
'Bacciflava'

Evergreen tree

'Bacciflava' is a female form of common holly with spiny, glossy, dark green leaves. With a male pollinator nearby, the tiny, insignificant flowers of spring and early summer will give rise to yellow berries that last into winter. It forms an erect, pyramidal tree that is good as a specimen and is also suitable for hedging. Trim hedges in summer. Plant in full sun or partial shade, in moist but well-drained, moderately fertile soil.

◊ ◊ ☼ ☀ ✽ ✽ ✽
‡ to 20m (70ft) ↔ to 6m (20ft)

JASMINUM NUDIFLORUM ♥

Deciduous shrub

The winter jasmine is one of the most popular of winter-flowering shrubs. It has arching, scrambling, dark green stems and dark green leaves, each divided into three leaflets. It is very free flowering, bearing bright yellow, six-petalled flowers, from mid-winter to early spring. It looks best when planted against a fence or trellis, but needs tying in to a support. Plant in full sun or partial shade, in fertile, well-drained soil. Trim after flowering to keep it dense, cutting back to strong buds.

◊ ☼ ☀ ✽ ✽ ✽
‡↔ to 3m (10ft)

LUZULA SYLVATICA
'Aurea'

Perennial

This golden form of greater woodrush
is a clump-forming evergreen rush, with
narrow, grass-like leaves. They are a
bright golden yellow in winter, fading
to yellow-green in summer. It is happy
in deep or partial shade, in humus-rich,
moist but well-drained, poor to
moderately fertile soil. It tolerates
dry soils. Use as ground cover or in a
woodland garden. It can be increased
by division autumn and spring.

◊ ◑ ☼ ☀ ❈ ❈ ❈
‡ to 80cm (32in) ↔ to 45cm (18in)

MAHONIA JAPONICA ♀

Evergreen shrub

A beautiful winter-flowering shrub
with upright branches clothed in spiny,
divided, dark green leaves. It bears
drooping spikes of strongly fragrant,
lemon yellow flowers from late autumn
to early spring. These are followed by
an abundant crop of bluish black
berries. It provides a long season of
interest in a shrub border or woodland
garden. Plant it in a slightly shaded
position, in humus-rich, moist but
well-drained soil.

◊ ◑ ☼ ❈ ❈ ❈
‡ to 2m (6ft) ↔ to 3m (10ft)

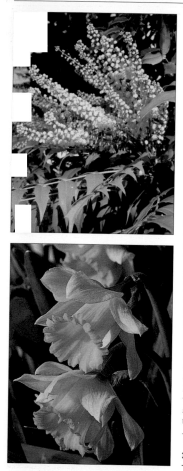

MAHONIA × MEDIA *'Charity'*

Evergreen shrub

This is one of the most attractive forms of the Oregon grape. It has large, dark green leaves divided into sharply toothed leaflets. Masses of sweetly scented, bright yellow flowers are borne in dense spikes from late autumn to early winter. Plant it in partial shade and moderately fertile, humus-rich, moist but well-drained soil. It makes an architectural specimen for planting in front of a wall, in a shrub border or woodland garden.

◊◊ ☼ ❄ ❄ ❄

‡ to 5m (15ft) ↔ to 4m (12ft)

NARCISSUS *'Rijnveld's Early Sensation'* ♀

Perennial bulb

This golden-yellow daffodil flowers in late winter, well before the other early flowering daffodils, such as 'February Gold'. It makes a valuable, long-flowering addition to the winter garden and should be planted in a bold group or naturalized in grass. Plant bulbs at one-and-a-half times their own depth in late summer. Grow in full sun, in fertile, well-drained soil. It often produces several flowers on each stem. Remove the dead flowers regularly.

◊ ☼ ❄ ❄ ❄

‡ to 35cm (14in)

PYRACANTHA
'Soleil d'Or'

Evergreen shrub

Pyracanthas have several seasons of
interest. This one has spiny red shoots
and glossy green leaves. In summer,
it produces sprays of small white
flowers, followed by yellow fruit that
last well into winter. Plant in full sun or
shade, in fertile, well-drained soil. It can
be trained against a wall or fence,
grown as a free-standing shrub and also
makes an excellent dense, impenetrable
hedge. Trim hedges in mid-spring and
summer.

◊ ☼ ☀ ❀ ❀ ❀
‡ to 3m (10ft) ↔ to 2.5m (8ft)

VIOLA × WITTROCKIANA
Universal Series ♀

Perennial

Universal pansies are among the most
prolific of all winter-flowering plants,
flowering almost non-stop from early
winter to mid-spring. The colour range
includes yellow, blue, mauve, maroon,
red and white, some with darker
patches at the centre. Plant in sun
in fertile, moist but well-drained soil.
Although perennial, they are usually
grown as annuals or biennials for
bedding. Use in borders, containers
or hanging baskets.

◊ ◊ ☼ ❀ ❀ ❀
‡↔ to 20cm (8in)

CALLUNA VULGARIS
'Boskoop'

Evergreen shrub

This dense and compact heather bears
spikes of lilac-pink flowers from
midsummer to late autumn. Then, the
foliage, which is golden throughout the
summer, begins to assume vibrant
orange-red winter tints that persist until
the new growth emerges in spring.
Grow in full sun in humus-rich, well-
drained acid soil. Clip plants lightly in
spring to keep them shapely. Excellent
for a rock garden, it associates well
with conifers and other heathers.

◊ ☼ ❉ ❉ ❉
‡ to 30cm (12in) ↔ to 40cm (16in)

ILEX AQUIFOLIUM
'Amber' ♀

Evergreen tree

This is one of the most attractive forms
of the common holly, with virtually
spine-free, glossy, bright green leaves.
The tiny, spring and early summer
flowers give rise to profuse clusters of
amber-yellow fruit. The tree is female
and needs a male to be planted nearby
to produce fruit. Plant it in full sun, in
well-drained, fertile soil. It can be
grown as a hedge or as an attractive
specimen tree. Trim in summer, if
grown as a hedge.

◊ ☼ ❉ ❉ ❉
‡ to 6m (20ft) ↔ to 2.5m (8ft)

IRIS FOETIDISSIMA ♀

Perennial

The stinking gladwyn is so called because the leaves smell unpleasantly when crushed. It forms clumps of evergreen leaves and, in early summer, bears dull-purple, yellow-tinged flowers. It really comes into its own, however, when the seed pods ripen in autumn. They split to reveal glistening orange-red seeds that remain in place until winter. Grow in well-drained, moderately fertile, neutral to acid soil. It is one of the toughest and most useful plants for dry shade.

○ ☼ ☀ ✽ ✽ ✽
‡ to 90cm (36in) ↔ indefinite

PYRACANTHA
'Orange Glow' ♀

Evergreen shrub

This is a vigorous, upright shrub with spiny stems and glossy, dark green leaves. In late spring, clusters of small white flowers are followed by masses of orange berries that last until winter. Plant in full sun or shade, in well-drained, moderately fertile soil. After flowering, shorten sideshoots back to two or three leaves to show off the berries. It can be trained against a wall, but also makes an intruder-proof hedge. Trim hedges in spring and summer.

○ ☼ ☀ ✽ ✽ ✽
‡↔ to 3m (10ft)

ALL SEASONS

IT IS A GOOD IDEA to include a few reliable, undemanding plants that remain attractive in every season. They give the garden shape and structure, and provide a backdrop for transient seasonal displays. Use them to liven up a border, or to create focal points, shapely conifers for example, can serve as topiary – without the work. The cabbage palm (*Cordyline*) and New Zealand flax (*Phormium*) may appear as tender exotics but are tougher than they look. Their spiky shapes are portable in containers, and in borders they enhance a colourful display.

Climbers, like ivy (*Hedera*), can be used to disguise fences and sheds, to shield an unsightly compost heap by training along a trellis, or for ground cover. Evergreen ground cover plants play a valuable role in helping to suppress weeds; low-growing junipers, silvery artemisias and heathers are all good choices as, with minimal care, their foliage provides interest all year round.

More visual punctuation may be obtained using grasses and bamboos, especially if you have plenty of space. Bamboos are normally grown as an elegant, rustling screen, but some, like *Phyllostachys flexuosa*, grace the garden with the changing colour of their stems.

A STRUCTURAL BACKBONE

Evergreen hedges and screens can surround the entire garden or divide it into sections. Box (*Buxus sempervirens*) and yew (*Taxus baccata*) are traditional choices for clipped formal hedging and topiary, but hollies (*Ilex*) and pyracanthas form superb, impenetrable hedges, and may also reward you with flowers and berries. Other conifers, apart from yew, will create a tall screen, but choose with care, as some can become a nuisance if they are allowed to grow too large. Leyland cypress can reach 35m (120ft), and there many more suitable for domestic situations.

ARTEMISIA ARBORESCENS

Evergreen shrub

This small, aromatic evergreen plant has very finely divided, silver-grey leaves that provide a foil for stronger flower colours in a sunny border or gravel garden. It also produces small yellow flowerheads in late summer and autumn. Plant it in a sunny situation, in moderately fertile, well-drained soil. It can become leggy and should be pruned hard in spring to keep it neat and compact. It dislikes cold, wet winters and in very cold areas is best grown close to a warm, sheltered wall.

◊ ☼ ❋ ❋ ❋

‡ to 1m (3ft) ↔ to 1.5m (5ft)

ARTEMISIA STELLERIANA
'Boughton Silver'

Perennial

This attractive evergreen forms a low, spreading clump of silver-grey leaves. It looks superb when planted against a background of darker foliage at the front of a border, or it can be used as path edging or in a gravel garden. The foliage looks better if the insignificant yellow flowers are removed before they open in late summer. It prefers a position in full sun, and well-drained, moderately fertile soil.

◊ ☼ ❋ ❋ ❋

‡ to 15cm (6in) ↔ to 45cm (18in)

BALLOTA ACETABULOSA ♛

Evergreen shrub

The upright, white-woolly stems of this compact, woody plant are clothed with rounded, greyish-green leaves. In the summer, it produces spires of small, purple-pink flowers. It grows well in hot, dry sites in full sun, and poor, very well-drained soil. It may not survive cold, wet winters, but where it does, cut it back hard in the spring to keep it bushy. Grow it as a background for bright flower colours in a raised bed, gravel garden, or sunny border. *Ballota pseudodictamnus* is hardier.

◊ ☼ ❈ ❈
‡ to 60cm (24in) ↔ to 75cm (30in)

BETULA UTILIS
'Silver Shadow' ♛

Deciduous tree

Birch trees are a year-round asset to a garden. They are valued for their graceful winter skeleton, attractive bark, yellow catkins in spring, and leaves that colour yellow in the autumn. 'Silver Shadow' has silvery bark and makes a beautiful specimen tree, especially against a dark background of evergreen trees or shrubs. Plant it in sun or dappled shade in fertile, moist, well-drained soil.

◊ ◊ ☼ ❈ ❈ ❈ ❈
‡ to 18m (60ft) ↔ to 10m (30ft)

CALLUNA VULGARIS
'Silver Queen' ♀

Evergreen shrub

This is one of many lings or heathers valued for year-round ground cover. It has silvery grey-green foliage and produces short spikes of pale mauve flowers in late summer and autumn. Plant lings in full sun in humus-rich, well-drained, acid (lime-free) soil, and clip the plants in spring to keep them compact and bushy. Grow them together with other heathers and acid-loving plants.

◊ ☼ ❀ ❀ ❀
‡ to 40cm (16in) ↔ to 55cm (22in)

CONVOLVULUS CNEORUM ♀

Evergreen shrub

This compact, bushy evergreen shrub has beautiful, silver-sheened leaves. It flowers from late spring to summer, producing delicate, funnel-shaped white flowers with yellow centres. Grow it in a warm, sunny, sheltered situation, in poor, gritty, very well-drained soil. It is an excellent plant for a rock garden, container, raised bed or sunny bank. In areas with cold, wet winters, grow it in pots of gritty compost and move it into a cool greenhouse for the winter. Trim after flowering to keep it compact.

◊ ☼ ❀ ❀
‡ to 60cm (24in) ↔ to 1m (3ft)

CORTADERIA SELLOANA
'Silver Comet'

Perennial grass

The arching clumps of tough, leathery evergreen leaves of pampas grass create an architectural presence throughout the year. The soft, silvery plumes arise in late summer and persist through the winter. Grow it as a specimen in well-drained, fertile soil in full sun. Remove the old flowerheads and dead foliage before growth begins in spring. The leaves are sharp-edged, so wear tough gloves to protect the hands.

○ ☼ ❋ ❋

‡ to 1.5m (5ft) ↔ to 1m (3ft)

EUONYMUS FORTUNEI
'Silver Queen'

Evergreen shrub

Valued for its year-round foliage, this compact shrub scrambles upwards if given support. The oval, leathery leaves are pale yellow when young, later becoming green with an irregular white margin that flushes pink during cold weather. Excellent for brightening a dull corner, it is also very effective when grown against a wall. Plant it in full sun or light shade in any but waterlogged soil. Trim shrubs in mid-spring to keep them within bounds.

○ ◐ ☼ ☀ ❋ ❋ ❋

‡ to 2.5m (8ft) ↔ to 1.5m (5ft)

HEBE PINGUIFOLIA
'Pagei' ♀

Evergreen shrub

The purple stems of this tough hebe are clothed in silvery, blue-grey leaves that remain attractive throughout the year. It produces short spikes of small white flowers over a long period, from late spring to summer. Plant it in full sun or partial shade, in moderately fertile, moist, well-drained soil. Use it at the front of a mixed border, in a rock garden or as ground cover.

◊ ◊ ☼ ☼ ✳ ✳ ✳
‡ to 30cm (12in) ↔ to 90cm (36in)

SEDUM SPATHULIFOLIUM
'Cape Blanco' ♀

Perennial

This evergreen stonecrop forms dense, low-growing mats of silvery-green foliage, comprised of rosettes of fleshy leaves covered in a waxy white bloom. The mats are spangled in summer with tiny, star-shaped yellow flowers. It is ideal for raised beds, troughs and the tops of dry stone walls. Grow it in gritty, poor to moderately fertile, very well-drained soil. The silvery foliage develops best in full sun, but the plant tolerates light shade.

◊ ☼ ✳ ✳ ✳
‡ to 10cm (4in) ↔ to 60cm (24in)

SEMPERVIVUM ARACHNOIDEUM ♀

Perennial

The cobweb houseleek is an evergreen mat-former with rosettes of fleshy, dark green, red-tipped leaves covered with a fine web of white hairs. In late summer it may produce sturdy stems with rose-red, star-shaped flowers at the tips. Each rosette dies after flowering, but new ones are readily formed to fill the gap. Plant it in full sun, in poor to moderately fertile, very well-drained soil. Grow it in a trough, pot, rock garden, or on a dry stone wall.

◊ ☼ ❋ ❋ ❋

‡ to 8cm (3in) ↔ to 30cm (12in)

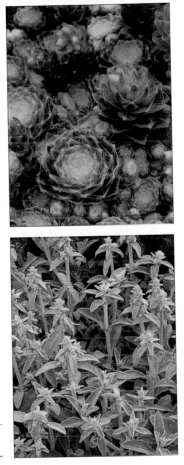

STACHYS BYZANTINA

Evergreen perennial

Lambs' ears form an evergreen, soft-textured mat of bright, silvery white-woolly leaves. In summer, it produces upright, hairy stems of pinkish purple flowers, but for the best foliage effect remove these before the blooms open. It makes an excellent ground cover plant beside a path, at the front of a border, or in a gravel garden. It can become rather straggly, and old growth should be cut back in early spring. Grow it in a sunny situation in moderately fertile, well-drained soil.

◊ ☼ ❋ ❋ ❋

‡ to 45cm (18in) ↔ to 60cm (24in)

AJUGA REPTANS
'Atropurpurea'

Perennial

This evergreen, mat-forming perennial is grown for its glossy, bronze-purple leaves, rather than the late spring spikes of blue flowers. The creeping stems root where they touch the soil, making this a superb ground-cover plant that is relatively easy to control. Grow it in a partially shaded or sunny site, in moist, moderately fertile soil. It is excellent in a woodland garden or shady border. 'Multicolor' has bronze-green and white leaves, heavily suffused with purple.

◗ ☼ ☀ ❀ ❀ ❀
‡ to 15cm (6in) ↔ to 1m (3ft)

CAREX COMANS
Bronze

Perennial

This attractive evergreen sedge forms a dense tussock of very narrow – almost hair-like – arching leaves in a warm, rich bronze-green. It will grow in sun or shade and in a wide range of soils, but looks best when it is placed in a sunny position, where the colour of its leaves will develop most fully. It produces rather inconspicuous brown flowers towards the end of the summer. Plant it beside a water garden or at the front of a herbaceous border.

◗ ☼ ☀ ❀ ❀ ❀
‡ to 35cm (14in) ↔ to 75cm (30in)

CORDYLINE AUSTRALIS
Purpurea Group

Evergreen tree

The New Zealand cabbage palm is an
architectural specimen with narrow,
purplish-green leaves. It develops a
trunk as it matures and may produce
creamy-white summer flowers. It will
survive outdoors in mild climates, and
sheltered urban gardens. Elsewhere,
grow it in a container of loam-based
compost and move under cover in
winter. Outdoors, grow it in sun or light
shade in fertile, well-drained soil, and
protect it over winter in its early years.

○ ☼ ☀ ✳ ✳
‡ to 3m (10ft) ↔ to 1m (3ft)

OPHIOPOGON PLANISCAPUS
'Nigrescens' ♀

Perennial

The black lilyturf is a clump-forming,
grass-like perennial with dark purple,
almost black leaves. It looks superb
when planted as edging or in pale-
coloured gravel. It is also suitable for
raised beds. In summer, it produces
spikes of tiny, bell-shaped, purple-
flushed white flowers. Plant it in full
sun or partial shade, in slightly acid,
moist but well-drained soil.

○ ◐ ☼ ☀ ✽ ✽ ✽
‡ to 20cm (8in) ↔ to 30cm (12in)

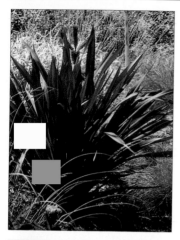

PHORMIUM TENAX
Purpureum Group ♀

Perennial

New Zealand flax is an evergreen with large, leathery, sword-shaped leaves in a rich copper or deep purple-red hue. In summer, tall, upright, architectural spikes of tubular, dark red flowers arise on plum-purple stems. Grow it as a specimen plant or in a border, in full sun and deep, fertile, moisture-retentive soil, with shelter from cold, dry winds. In cold, wet areas, provide a deep, dry mulch in winter. Phormiums do well in coastal gardens.

◐ ☼ ❄ ❄
‡ to 2.5m (8ft) ↔ to 1m (3ft)

PITTOSPORUM TENUIFOLIUM
'Purpureum'

Evergreen shrub

The kohuhu is an evergreen shrub or small tree, with black stems and wavy-edged, leathery, purple leaves. In late spring, it has tiny, scented, dark red, bell-shaped flowers. Plant it in full sun or partial shade in fertile, moist, well-drained soil. The leaf colour is most intense in full sun, and the plant should be protected from cold winds. It is a superb hedge for coastal gardens, and the foliage is used in floral displays. Trim hedges in spring and early autumn.

◐◐ ☼ ❄ ❄
‡ to 10m (30ft) ↔ to 5m (15ft)

SALVIA OFFICINALIS
'Purpurascens' ♛

Evergreen shrub

The purple sage forms a shrubby
mound of aromatic, red-purple leaves,
with spikes of purple summer flowers
which are very attractive to bees. It can
be grown in a herb garden for culinary
use, and it is also a useful foliage foil in
a sunny border or gravel garden, where
it associates well with silver-leaved
plants. Grow it in full sun in moderately
fertile, light, well-drained soil. Clip it
over in spring and after flowering to
keep it shapely.

◊ ☼ ❁ ❁ ❁
‡ to 80cm (32in) ↔ to 1m (3ft)

SEDUM SPATHULIFOLIUM
'Purpureum'

Evergreen perennial

This low-growing evergreen forms tight,
dense mats of ground-covering foliage,
studded with starry yellow flowers in
summer. The rosettes of fleshy, silvery-
grey leaves are flushed with purple and
covered in a thick, waxy bloom. Grow
it in a rock garden, a trough, on top
of a dry stone wall, or in a raised bed.
It grows best in full sun in gritty, very
well-drained, poor to moderately fertile
soil. It can easily be trimmed back
occasionally to restrict its spread.

◊ ☼ ❁ ❁ ❁
‡ to 10cm (4in) ↔ to 60cm (24in)

FESTUCA GLAUCA
'Elijah Blue'

Perennial grass

This densely tufted evergreen grass forms a rounded clump of narrow, blue leaves with matching spikes of flowers in early summer. It makes a valuable colour foil at the front of a border, or in a gravel or rock garden. The best effects are achieved by planting it in drifts of 3–5 plants. Grow it in full sun, in poor to slightly fertile, well-drained, rather dry soil. Divide and replant it every 2–3 years in spring.

◊ ☼ ❈ ❈ ❈
‡ to 30cm (12in) ↔ to 25cm (10in)

JUNIPERUS SQUAMATA
'Blue Star' ♀

Evergreen shrub

This low-growing conifer forms dense, compact mounds of sharply pointed greyish-blue leaves that retain their colour throughout the year. The older stems have attractive reddish brown bark. It is ideal for growing as ground cover on a bank or in a gravel garden, and combines well with other dwarf conifers and heathers. Plant it in full sun or dappled shade, in fertile, well-drained soil. It seldom needs pruning.

◊ ☼ ☼ ❈ ❈ ❈
‡ to 40cm (16in) ↔ to 1m (3ft)

LEYMUS ARENARIUS

Perennial grass

This robust, tufted grass forms loose clumps of rather stiff, bright steel blue leaves, adorned in summer by strong-stemmed heads of blue-grey flowers that age to buff. It spreads rapidly but can be confined in a container. It will develop the best colour when grown in full sun in light, well-drained, slightly fertile soil, and it is ideal for creating foliage contrasts in a herbaceous or mixed border. Cut down the faded growth in spring, and trim back before flowering for improved foliage.

◊ ☼ ✿ ✿ ✿

‡ to 1.5m (5ft) ↔ indefinite

RUTA GRAVEOLENS
'Jackman's Blue'

Evergreen shrub

This rounded shrub is grown for its deeply lobed, aromatic, blue-green leaves. In summer, it produces small yellow flowers, but these should be removed before they bloom for the best foliage effect. It will grow well in a sunny position in a gravel garden, when planted in moderately fertile, well-drained soil. It can also be grown in a herb garden, or in a mixed or herbaceous border. Contact with the sap can cause a severe skin reaction.

∧ ☼ ✿ ✿ ✿

‡ ↔ to 60cm (24in)

ASPLENIUM SCOLOPENDRIUM ♀

Perennial fern

The hart's tongue fern forms shuttlecock-like clumps of emerald green, lance-shaped fronds, which often have wavy margins. In summer, rust-coloured spore cases are arranged herringbone-fashion on the undersides of the fronds. A beautiful fern for a damp, shady wall, crevice, or border, it is also suitable for a woodland garden. Grow it in partial shade in a moist, preferably alkaline, well-drained soil. Divide large clumps in spring.

○ ◊ ☼ ❀ ❀ ❀
‡ to 75cm (30in) ↔ to 45cm (18in)

BLECHNUM PENNA-MARINA ♀

Perennial fern

A tough but delicate-looking fern, this variety has long, slender fronds with many small, triangular, glossy, dark green leaflets. It spreads by means of underground stems and can form large, extensive colonies in ideal conditions. It forms good year-round ground cover in a woodland garden or a damp border, or plant it in a shady niche by a wall. Grow it in partial shade in moist, fertile, slightly acid soil.

◊ ☼ ❀ ❀ ❀
‡ to 20cm (8in) ↔ indefinite

BUXUS SEMPERVIRENS ♀

Evergreen shrub

The common box is a slow-growing
shrub with small, dark green leaves. It
is widely grown as a hedge, planted in
pots, or trimmed into balls, pyramids or
other topiary shapes. If left unpruned,
it eventually forms a small bushy tree.
'Suffruticosa' is best for dwarf hedges
or for edging beds. Box prefers partial
shade, but will tolerate full sun as long
the soil does not dry out. Grow it in
moist, well-drained soil; it thrives on
chalky soil, or in pots of loam-based
compost. Trim once a year in summer.

○ ◐ ☼ ❋ ❋ ❋
↕↔ to 5m (15ft)

CHUSQUEA CULEOU ♀

Evergreen bamboo

This useful slow-growing bamboo is
less invasive than most, and forms a
fountain-shaped clump of cylindrical
yellowish green stems, with whiskery
sheaves of narrow leaves arising at
intervals on the stems. Plant it in sun or
partial shade, in moist but well-drained
soil. Grow it in a sheltered site, where
it is protected from cold, dry winds,
such as in a woodland garden or to
disguise a fence. Old canes can be cut
out and used for staking other plants.

○ ◐ ☼ ❋ ❋ ❋
↕ to 6m (20ft) ↔ to 2.5m (8ft)

EUCALYPTUS PAUCIFLORA
SUBSP. NIPHOPHILA ♥

Evergreen tree

The alpine snow gum is fast-growing once established, and has attractive bark that peels to form a patchwork of green, grey and cream. The leaves are blue-green and rounded in the juvenile form, lance-shaped when mature. Plant it in full sun in fertile, moist, well-drained soil. Grow it as a specimen tree or, in small gardens and borders, prune it hard every year in spring to produce a shrub with colourful young foliage. Feed and mulch after pruning.

◊ ◊ ☼ ❀ ❀ ❀
↕↔ to 6m (20ft)

FARGESIA NITIDA

Evergreen bamboo

The fountain bamboo is slow-growing and produces erect, purplish-green canes, topped by narrow, lance-shaped, dark green leaves. It can be grown in a wild garden, but its spread may need to be restricted elsewhere. To achieve this, plant it in a large, bottomless container plunged up to its rim in the ground. Alternatively, chop back the rootstock using a sharpened spade every couple of years. Plant this bamboo in dappled shade in fertile, moist soil, and protect it from cold, drying winds.

◊ ☼ ❀ ❀ ❀
↕ to 5m (15ft) ↔ to 1.5m (5ft) or more

FATSIA JAPONICA ♀

Evergreen shrub

A superb architectural shrub with huge, deeply lobed leaves. In the summer, it produces large heads of creamy-white flowers. Plant it in full sun or partial shade in fertile, moist but well-drained soil. It is hardy but needs a sheltered position away from cold drying winds, which can damage the large leaves. It also benefits from a deep mulch to give some winter protection in the early years. Tolerant of pollution, it is suitable for urban gardens, and can be grown successfully by the coast too.

◊ ◐ ☼ ☀ ❋ ❋ ❋
‡↔ to 4m (12ft)

GRISELINIA LITTORALIS ♀

Evergreen shrub

This vigorous shrub can become tree-like in mild areas, but is more often grown as a hedge, valued for its rather leathery, glossy, emerald-green leaves. Plant it in full sunshine, in well-drained, fertile soil. Cold, drying winds can damage it in exposed inland gardens, but it makes a good windbreak in mild coastal areas. Clip hedges in spring, or for a more informal effect, prune back with secateurs.

◊ ☼ ❋ ❋ ❋
‡ to 8m (25ft) ↔ to 5m (15ft)

HEBE CUPRESSOIDES
'Boughton Dome'

Evergreen shrub

A compact, dwarf hebe, this variety
forms a dense, rounded mound of
bright green leaves. Mature plants may
produce small spikes of white flowers.
It makes a neat specimen that needs no
pruning, or can be used in a container,
rock garden or raised bed. Plant it in
full sun or partial shade, in poor to
slightly fertile, moist, well-drained,
neutral to alkaline soil. It is also tolerant
of coastal conditions and salt spray.

○ ◐ ☼ ☀ ❋ ❋ ❋
↕ to 30cm (12in) ↔ to 60cm (24in)

HEDERA HELIX
'Erecta' ♀

Evergreen shrub

'Erecta' is an unusual ivy in that it is a
non-climbing form. It is shrub-like, with
stiffly upright, spire-like stems clothed
in arrow-shaped, dark green leaves. It
can be grown in a shrub border or as
ground cover between trees, and looks
especially effective at the foot of tree
stumps or boulders. Plant it in fertile,
preferably alkaline, moist, well-drained
soil, in sun or partial shade. It needs
very little pruning.

○ ◐ ☼ ☀ ❋ ❋ ❋
↕ to 1m (3ft) ↔ to 1.2m (4ft)

HEDERA HIBERNICA ♛

Climber

The Irish ivy is a vigorous, self-clinging, evergreen climber, ideal for clothing unsightly walls, growing through large trees, or for using as fast-growing ground cover. It has lobed, broadly oval, glossy dark green leaves with distinct, paler grey-green veins. Grow it in moist but well-drained, fertile, preferably alkaline soil, in deep or partial shade. It needs no regular pruning, but can be cut back hard at any time of year if it becomes necessary to restrict its spread.

◊ ◊ ☼ ☀ ❆ ❆ ❆
‡ to 10m (30ft)

JUNIPERUS COMMUNIS
'Hibernica' ♛

Evergreen shrub

This juniper forms a narrow, tapering column of dense, prickly, bluish-green foliage. It will grow happily in most well-drained soils, including chalky conditions. While many junipers tolerate some degree of shade, 'Hibernica' may become misshapen if not provided with a sunny position. It suits formal gardens or plant it as a vertical accent in a large rock garden or a gravel garden. It does not need to be pruned.

◊ ☼ ❆ ❆ ❆
‡ to 5m (15ft) ↔ to 30cm (12in)

JUNIPERUS PROCUMBENS

Evergreen shrub

The Bonin Island juniper is a creeping, low-growing conifer that forms a ground-hugging mound of yellowish green, needle-like leaves. It makes a superb ground-cover plant for a bank, or for the edge of a gravel garden or a patio. It associates well with heathers and more upright dwarf conifers, and will grow well in full sun or partial shade in any well-drained soil; it thrives in sandy, chalky and dry soils. It needs no pruning and should be given space to spread.

◊ ☼ ☀ ❋ ❋ ❋
‡ to 75cm (30in) ↔ to 2m (6ft)

LONICERA PILEATA

Evergreen shrub

The privet honeysuckle has glossy, dark green, oval- to lance-shaped leaves. In late spring, it produces clusters of creamy-white, funnel-shaped flowers, which are followed by small, violet, translucent berries in summer. Plant it in full sun or partial shade, in any well-drained soil. It makes a good ground-cover plant that requires little attention, and is suitable for coastal gardens since it tolerates salt spray. In cold winters it may lose some of its leaves.

◊ ☼ ☀ ❋ ❋ ❋
‡ to 60cm (24in) ↔ to 2.5m (8ft)

PICEA MARIANA
'Nana' ♀

Evergreen shrub

This is a slow-growing, dwarf form of
the black spruce, and bears bluish-grey
leaves. It forms a neat, rounded bush
that is suitable for growing in a gravel
or rock garden, on a patio, or with
heathers. Plant it in full sun, in neutral
to slightly acid, moderately fertile, well-
drained soil. It occasionally produces
vigorous upright shoots, which mar the
appearance of the plant. Cut them back
to the base as soon as they appear.

◊ ☼ ❁ ❁ ❁
‡↔ to 50cm (20in)

PHYLLOSTACHYS FLEXUOSA

Evergreen bamboo

The zigzag bamboo forms clumps of
slender, arching canes. The canes are
bright green when they emerge, later
becoming golden brown and finally
almost black as they mature. Grow in a
sheltered situation, such as a woodland
garden, and plant it in fertile, humus-
rich, moist, well-drained soil, in sun or
dappled shade. In mild areas clumps
will grow fast and require cutting back
with a sharp spade every 2-3 years.

◊ ◊ ☼ ☀ ❁ ❁ ❁
↓ to 10m (30ft) ↔ indefinite

PINUS MUGO
'Mops' ♀

Evergreen shrub

A diminutive selection of the Japanese dwarf mountain pine, 'Mops' forms a small, almost spherical shrub with upright branches covered in deep green, needle-like leaves. It produces tiny, oval, dark brown cones. Very slow growing, it is suitable for planting in a rock garden or with heathers and other dwarf conifers. Choose a site in full sun with well-drained soil. It requires very little or no pruning.

○ ☼ ❀ ❀ ❀
‡ to 1m (3ft) ↔ to 2m (6ft)

PITTOSPORUM TOBIRA ♀

Evergreen shrub

The Japanese mock orange forms an upright shrub or small tree that bears leathery, shiny, dark green leaves. In the late spring and early summer, it produces clusters of scented, creamy-white flowers. In mild areas, grow it outdoors in a sunny, sheltered site in fertile, moist, well-drained soil, and mulch in winter with straw or bracken. In colder gardens, grow it in a large container of loam-based compost, and move it to a cool conservatory or greenhouse over winter.

○ ◑ ☼ ❀ ❀
‡ to 10m (30ft) ↔ to 3m (10ft)

POLYSTICHUM SETIFERUM
Divisilobum Group

Perennial fern

One of the most beautiful of all hardy
ferns, this variety forms a spreading,
evergreen plant with soft, feathery
fronds, divided several times into tiny
pale green leaflets. It will flourish when
planted in full or partial shade in fertile,
moist but well-drained soil. Grow it in a
mixed border beneath shrubs, a dark,
shady corner, or in a woodland garden.

◊ ◊ ☼ ☀ ❋ ❋ ❋
‡ to 60cm (24in) ↔ to 45cm (18in)

SASA VEITCHII

Evergreen bamboo

This spreading bamboo needs plenty of
space. Its purple canes bear dark green
leaves during summer, but later in the
year, the margins dry out so that they
appear variegated. Grow it in fertile,
moist, well-drained soil in partial to
deep shade; it tolerates sun in reliably
moist soil. It is suitable for a woodland
garden; elsewhere, to restrict it, plant it
in a large bottomless container, plunged
in the ground to the rim. Alternatively,
chop back clumps with a sharp spade
every couple of years.

◊ ◊ ☼ ☀ ❋ ❋ ❋
‡ to 1.2m (4ft) ↔ indefinite

STIPA GIGANTEA ♀

Perennial grass

Golden oats is a magnificent, evergreen grass that forms dense clumps of very narrow, dark green leaves. In summer, tall, slender but strong stems appear bearing clouds of tiny, glistening, purple-green flowers that age to gleaming gold. They make an attractive feature in the garden over winter, so wait until early spring to cut them down, along with any dead leaves. Grow as a specimen or as a gauzy screen at the back of a border. Best in full sun in fertile, well-drained soil.

◊ ☼ ❄ ❄ ❄
‡ to 2.5m (8ft) ↔ to 1.2m (4ft)

TAXUS BACCATA ♀

Evergreen tree

The common yew makes a large specimen tree but it is also one of the finest species for hedging and topiary. It forms a dense, dark green hedge and impenetrable barrier. Wherever possible, use plants grown from cuttings, because seedlings can vary slightly in colour. Plant in full sun or partial shade, in fertile, moist but well-drained soil. Yew also grows well on chalk. Trim hedges once a year in late summer; renovate overgrown or misshapen hedges by cutting back hard in late summer.

◊ ◑ ☼ ☼ ❄ ❄ ❄
‡ to 20m (70ft) ↔ to 10m (30ft)

THUJA ORIENTALIS
'Aurea Nana'

Evergreen shrub

This is a dwarf, globe-shaped conifer, with upright sprays of yellowish green leaves that become bronzed in autumn and winter. It is ideal for a raised bed or rock garden, for planting with heathers and for growing as part of a collection of dwarf conifers. Plant it in full sun, in moderately fertile, moist but well-drained soil. It needs little or no pruning.

○ ◑ ☼ ❀ ❀ ❀
↕↔ to 60cm (24in)

VINCA MINOR

Evergreen shrub

This scrambling plant has glossy, dark green leaves and violet-blue flowers from spring to autumn. A few flowers often appear in the colder months of the year. It makes an excellent ground-cover plant, with spreading stems that root wherever they touch the ground – it is, however, fairly easy to control. It grows well in any moderately fertile, well-drained soil, in partial or dappled shade, but it flowers most freely in sun. *V. major* is more invasive.

○ ☼ ❀ ❀ ❀
↕ to 20cm (8in) ↔ indefinite

ABIES NORDMANNIANA
'Golden Spreader' ♀

Evergreen shrub

The common Nordmann fir forms a
very large ornamental tree, but 'Golden
Spreader' is a dwarf, slow-growing form
with spreading branches. The leaves on
the inner parts of the plant are green,
but those on the tips are bright golden-
yellow, giving a very attractive two-tone
effect. It is suitable for growing in a
rock or gravel garden. Plant in full sun,
in fertile, moist but well-drained, neutral
or acid (lime-free) soil.

◊ ◊ ☼ ❋ ❋ ❋
‡ to 1m (3ft) ↔ to 1.5m (5ft)

AUCUBA JAPONICA
'Gold Dust'

Evergreen shrub

The spotted laurel is a rounded shrub
with glossy green leaves variably spotted
and splashed with golden yellow. If
grown with a male plant, this female
plant bears bright red berries in the
autumn. Aucubas are happy in most
soils and tolerant of pollution and salt
spray. It prefers partial shade but will
tolerate deep shade and grows in any
soil, except waterlogged. It can be
planted as a hedge, which should
be pruned with secateurs in spring.

◊ ◊ ☼ ❋ ❋ ❋
‡↔ to 3m (10ft)

BUXUS SEMPERVIRENS
'Elegantissima' ♀

Evergreen shrub

This variegated form of the common
box makes a neat, dome-shaped bush
that can also be used for hedging and
topiary. It grows best in dappled shade,
but will also tolerate full sun. Grow
in any well-drained, fertile soil, or as
trimmed shapes in pots of loam-based
compost. Trim hedging in summer. If
older bushes become untidy, they can
be rejuvenated by hard pruning in
spring, followed by an application
of general purpose fertilizer.

○ ☼ ❊ ❊ ❊
↕↔ to 1.5m (5ft)

CALLUNA VULGARIS
'Gold Haze' ♀

Evergreen shrub

There are several forms of ling or Scots
heather with golden-yellow foliage.
'Gold Haze' retains its brilliant colour
all year and in summer produces long
spikes of pure white flowers. 'Ruth
Sparkes' is more compact, with double
white flowers. The golden leaves of
'Spitfire' turn red during winter. All
three are useful ground-cover plants.
Plant in full sun, in acid, moist but well-
drained, fertile soil. Clip over in spring
to keep compact and bushy.

○ ◐ ☼ ❊ ❊ ❊
↕ to 45cm (18in) ↔ to 60cm (24in)

CAREX OSHIMENSIS
'Evergold' ♀

Perennial

This sedge forms tussocks of narrow, arching, brightly variegated leaves. The leaves are dark green with a central stripe of rich golden yellow. In mid- to late spring, it also produces spikes of dark brown flowers. Plant it in full sun or partial shade, in fertile, moist but well-drained soil, although it tolerates dry conditions. It looks very good in containers, near water and towards the front of a mixed or herbaceous border.

◊ ◊ ◐ ☼ ☼ ✿ ✿ ✿
‡ to 30cm (12in) ↔ to 35cm (14in)

CHAMAECYPARIS OBTUSA
'Crippsii' ♀

Evergreen tree

A slow-growing form of the Hinoki cypress, this lovely specimen tree forms a broad column. The rich golden-yellow colour of its leaves is most strongly emphasized if it is planted against a background of darker foliage, such as a yew hedge. Plant it in full sun, in fertile, moist but well-drained, neutral or slightly acid soil. It will also grow on deep chalky soil. Pruning is unnecessary.

◊ ◊ ☼ ✿ ✿ ✿
‡ to 15m (50ft) ↔ to 8m (25ft)

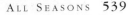

CHAMAECYPARIS PISIFERA *'Sungold'*

Evergreen tree

A form of Sawara cypress, this irregularly conical conifer has tiers of slightly drooping, thread-like, golden-yellow shoots. There are several other cultivars with golden-yellow foliage, but they tend to be scorched by cold winds and strong sunshine. Plant 'Sungold' in fertile, moist but well-drained, neutral to slightly acid soil. A pretty specimen tree, it looks its best when planted against the dark background of an evergreen hedge, such as yew.

◊ ◊ ☼ ☀ ❄ ❄ ❄
↕ to 12m (40ft) ↔ to 5m (15ft)

CHOISYA TERNATA *Sundance* ♀

Evergreen shrub

With its bright yellow leaves boldly divided into three leaflets, Sundance is one of the most dramatic evergreen shrubs for a mixed or shrub border. The colour is more vibrant if it is planted in full sun, as the leaves become yellowish green in shade. Plant in well-drained, fertile soil and provide shelter from cold, drying winds – against a warm wall is ideal.

◊ ☼ ❄ ❄
↕↔ to 2.5m (8ft)

CORDYLINE AUSTRALIS
'Torbay Dazzler' ♀

Evergreen tree

A decorative form of New Zealand cabbage palm, 'Torbay Dazzler' develops a slender trunk that bears a large cluster of creamy-white variegated, sword-shaped leaves. In summer, it may produce creamy-white flowers. Plant it in fertile, well-drained soil in full sun or partial shade. Dry mulch for winter protection in its early years. In cold areas it is better grown as a container plant and over-wintered in a frost-free conservatory or greenhouse.

◊ ☼ ☀ ❄ ❄
‡ to 3m (10ft) ↔ to 1m (3ft)

CRYPTOMERIA JAPONICA
'Sekkan-sugi'

Evergreen shrub

This is a slow-growing type of Japanese cedar with creamy-yellow foliage that turns almost white in winter. It is best planted in partial shade because the pale foliage is easily scorched in strong sunshine. Plant it in fertile, moist but well-drained soil. It is best planted as a specimen tree. Unusually for a conifer, if it is cut back hard it will sprout again, so it can be safely pruned if it outgrows its allotted space.

◊ ◊ ☀ ❄ ❄ ❄
‡ to 8m (25ft) ↔ to 5m (15ft)

CUPRESSUS MACROCARPA
'Goldcrest' ♀

Evergreen tree

'Goldcrest' is a striking conifer that forms
a narrow, column-shaped tree with
bright golden-yellow leaves. Suitable for
a coastal garden, plant it in full sun, in
any well-drained soil. Although it is fully
hardy, in its early years it needs
protection from severe frost. It also
needs shelter from cold, drying winds
which may scorch the foliage. It makes
an attractive hedge that needs only
gentle trimming in late summer – take
care not to cut back into old wood.

◊ ☼ ❄ ❄ ❄
‡ to 5m (15ft) ↔ to 2.5m (8ft)

ELAEAGNUS PUNGENS
'Maculata'

Evergreen shrub

This vigorous shrub has dark green,
glossy, leathery leaves with a bold,
central yellow blotch. In autumn, it bears
clusters of small white flowers. Remove
any shoots that revert to plain green as
soon as they appear and, in spring, trim
any stray stems that spoil the shape of
the plant. Suitable for hedging, it is also
tolerant of coastal conditions. If grown
as a hedge, trim it in summer. Plant it
in full sun or partial shade, in fairly
fertile, well-drained soil.

◊ ☼ ☼ ❄ ❄ ❄
‡ to 4m (12ft) ↔ to 5m (15ft)

ERICA CARNEA
'Foxhollow' ♀

Evergreen shrub

Some heaths have especially attractive foliage, such as 'Foxhollow' which is yellow-green and has bronze-tipped young shoots. In cold winters, its leaves are infused with shades of pinkish orange and red. In late winter and early spring it bears purple-pink flowers. Plant in full sun, in moist but well-drained, fertile, acid soil. It will also tolerate slightly alkaline soil. A lovely ground-cover plant, give it a light clipping after flowering to keep it neat.

◊ ◊ ☼ ❁ ❁ ❁
↕ to 15cm (6in) ↔ to 40cm (16in)

EUONYMUS FORTUNEI
'Emerald 'n' Gold' ♀

Evergreen shrub

This robust and easily grown, bushy shrub has glossy green leaves with bright yellow margins; during the cold winter months they take on pinkish tints. It grows in any soil, except waterlogged, and while it will tolerate shade, the leaf colour is richer and stronger in full sun. A superb ground-cover plant, it can also be grown in containers, or as a low hedge needing only a light trim in summer to keep it in shape.

◊ ◊ ☼ ❁ ❁ ❁
↕ to 60cm (24in) ↔ to 90cm (36in)

HEBE OCHRACEA
'James Stirling' ♥

Evergreen shrub

The tiny, scale-like leaves of the whipcord hebe give it the appearance of a dwarf conifer. The rich ochre-yellow leaves look particularly attractive in winter. In late spring and early summer it bears clusters of small white flowers. Plant it in a raised bed or on a rock garden in full sun or partial shade, in moderately fertile, moist but well-drained soil. It is a tough shrub that is ideally suited to the conditions in a coastal garden.

◊ ◑ ☼ ☀ ❀ ❀ ❀
‡ to 45cm (18in) ↔ to 60cm (24in)

HEDERA COLCHICA
'Sulphur Heart' ♥

Climber

Persian ivy is a vigorous, self-clinging climber with large, glossy, evergreen leaves that are marked with a central blotch of soft sulphur yellow. It provides excellent, fast-growing cover for a shady wall and can also be used as a ground cover plant. Grow it in full sun or partial shade, in fertile, moist but well-drained, preferably alkaline soil. It develops the most intense leaf colour in a sunny position. Clip back at any time of year if necessary.

◊ ◑ ☼ ☀ ❀ ❀ ❀
‡ to 5m (15ft)

HEDERA HELIX
'Buttercup' ♀

Climber

An extremely attractive form of the common ivy, this self-clinging evergreen climber has large, lobed, bright butter-yellow leaves. In full sun the leaves really colour up, while in shade they are a pale green. This makes for some interesting colour effects as the leaves overlap each other. Grow in fertile, moist but well-drained, preferably alkaline soil. An excellent wall plant, trim it back at any time of year if it exceeds its allotted space

◊ ◊ ☼ ☼ ✳ ✳ ✳
‡ to 2m (6ft)

ILEX AQUIFOLIUM
'Golden Milkboy'

Evergreen tree

A dense, upright tree, this striking holly makes a fine specimen or hedge. Its spiny, dark green leaves have irregular, golden-yellow markings in the centre. 'Golden Milkboy' is a male plant and does not produce berries, but it makes a good pollinator for female, berrying hollies. Plant in full sun or partial shade, in fertile, moist but well-drained soil. For best leaf colour, plant in full sun. Trim hedges in summer.

◊ ◊ ☼ ☼ ✳ ✳ ✳ ✳
‡ to 6m (20ft) ↔ to 4m (12ft)

OSMANTHUS HETEROPHYLLUS 'Aureomarginatus'

Evergreen shrub

This rounded, slow-growing shrub has pretty, glossy, holly-like leaves with irregular dark green centres and bright golden-yellow margins. In late summer and autumn, it produces clusters of small but very fragrant white flowers. A welcome addition to the shrub border, in milder areas it makes a very good evergreen hedge. Grow in full sun, in fertile, well-drained soil with some shelter from cold, drying winds. Trim hedges lightly in summer.

○ ◌ ☼ ❉ ❉ ❉
‡↔ to 5m (15ft)

PHORMIUM TENAX 'Yellow Wave' ♀

Perennial

The arching, sword-shaped leaves of this large clump-forming evergreen make a bold focal point. They are a vibrant yellow-green with a broad, central green stripe. In summer, tall spikes of red-purple flowers may appear. Plant in full sun, in moist but well-drained, fertile soil. During winter in colder areas, protect the crown by tucking in a thick layer of dry mulch among the leaves. Use as a specimen plant or in a mixed border. Suitable for coastal gardens.

○ ◑ ☼ ❉ ❉
‡ to 3m (10ft) ↔ to 2m (6ft)

PINUS SYLVESTRIS
'Gold Coin'

Evergreen shrub

A diminutive, slow-growing version of
the Scots pine, this dwarf conifer has
greenish yellow, needle-like leaves that
turn an intense shade of golden yellow
in winter. A small rounded shrub, it is a
good choice for an urban garden where
space is limited; it is also ideally suited
to a rock or gravel garden. Plant it in
full sun, in any moderately fertile, well-
drained soil. It needs no pruning.

◊ ☼ ❁ ❁ ❁
‡↔ to 2m (6ft)

PITTOSPORUM TENUIFOLIUM
'Abbotsbury Gold'

Evergreen shrub

This kohuhu is valued for its green-
margined, golden leaves. A bushy shrub
or small tree, it is suitable for smaller
gardens where it will thrive against
a sunny wall. It can also be used for
hedging, especially in coastal gardens,
needing a trim once only in spring to
keep it in shape. Grow in fertile, moist
but well-drained soil. Provide shelter
from cold, drying winds; in areas where
winters are severe, grow in containers
and bring in under cover.

◊ ◊ ☼ ☼ ❁ ❁
‡ to 3m (10ft) ↔ to 1.5m (5ft)

PITTOSPORUM TENUIFOLIUM
'Irene Patterson' ♀

Evergreen shrub

The emergent spring foliage of this
attractive shrub is cream, gradually
becoming marbled with dark green.
Slow-growing and mound-forming,
it makes an attractive specimen but
it is also suitable as a hedging plant,
especially in wild and coastal gardens.
Trim to shape in spring. Plant in moist
but well-drained, fertile soil, in full sun
or partial shade. Protect from cold,
drying winds and mulch young
plants over winter.

○ ◐ ☼ ☀ ❀ ❀
‡ to 1.2m (4ft) ↔ to 60cm (24in)

THUJA PLICATA
'Stoneham Gold' ♀

Evergreen shrub

A small cone-shaped bush, this is a
dwarf form of the Western red cedar.
The irregularly arranged sprays of
foliage are coppery bronze, becoming
golden yellow and then green as it
ages. It is slow-growing and makes a
good plant for a rock garden. Plant in
moist but well-drained, fertile soil in full
sun. It needs to be protected from cold,
drying winds to avoid foliage scorch,
especially in its early years.

○ ◐ ☼ ❀ ❀ ❀
‡↔ to 2m (6ft)

INDEX

S

ACKNOWLEDGEMENTS

Picture research: Samantha Nunn
Picture library: Richard Dabb, Lucy
Claxton, Charlotte Oster
Index: Michèle Clarke

The publisher would like to thank the
following for their kind permission to
reproduce their photographs:
(key: t=top, b=bottom)

17: Andrew Butler (b), Photos
Horticultural (t); 27: Harry Smith
Collection (t); 28: Garden Matters (t); 29:
Garden Matters (b), James Young (t); 30:
Andrew Lawson (t); 32: Juliette Wade (t);
33: John Glover (b), Harry Smith
Collection (t); 34: Juliette Wade (b); 38:
Garden Matters (t); 42: A-Z Botanical
Collection/Adrian Thomas (t), A-Z
Botanical Collection/Andrew Ackerley (b);
43: Garden Matters (t); 45: GPL/Sunniva
Harte (b); 51: Clive Nichols (b); 52: Photos
Horticultural (t); 58: GPL/Brian Carter (b);
65: RHS Garden Wisley (t); 77: Martin
Page (t); 78: James Young (t); 79: Photos
Horticultural (b); 81: GPL/Christopher
Fairweather (t); 91: Garden Matters (t);
106: GPL/Jacqui Hurst (b); 107: Martin
Page (b), Harry Smith Collection (t); 109:
James Young (t); 110:Garden Matters (t);
112: Roger Smith/DK (t); 117: Garden
Matters (t); 118: A-Z Botanical Collection
(b), 120. Photos Horticultural (t); 121:
Photos Horticultural (b, t); 122: John
Fielding (b); 123: Eric Crichton Photos (b);
124: A-Z Botanical Collection/Adrian
Thomas (b), 125. Andrew Lawson (b); 127:
Photos Horticultural (b); 130: GPL/Jacqui
Hurst (b), 132. James Young (b); 135:
Juliette Wade (t); 136: Martin Page (b);
137: A-Z Botanical Collection/Nina

McKenna (b); 141: Andrew Butler (t); 143:
A-Z Botanical Collection/Jack Coulthard
(t); 144: Roger Smith/DK (t); 149: Harry Smith
Collection (b); 160: John Fielding (b); 162:
Harry Smith Collection (t); 166: Andrew
Butler (t); 168: Juliette Wade (b); 173: C.
Andrew Henley (b); 174: Martin Page (b);
176: Roger Smith/DK (b); 185: Christine M.
Douglas (t); 188: Photos Horticultural (b);
192: Martin Page (t); 194: Photos
Horticultural (t), Roger Smith/DK (b); 196:
Roger Smith/DK (t); 198: Roger Smith/DK
(t); 200: Harry Smith Collection (b); 201:
Beth Chatto (t), Photos Horticultural (t);
202: GPL/Juliet Greene (t); 204: Eric
Crichton Photos (t); 205: GPL/Howard
Rice (t); 214: James Young (b); 217: Martin
Page (b); 220: James Young (b, t); 223:
Roger Smith/DK (t); 228: Garden Matters
(t); 229: Photos Horticultural (b); 232:
Photos Horticultural (b); 233: Harry Smith
Collection (b); 235: Photos Horticultural
(b); 239: GPL/Kim Blaxland (b); 240:
GPL/John Glover (t), Harry Smith
Collection (t); 246: Roger Smith/DK
(b), Harry Smith Collection (t); 253:
Michael Booher (b); 258: GPL/Linda
Burgess (b); 266: John Glover (t); 267:
Harry Smith Collection (t); 269: C. Andrew
Henley (b); 274: Harry Smith Collection
(t); 275: Roger Smith/DK (b); 278: A-Z
Botanical Collection/Derick Ditchburn (t);
285: GPL/Jacqui Hurst (b); 286: Harry
Smith Collection (t); 300: Clive Nichols (b);
311: Christine M. Douglas (b), GPL/J. S
Sira (t); 313: Photos Horticultural (t); 315:
Clive Nichols (b); 317: Harry Smith
Collection (b); 331: GPL/Eric Crichton (t),
Harry Smith Collection (b); 337: C.
Andrew Henley (b), Photos Horticultural
(t); 338: Harry Smith Collection (b); 342:
Martin Page (b); 344: Harry Smith

Collection (b); 345: Photos Horticultural (b); 347: Photos Horticultural (b); 352: Photos Horticultural (b); 355: Photos Horticultural (b); 356: Photos Horticultural (b); 358: Eric Crichton Photos (b); 360: Clive Nichols (t); 361: Photos Horticultural (b); 362: Photos Horticultural (t); 363: Harry Smith Collection (t); 367: Harry Smith Collection (t); 368: Harry Smith Collection (t); 373: GPL/Howard Rice (b); 374: Juliette Wade (b); 379: Andrew Butler (t); 383: Photos Horticultural (b); 397: GPL/John Glover (t), GPL/Philippe Bonduel (b); 398: Harry Smith Collection (t);401: Clive Nichols/Jane Nichols (b); 406: Andrew Butler (b), Photos Horticultural (t); 408: Harry Smith Collection (t); 414: Clive Nichols (b); 422: Andrew Butler (b); 423: Juliette Wade (t); 424: Harry Smith Collection (t); 427: GPL/Ron Evans (t); 429: John Fielding (t); 430: Photos Horticultural (b); 431: Christine M. Douglas (t); 435: Andrew Lawson (b); 436: Clive Nichols (t); 437: Andrew Butler (b); 439: Andrew Lawson (t); 442: Andrew Butler (t); 445: Andrew Butler (t); 446: Roger Smith/DK (t); 458: Andrew Butler (t); 459: Beth Chatto (t), C. Andrew Henley (b); 462: Martin Page (b); 467: Photos Horticultural (t), Harry Smith Collection (b); 470: Andrew Butler (t); 472: Andrew Lawson; 478: GPL/Howard Rice (b); 480: GPL/Howard Rice (t); 482: Andrew Butler (b); 483: Clive Nichols (b), Photos Horticultural (t); 485: GPL/Neil Holmes (t); 486: Eric Crichton Photos (b); 487: Photos Horticultural (t); 489: Harry Smith Collection (t); 490: John Glover (b),

Photos Horticultural (t); 491: Andrew Lawson (t); 493: Photos Horticultural (b); 495: John Glover (b); 496: GPL/Howard Rice (t, Photos Horticultural (b); 499: Andrew Lawson (t); 502: Harry Smith Collection (t); 504: Roger Smith/DK (t); 506: John Glover (b); 509: Photos Horticultural (t); 512: Photos Horticultural (b); 513: Beth Chatto (b); 514: Martin Page (t); 518: Harry Smith Collection (b); 520: Roger Smith/DK (t); 521: Roger Smith/DK (t); 522: James Young (b); 523: Harry Smith Collection (t); 527: James Young (b); 531: James Young (t); 532: John Fielding (b); 536: GPL/J. S. Sira (b); 537: GPL/Jerry Pavia (t); 538: James Young (b); 539: Juliette Wade (b), GPL/Lamontagne (t); 540: John Glover (b); 542: James Young (t); 543: Photos Horticultural (t); 546: Andrew Butler (b); 547: Andrew Butler (t).

All other images © Dorling Kindersley.

For further information see: www.dkimages.com

Dorling Kindersley would also like to thank the following for editorial assistance: Zia Allaway, Chris Dyer, Lin Hawthorne, Letitia Luff, Robin Pridy; at the Royal Horticultural Society, Vincent Square: Barbara Haynes, Susanne Mitchell and Simon Maughan.

Visit the RHS on the internet at **www.rhs.org.uk**